SPOTLIGHT!! HERE!
OVER HERE!!

岸本斉史

Main character Naruto finally returns to center stage in this volume! I'm so glad to be able to draw the titular character again! I was told by someone that this was "a manga where the main character ~~isn't very involved~~ is used quite stingily," but he'll be really active from here on out!! ...I think! ...Er... Hmm, I wonder... I don't really know about the future... Well...

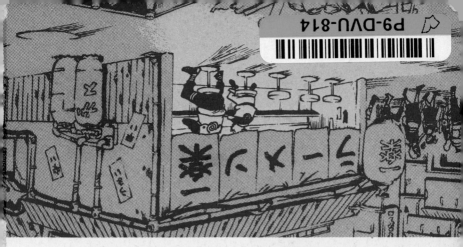

—Masashi Kishimoto, 2011

Author/artist Masashi Kishimoto was born in 1974 in rural Okayama Prefecture, Japan. After spending time in art college, he won the Hop Step Award for new manga artists with his manga **Karakuri** (Mechanism). Kishimoto decided to base his next story on traditional Japanese culture. His first version of **Naruto**, drawn in 1997, was a one-shot story about fox spirits; his final version, which debuted in **Weekly Shonen Jump** in 1999, quickly became the most popular ninja manga in Japan.

ラーメン一楽

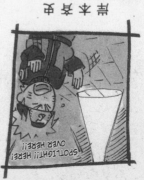

NARUTO VOL. 57
SHONEN JUMP Manga Edition

STORY AND ART BY MASASHI KISHIMOTO

Translation/Mari Morimoto
English Adaptation/Joel Enos
Touch-up Art & Lettering/Sabrina Heep
Design/Sam Elzway
Editor/Joel Enos

NARUTO © 1999 by Masashi Kishimoto. All rights reserved. First
published in Japan in 1999 by SHUEISHA Inc., Tokyo. English translation
rights arranged by SHUEISHA Inc.

The rights of the author(s) of the work(s) in this publication to be so
identified have been asserted in accordance with the Copyright, Designs
and Patents Act 1988. A CIP catalogue record for this book is available
from the British Library.

Printed in the U.S.A.

Published by VIZ Media, LLC
P.O. Box 77010
San Francisco, CA 94107

10 9 8 7 6 5 4 3 2 1

First printing, July 2012

www.shonenjump.com

www.viz.com

SHONEN JUMP MANGA EDITION

NARUTO

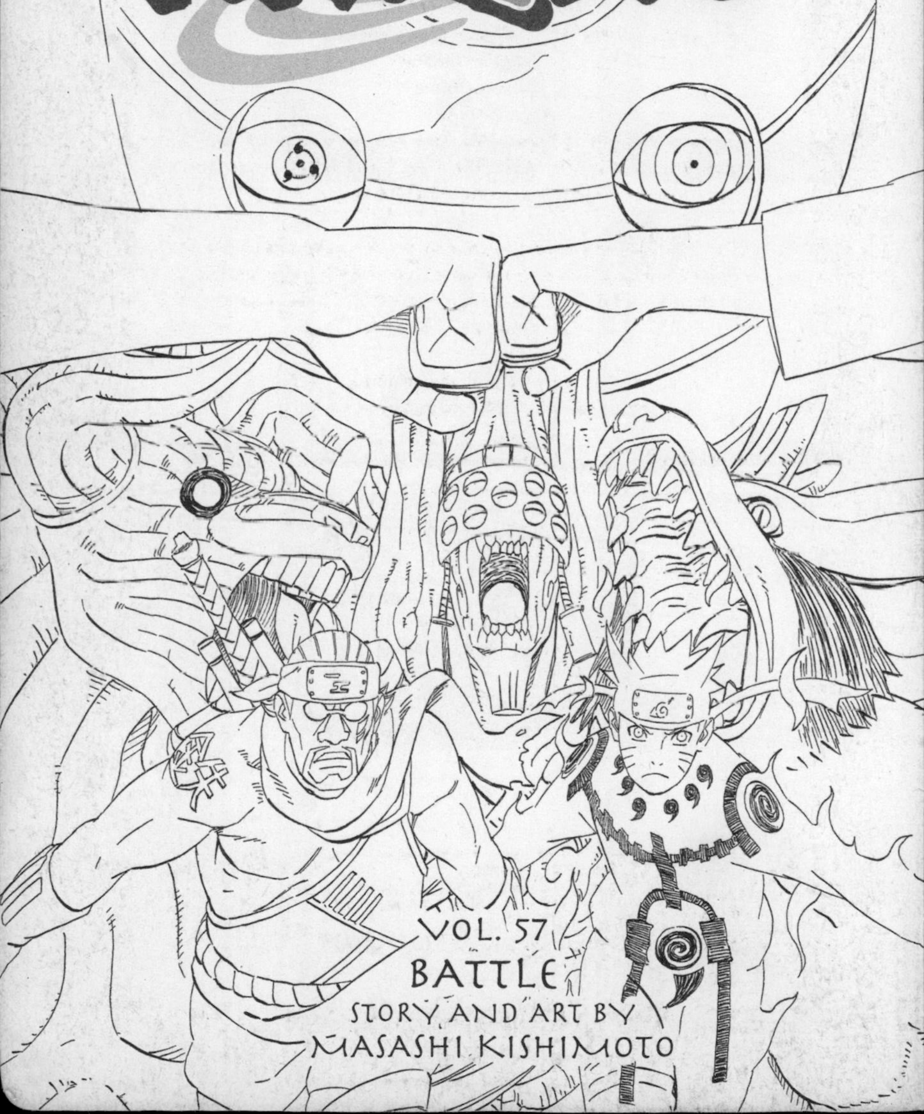

VOL. 57

BATTLE

STORY AND ART BY
MASASHI KISHIMOTO

CHARACTERS

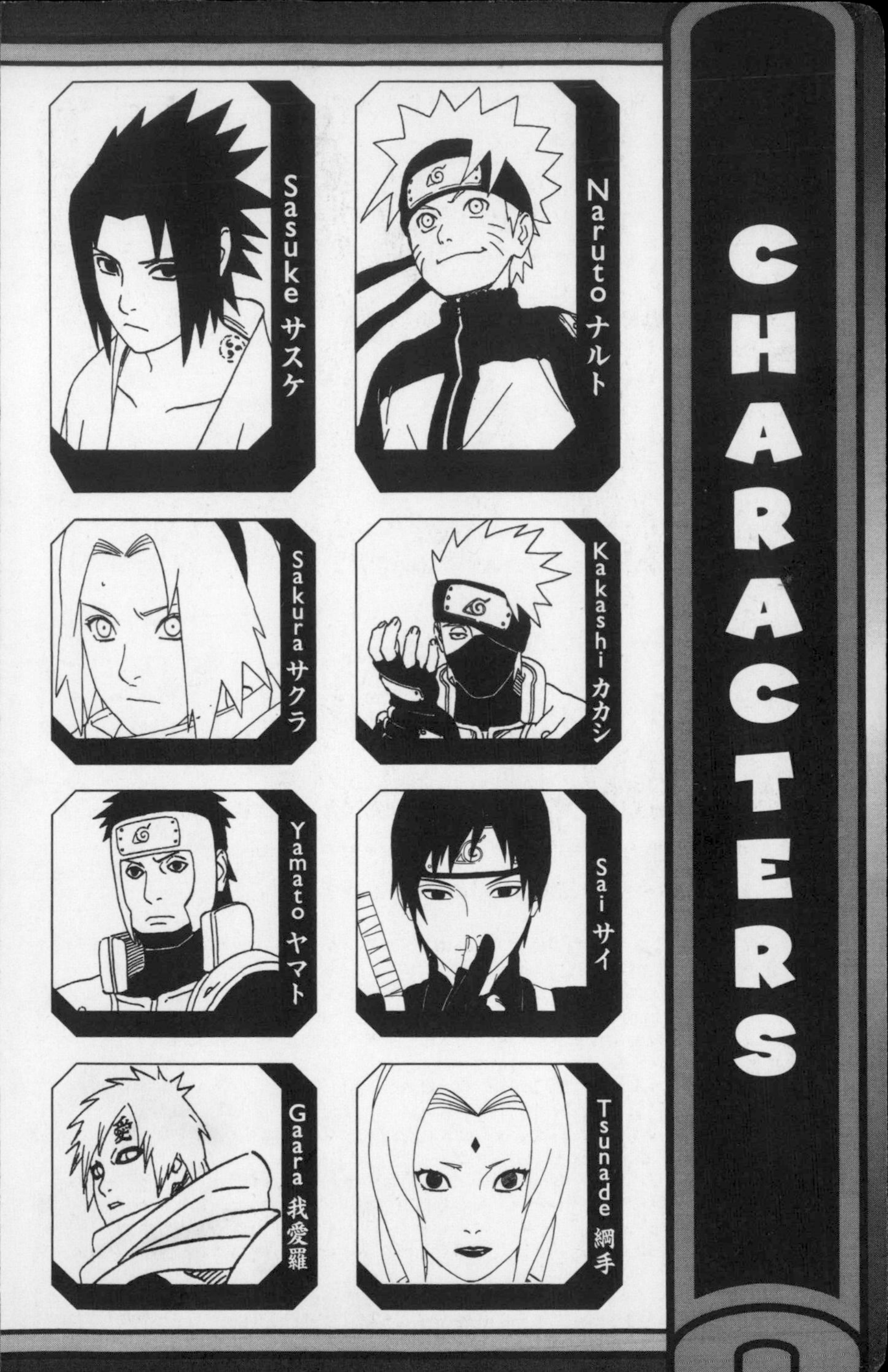
Naruto ナルト
Sasuke サスケ
Kakashi カカシ
Sakura サクラ
Sai サイ
Yamato ヤマト
Tsunade 綱手
Gaara 我愛羅

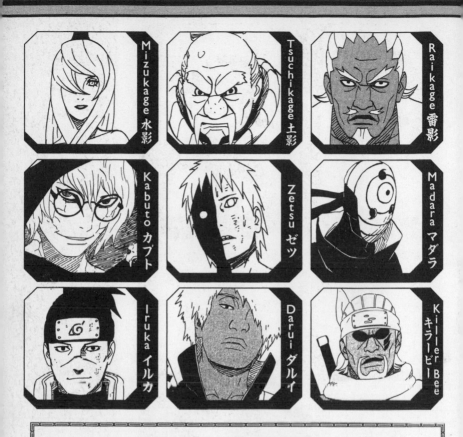

Mizukage 水影

Tsuchikage 土影

Raikage 雷影

Kabuto カブト

Zetsu ゼツ

Madara マダラ

Iruka イルカ

Darui ダルイ

Killer Bee キラービー

THE STORY SO FAR...

Naruto, the biggest troublemaker at the Ninja Academy in the Village of Kono-hagakure, finally becomes a full-fledged ninja. With his classmates Sasuke and Sakura, he endures countless trials and battles, growing ever stronger. However, Sasuke, unable to give up his quest for vengeance for the death of his family, leaves Konoha to seek out the rogue ninja Orochimaru, who he believes will give him great power.

As two years pass, Naruto battles the Tailed Beast-targeting Akatsuki organization while Sasuke triumphs over his murderous brother, Itachi. But new intel sets Sasuke, now aligned with the Akatsuki, on a new mission of revenge, this time against the village of Konoha.

Madara of the Akatsuki declares war on the Five Great Nations, prompting the Gokage, the five great leaders, to create an Allied Shinobi Force. The Fourth Great Ninja War begins. The Allied Forces confront an army of resurrected dead heroes and Naruto, still in the midst of training, attempts to sneak out and join the fray.

NARUTO

VOL. 57
BATTLE

CONTENTS

Number 535: Iruka's Impact

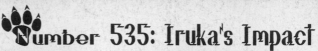

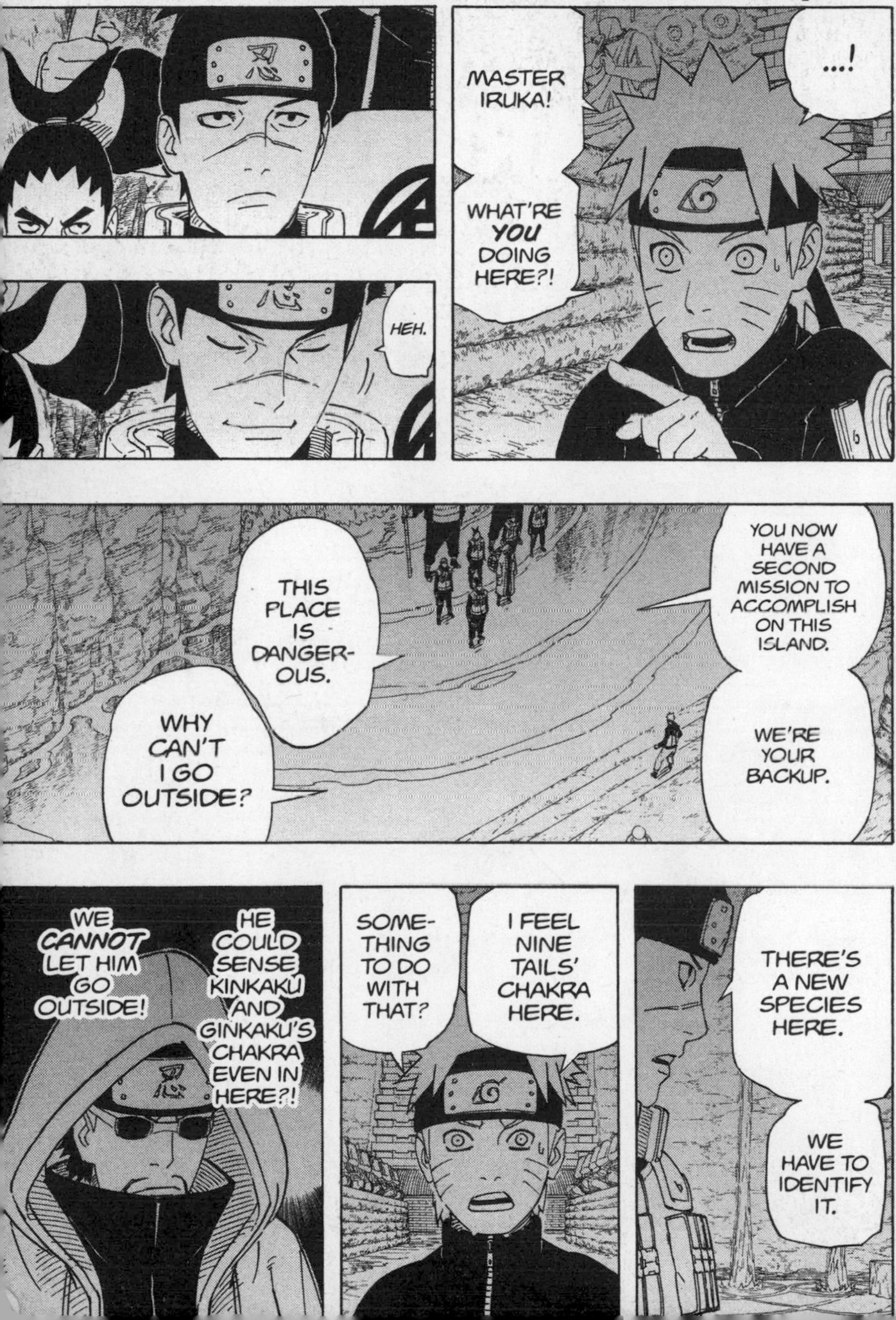
...!
MASTER IRUKA!
WHAT'RE YOU DOING HERE?!
HEH.
YOU NOW HAVE A SECOND MISSION TO ACCOMPLISH ON THIS ISLAND.
WE'RE YOUR BACKUP.
THIS PLACE IS DANGEROUS.
WHY CAN'T I GO OUTSIDE?
THERE'S A NEW SPECIES HERE.
WE HAVE TO IDENTIFY IT.
I FEEL NINE TAILS' CHAKRA HERE.
SOMETHING TO DO WITH THAT?
HE COULD SENSE KINKAKU AND GINKAKU'S CHAKRA EVEN IN HERE?!
WE CANNOT LET HIM GO OUTSIDE!

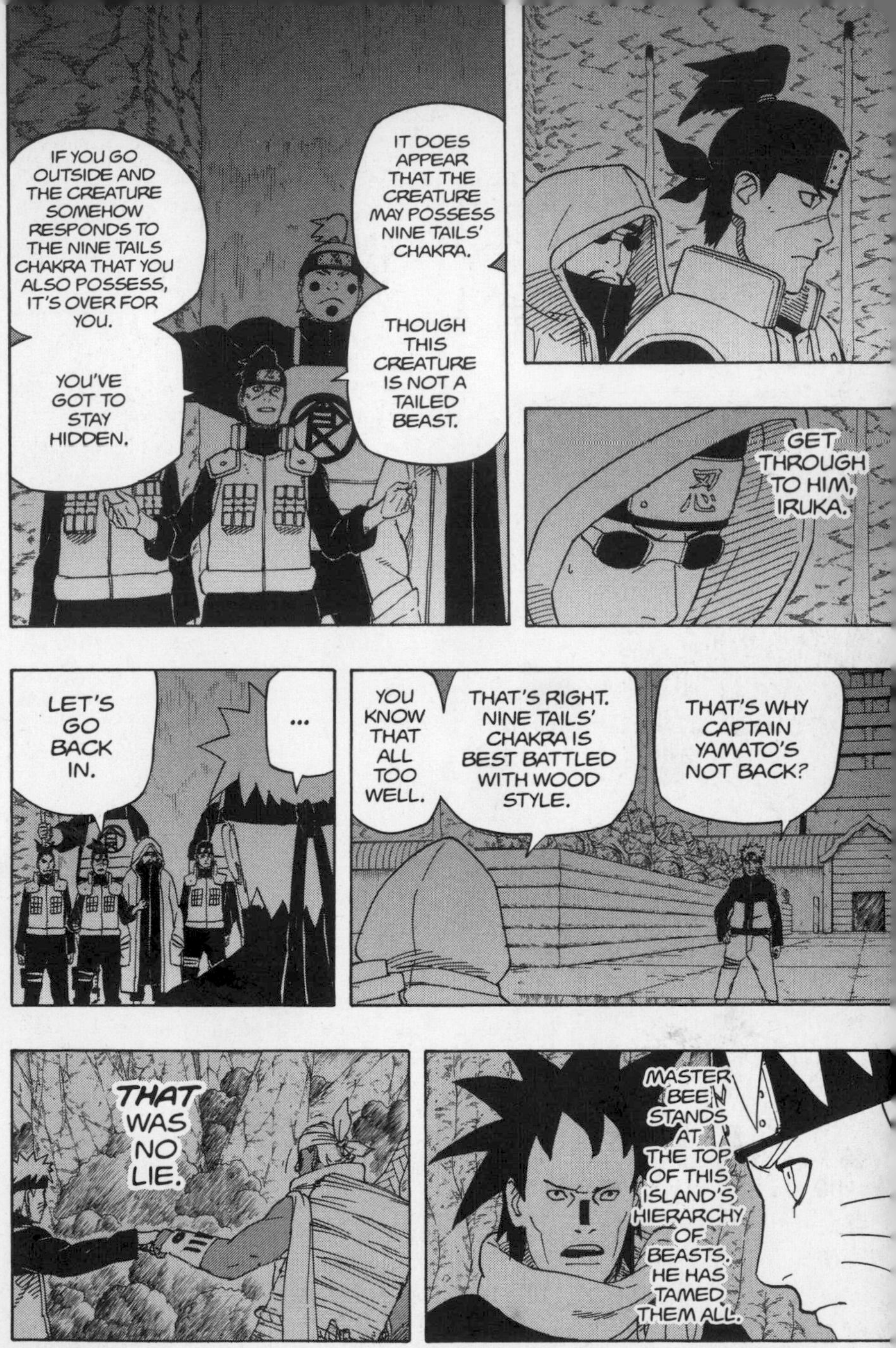
GET THROUGH TO HIM, IRUKA.
IT DOES APPEAR THAT THE CREATURE MAY POSSESS NINE TAILS' CHAKRA.
THOUGH THIS CREATURE IS NOT A TAILED BEAST.
IF YOU GO OUTSIDE AND THE CREATURE SOMEHOW RESPONDS TO THE NINE TAILS CHAKRA THAT YOU ALSO POSSESS, IT'S OVER FOR YOU.
YOU'VE GOT TO STAY HIDDEN.
THAT'S WHY CAPTAIN YAMATO'S NOT BACK?
THAT'S RIGHT. NINE TAILS' CHAKRA IS BEST BATTLED WITH WOOD STYLE.
YOU KNOW THAT ALL TOO WELL.
...
LET'S GO BACK IN.
MASTER BEE STANDS AT THE TOP OF THIS ISLAND'S HIERARCHY OF BEASTS. HE HAS TAMED THEM ALL.
THAT WAS NO LIE.

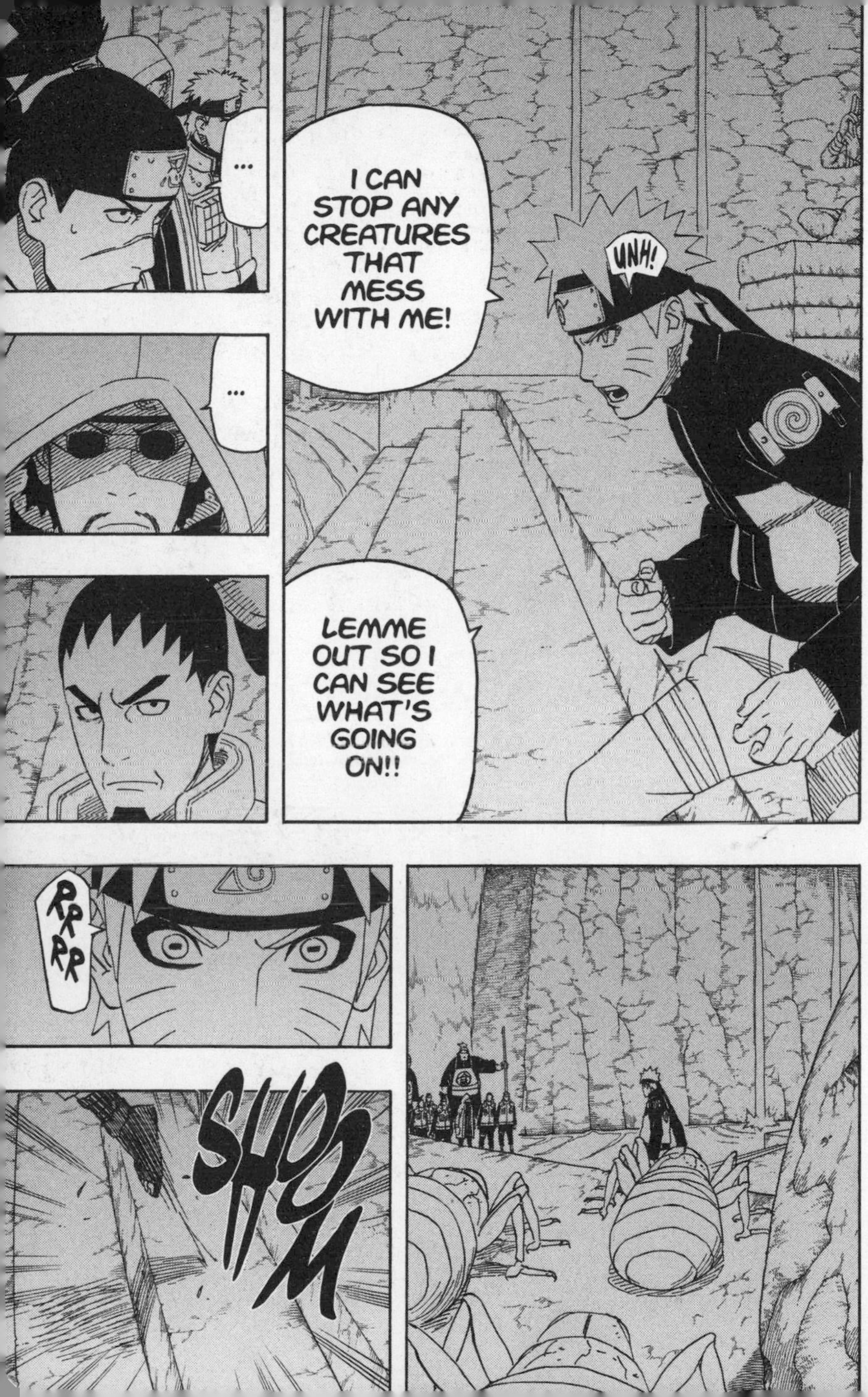
I CAN STOP ANY CREATURES THAT MESS WITH ME!
UNH!
LEMME OUT SO I CAN SEE WHAT'S GOING ON!!
...
...
RRRR
SHOOM

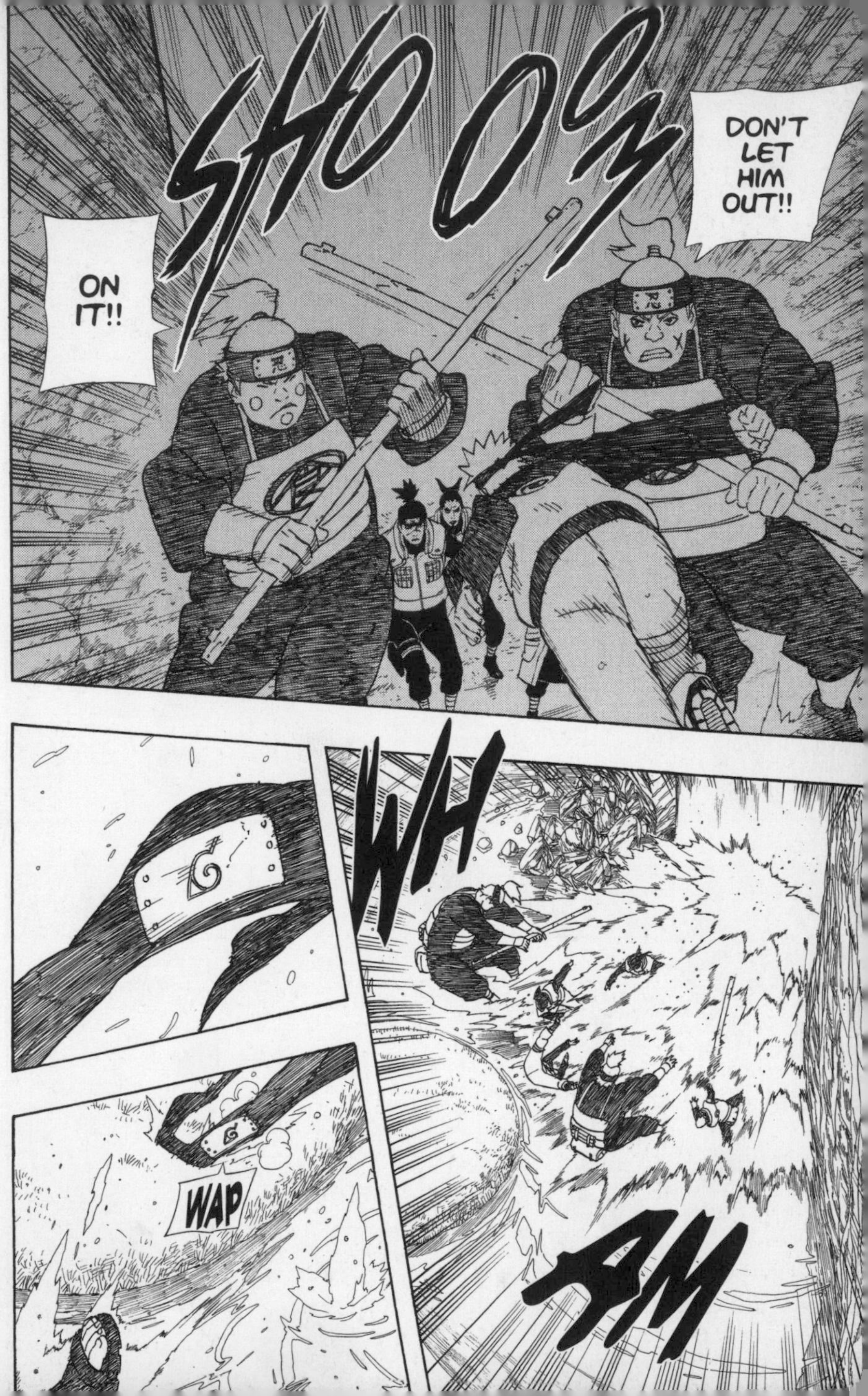
SHOOP
DON'T LET HIM OUT!!
ON IT!!
WH
AM
WAP

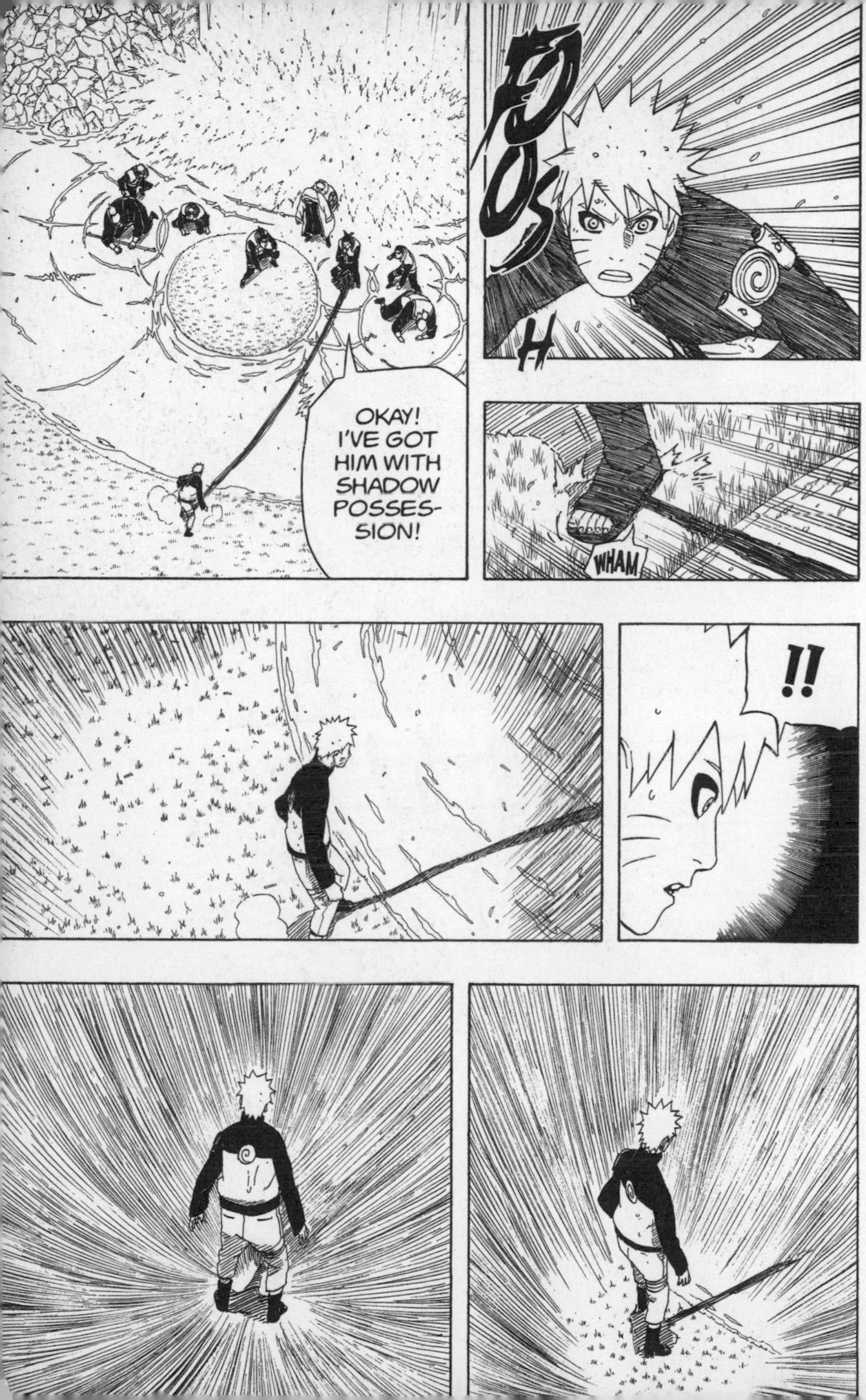
FOOSH
WHAM
OKAY! I'VE GOT HIM WITH SHADOW POSSESSION!
!!

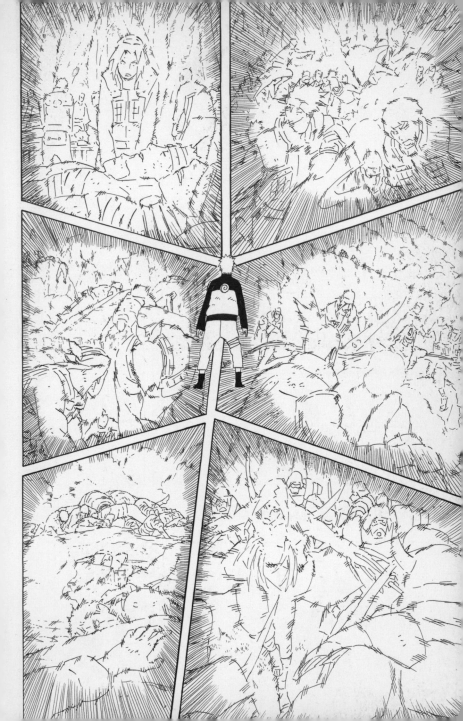

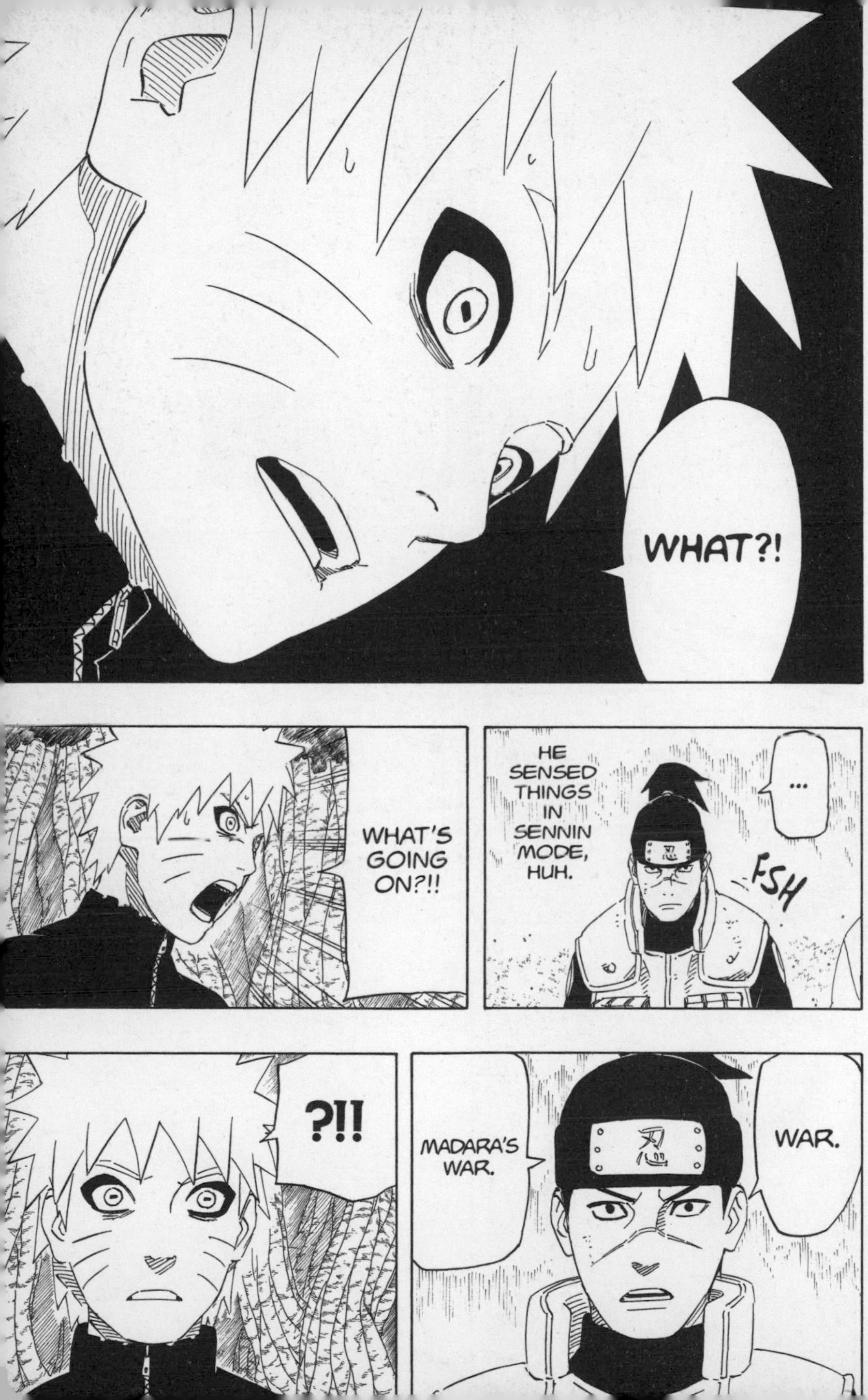
WHAT?!
...
FSH
HE SENSED THINGS IN SENNIN MODE, HUH.
WHAT'S GOING ON?!!
WAR.
MADARA'S WAR.
?!!

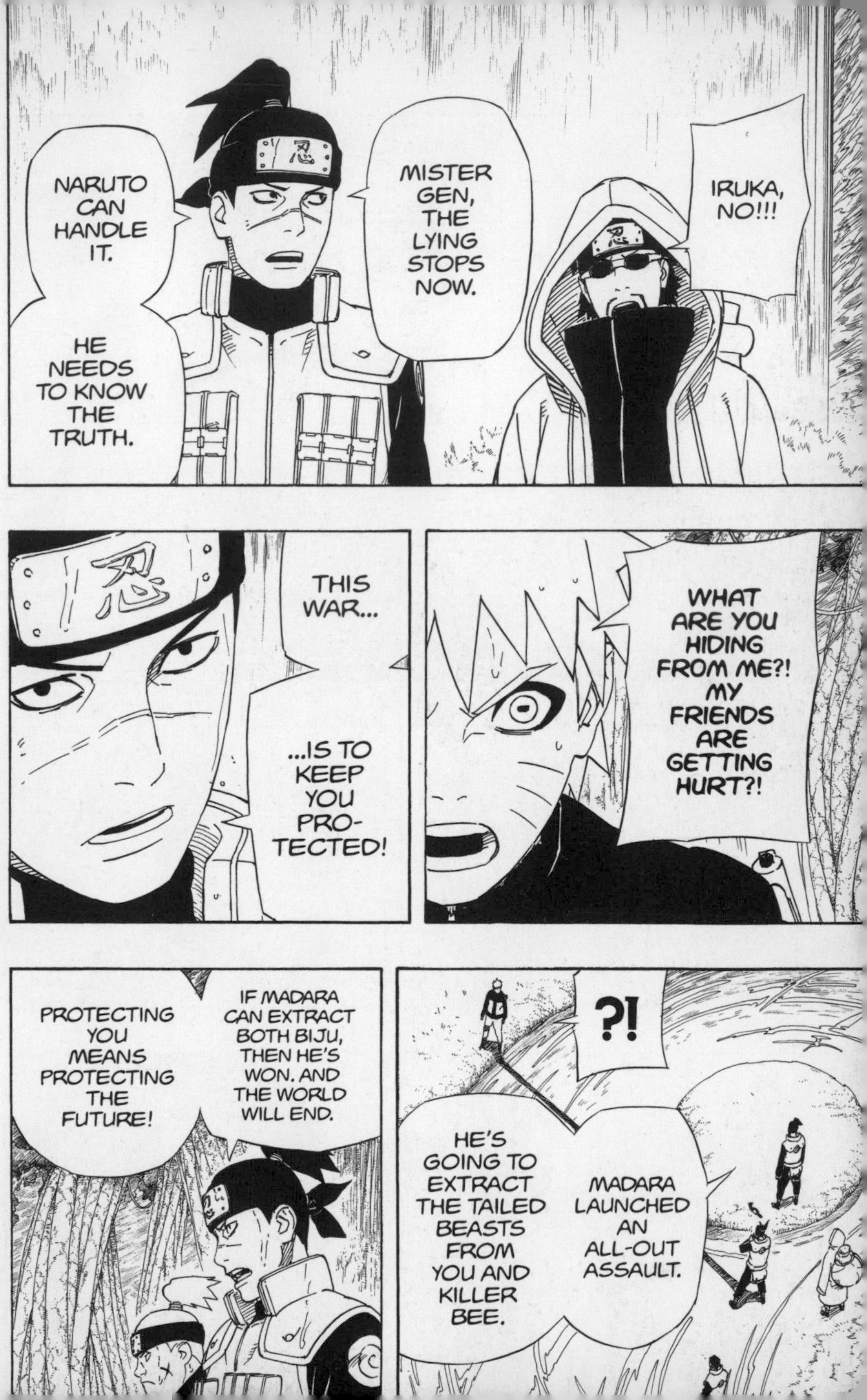
IRUKA, NO!!!
MISTER GEN, THE LYING STOPS NOW.
NARUTO CAN HANDLE IT.
HE NEEDS TO KNOW THE TRUTH.
WHAT ARE YOU HIDING FROM ME?! MY FRIENDS ARE GETTING HURT?!
THIS WAR...
...IS TO KEEP YOU PRO-TECTED!
?!
MADARA LAUNCHED AN ALL-OUT ASSAULT.
HE'S GOING TO EXTRACT THE TAILED BEASTS FROM YOU AND KILLER BEE.
IF MADARA CAN EXTRACT BOTH BIJU, THEN HE'S WON. AND THE WORLD WILL END.
PROTECTING YOU MEANS PROTECTING THE FUTURE!

READ THIS WAY

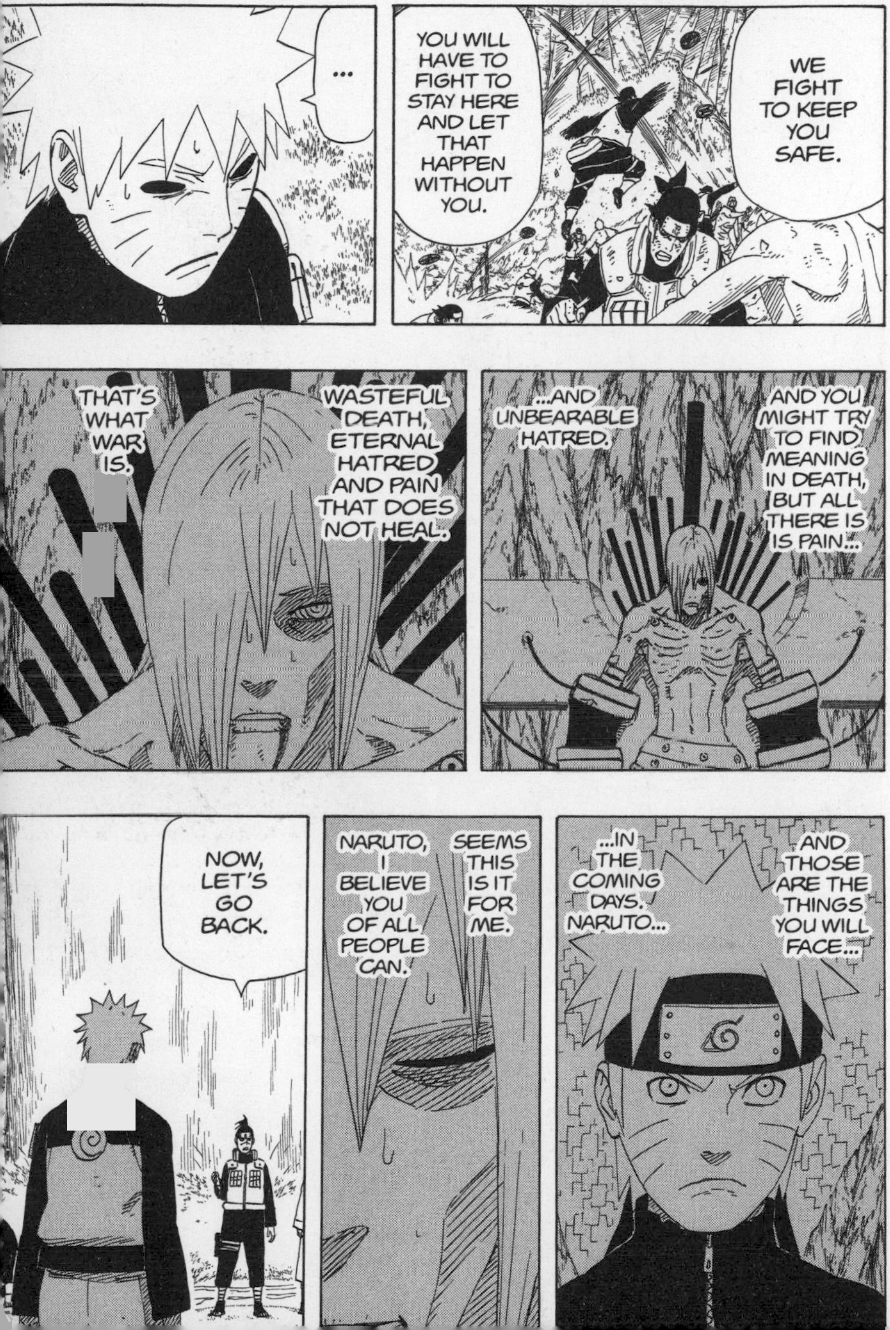
WE FIGHT TO KEEP YOU SAFE.
YOU WILL HAVE TO FIGHT TO STAY HERE AND LET THAT HAPPEN WITHOUT YOU.
...
AND YOU MIGHT TRY TO FIND MEANING IN DEATH, BUT ALL THERE IS IS PAIN...
...AND UNBEARABLE HATRED.
WASTEFUL DEATH, ETERNAL HATRED AND PAIN THAT DOES NOT HEAL.
THAT'S WHAT WAR IS.
AND THOSE ARE THE THINGS YOU WILL FACE...
...IN THE COMING DAYS. NARUTO...
SEEMS THIS IS IT FOR ME.
NARUTO, I BELIEVE YOU OF ALL PEOPLE CAN.
NOW, LET'S GO BACK.

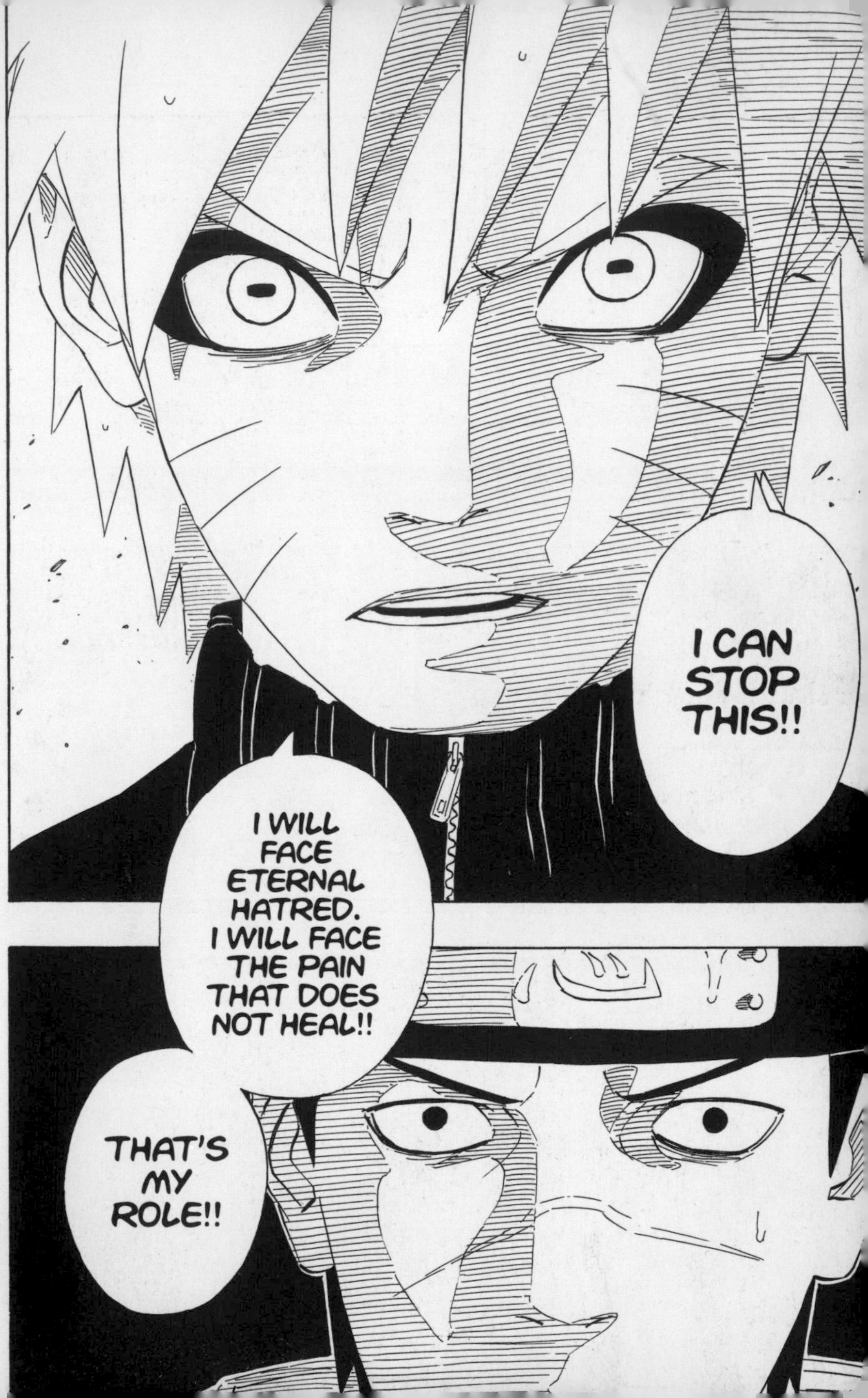
I CAN STOP THIS!!
I WILL FACE ETERNAL HATRED. I WILL FACE THE PAIN THAT DOES NOT HEAL!!
THAT'S MY ROLE!!

READ THIS WAY

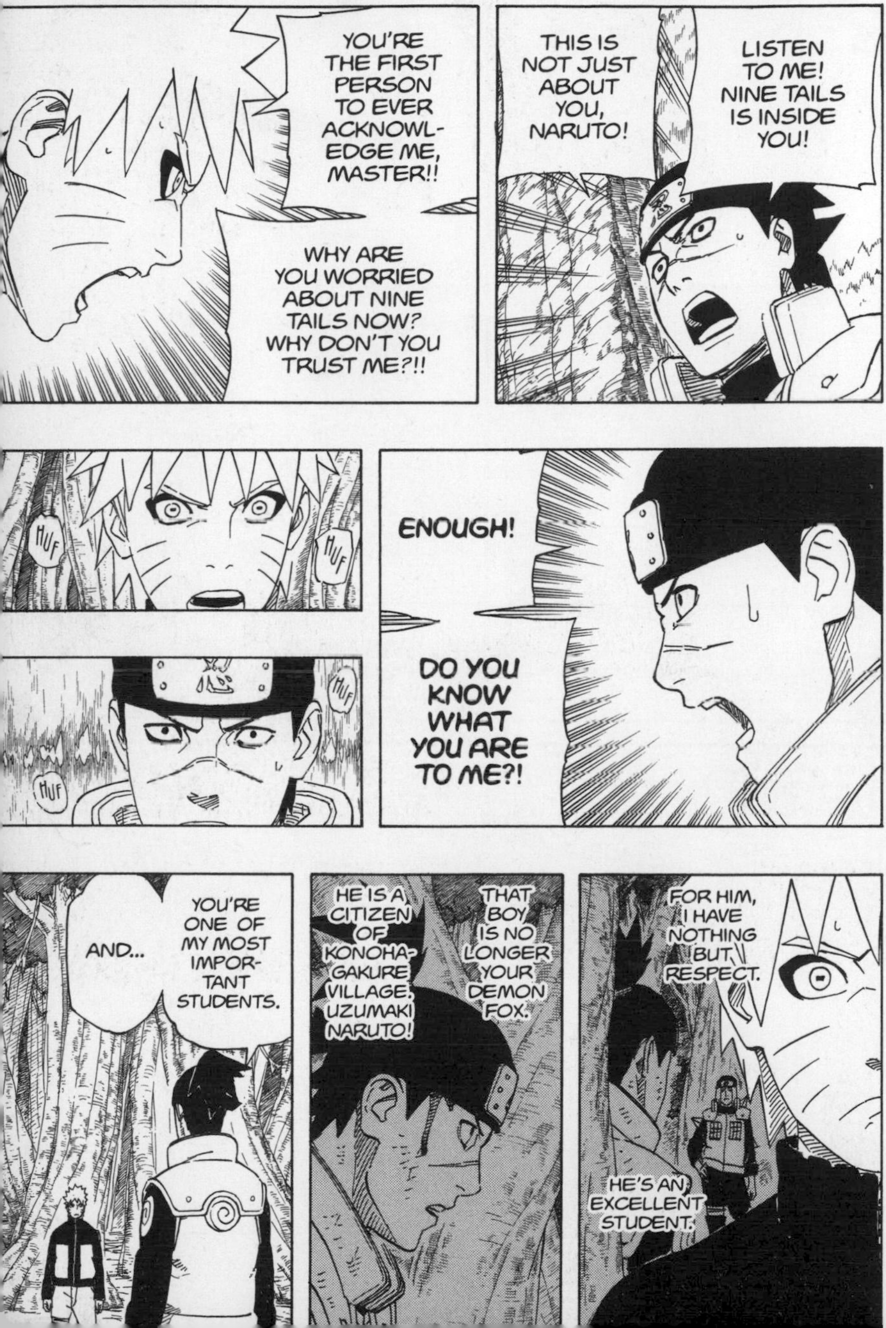
LISTEN TO ME! NINE TAILS IS INSIDE YOU!
THIS IS NOT JUST ABOUT YOU, NARUTO!
YOU'RE THE FIRST PERSON TO EVER ACKNOWLEDGE ME, MASTER!!
WHY ARE YOU WORRIED ABOUT NINE TAILS NOW? WHY DON'T YOU TRUST ME?!!
ENOUGH!
DO YOU KNOW WHAT YOU ARE TO ME?!
HUF
HUF
HUF
HUF
FOR HIM, I HAVE NOTHING BUT RESPECT.
HE'S AN EXCELLENT STUDENT.
THAT BOY IS NO LONGER YOUR DEMON FOX.
HE IS A CITIZEN OF KONOHAGAKURE VILLAGE. UZUMAKI NARUTO!
YOU'RE ONE OF MY MOST IMPORTANT STUDENTS.
AND...

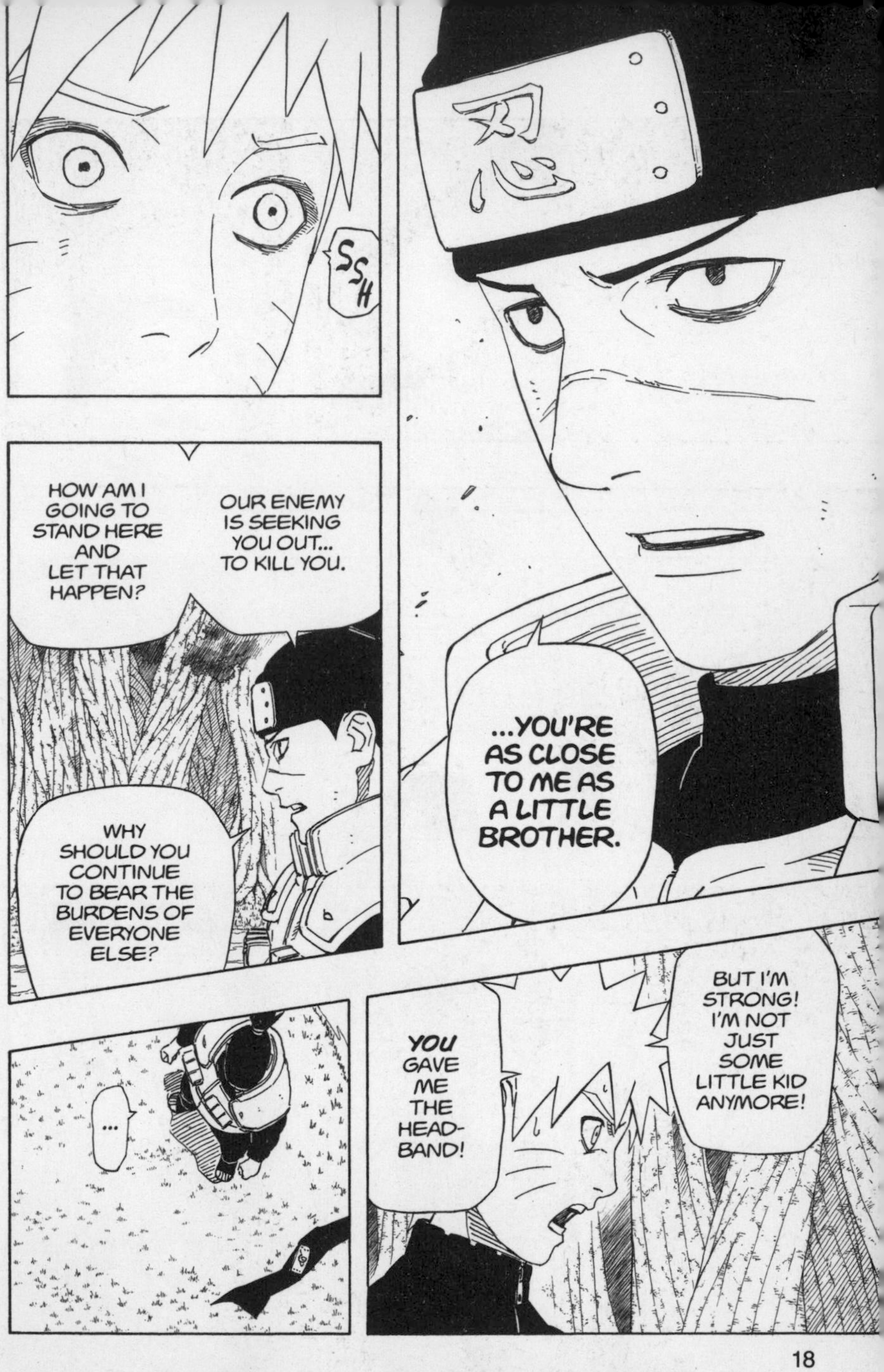
...YOU'RE AS CLOSE TO ME AS A LITTLE BROTHER.
SSH
OUR ENEMY IS SEEKING YOU OUT... TO KILL YOU.
HOW AM I GOING TO STAND HERE AND LET THAT HAPPEN?
WHY SHOULD YOU CONTINUE TO BEAR THE BURDENS OF EVERYONE ELSE?
BUT I'M STRONG! I'M NOT JUST SOME LITTLE KID ANYMORE!
YOU GAVE ME THE HEAD-BAND!
...

READ THIS WAY

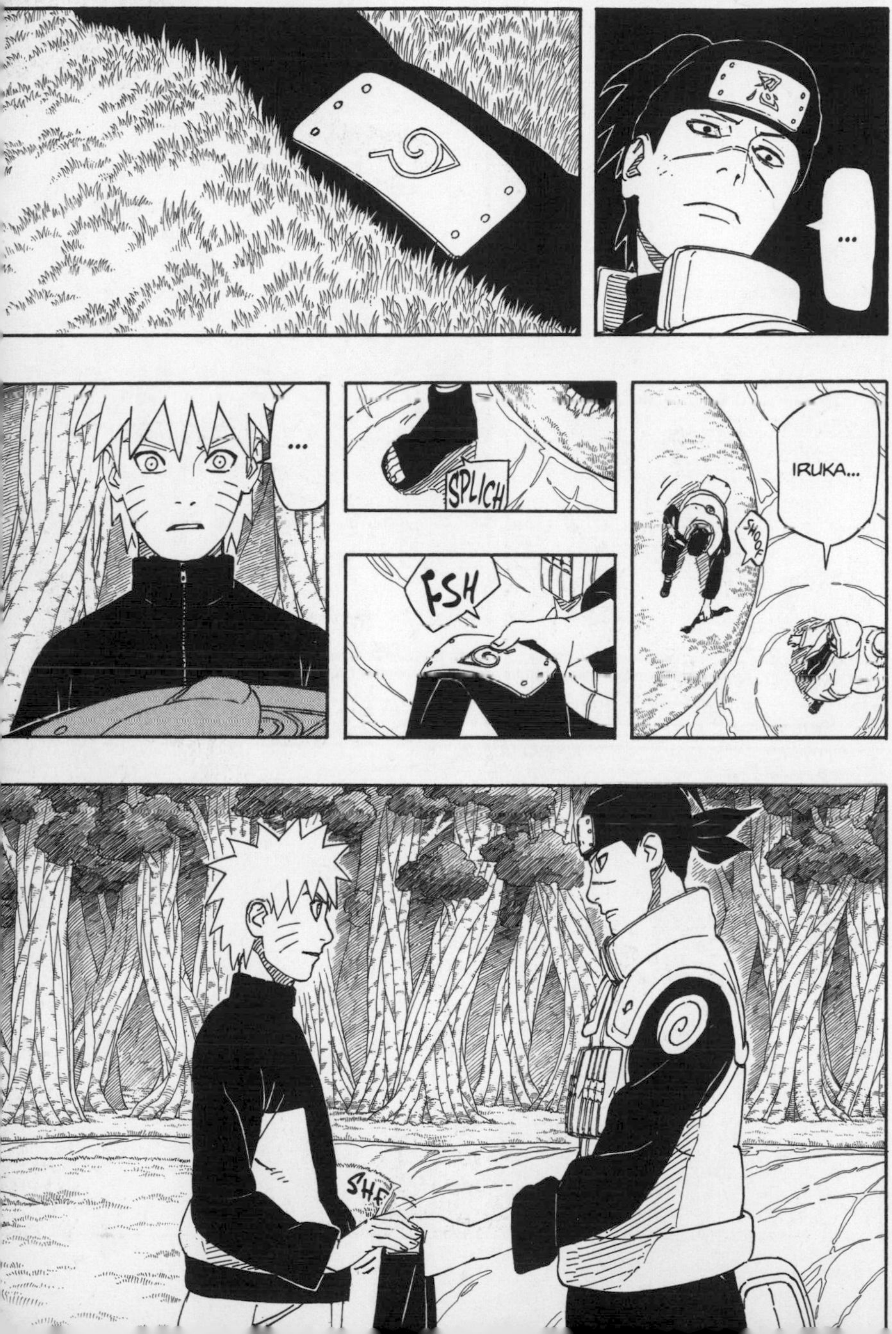
...
IRUKA...
SHOOF
SPLICH
FSH
...
SHF

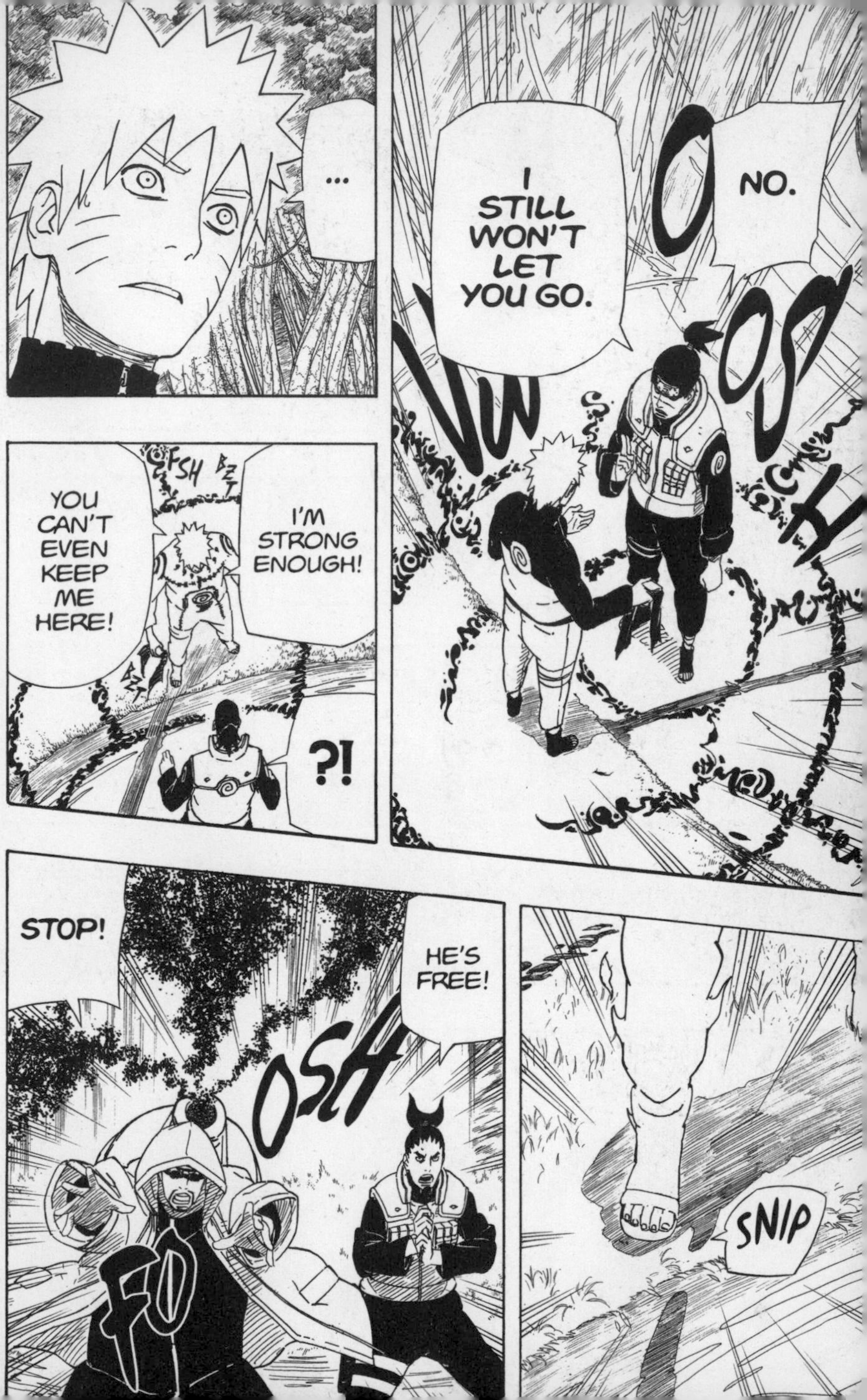
NO.
I STILL WON'T LET YOU GO.
WHOOSH
...
I'M STRONG ENOUGH!
YOU CAN'T EVEN KEEP ME HERE!
FSH
BZT
BZT
?!
SNIP
HE'S FREE!
STOP!
FOSH

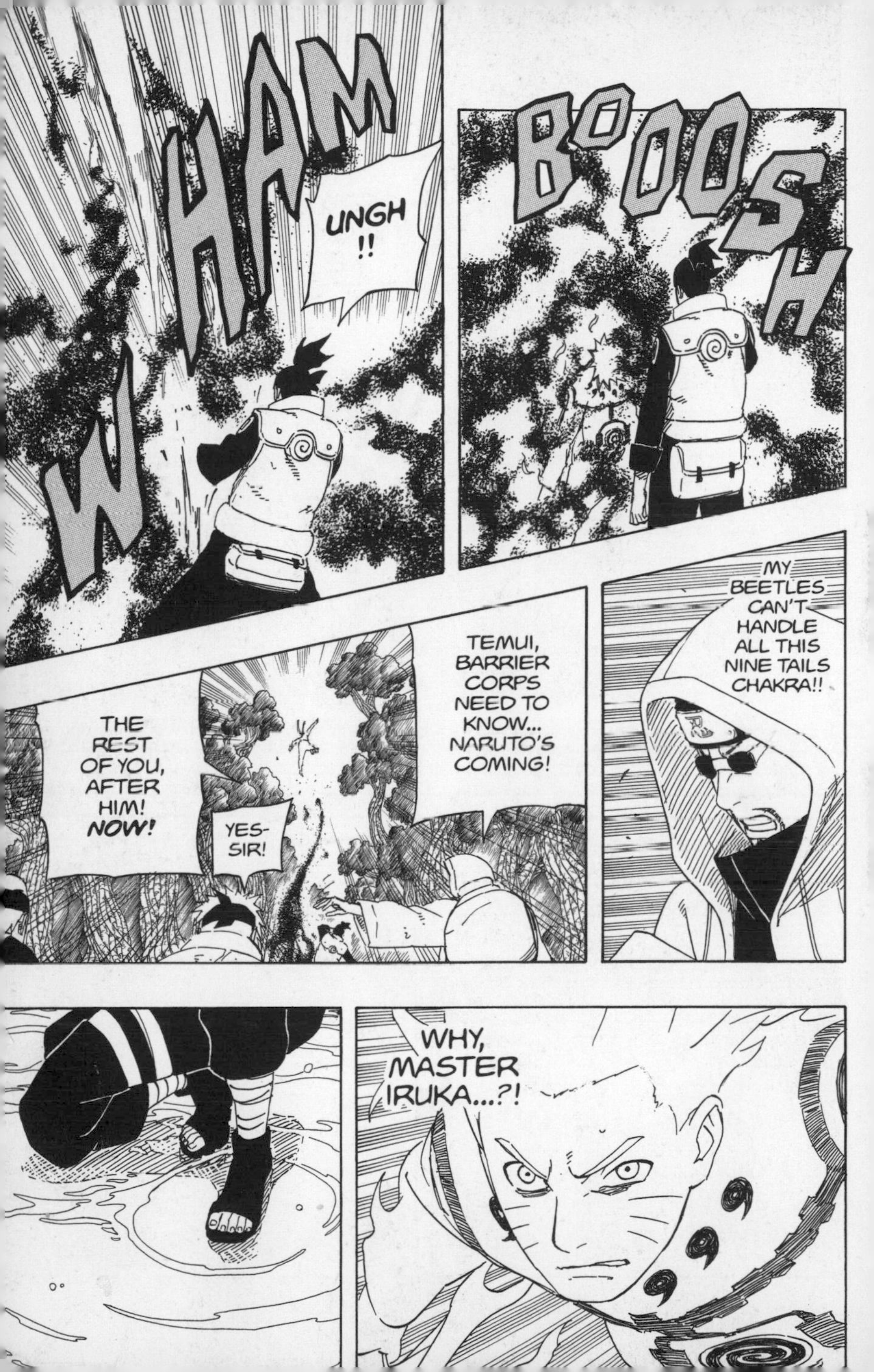
BOOOSH
WHAM
UNGH !!
MY BEETLES CAN'T HANDLE ALL THIS NINE TAILS CHAKRA!!
TEMUI, BARRIER CORPS NEED TO KNOW... NARUTO'S COMING!
THE REST OF YOU, AFTER HIM! **NOW!**
YES-SIR!
WHY, MASTER IRUKA...?!

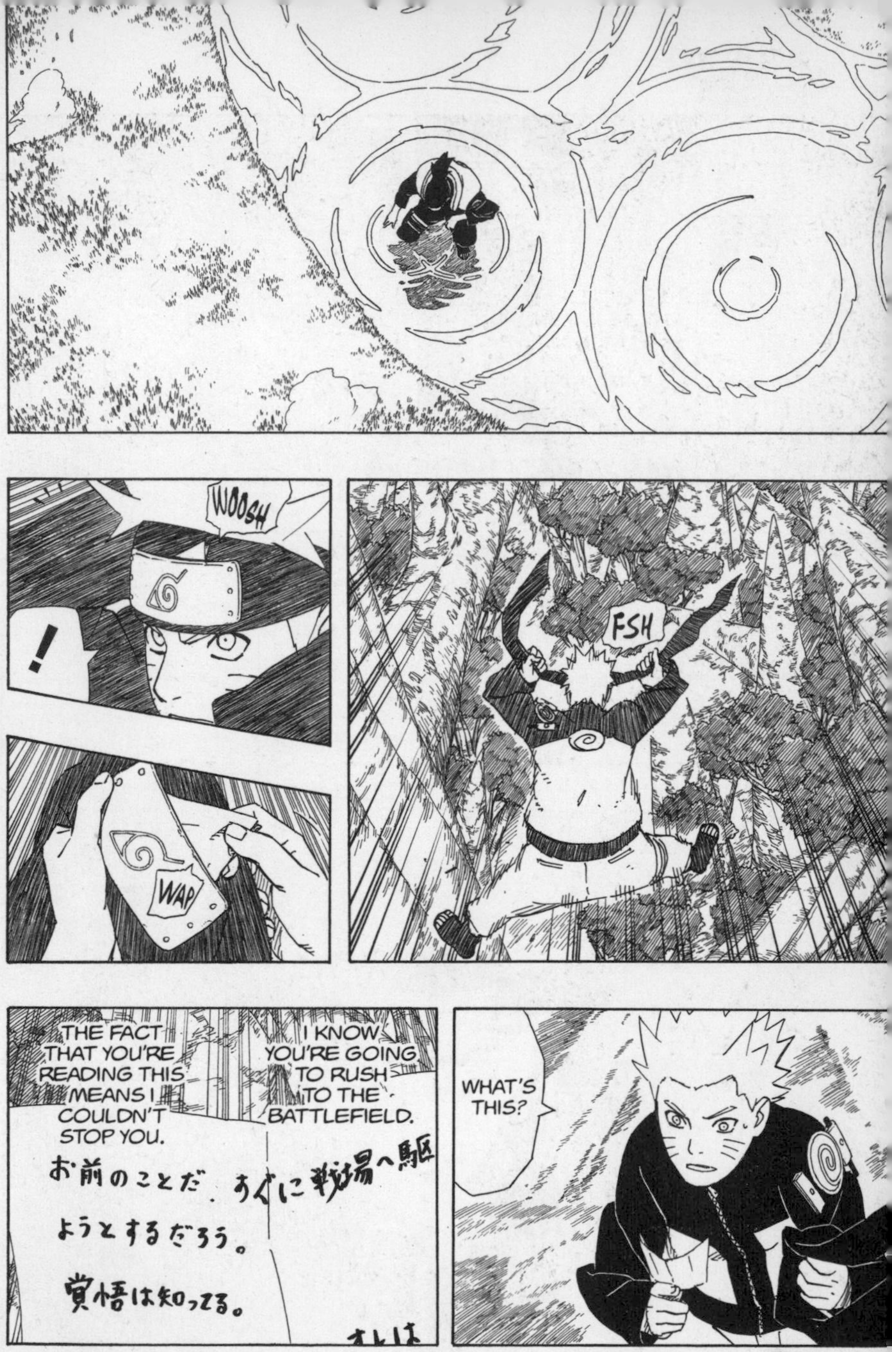
FSH
WOOSH
!
WAP
WHAT'S THIS?
I KNOW YOU'RE GOING TO RUSH TO THE BATTLEFIELD.
THE FACT THAT YOU'RE READING THIS MEANS I COULDN'T STOP YOU.
お前のことだ. すぐに戦場へ駆
ようとするだろう。
覚悟は知ってる。
オレは

READ THIS WAY

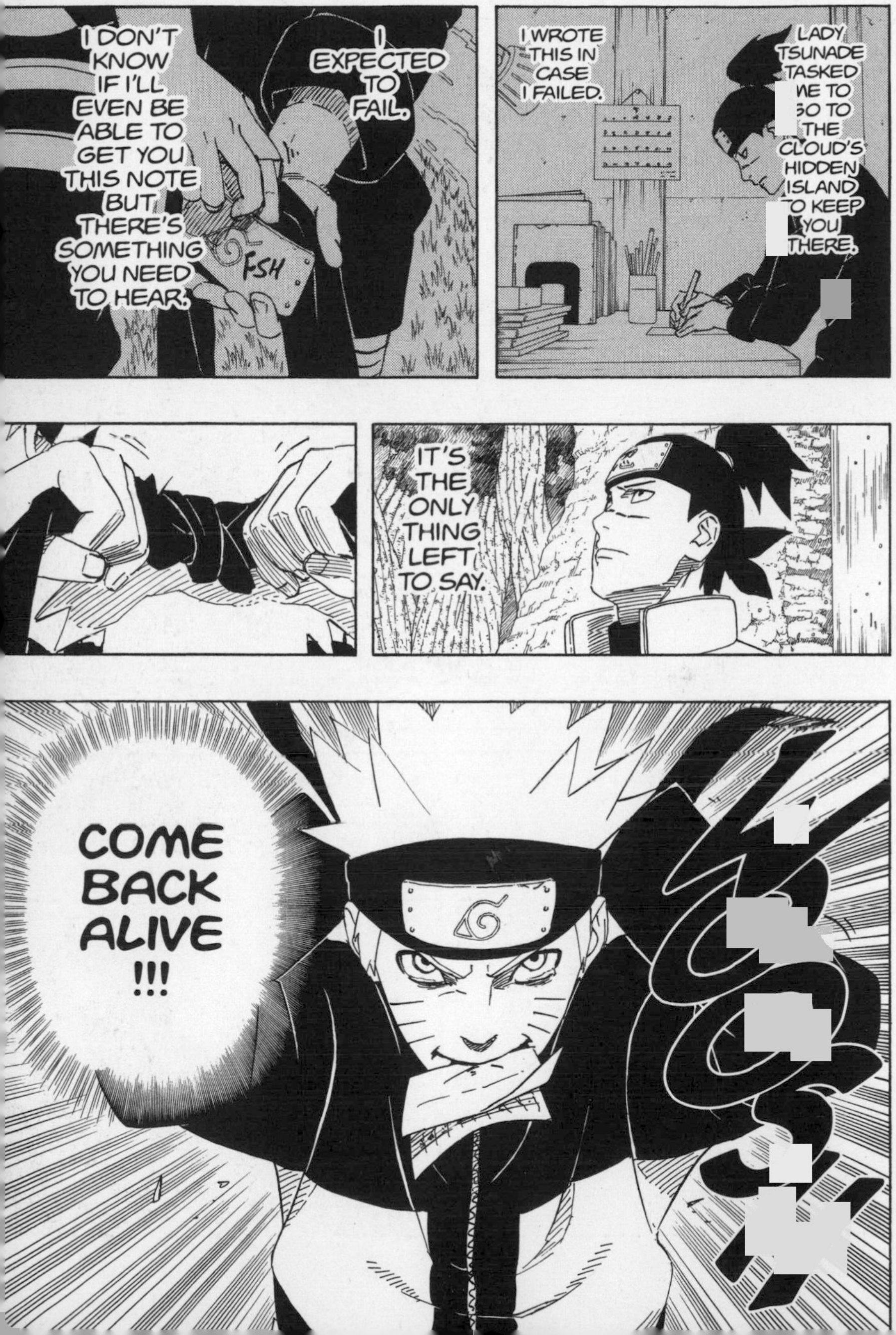
LADY TSUNADE TASKED ME TO GO TO THE CLOUD'S HIDDEN ISLAND TO KEEP YOU THERE.
I WROTE THIS IN CASE I FAILED.
I EXPECTED TO FAIL.
I DON'T KNOW IF I'LL EVEN BE ABLE TO GET YOU THIS NOTE BUT THERE'S SOMETHING YOU NEED TO HEAR.
FSH
IT'S THE ONLY THING LEFT TO SAY.
COME BACK ALIVE!!!

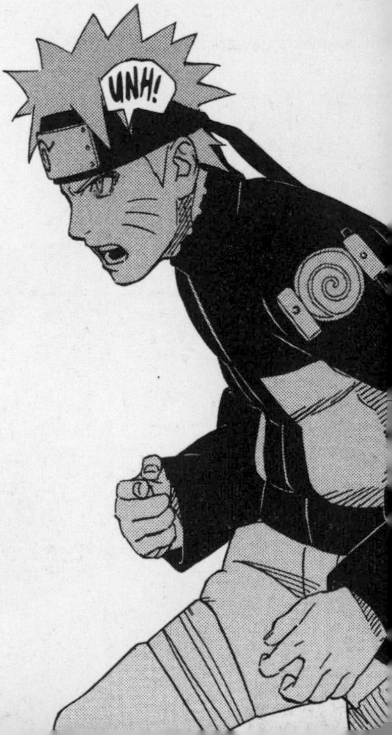
UNH!

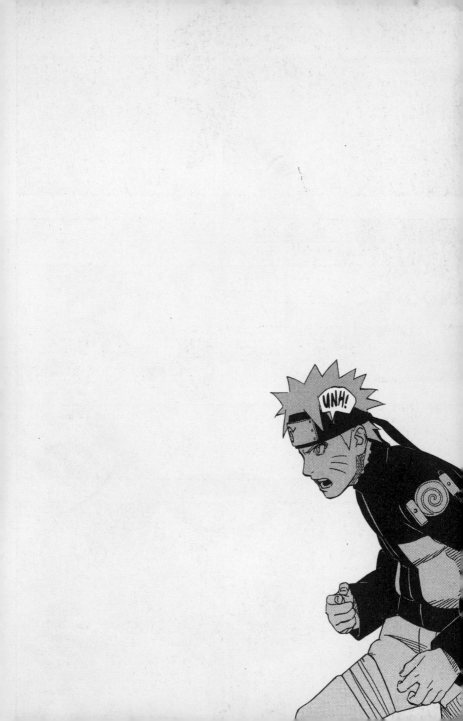

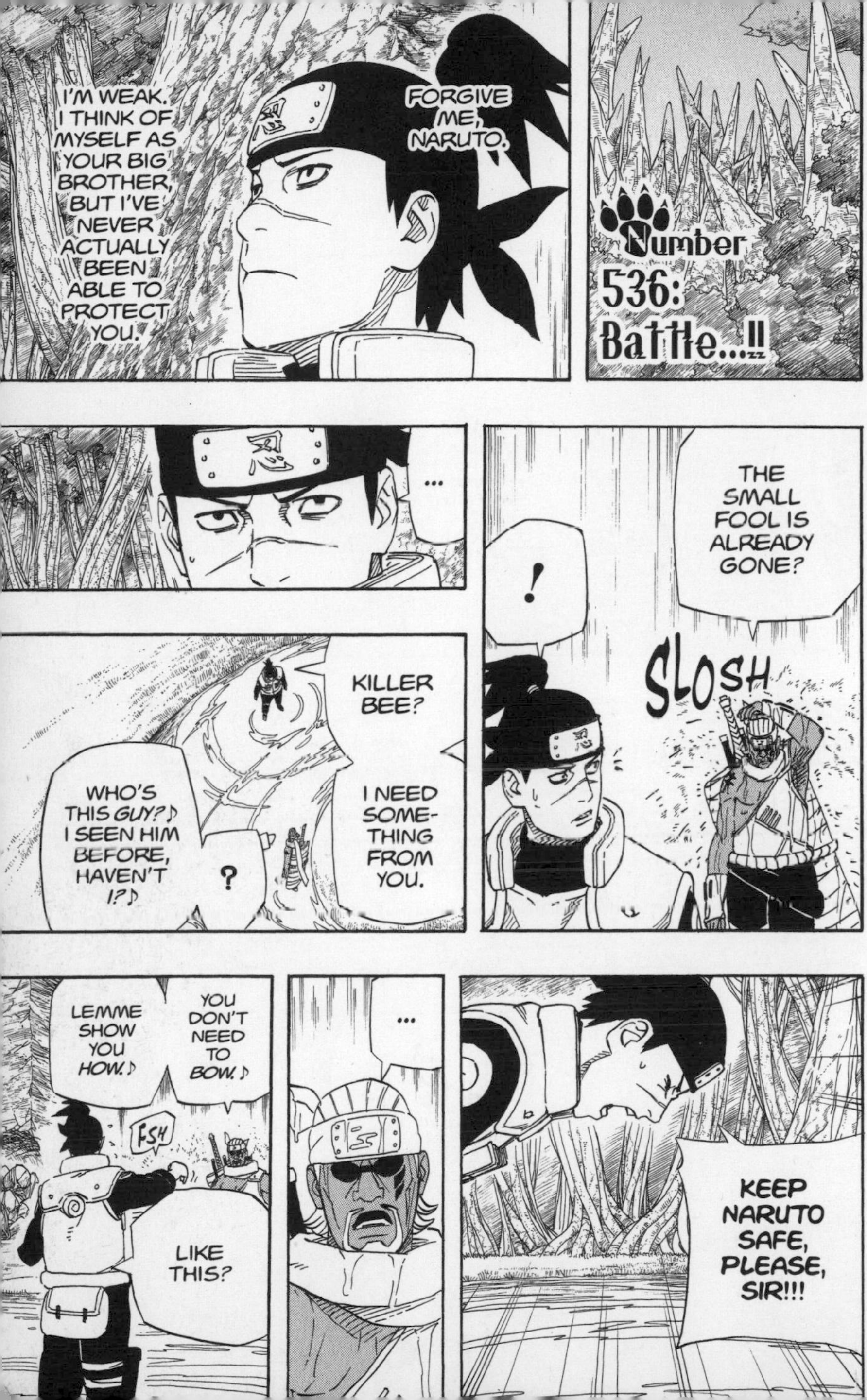
Number 536: Battle...!!
FORGIVE ME, NARUTO.
I'M WEAK. I THINK OF MYSELF AS YOUR BIG BROTHER, BUT I'VE NEVER ACTUALLY BEEN ABLE TO PROTECT YOU.
THE SMALL FOOL IS ALREADY GONE?
!
SLOSH
...
KILLER BEE?
I NEED SOME-THING FROM YOU.
?
WHO'S THIS GUY?♪ I SEEN HIM BEFORE, HAVEN'T I?♪
KEEP NARUTO SAFE, PLEASE, SIR!!!
...
YOU DON'T NEED TO BOW.♪
LEMME SHOW YOU HOW.♪
FSH
LIKE THIS?

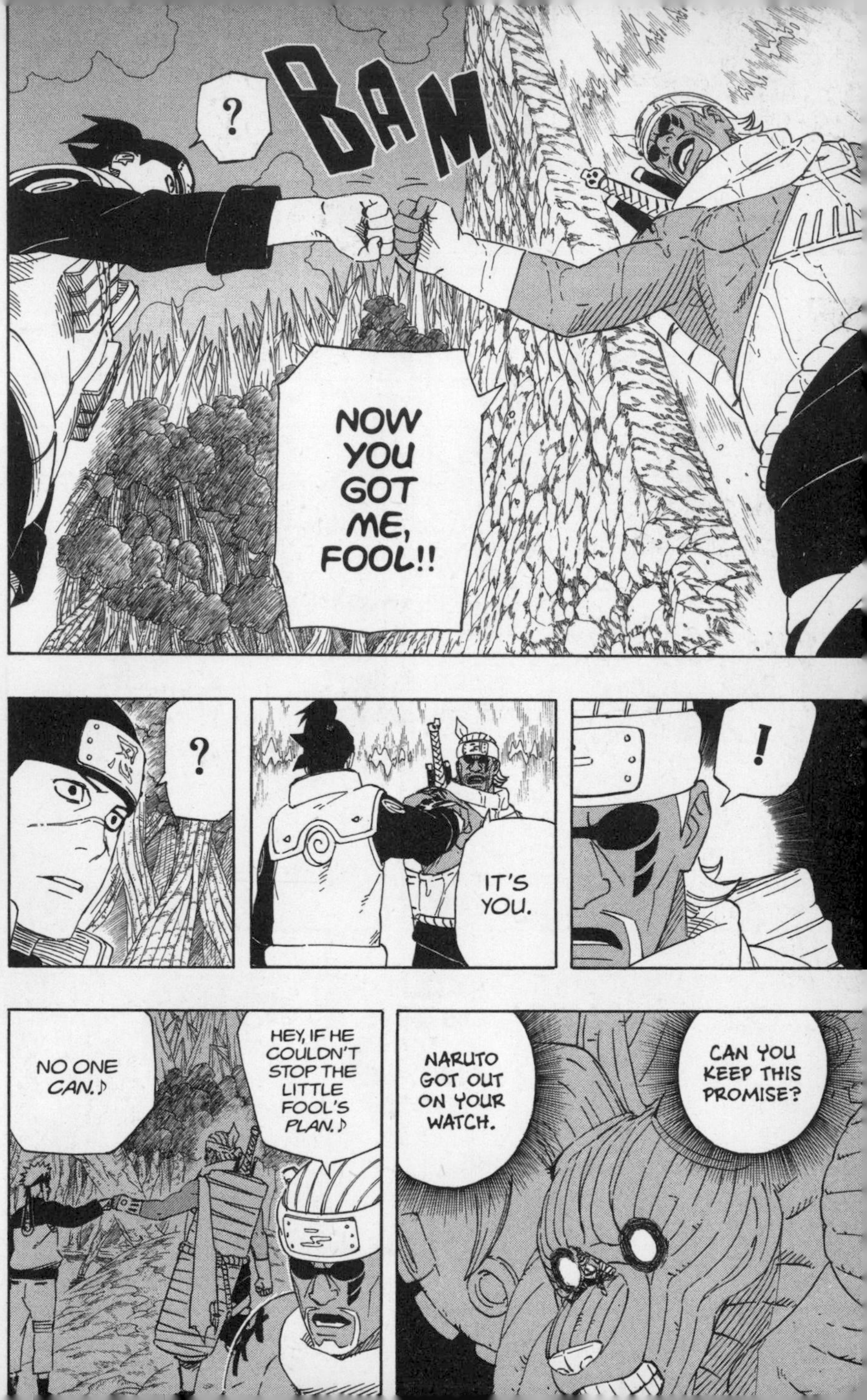
BAM
?
NOW YOU GOT ME, FOOL!!
!
IT'S YOU.
?
CAN YOU KEEP THIS PROMISE?
NARUTO GOT OUT ON YOUR WATCH.
HEY, IF HE COULDN'T STOP THE LITTLE FOOL'S PLAN.♪
NO ONE CAN.♪

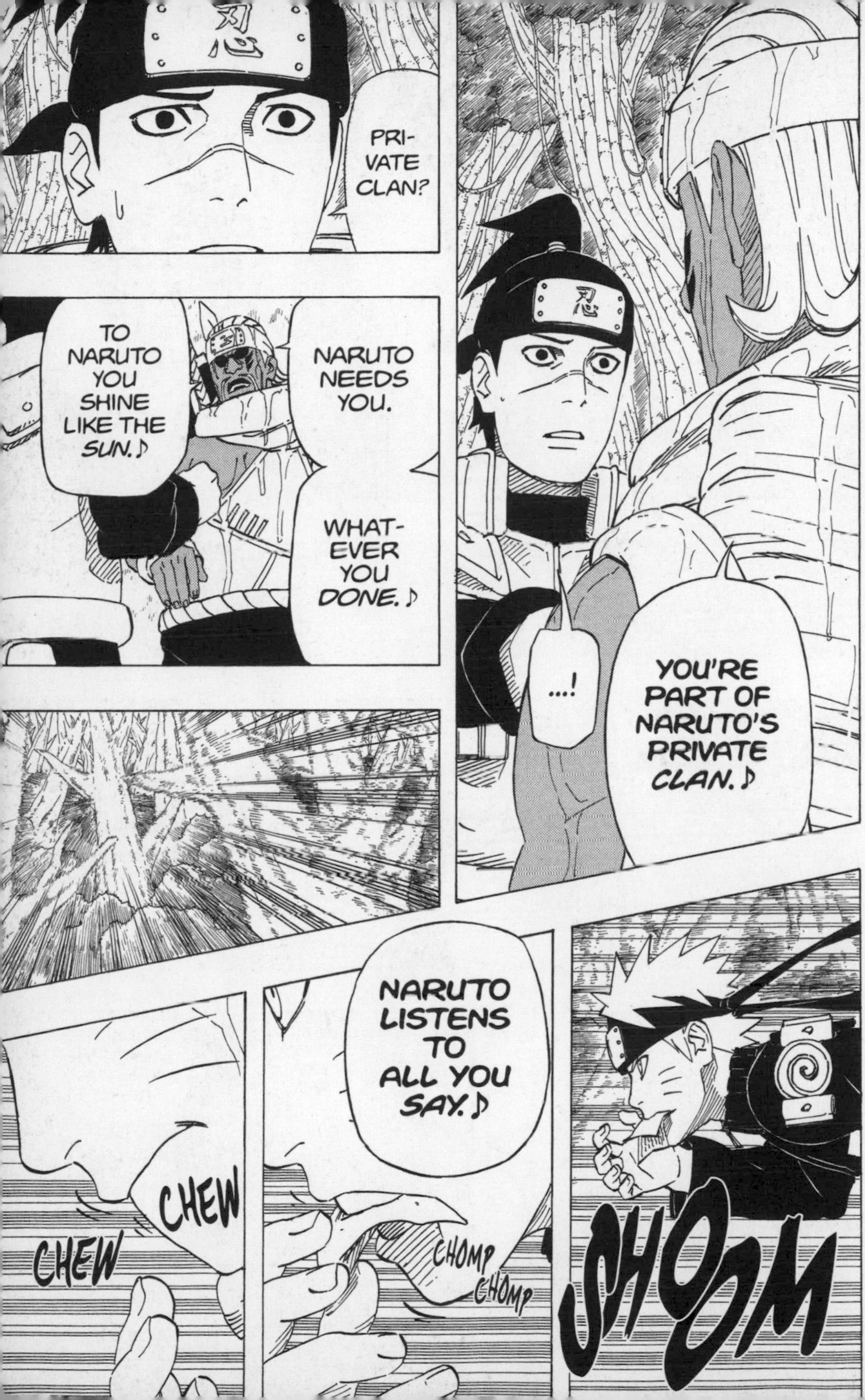
YOU'RE PART OF NARUTO'S PRIVATE CLAN.♪
...!
PRI-VATE CLAN?
NARUTO NEEDS YOU.
WHAT-EVER YOU DONE.♪
TO NARUTO YOU SHINE LIKE THE SUN.♪
SHOOM
NARUTO LISTENS TO ALL YOU SAY.♪
CHOMP
CHOMP
CHEW
CHEW

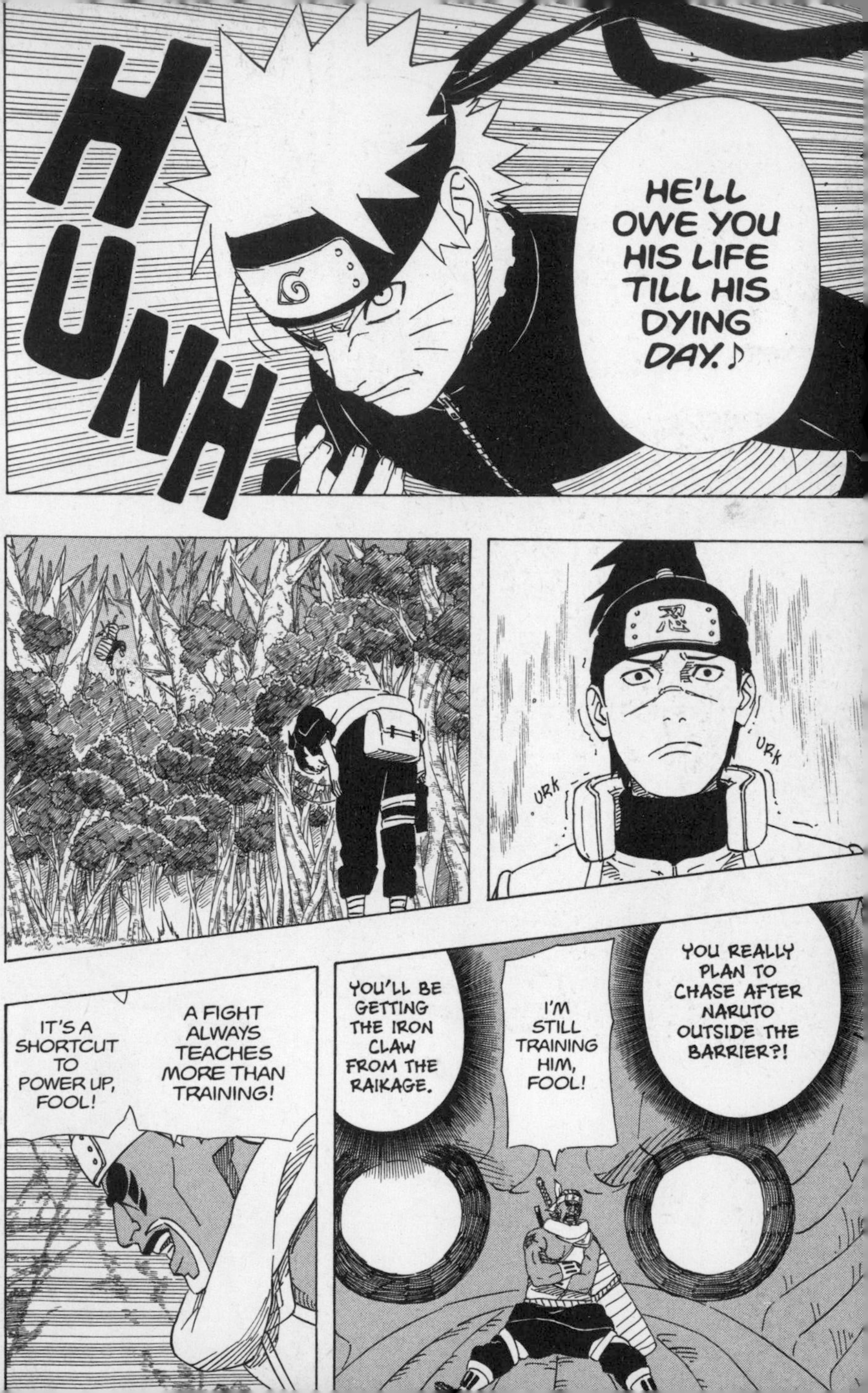
HE'LL OWE YOU HIS LIFE TILL HIS DYING DAY.♪
HUNH
URK
URK
YOU REALLY PLAN TO CHASE AFTER NARUTO OUTSIDE THE BARRIER?!
I'M STILL TRAINING HIM, FOOL!
YOU'LL BE GETTING THE IRON CLAW FROM THE RAIKAGE.
A FIGHT ALWAYS TEACHES MORE THAN TRAINING!
IT'S A SHORTCUT TO POWER UP, FOOL!

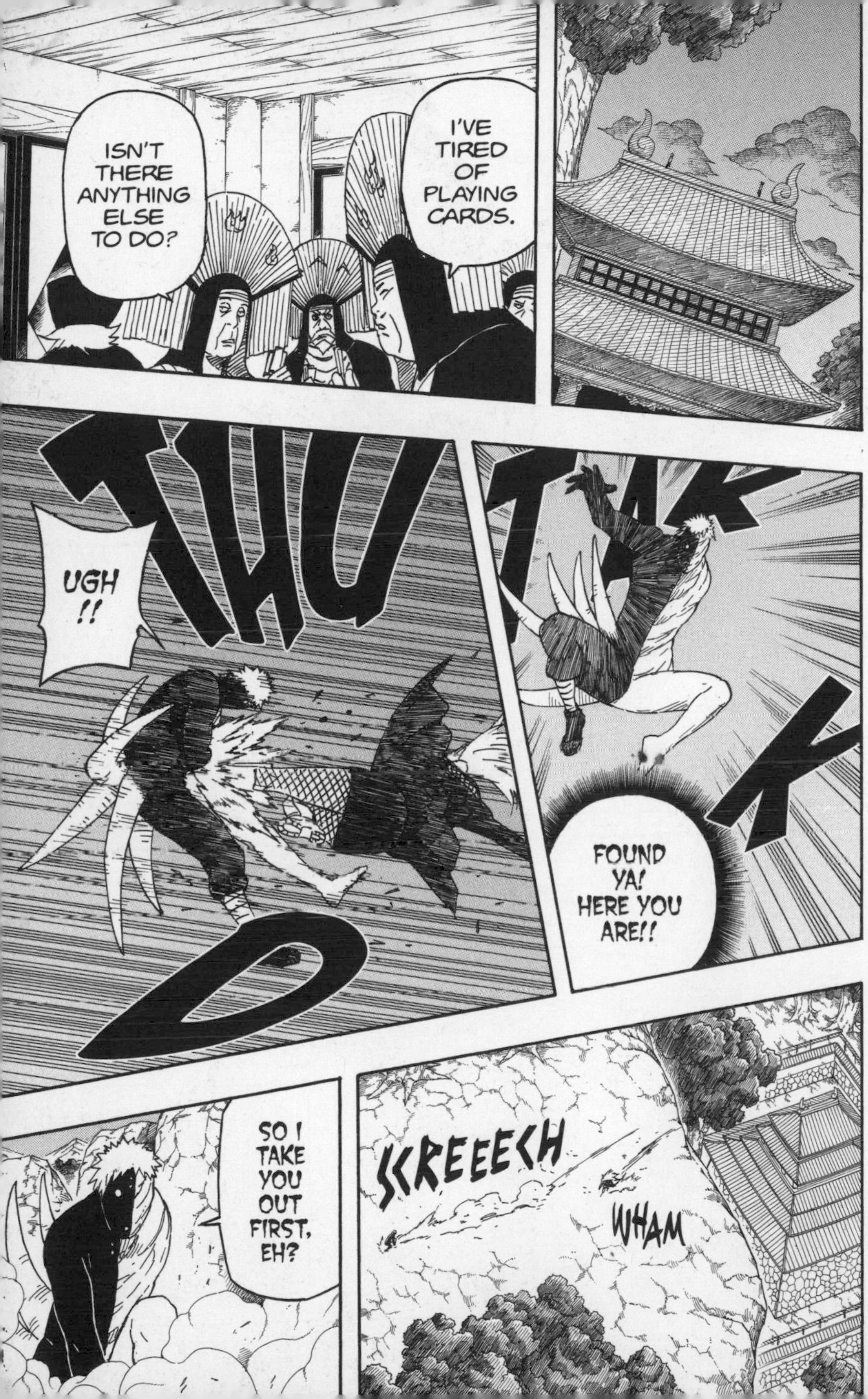
I'VE TIRED OF PLAYING CARDS.
ISN'T THERE ANYTHING ELSE TO DO?
TAK
FOUND YA! HERE YOU ARE!!
THUD
UGH !!
SCREEECH
WHAM
SO I TAKE YOU OUT FIRST, EH?

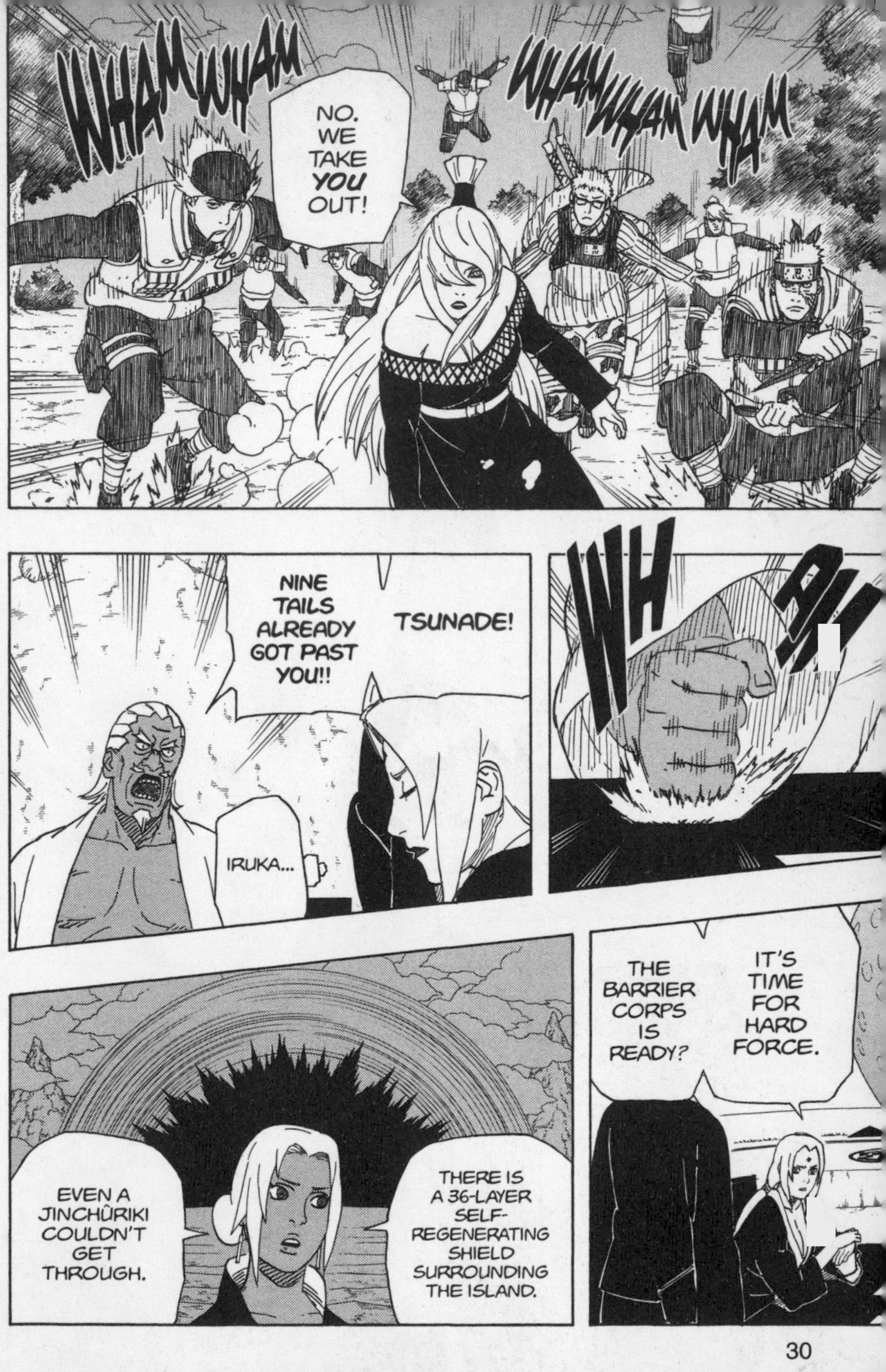
WHAM WHAM WHAM
NO. WE TAKE YOU OUT!
WHAM WHAM
WHAM
TSUNADE!
NINE TAILS ALREADY GOT PAST YOU!!
IRUKA...
IT'S TIME FOR HARD FORCE.
THE BARRIER CORPS IS READY?
THERE IS A 36-LAYER SELF-REGENERATING SHIELD SURROUNDING THE ISLAND.
EVEN A JINCHÛRIKI COULDN'T GET THROUGH.

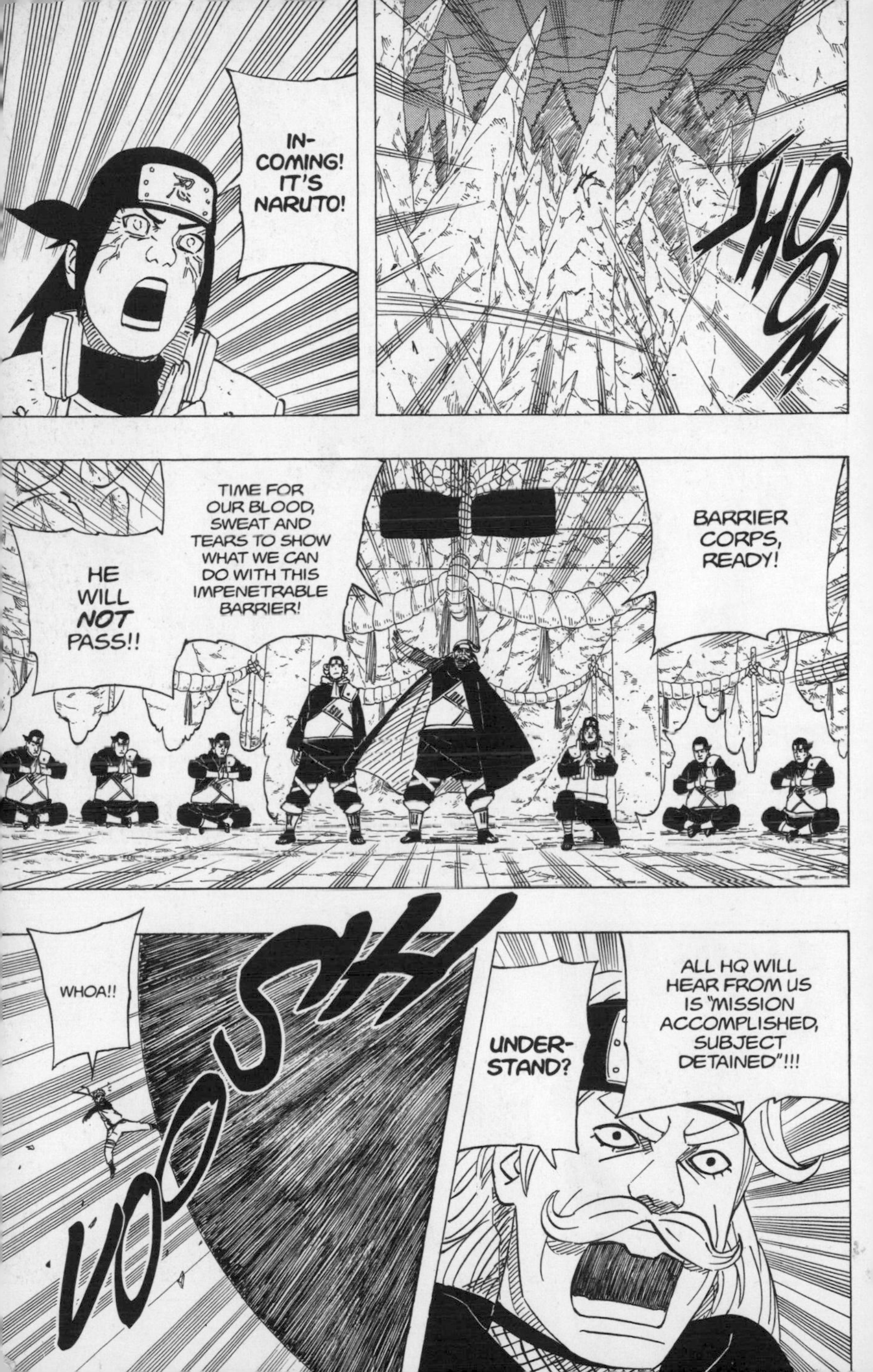
SHOOM
IN-COMING! IT'S NARUTO!
BARRIER CORPS, READY!
TIME FOR OUR BLOOD, SWEAT AND TEARS TO SHOW WHAT WE CAN DO WITH THIS IMPENETRABLE BARRIER!
HE WILL NOT PASS!!
ALL HQ WILL HEAR FROM US IS "MISSION ACCOMPLISHED, SUBJECT DETAINED"!!!
UNDER-STAND?
VOOSH
WHOA!!

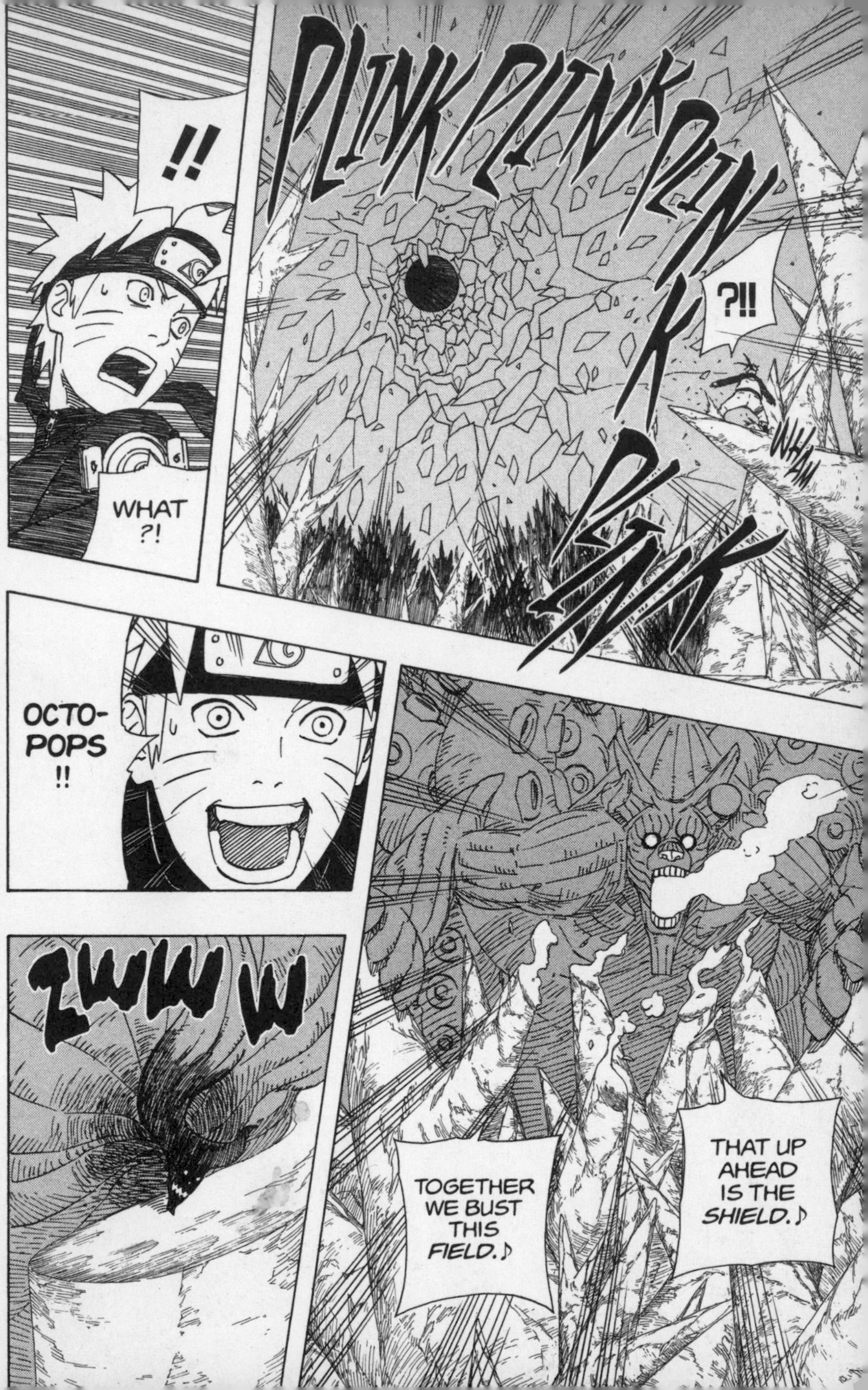
PLINK PLINK PLINK PLINK
?!!
WHAM
!!
WHAT ?!
THAT UP AHEAD IS THE SHIELD.♪
TOGETHER WE BUST THIS FIELD.♪
OCTO-POPS !!
ZWWW

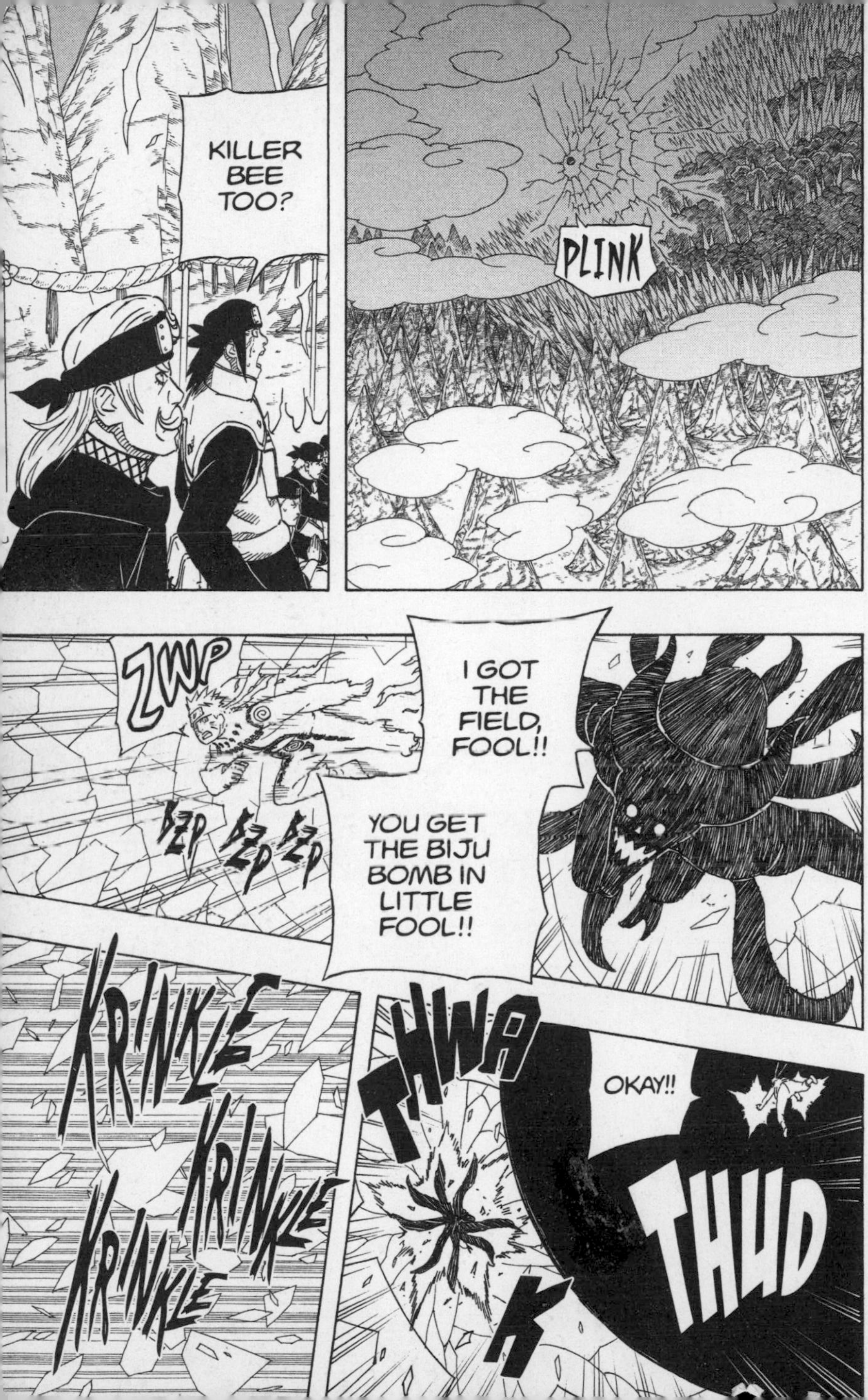
PLINK
KILLER BEE TOO?
I GOT THE FIELD, FOOL!!
YOU GET THE BIJU BOMB IN LITTLE FOOL!!
ZWP
BZP BZP BZP
OKAY!!
THUD
THWAK
KRINKLE KRINKLE KRINKLE

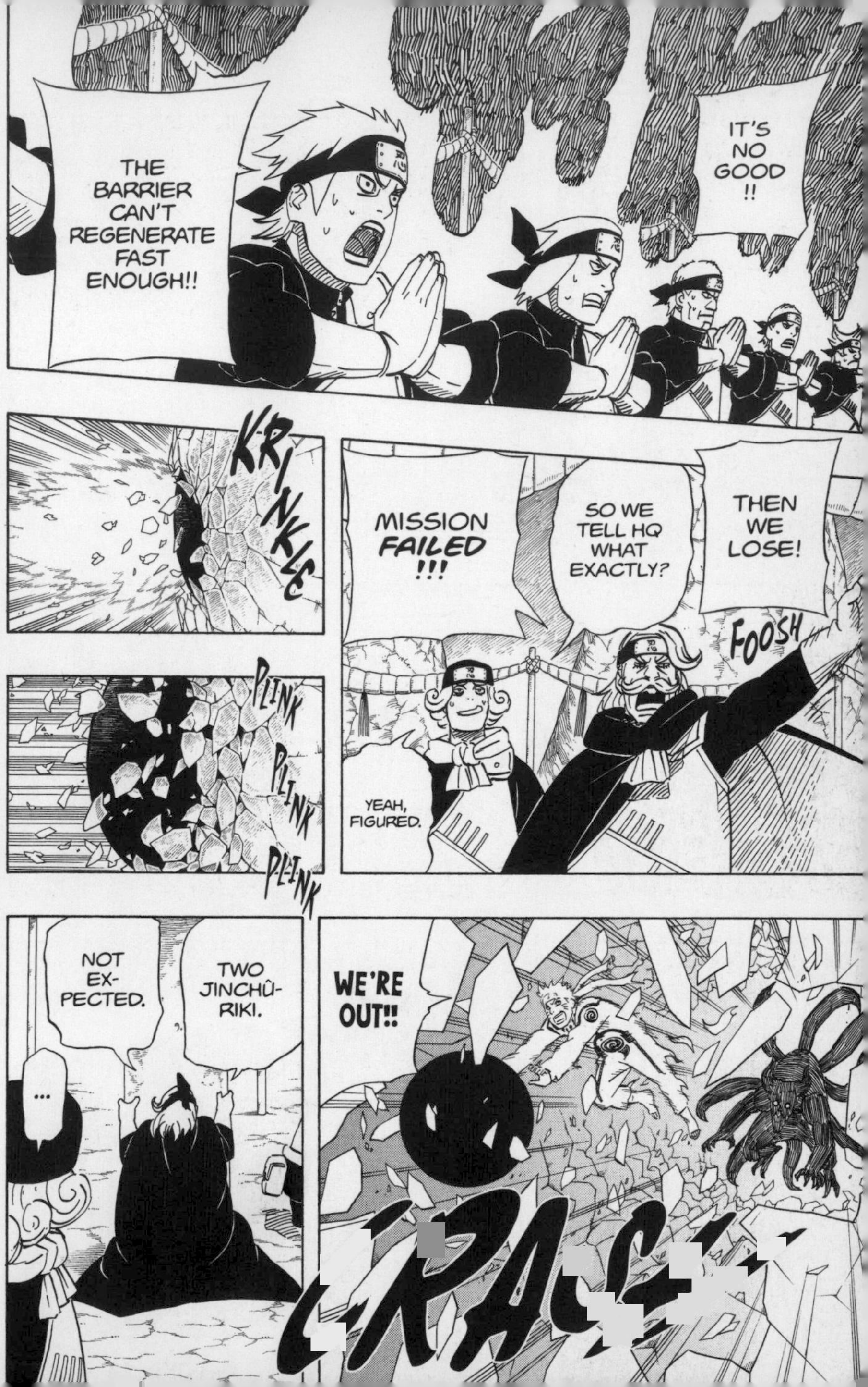
IT'S NO GOOD!!
THE BARRIER CAN'T REGENERATE FAST ENOUGH!!
THEN WE LOSE!
SO WE TELL HQ WHAT EXACTLY?
MISSION FAILED!!!
FOOSH
YEAH, FIGURED.
KRINKLE
PLINK
PLINK
PLINK
WE'RE OUT!!
TWO JINCHÛ-RIKI.
NOT EX-PECTED.
...

READ THIS WAY

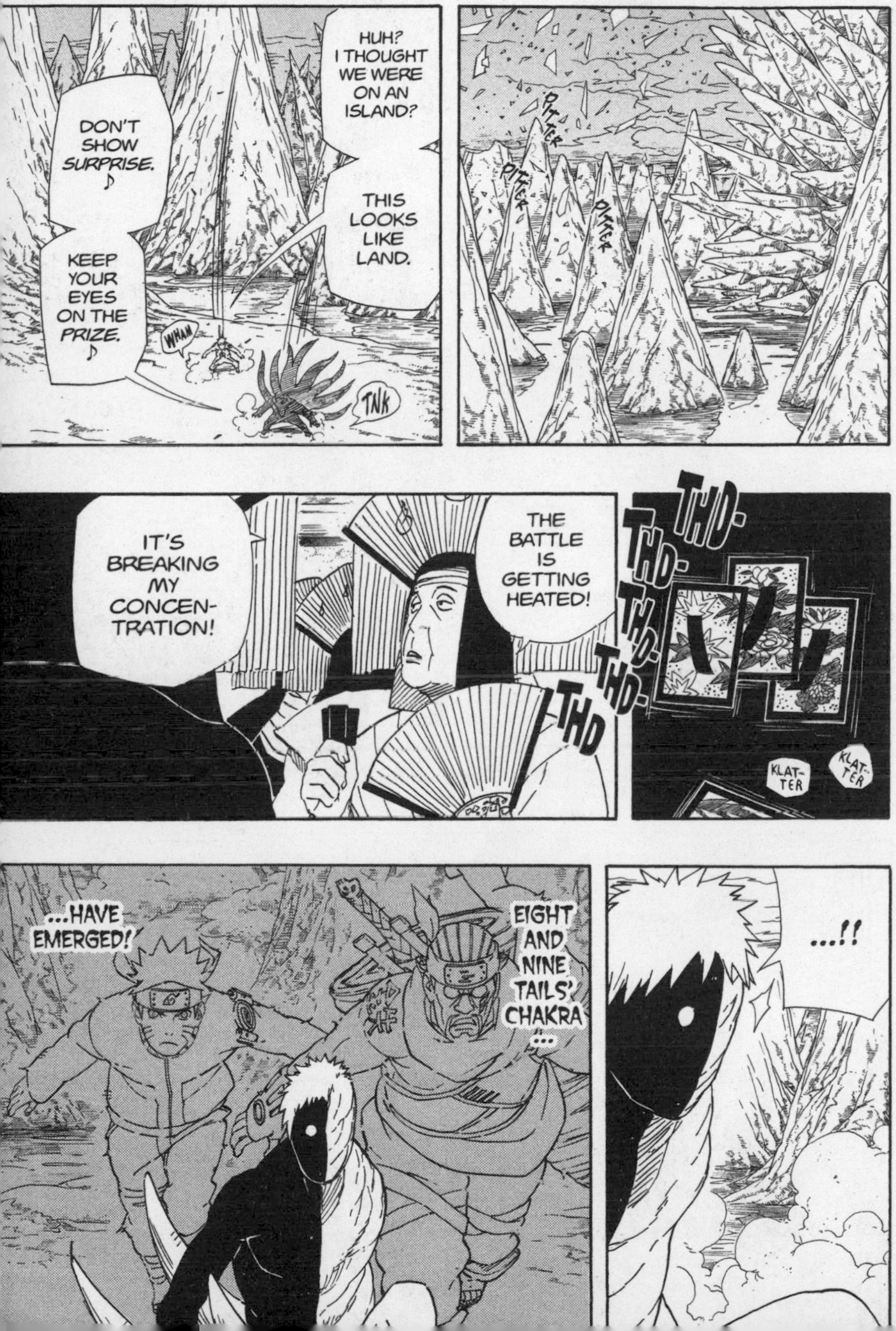
PITTER
PITTER
PITTER
HUH? I THOUGHT WE WERE ON AN ISLAND?
THIS LOOKS LIKE LAND.
DON'T SHOW SURPRISE. ♪
KEEP YOUR EYES ON THE PRIZE. ♪
WHAM
TNK
THD-THD-THD-THD-THD-THD
KLATTER
KLATTER
THE BATTLE IS GETTING HEATED!
IT'S BREAKING MY CONCENTRATION!
...!!
EIGHT AND NINE TAILS' CHAKRA...
...HAVE EMERGED!

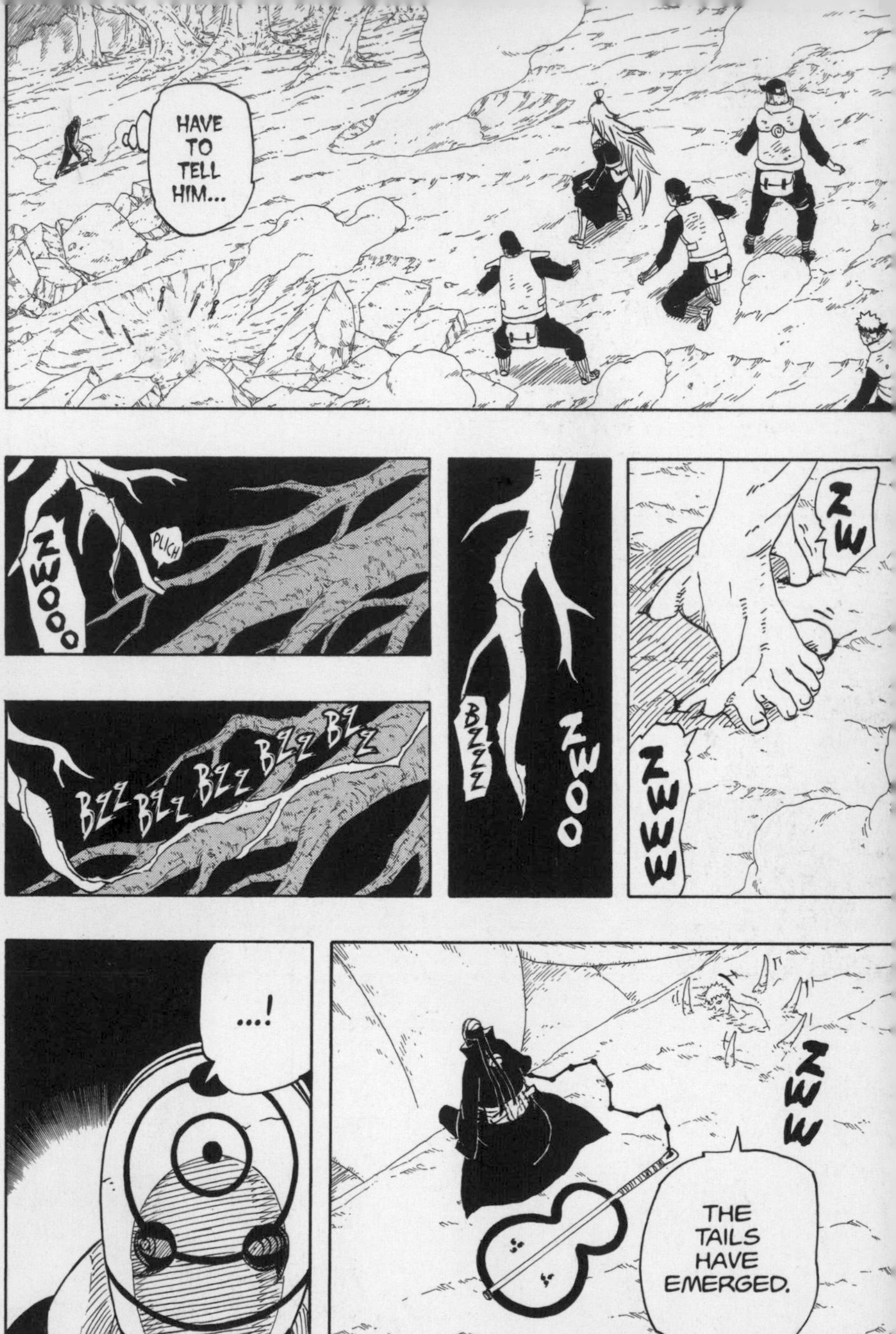
HAVE TO TELL HIM...
ZW
ZWWW
BZZZ
ZWOO
ZWOOO
PLICH
BZZ BZZ BZZ BZZ BZZ
ZWW
THE TAILS HAVE EMERGED.
...!

READ THIS WAY

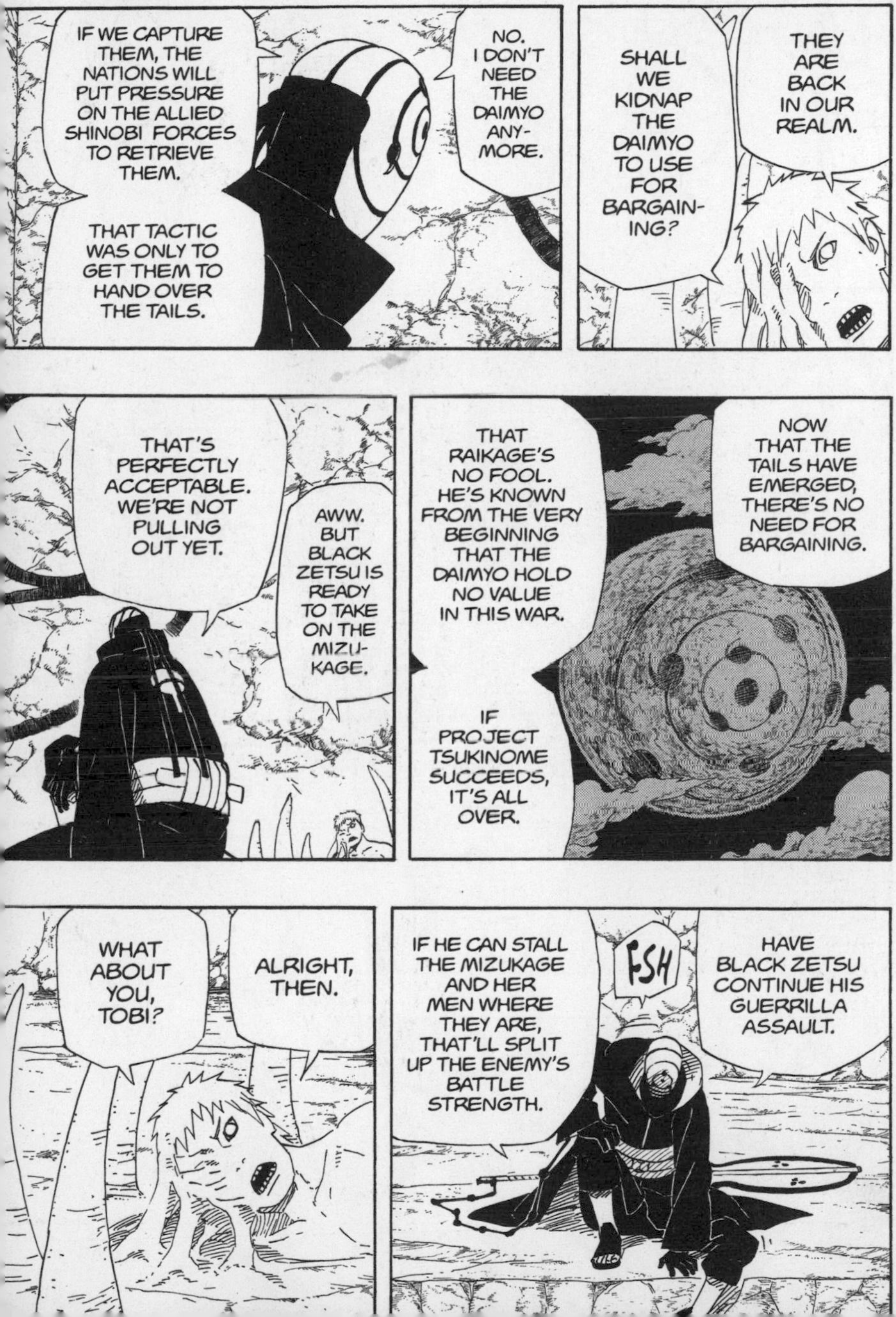

THEY ARE BACK IN OUR REALM.
SHALL WE KIDNAP THE DAIMYO TO USE FOR BARGAINING?
NO. I DON'T NEED THE DAIMYO ANYMORE.
IF WE CAPTURE THEM, THE NATIONS WILL PUT PRESSURE ON THE ALLIED SHINOBI FORCES TO RETRIEVE THEM.
THAT TACTIC WAS ONLY TO GET THEM TO HAND OVER THE TAILS.
NOW THAT THE TAILS HAVE EMERGED, THERE'S NO NEED FOR BARGAINING.
THAT RAIKAGE'S NO FOOL. HE'S KNOWN FROM THE VERY BEGINNING THAT THE DAIMYO HOLD NO VALUE IN THIS WAR.
IF PROJECT TSUKINOME SUCCEEDS, IT'S ALL OVER.
AWW. BUT BLACK ZETSU IS READY TO TAKE ON THE MIZUKAGE.
THAT'S PERFECTLY ACCEPTABLE. WE'RE NOT PULLING OUT YET.
HAVE BLACK ZETSU CONTINUE HIS GUERRILLA ASSAULT.
FSH
IF HE CAN STALL THE MIZUKAGE AND HER MEN WHERE THEY ARE, THAT'LL SPLIT UP THE ENEMY'S BATTLE STRENGTH.
ALRIGHT, THEN.
WHAT ABOUT YOU, TOBI?

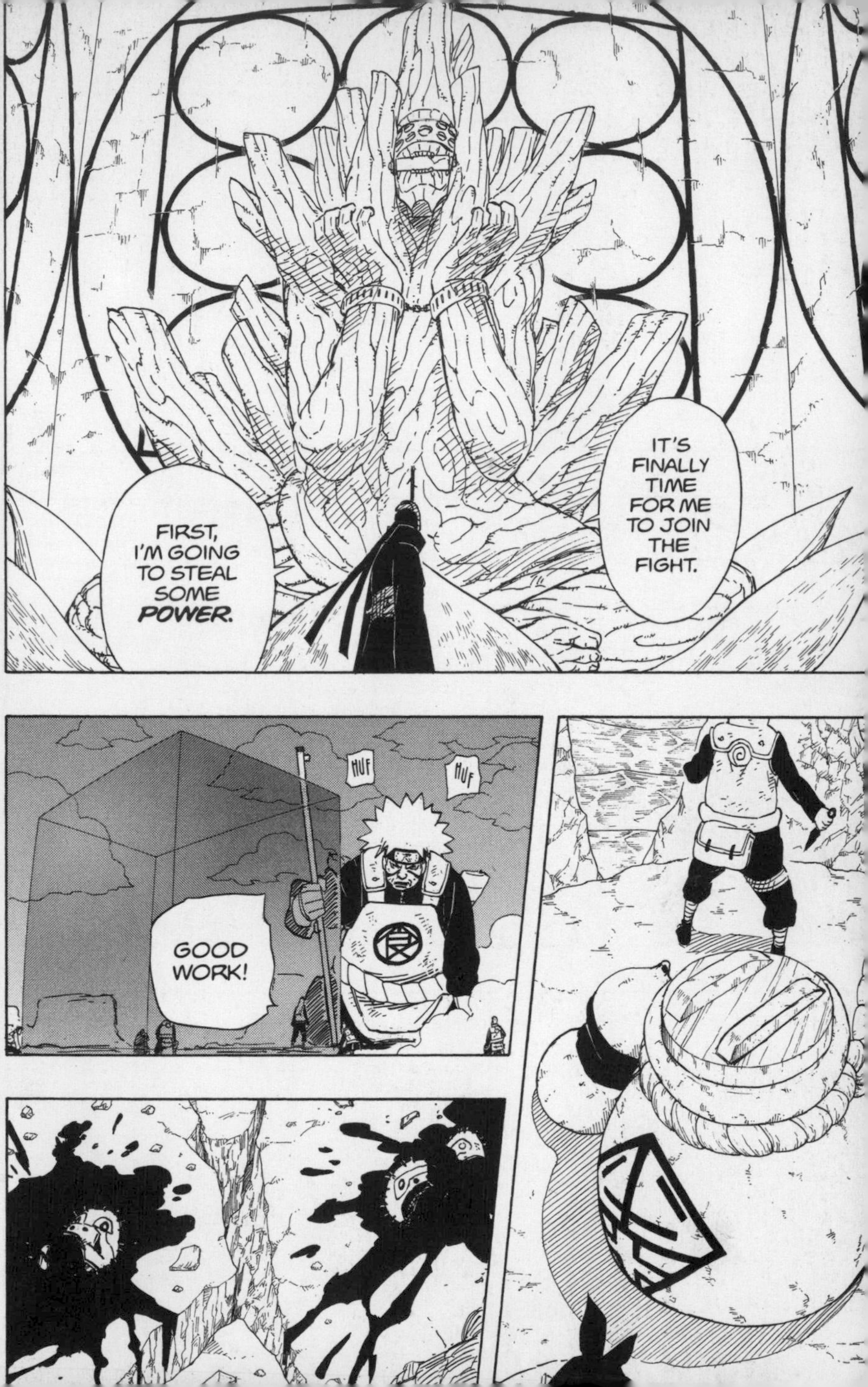
IT'S FINALLY TIME FOR ME TO JOIN THE FIGHT.
FIRST, I'M GOING TO STEAL SOME *POWER.*
HUF
HUF
GOOD WORK!

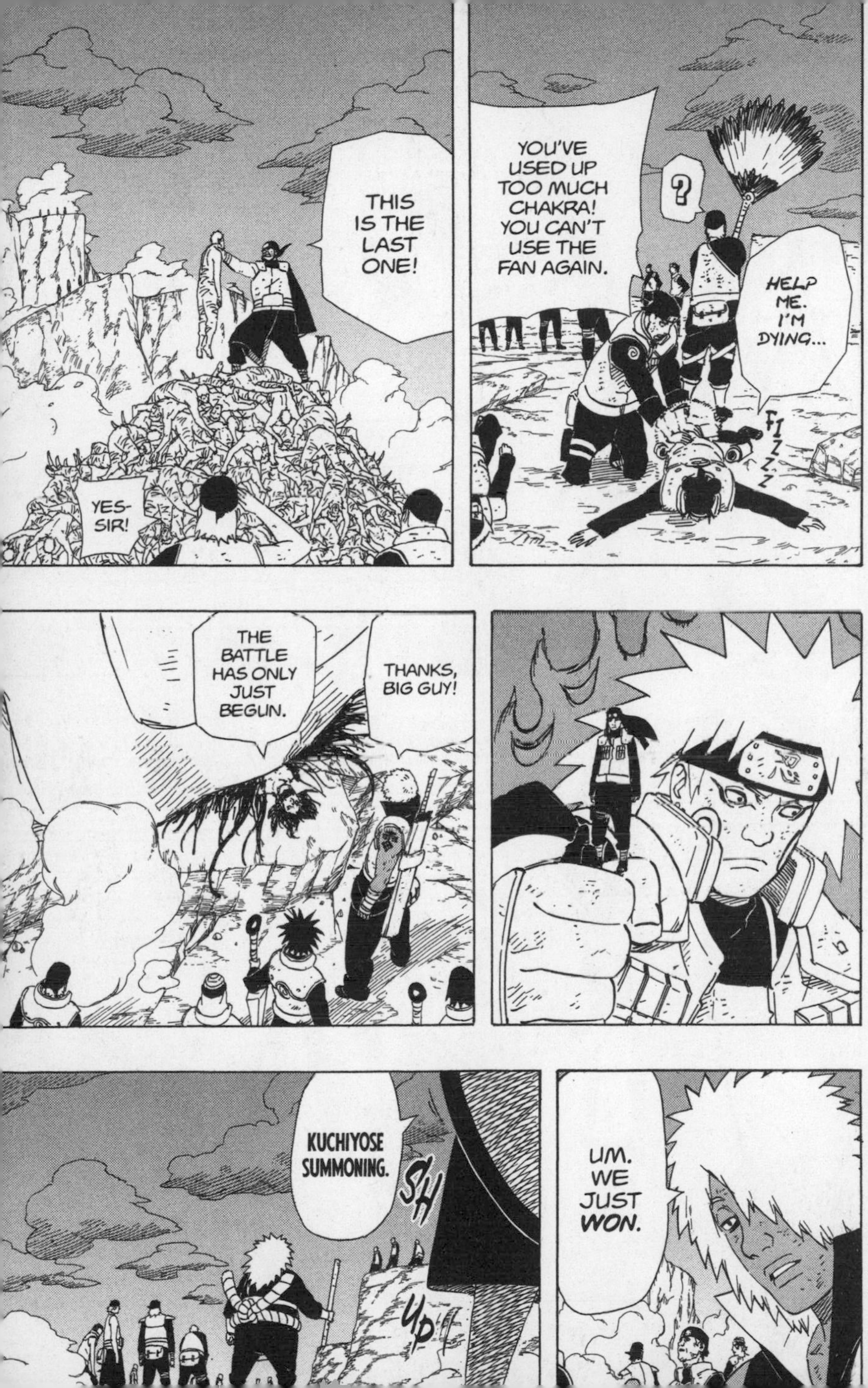
YOU'VE USED UP TOO MUCH CHAKRA! YOU CAN'T USE THE FAN AGAIN.
?
HELP ME. I'M DYING...
FIZZZ
THIS IS THE LAST ONE!
YES-SIR!
THANKS, BIG GUY!
THE BATTLE HAS ONLY JUST BEGUN.
UM. WE JUST **WON**.
KUCHIYOSE SUMMONING.
SHUP

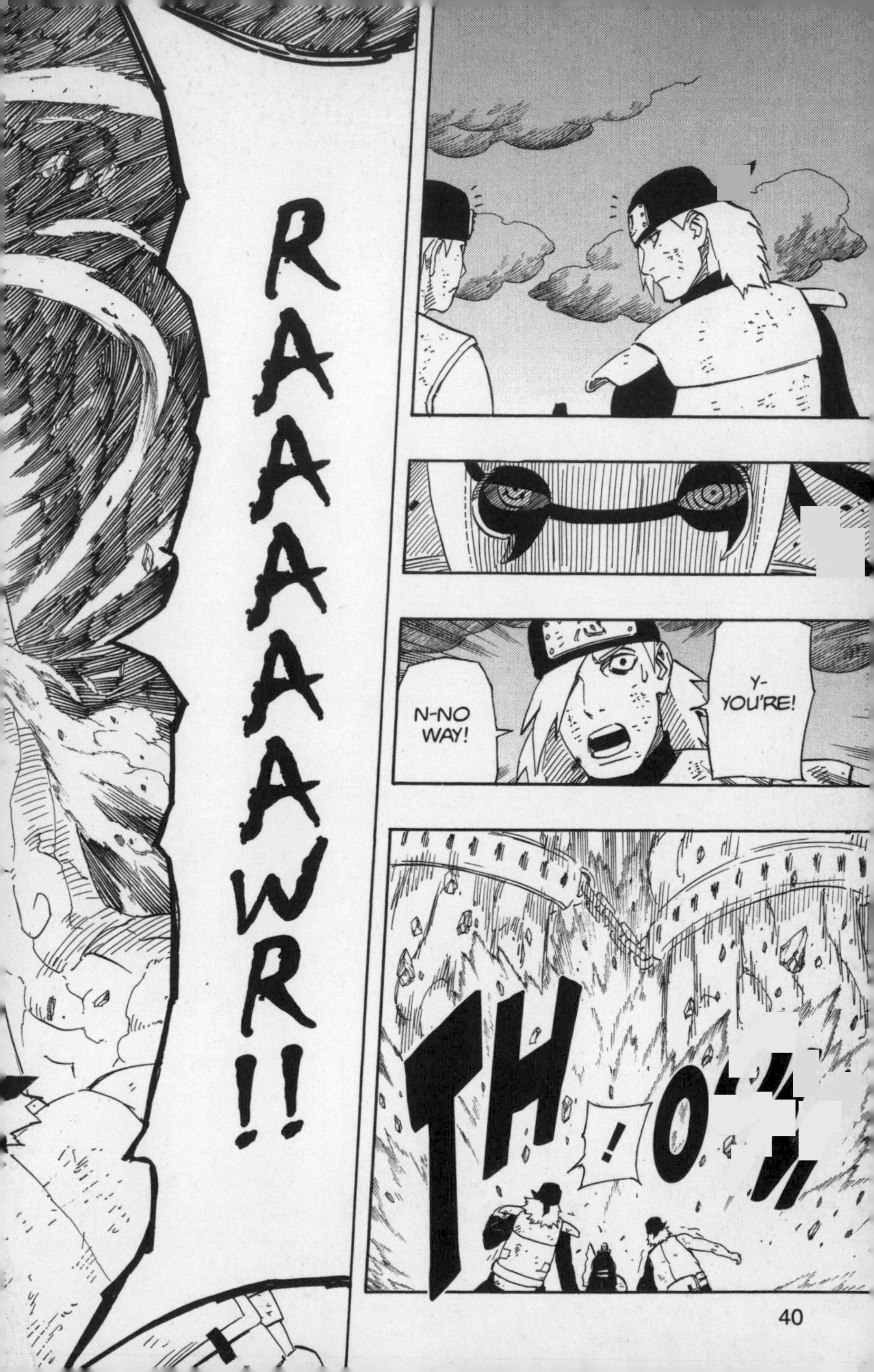
Y-
YOU'RE!
N-NO
WAY!
THO
!
RAAAAAWR!!

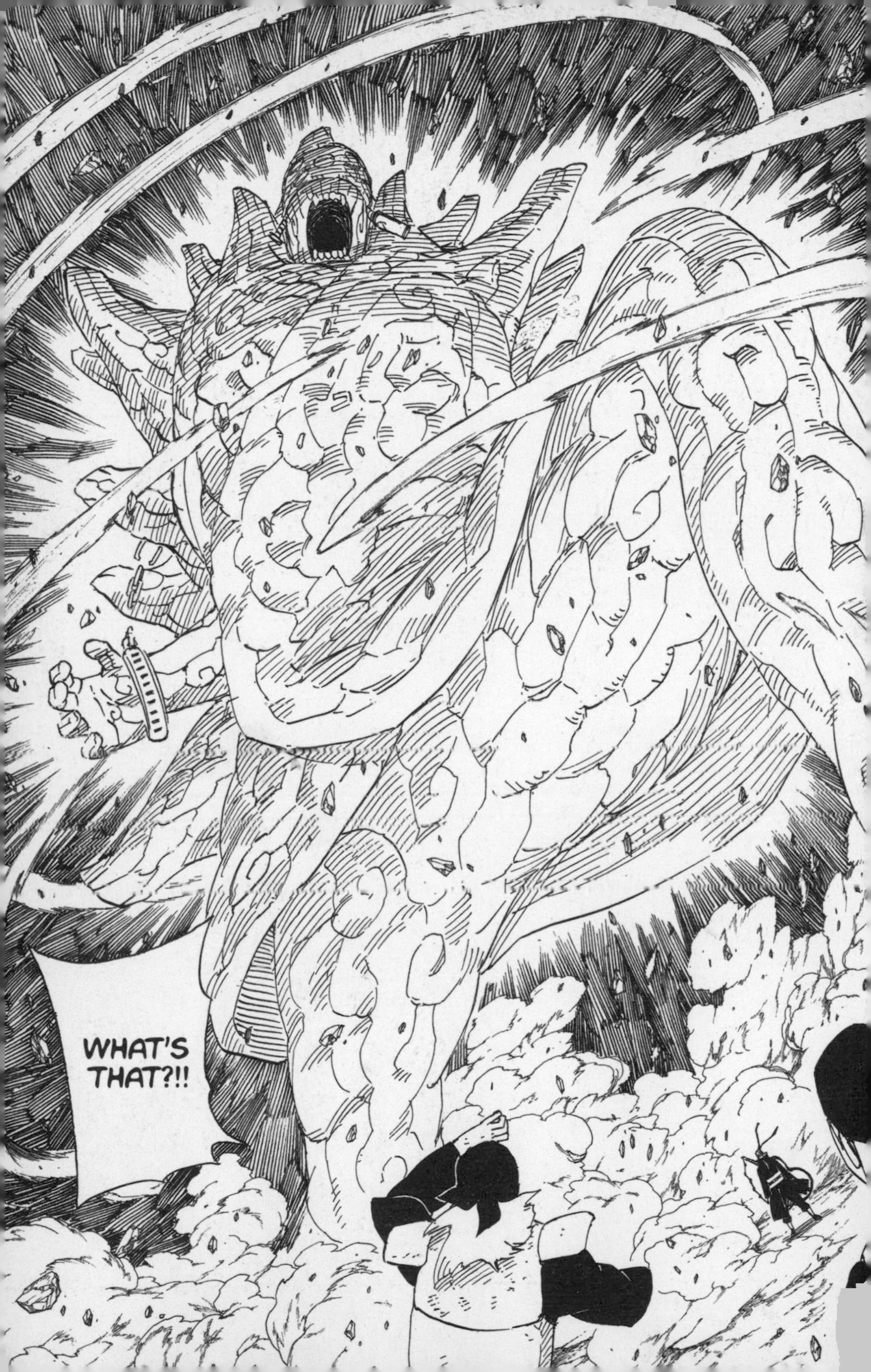
WHAT'S THAT?!!

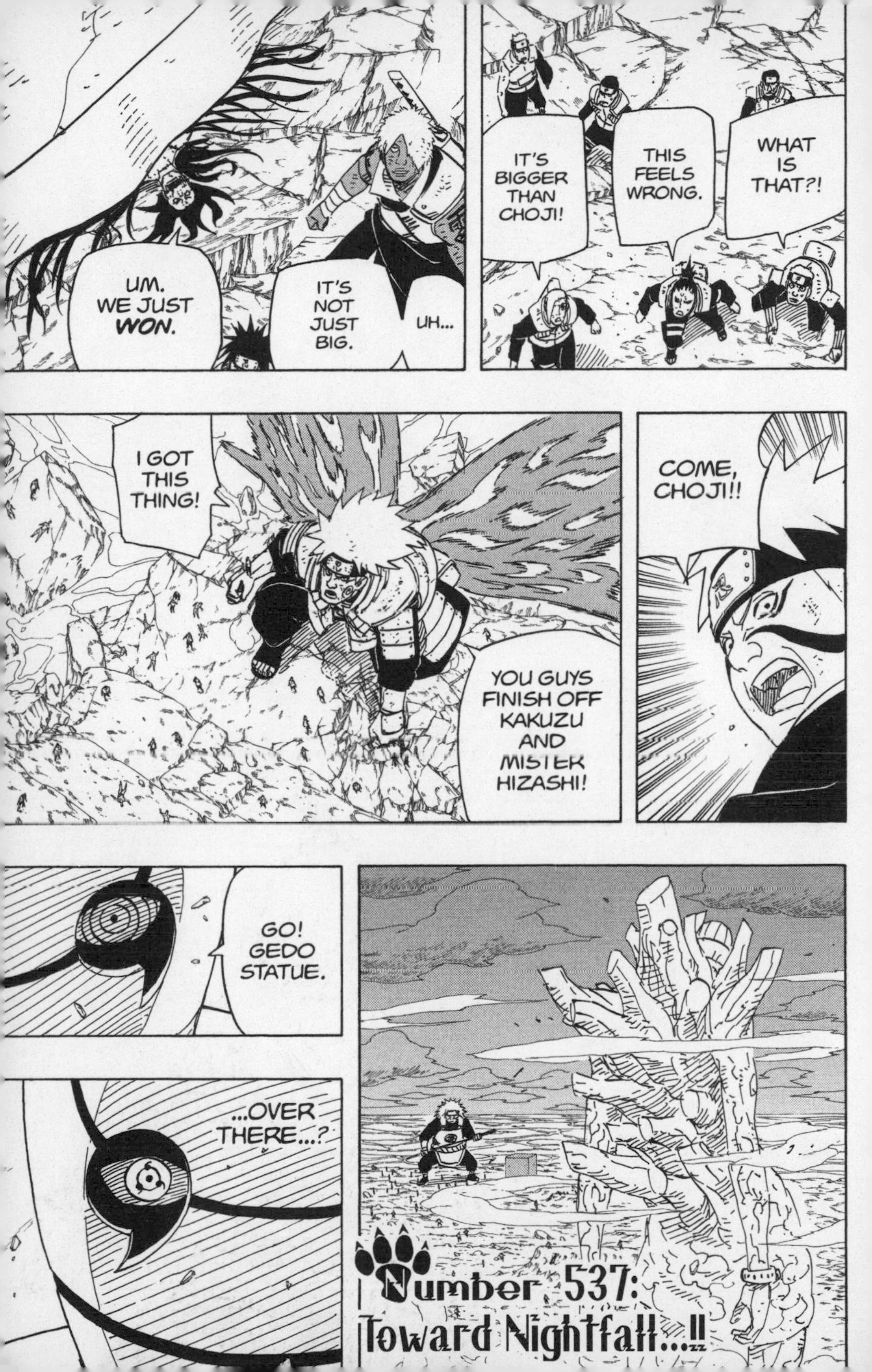
WHAT IS THAT?!
THIS FEELS WRONG.
IT'S BIGGER THAN CHOJI!
UH...
IT'S NOT JUST BIG.
UM. WE JUST WON.
COME, CHOJI!!
I GOT THIS THING!
YOU GUYS FINISH OFF KAKUZU AND MISTER HIZASHI!
Number 537: Toward Nightfall...!!
GO! GEDO STATUE.
...OVER THERE...?

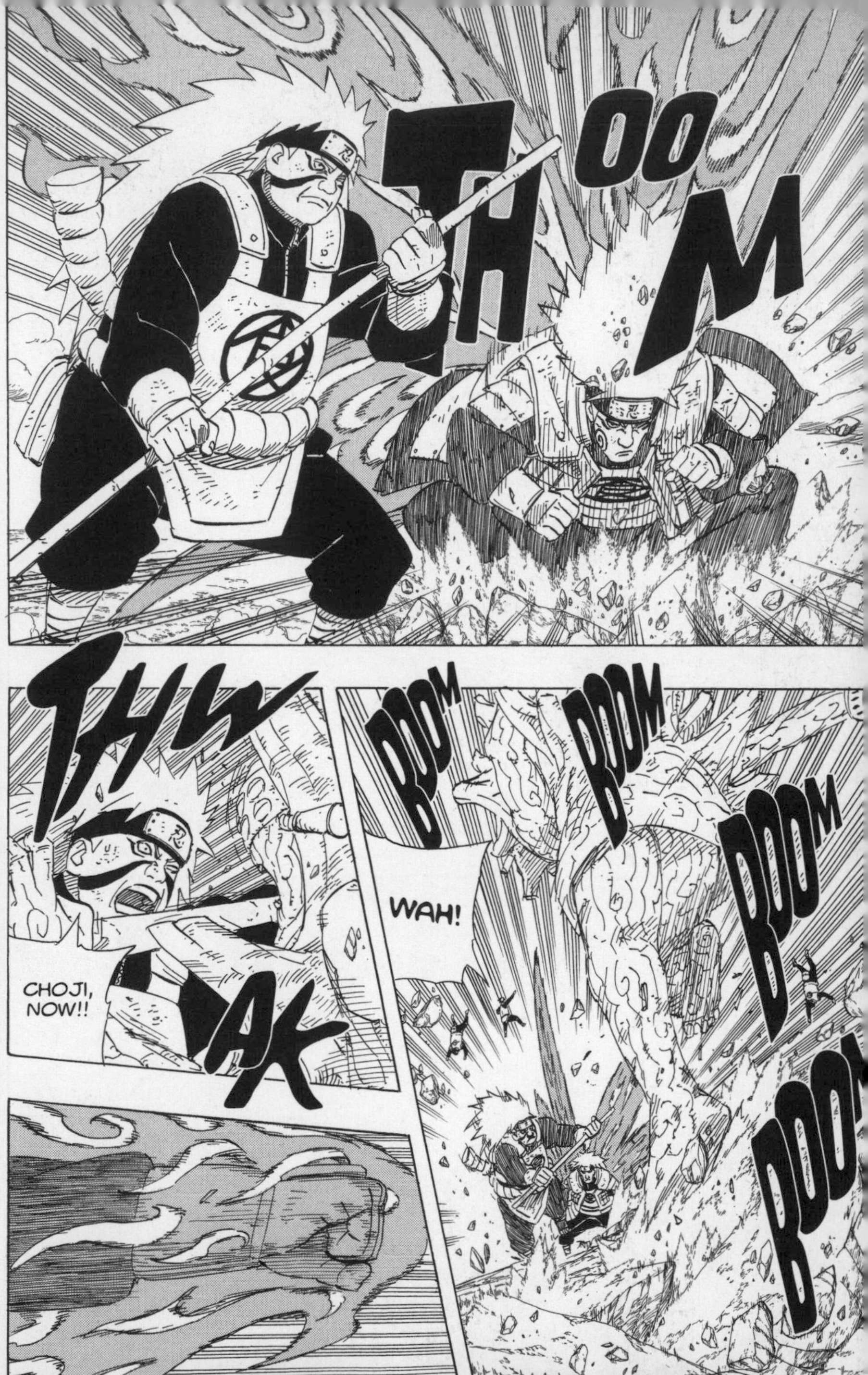
THOOM
BOOM
BOOM
BOOM
BOO
WAH!
THWAK
CHOJI, NOW!!

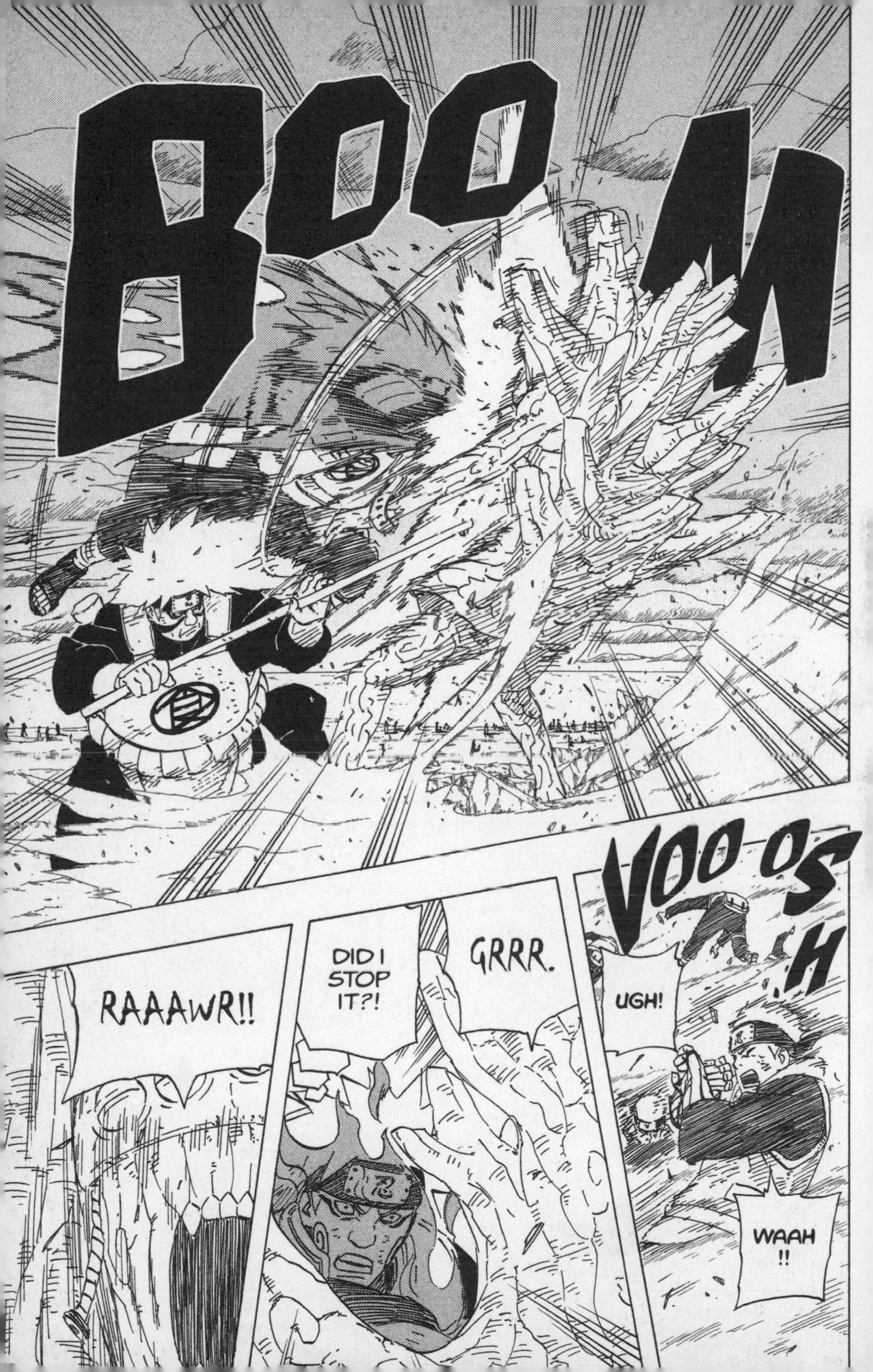
BOOM
VOOOSH
UGH!
WAAH!!
GRRR.
DID I STOP IT?!
RAAAWR!!

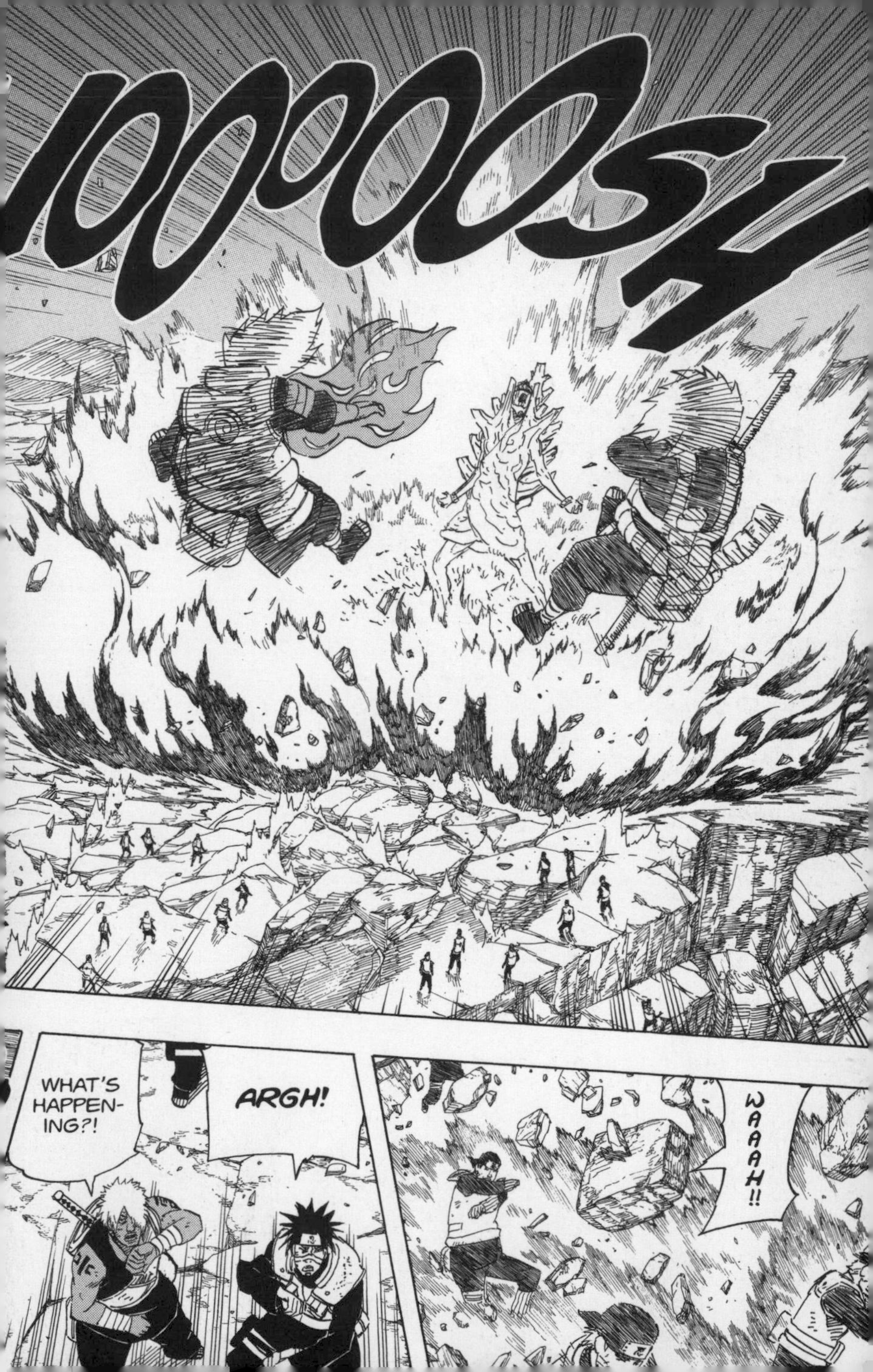
WOOOOSH
WAAAAH!!
ARGH!
WHAT'S HAPPEN-ING?!

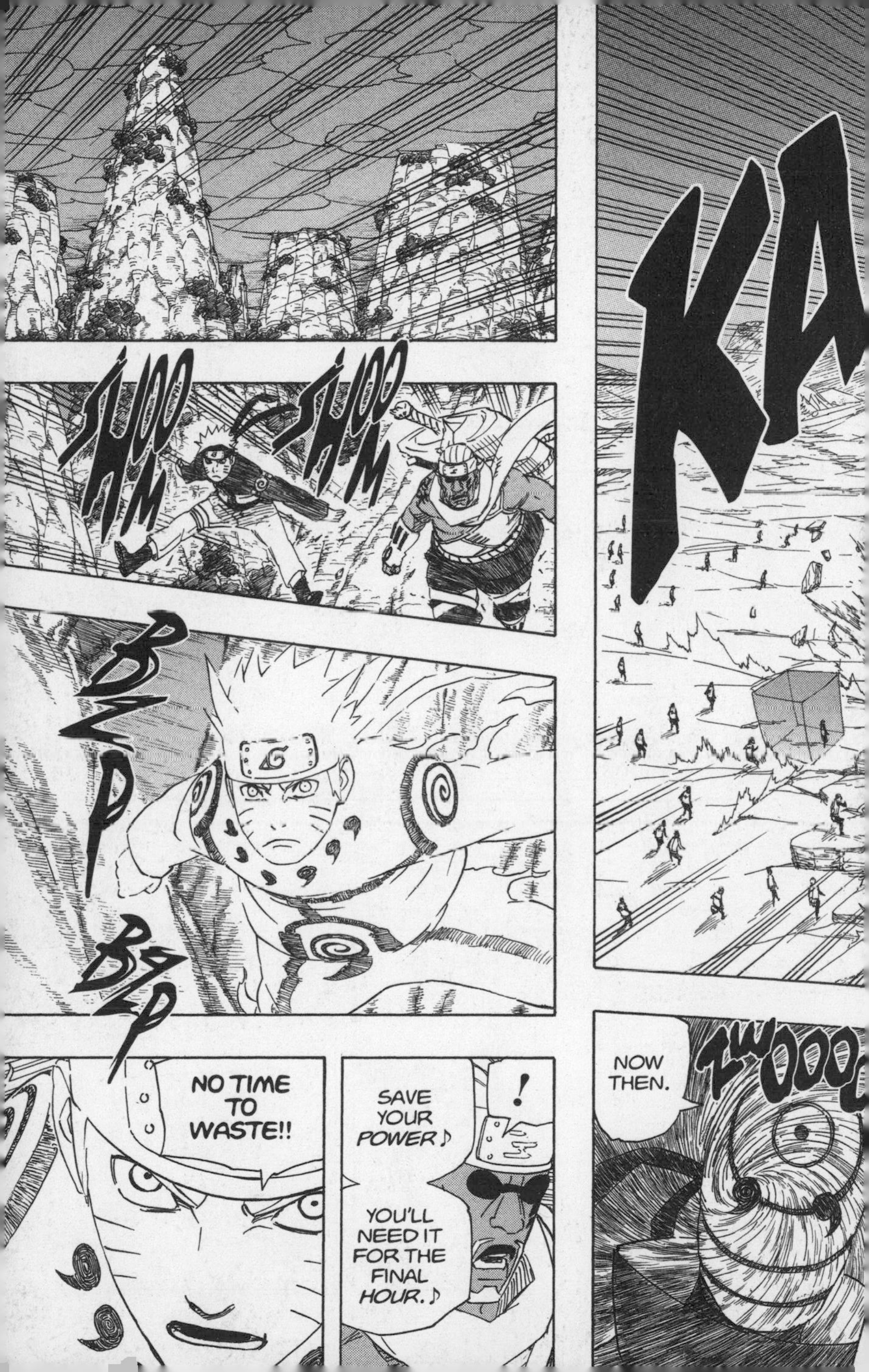
KA
NOW THEN.
ZWOOO
SHOOM
SHOOM
BZZP
BZZP
!
SAVE YOUR POWER♪
YOU'LL NEED IT FOR THE FINAL HOUR.♪
NO TIME TO WASTE!!

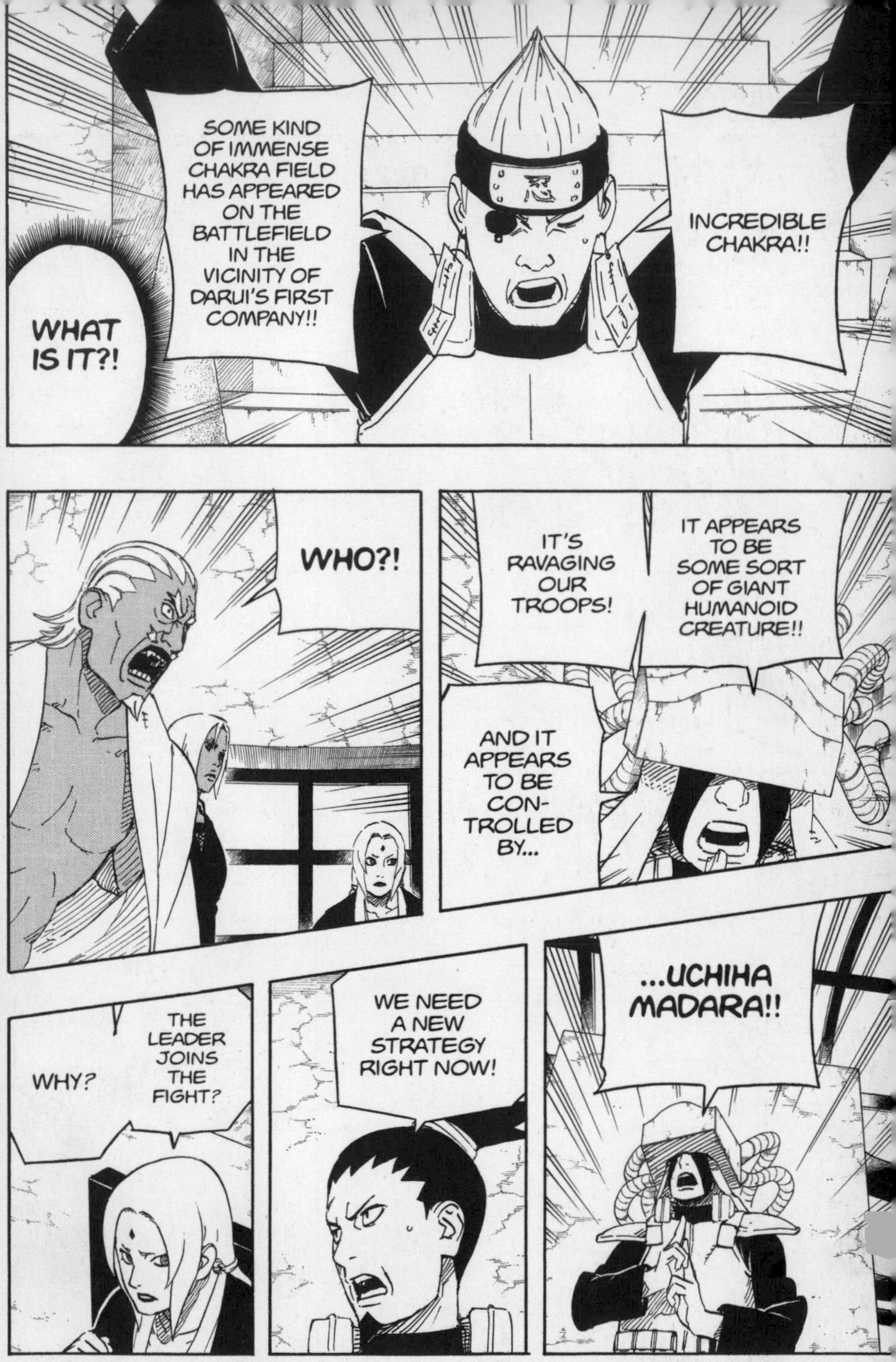
INCREDIBLE CHAKRA!!
SOME KIND OF IMMENSE CHAKRA FIELD HAS APPEARED ON THE BATTLEFIELD IN THE VICINITY OF DARUI'S FIRST COMPANY!!
WHAT IS IT?!
IT APPEARS TO BE SOME SORT OF GIANT HUMANOID CREATURE!!
IT'S RAVAGING OUR TROOPS!
AND IT APPEARS TO BE CON-TROLLED BY...
WHO?!
...UCHIHA MADARA!!
WE NEED A NEW STRATEGY RIGHT NOW!
THE LEADER JOINS THE FIGHT?
WHY?

READ THIS WAY

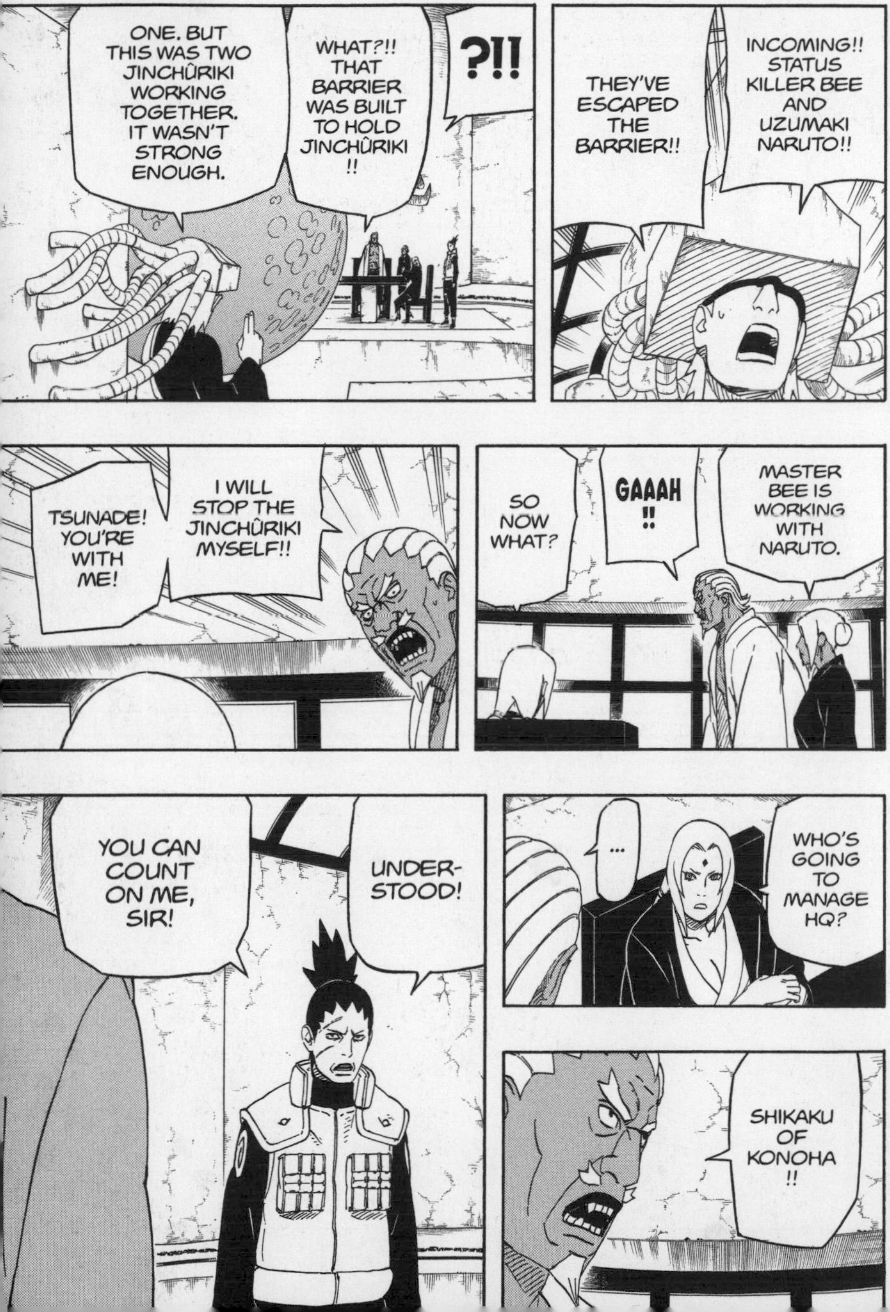

INCOMING!! STATUS KILLER BEE AND UZUMAKI NARUTO!!
THEY'VE ESCAPED THE BARRIER!!
?!!
WHAT?!! THAT BARRIER WAS BUILT TO HOLD JINCHÛRIKI !!
ONE. BUT THIS WAS TWO JINCHÛRIKI WORKING TOGETHER. IT WASN'T STRONG ENOUGH.
MASTER BEE IS WORKING WITH NARUTO.
GAAAH !!
SO NOW WHAT?
I WILL STOP THE JINCHÛRIKI MYSELF!!
TSUNADE! YOU'RE WITH ME!
WHO'S GOING TO MANAGE HQ?
...
SHIKAKU OF KONOHA !!
UNDER-STOOD!
YOU CAN COUNT ON ME, SIR!

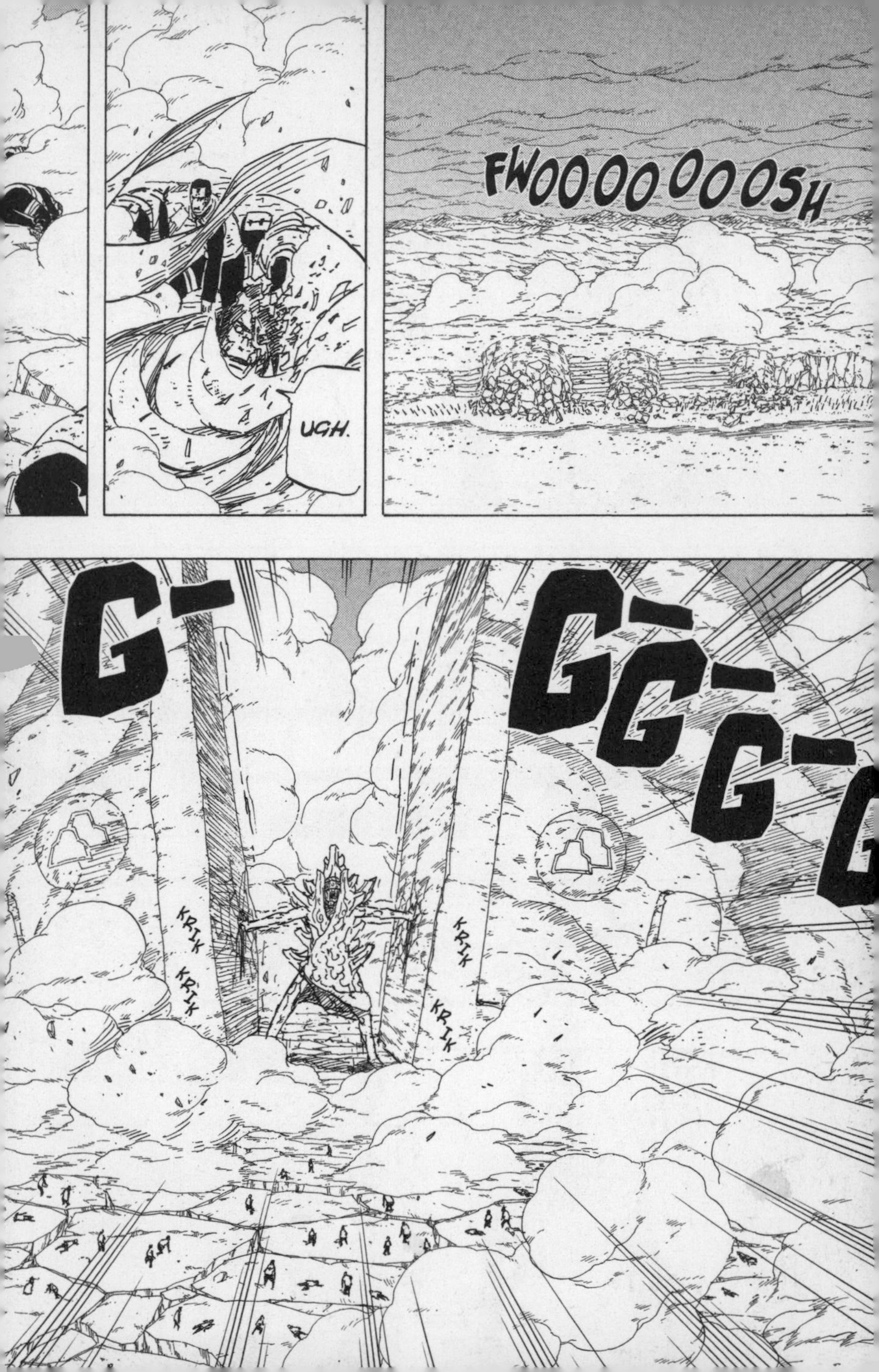
FWOOOOOOOOSH
UGH.
G-
G-G-G-G
KRIK
KRIK
KRIK
KRIK

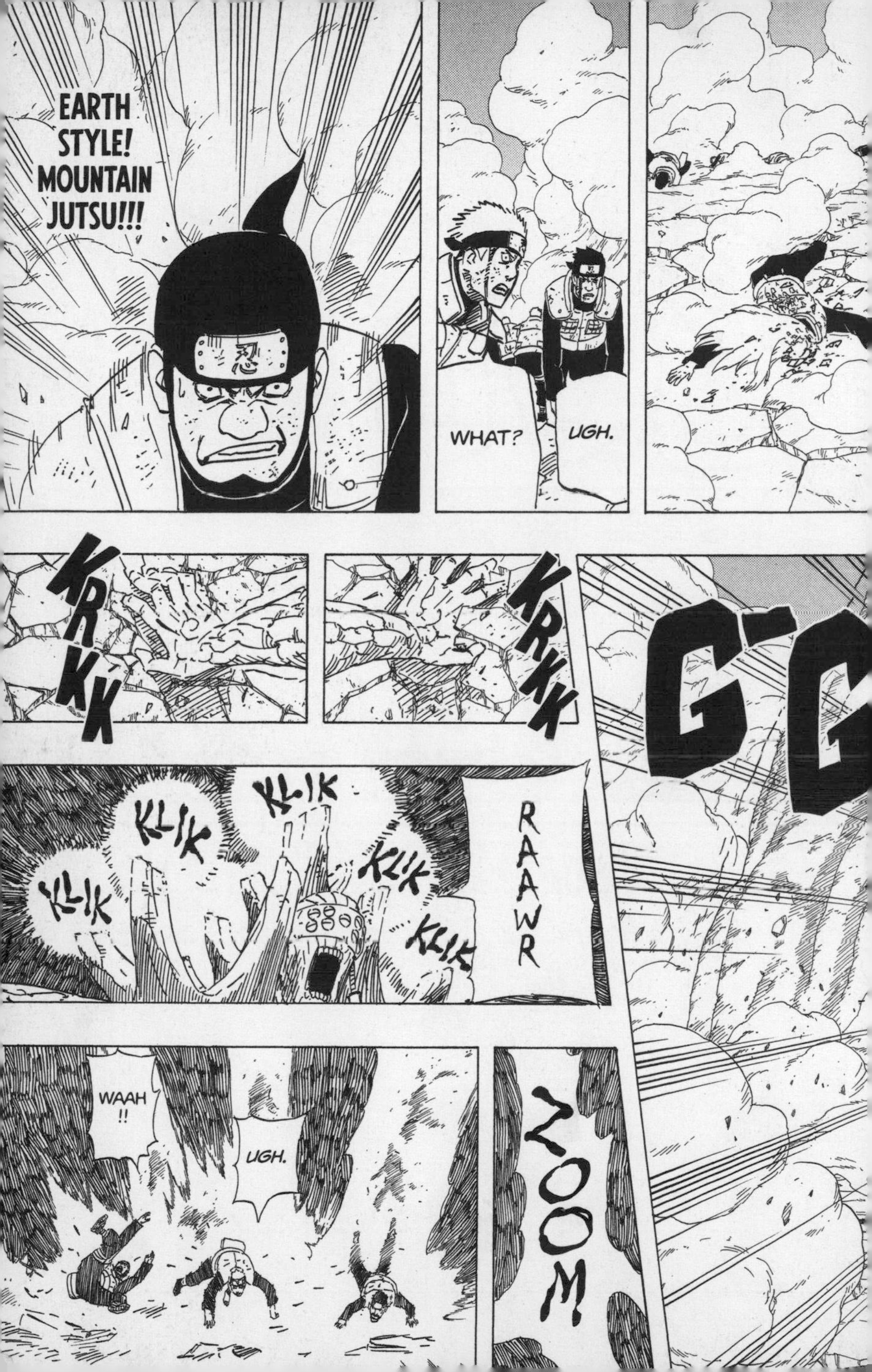
UGH.
WHAT?
EARTH STYLE! MOUNTAIN JUTSU!!!
GG
KRKK
KRKK
RAAAWR
KLIK
KLIK
KLIK
KLIK
KLIK
ZOOM!
UGH.
WAAH!!

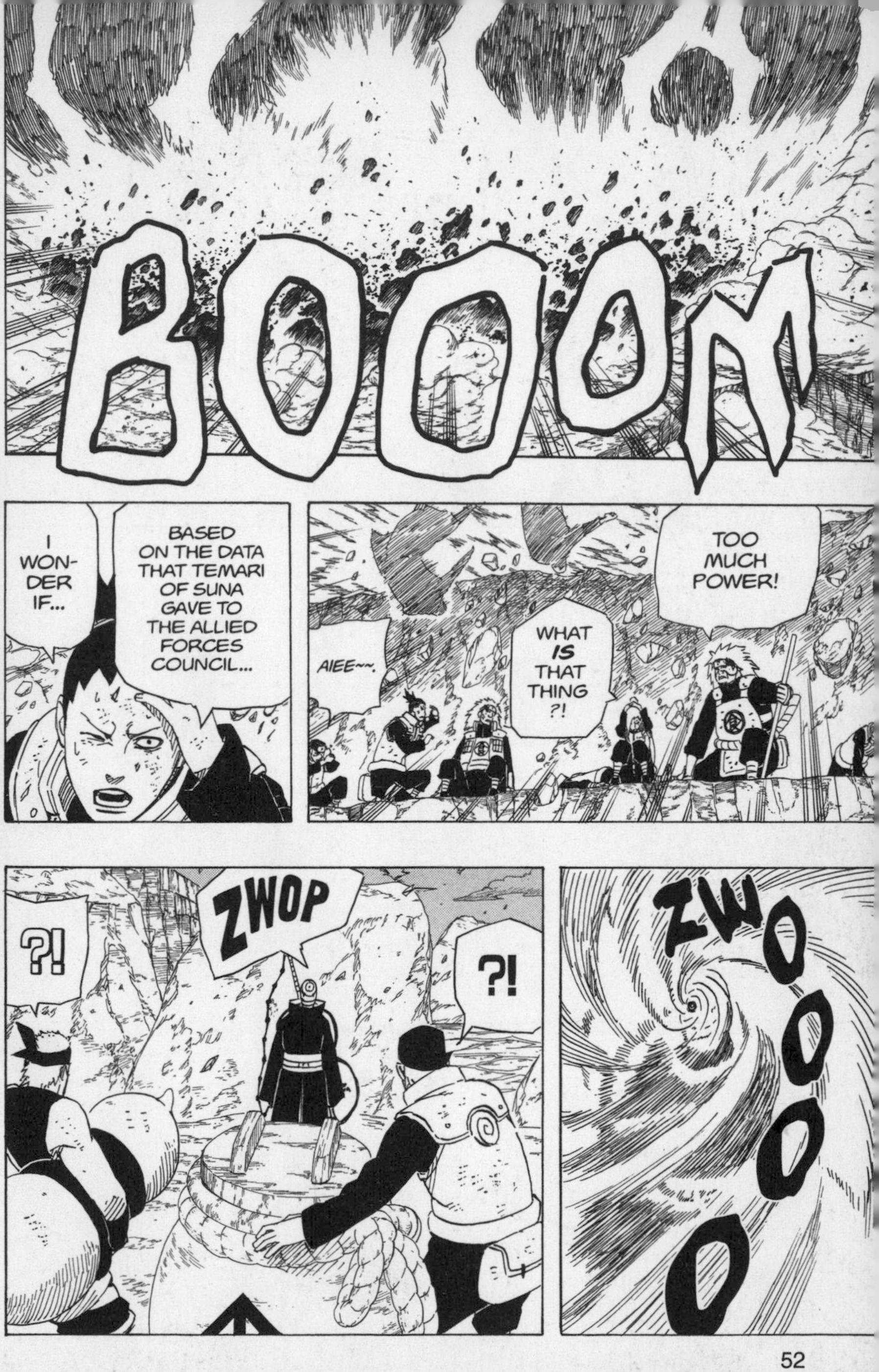
BOOOM
TOO MUCH POWER!
WHAT IS THAT THING?!
AIEE~~.
BASED ON THE DATA THAT TEMARI OF SUNA GAVE TO THE ALLIED FORCES COUNCIL...
I WONDER IF...
ZWOOOO
ZWOP
?!
?!

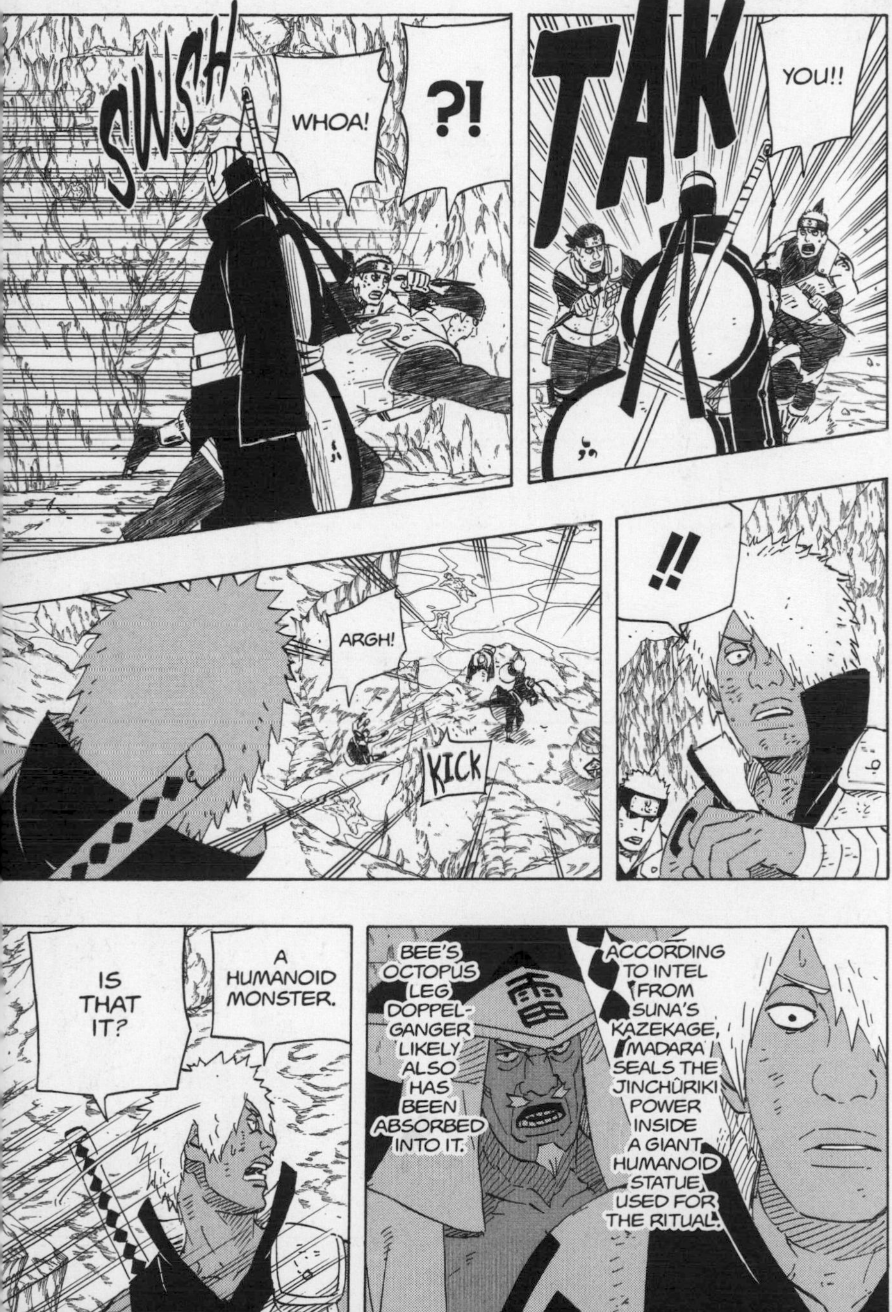
TAK
YOU!!
?!
WHOA!
SWSH
!!
ARGH!
KICK
ACCORDING TO INTEL FROM SUNA'S KAZEKAGE, MADARA SEALS THE JINCHÛRIKI POWER INSIDE A GIANT HUMANOID STATUE USED FOR THE RITUAL.
BEE'S OCTOPUS LEG DOPPELGANGER LIKELY ALSO HAS BEEN ABSORBED INTO IT.
A HUMANOID MONSTER.
IS THAT IT?

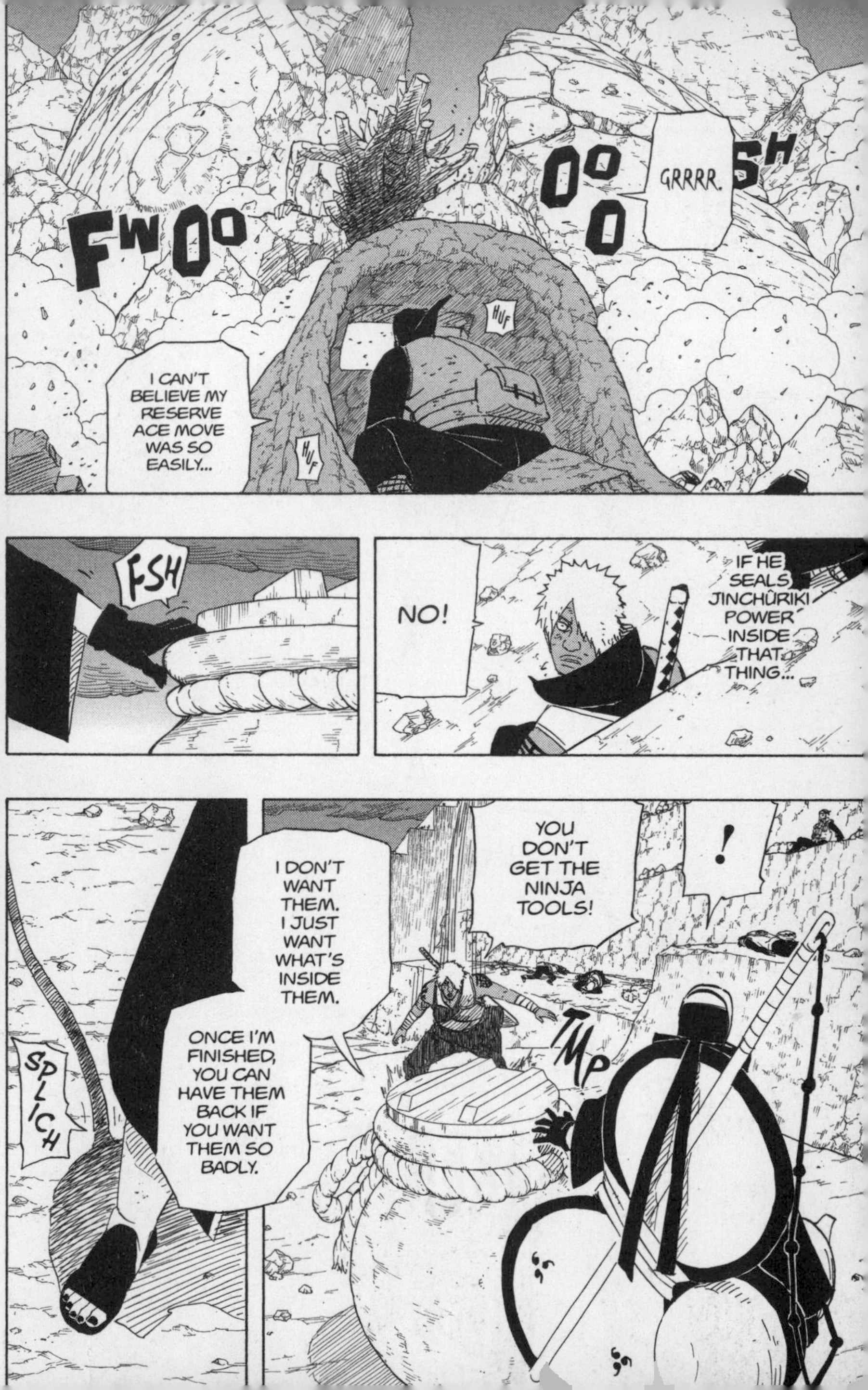

GRRRR.
FWOO OOO SH
HUF
I CAN'T BELIEVE MY RESERVE ACE MOVE WAS SO EASILY...
HUF
IF HE SEALS JINCHŪRIKI POWER INSIDE THAT THING...
NO!
FSH
!
YOU DON'T GET THE NINJA TOOLS!
I DON'T WANT THEM. I JUST WANT WHAT'S INSIDE THEM.
ONCE I'M FINISHED, YOU CAN HAVE THEM BACK IF YOU WANT THEM SO BADLY.
TMP
SPLICH

READ THIS WAY

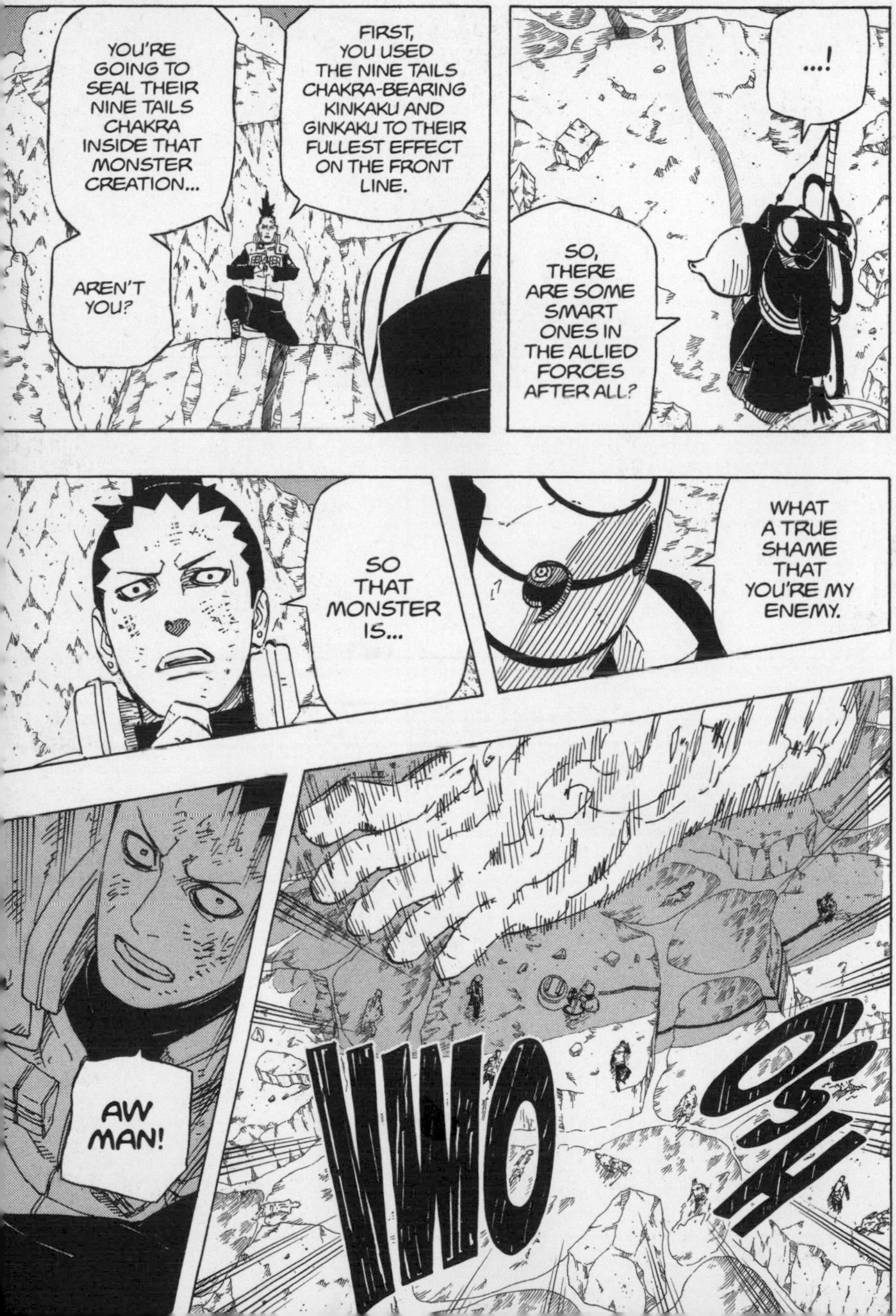

...!
SO, THERE ARE SOME SMART ONES IN THE ALLIED FORCES AFTER ALL?
FIRST, YOU USED THE NINE TAILS CHAKRA-BEARING KINKAKU AND GINKAKU TO THEIR FULLEST EFFECT ON THE FRONT LINE.
YOU'RE GOING TO SEAL THEIR NINE TAILS CHAKRA INSIDE THAT MONSTER CREATION...
AREN'T YOU?
WHAT A TRUE SHAME THAT YOU'RE MY ENEMY.
SO THAT MONSTER IS...
VWO
OSH
AW MAN!

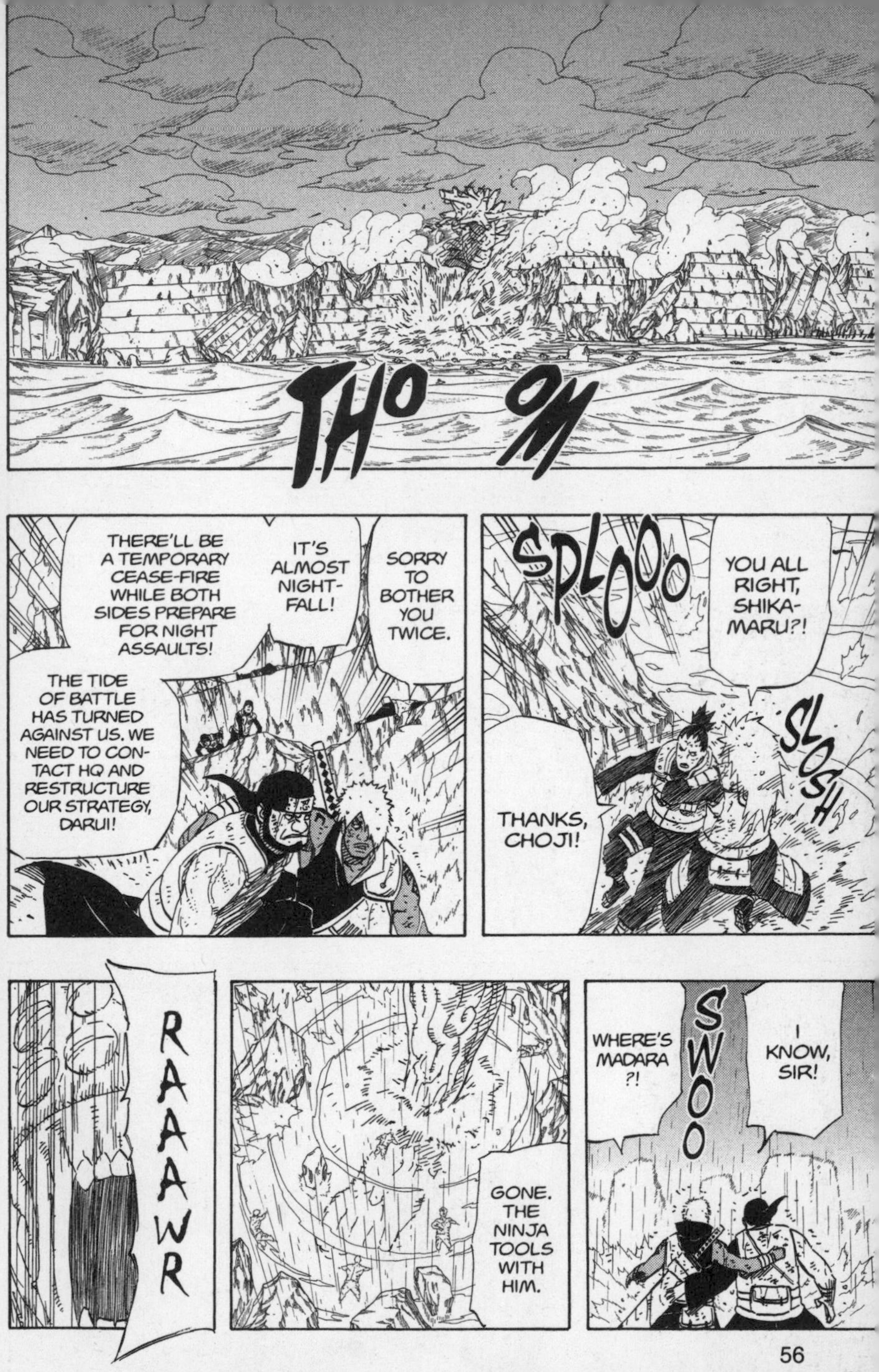
THOOM
SPLOOO
YOU ALL RIGHT, SHIKAMARU?!
THANKS, CHOJI!
SLOSH
SORRY TO BOTHER YOU TWICE.
IT'S ALMOST NIGHTFALL!
THERE'LL BE A TEMPORARY CEASE-FIRE WHILE BOTH SIDES PREPARE FOR NIGHT ASSAULTS!
THE TIDE OF BATTLE HAS TURNED AGAINST US. WE NEED TO CONTACT HQ AND RESTRUCTURE OUR STRATEGY, DARUI!
I KNOW, SIR!
SWOO
WHERE'S MADARA?!
GONE. THE NINJA TOOLS WITH HIM.
RAAAWR

READ THIS WAY

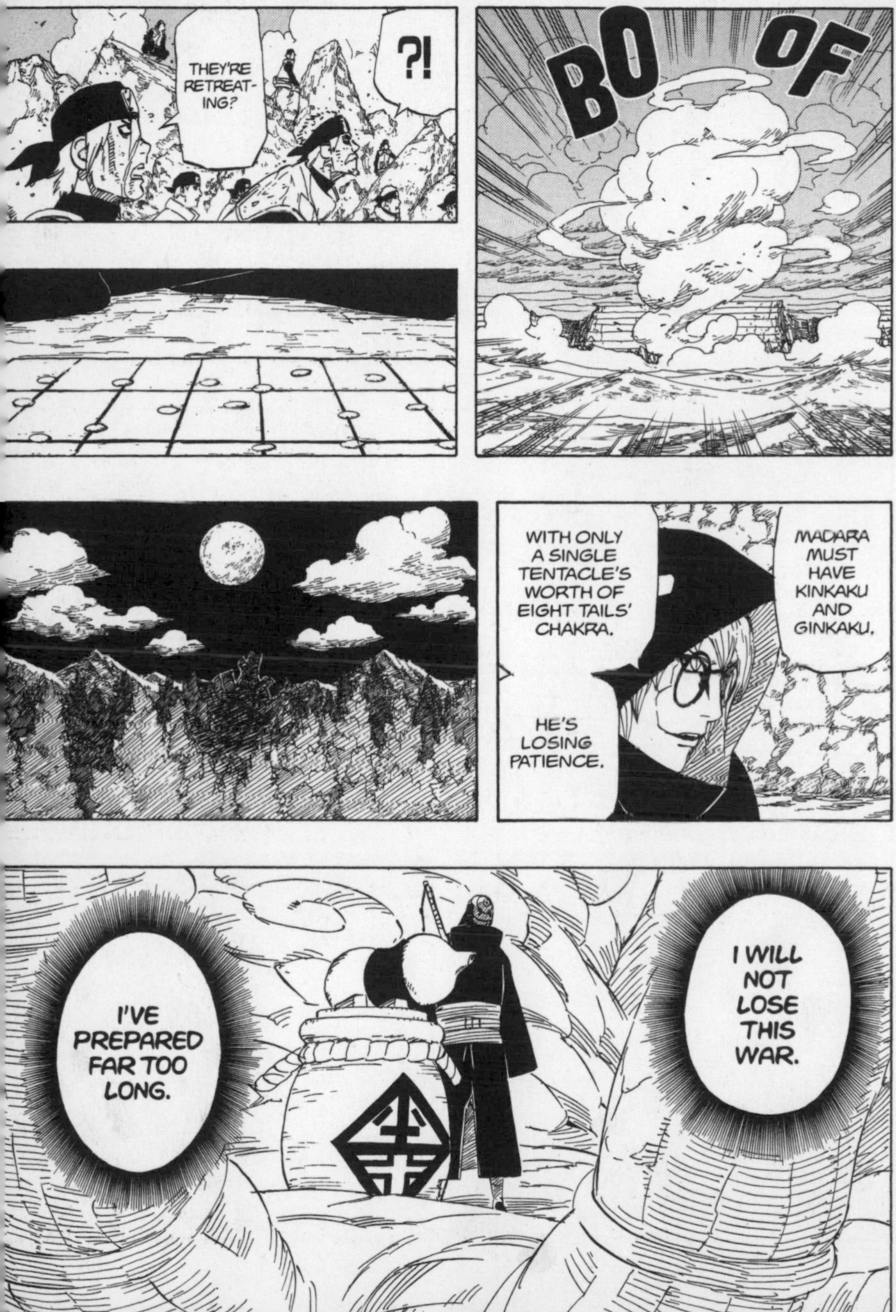
BO OF
?!
THEY'RE RETREATING?
MADARA MUST HAVE KINKAKU AND GINKAKU.
WITH ONLY A SINGLE TENTACLE'S WORTH OF EIGHT TAILS' CHAKRA.
HE'S LOSING PATIENCE.
I WILL NOT LOSE THIS WAR.
I'VE PREPARED FAR TOO LONG.

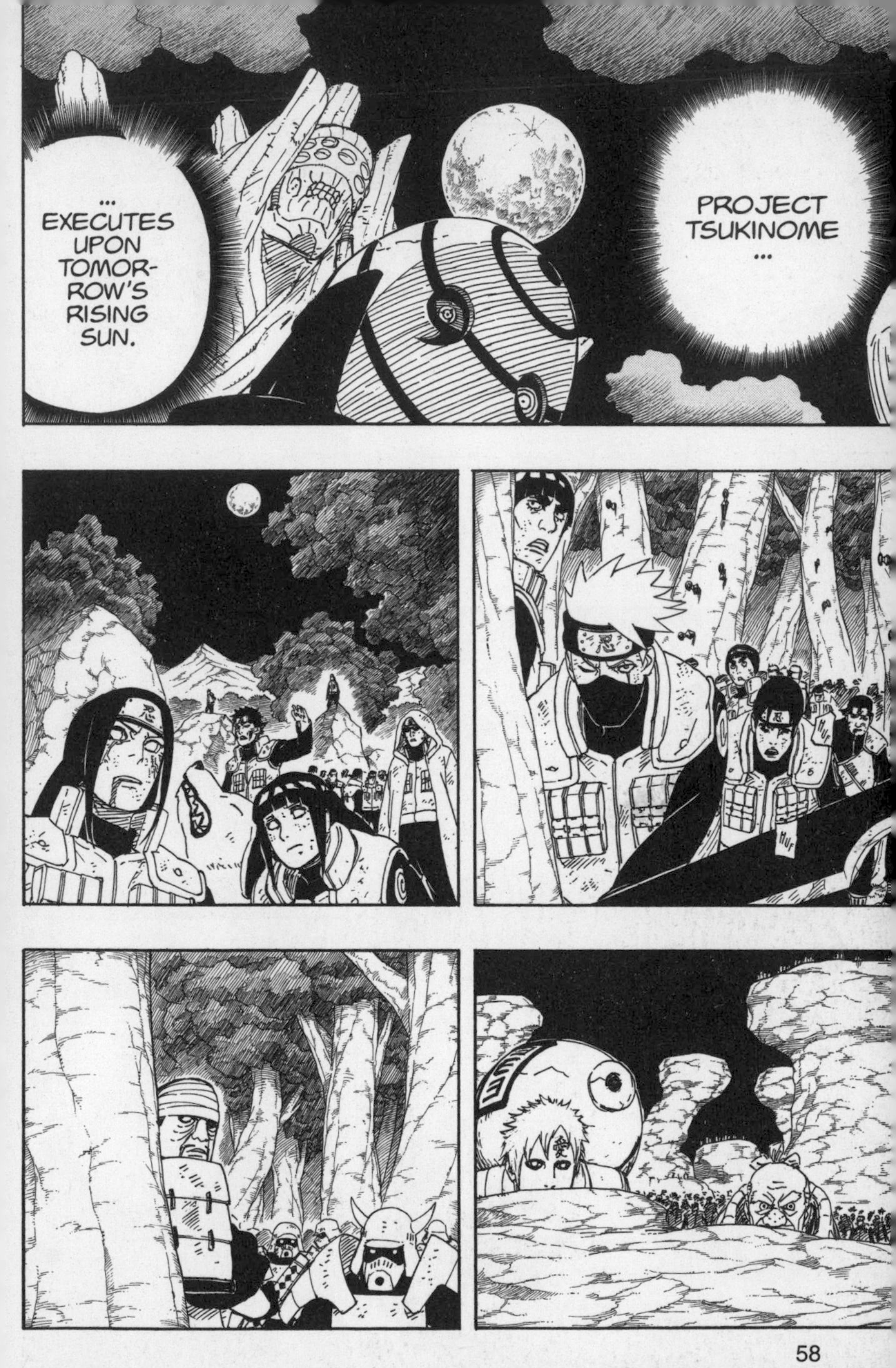
PROJECT TSUKINOME ...
... EXECUTES UPON TOMOR-ROW'S RISING SUN.

READ THIS WAY

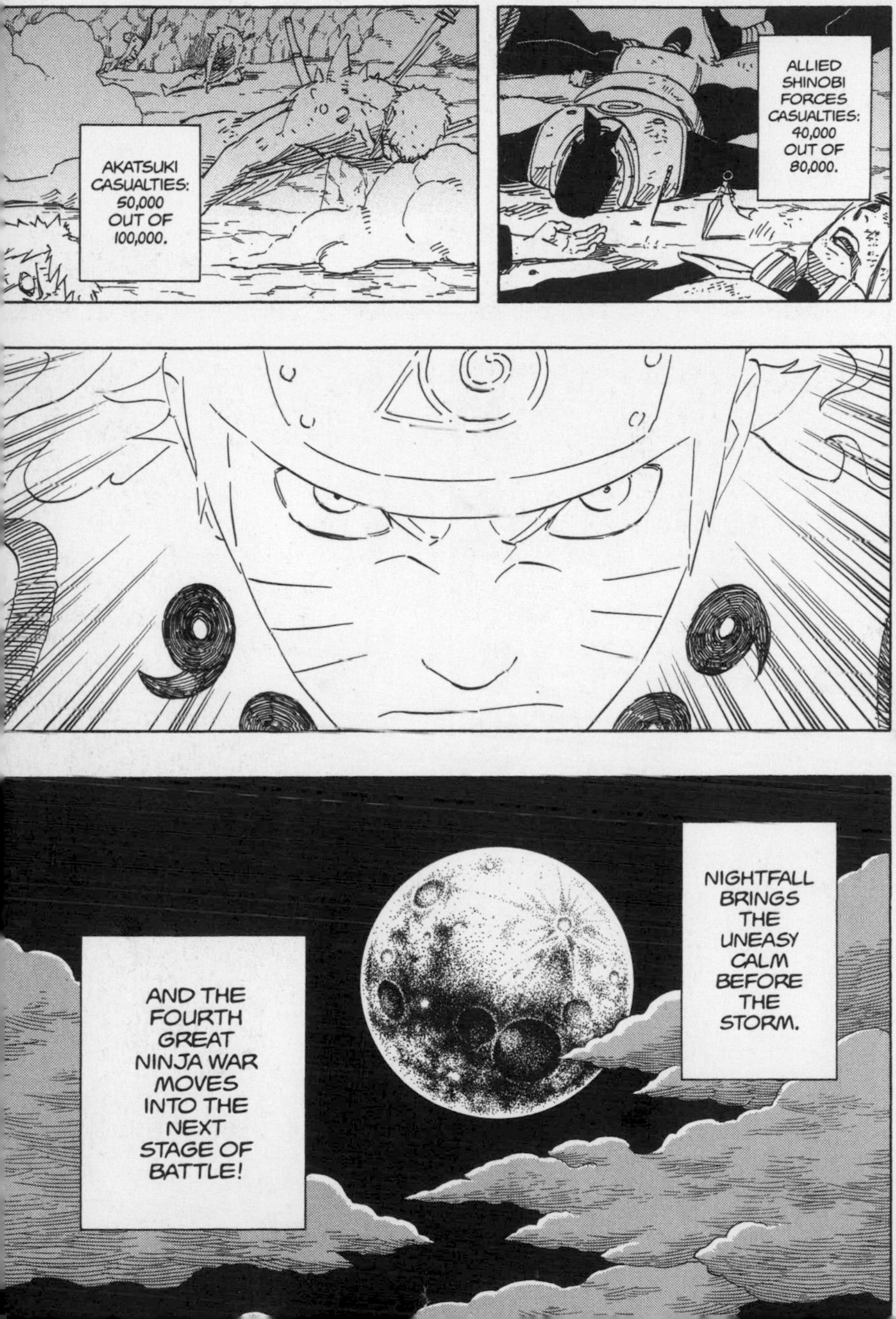
ALLIED SHINOBI FORCES CASUALTIES: 40,000 OUT OF 80,000.
AKATSUKI CASUALTIES: 50,000 OUT OF 100,000.
NIGHTFALL BRINGS THE UNEASY CALM BEFORE THE STORM.
AND THE FOURTH GREAT NINJA WAR MOVES INTO THE NEXT STAGE OF BATTLE!

NARUTO

Number 538: Cross-Examination

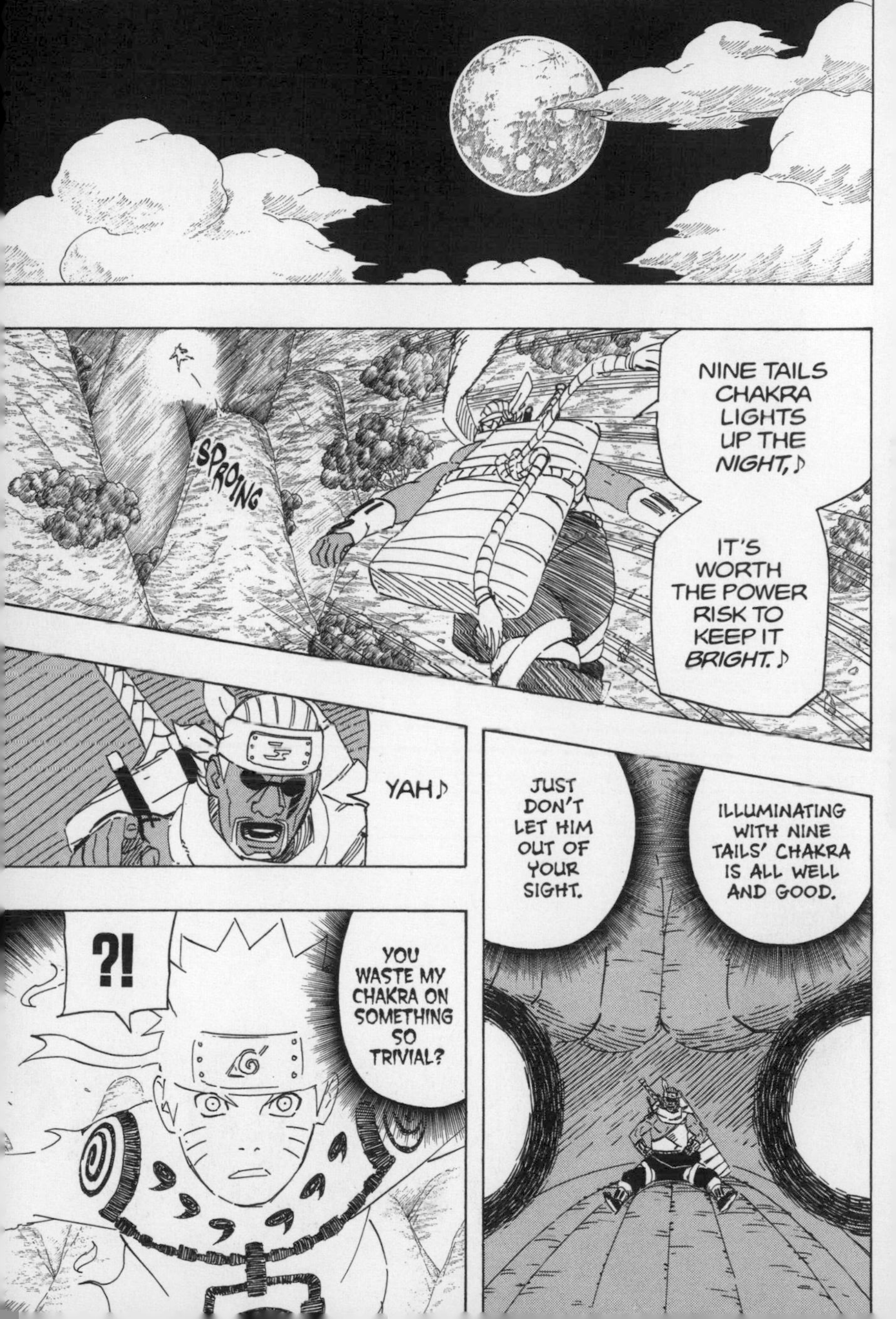

NINE TAILS CHAKRA LIGHTS UP THE *NIGHT,*♪
IT'S WORTH THE POWER RISK TO KEEP IT *BRIGHT.*♪
SPROING
ILLUMINATING WITH NINE TAILS' CHAKRA IS ALL WELL AND GOOD.
JUST DON'T LET HIM OUT OF YOUR SIGHT.
YAH♪
YOU WASTE MY CHAKRA ON SOMETHING SO TRIVIAL?
?!

Number 538: Cross-Examination

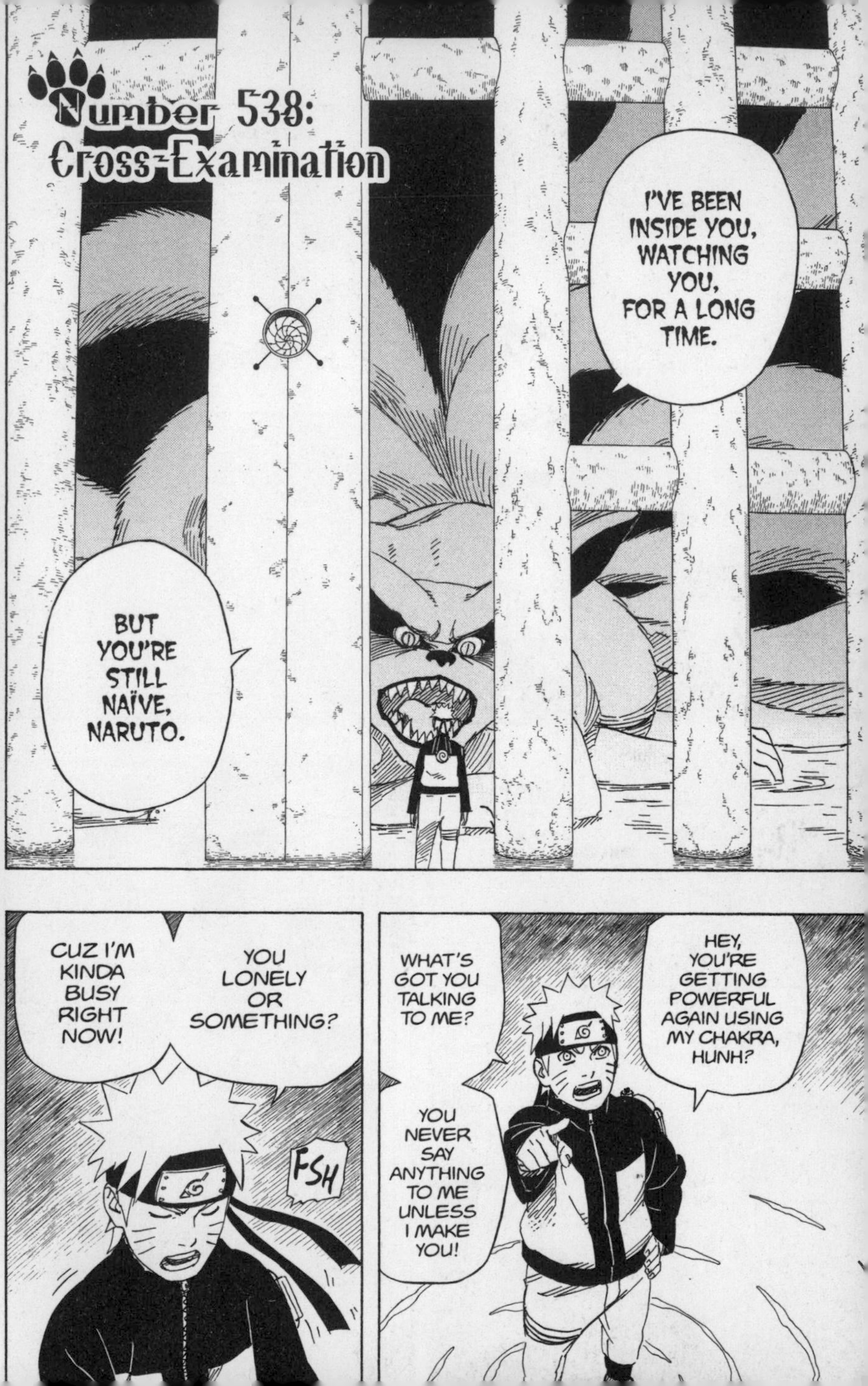
I'VE BEEN INSIDE YOU, WATCHING YOU, FOR A LONG TIME.
BUT YOU'RE STILL NAÏVE, NARUTO.
HEY, YOU'RE GETTING POWERFUL AGAIN USING MY CHAKRA, HUNH?
WHAT'S GOT YOU TALKING TO ME?
YOU NEVER SAY ANYTHING TO ME UNLESS I MAKE YOU!
YOU LONELY OR SOMETHING?
CUZ I'M KINDA BUSY RIGHT NOW!
FSH

READ THIS WAY

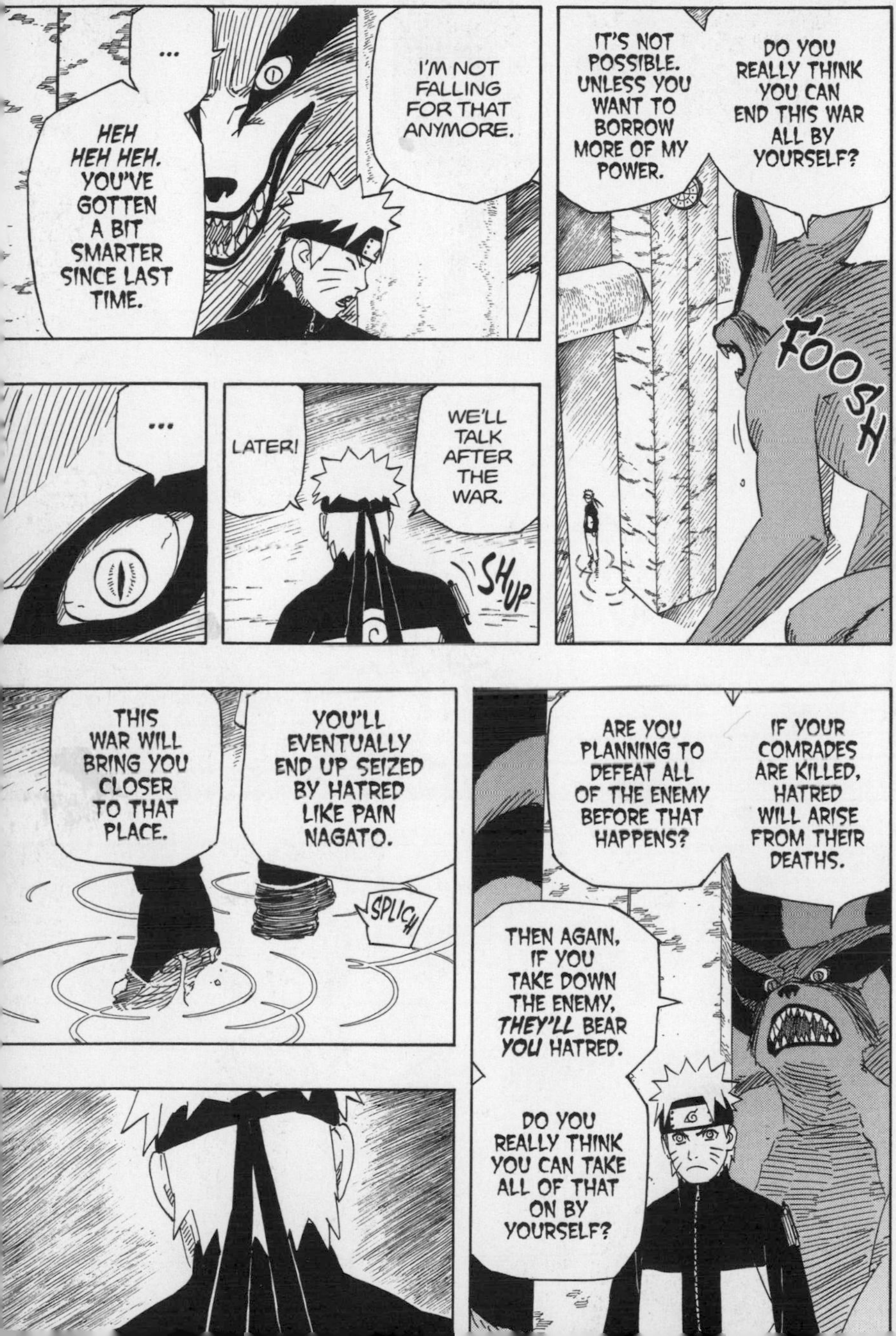
DO YOU REALLY THINK YOU CAN END THIS WAR ALL BY YOURSELF?
IT'S NOT POSSIBLE. UNLESS YOU WANT TO BORROW MORE OF MY POWER.
FOOSH
I'M NOT FALLING FOR THAT ANYMORE.
...
HEH HEH HEH. YOU'VE GOTTEN A BIT SMARTER SINCE LAST TIME.
WE'LL TALK AFTER THE WAR.
LATER!
SHUP
...
IF YOUR COMRADES ARE KILLED, HATRED WILL ARISE FROM THEIR DEATHS.
ARE YOU PLANNING TO DEFEAT ALL OF THE ENEMY BEFORE THAT HAPPENS?
THEN AGAIN, IF YOU TAKE DOWN THE ENEMY, *THEY'LL* BEAR *YOU* HATRED.
DO YOU REALLY THINK YOU CAN TAKE ALL OF THAT ON BY YOURSELF?
YOU'LL EVENTUALLY END UP SEIZED BY HATRED LIKE PAIN NAGATO.
THIS WAR WILL BRING YOU CLOSER TO THAT PLACE.
SPLICH

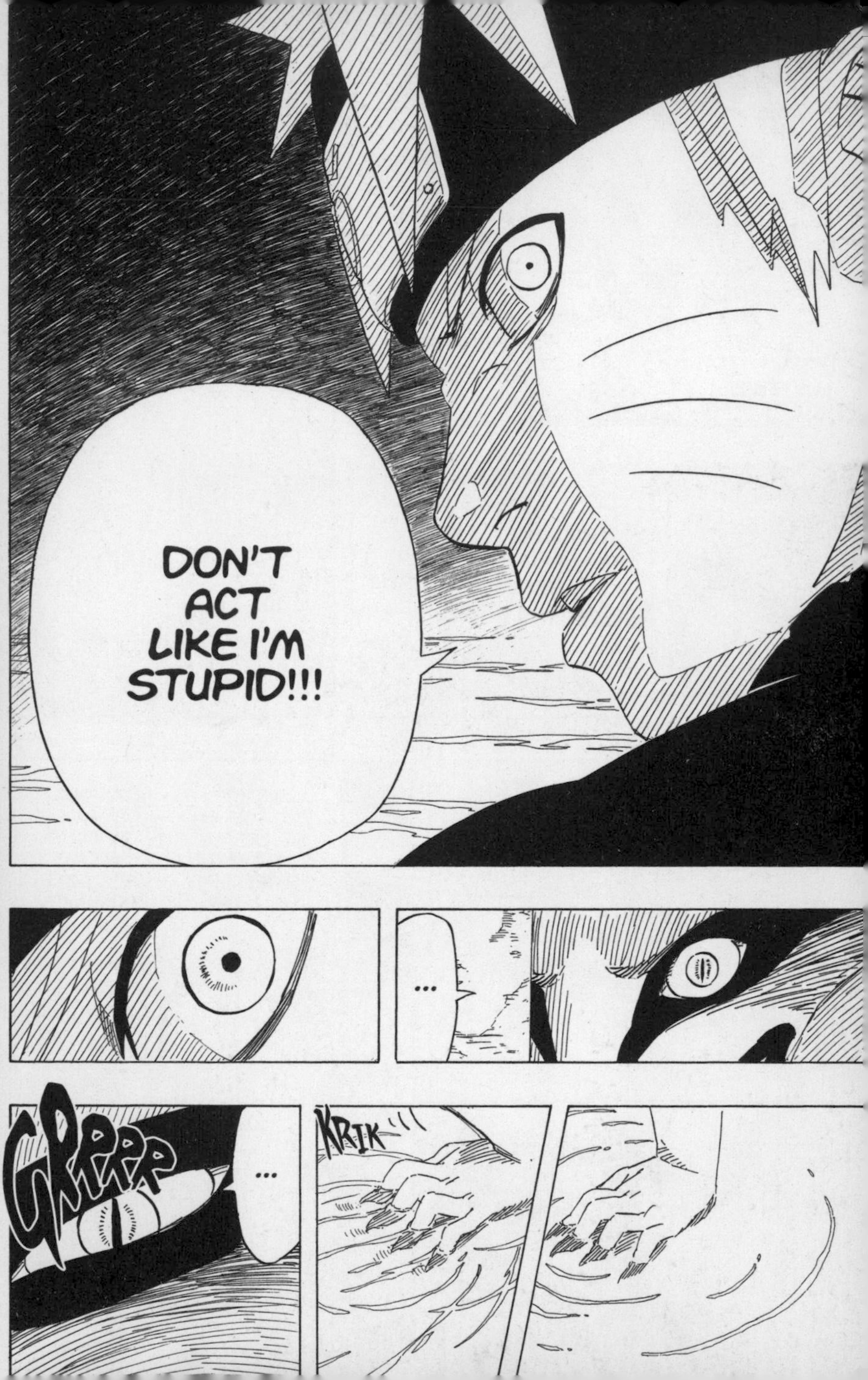
DON'T ACT LIKE I'M STUPID!!!
...
KRIK
GRRRR
...

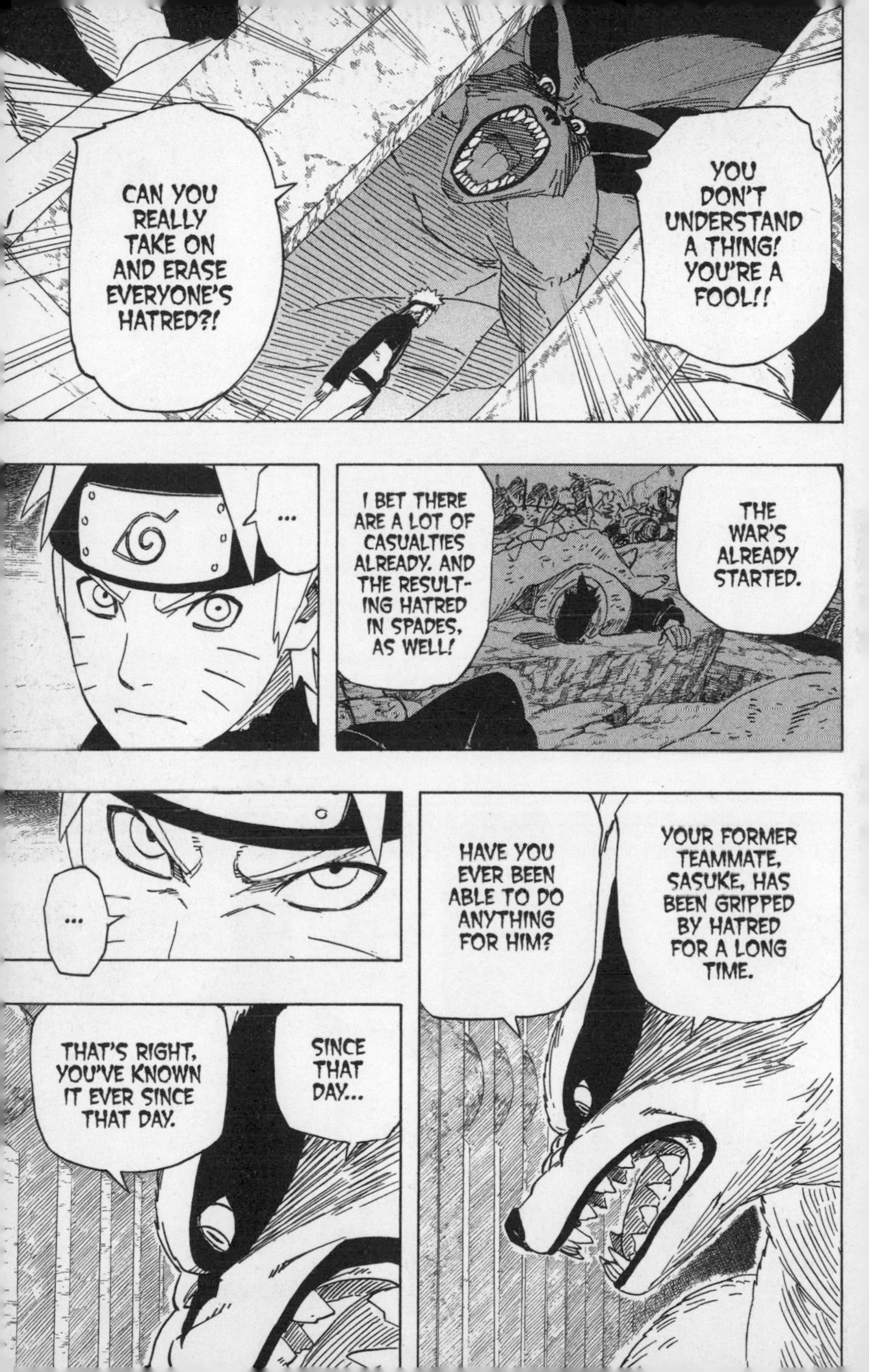
YOU DON'T UNDERSTAND A THING! YOU'RE A FOOL!!
CAN YOU REALLY TAKE ON AND ERASE EVERYONE'S HATRED?!
THE WAR'S ALREADY STARTED.
I BET THERE ARE A LOT OF CASUALTIES ALREADY. AND THE RESULTING HATRED IN SPADES, AS WELL!
...
YOUR FORMER TEAMMATE, SASUKE, HAS BEEN GRIPPED BY HATRED FOR A LONG TIME.
HAVE YOU EVER BEEN ABLE TO DO ANYTHING FOR HIM?
...
SINCE THAT DAY...
THAT'S RIGHT, YOU'VE KNOWN IT EVER SINCE THAT DAY.

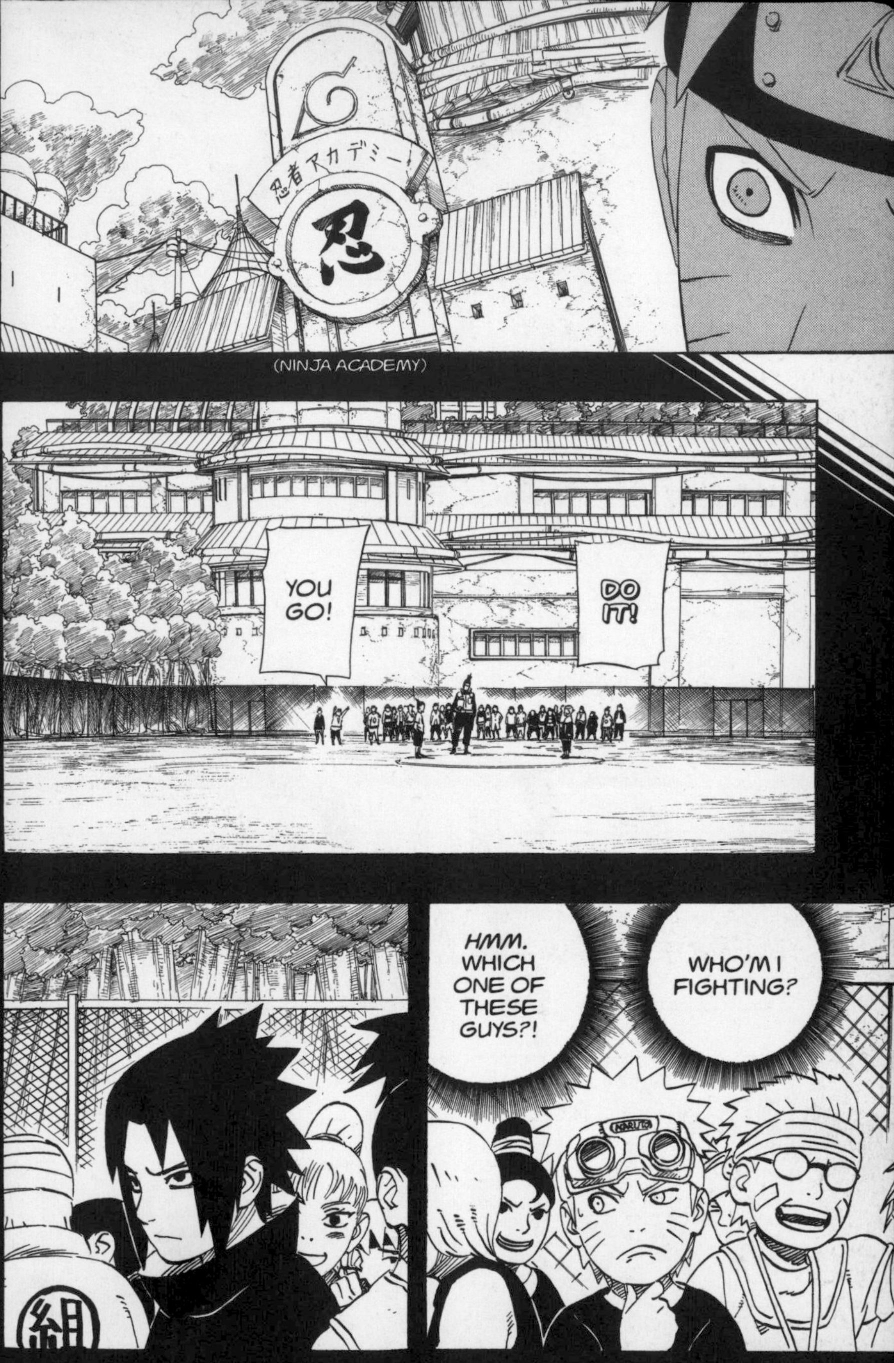

忍者アカデミー
忍
(NINJA ACADEMY)
DO IT!
YOU GO!
WHO'M I FIGHTING?
HMM. WHICH ONE OF THESE GUYS?!
組

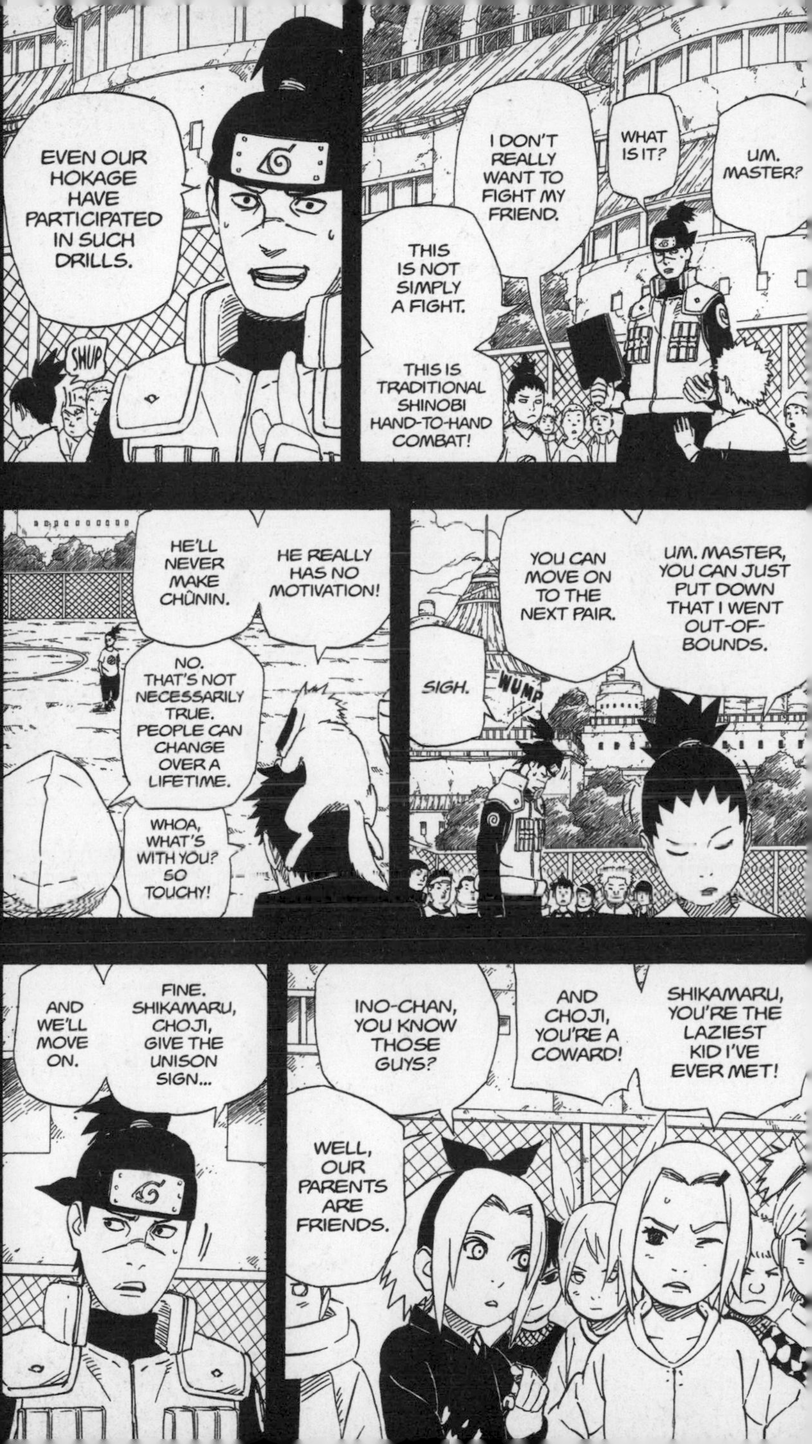
UM. MASTER?
WHAT IS IT?
I DON'T REALLY WANT TO FIGHT MY FRIEND.
THIS IS NOT SIMPLY A FIGHT.
THIS IS TRADITIONAL SHINOBI HAND-TO-HAND COMBAT!
EVEN OUR HOKAGE HAVE PARTICIPATED IN SUCH DRILLS.
SHUP
UM. MASTER, YOU CAN JUST PUT DOWN THAT I WENT OUT-OF-BOUNDS.
YOU CAN MOVE ON TO THE NEXT PAIR.
SIGH.
WUMP
HE REALLY HAS NO MOTIVATION!
HE'LL NEVER MAKE CHŪNIN.
NO. THAT'S NOT NECESSARILY TRUE. PEOPLE CAN CHANGE OVER A LIFETIME.
WHOA, WHAT'S WITH YOU? SO TOUCHY!
SHIKAMARU, YOU'RE THE LAZIEST KID I'VE EVER MET!
AND CHOJI, YOU'RE A COWARD!
INO-CHAN, YOU KNOW THOSE GUYS?
WELL, OUR PARENTS ARE FRIENDS.
FINE. SHIKAMARU, CHOJI, GIVE THE UNISON SIGN...
AND WE'LL MOVE ON.

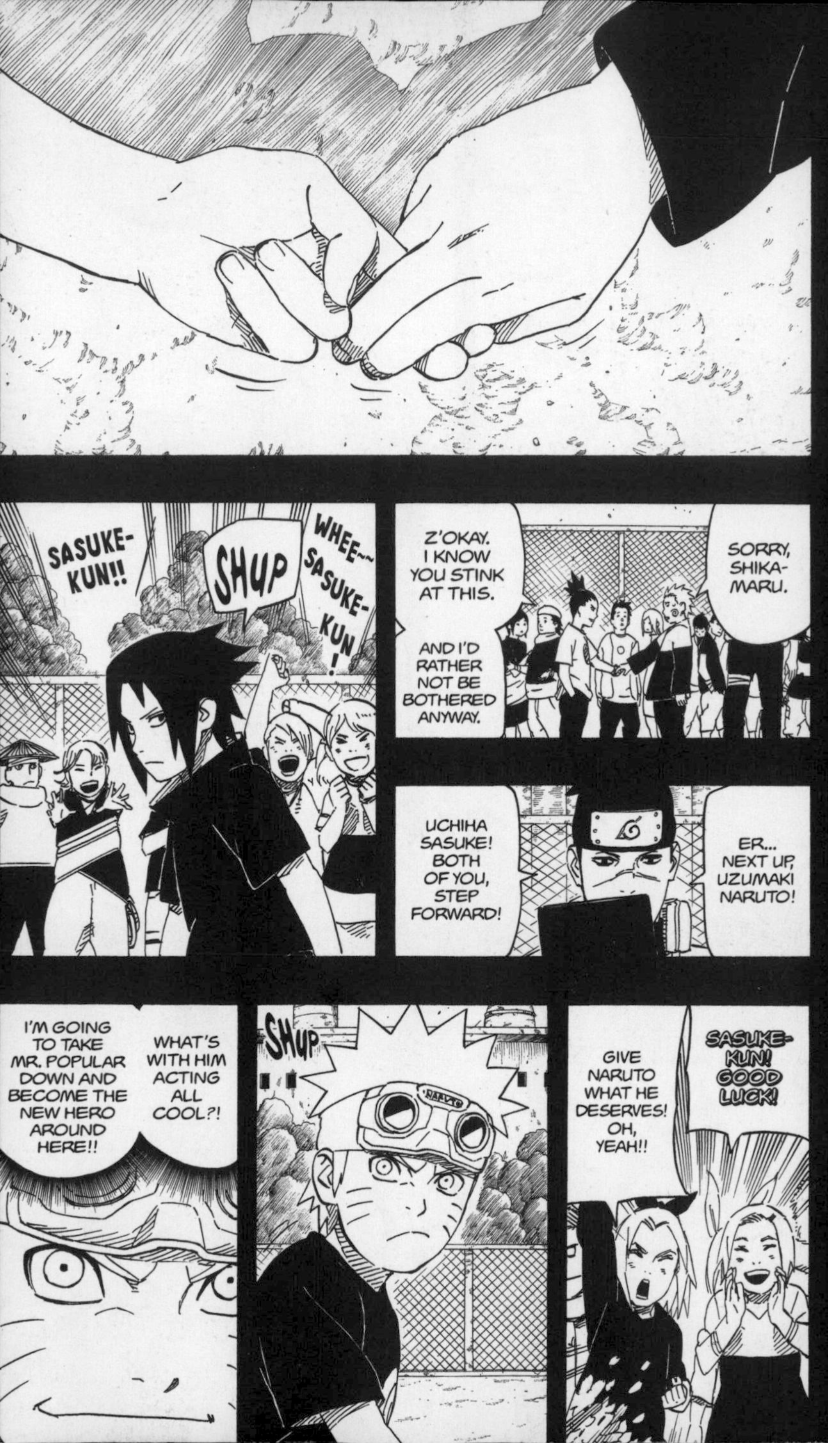
SORRY, SHIKAMARU.
Z'OKAY. I KNOW YOU STINK AT THIS.
AND I'D RATHER NOT BE BOTHERED ANYWAY.
ER... NEXT UP, UZUMAKI NARUTO!
UCHIHA SASUKE! BOTH OF YOU, STEP FORWARD!
WHEE~~ SASUKE-KUN!
SHUP
SASUKE-KUN!!
SASUKE-KUN! GOOD LUCK!
GIVE NARUTO WHAT HE DESERVES! OH, YEAH!!
SHUP
WHAT'S WITH HIM ACTING ALL COOL?!
I'M GOING TO TAKE MR. POPULAR DOWN AND BECOME THE NEW HERO AROUND HERE!!

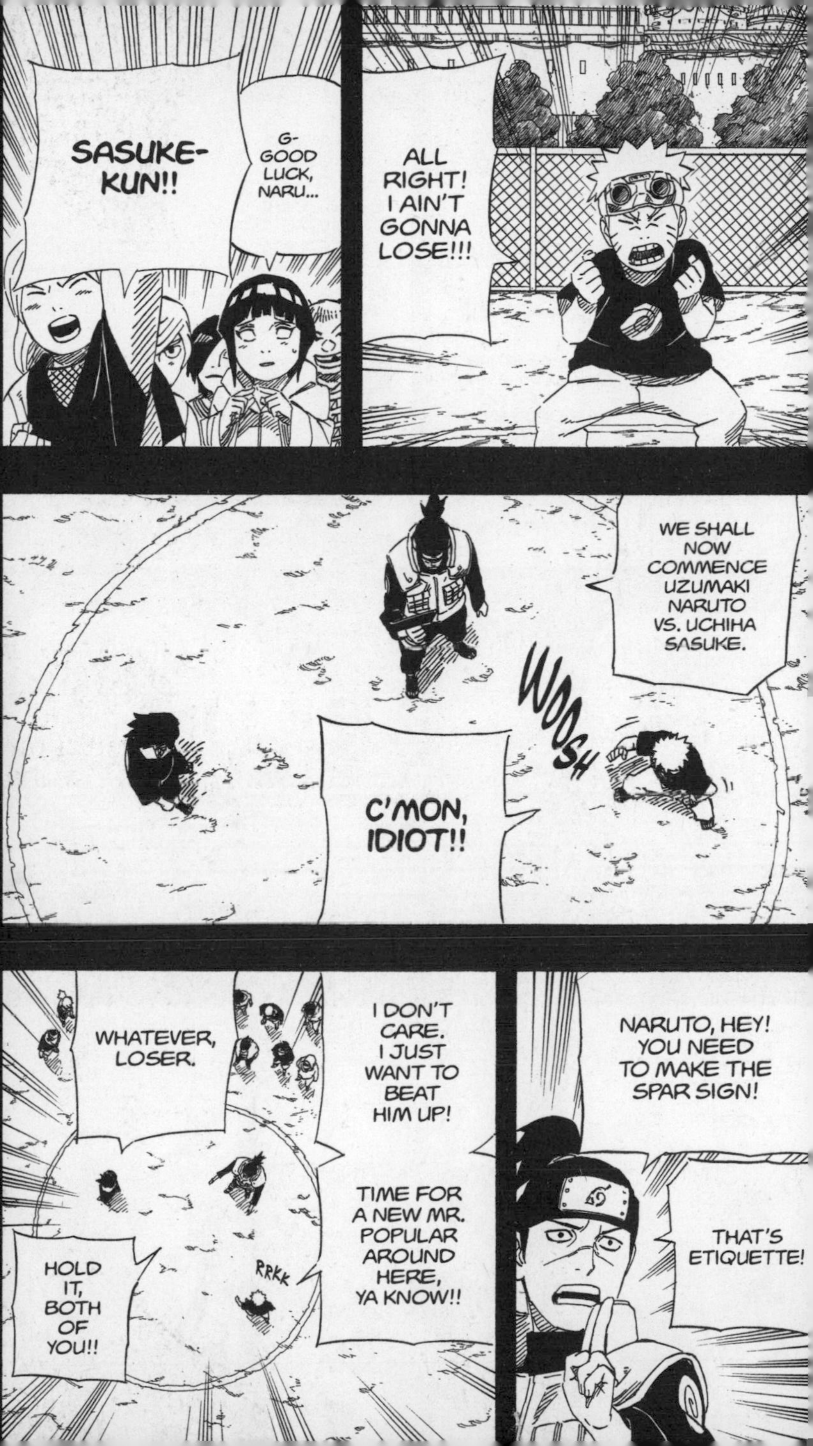
ALL RIGHT! I AIN'T GONNA LOSE!!!
G-GOOD LUCK, NARU...
SASUKE-KUN!!
WE SHALL NOW COMMENCE UZUMAKI NARUTO VS. UCHIHA SASUKE.
WOOSH
C'MON, IDIOT!!
NARUTO, HEY! YOU NEED TO MAKE THE SPAR SIGN!
THAT'S ETIQUETTE!
I DON'T CARE. I JUST WANT TO BEAT HIM UP!
WHATEVER, LOSER.
TIME FOR A NEW MR. POPULAR AROUND HERE, YA KNOW!!
RRKK
HOLD IT, BOTH OF YOU!!

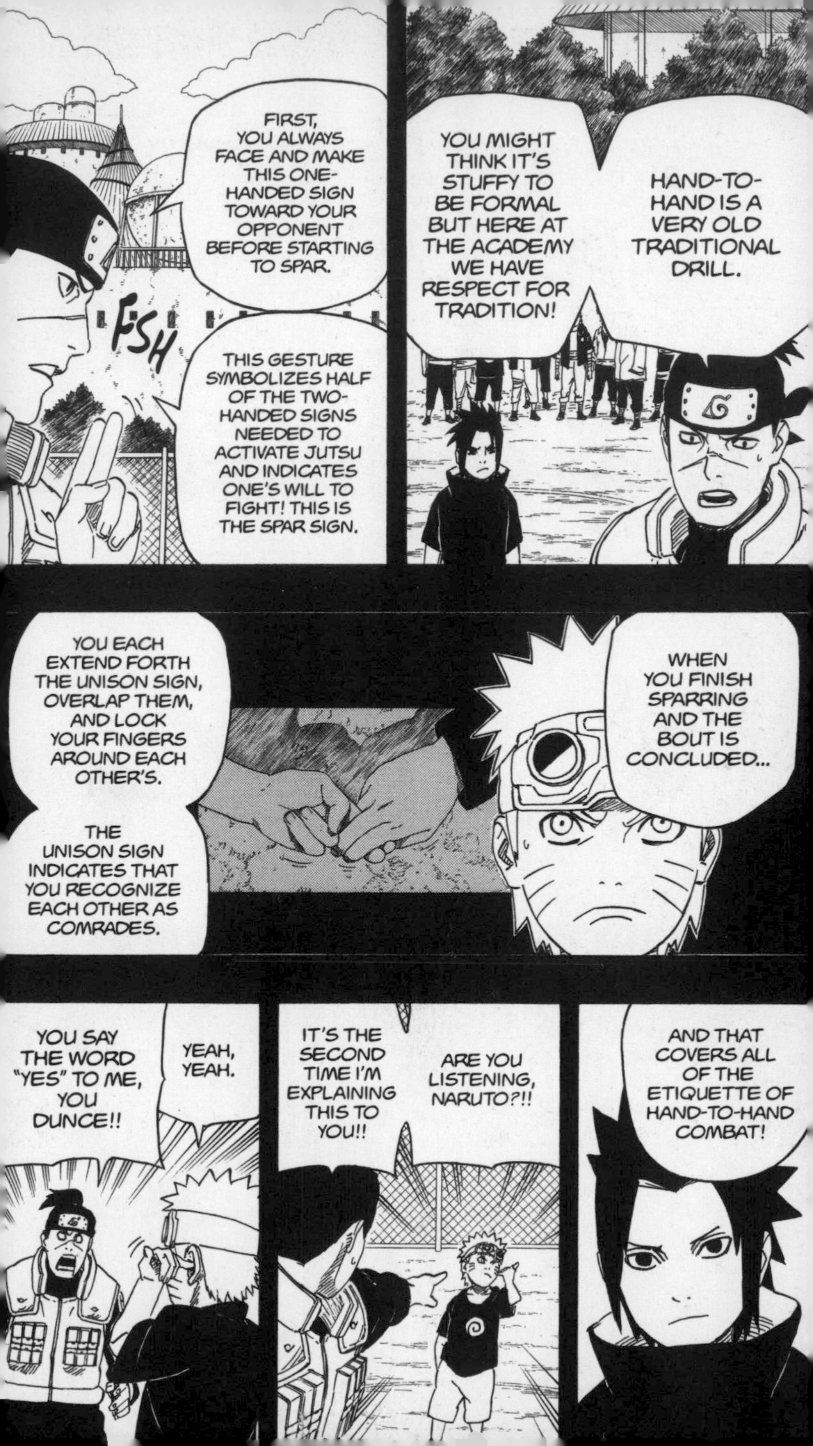
HAND-TO-HAND IS A VERY OLD TRADITIONAL DRILL.
YOU MIGHT THINK IT'S STUFFY TO BE FORMAL BUT HERE AT THE ACADEMY WE HAVE RESPECT FOR TRADITION!
FIRST, YOU ALWAYS FACE AND MAKE THIS ONE-HANDED SIGN TOWARD YOUR OPPONENT BEFORE STARTING TO SPAR.
FSH
THIS GESTURE SYMBOLIZES HALF OF THE TWO-HANDED SIGNS NEEDED TO ACTIVATE JUTSU AND INDICATES ONE'S WILL TO FIGHT! THIS IS THE SPAR SIGN.
WHEN YOU FINISH SPARRING AND THE BOUT IS CONCLUDED...
YOU EACH EXTEND FORTH THE UNISON SIGN, OVERLAP THEM, AND LOCK YOUR FINGERS AROUND EACH OTHER'S.
THE UNISON SIGN INDICATES THAT YOU RECOGNIZE EACH OTHER AS COMRADES.
AND THAT COVERS ALL OF THE ETIQUETTE OF HAND-TO-HAND COMBAT!
ARE YOU LISTENING, NARUTO?!!
IT'S THE SECOND TIME I'M EXPLAINING THIS TO YOU!!
YEAH, YEAH.
YOU SAY THE WORD "YES" TO ME, YOU DUNCE!!

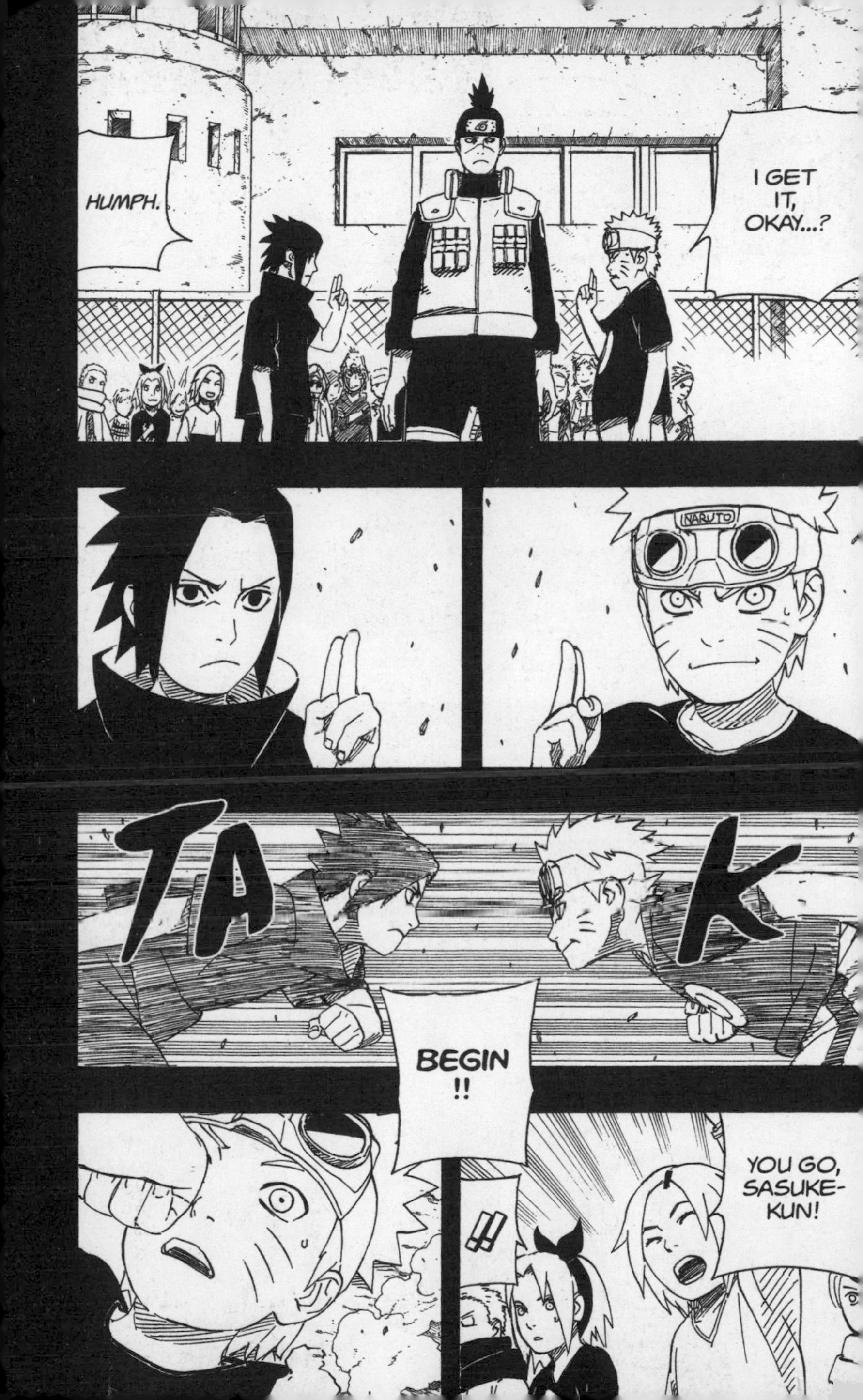
I GET IT, OKAY...?
HUMPH.
NARUTO
TA
K
BEGIN !!
YOU GO, SASUKE-KUN!
!!

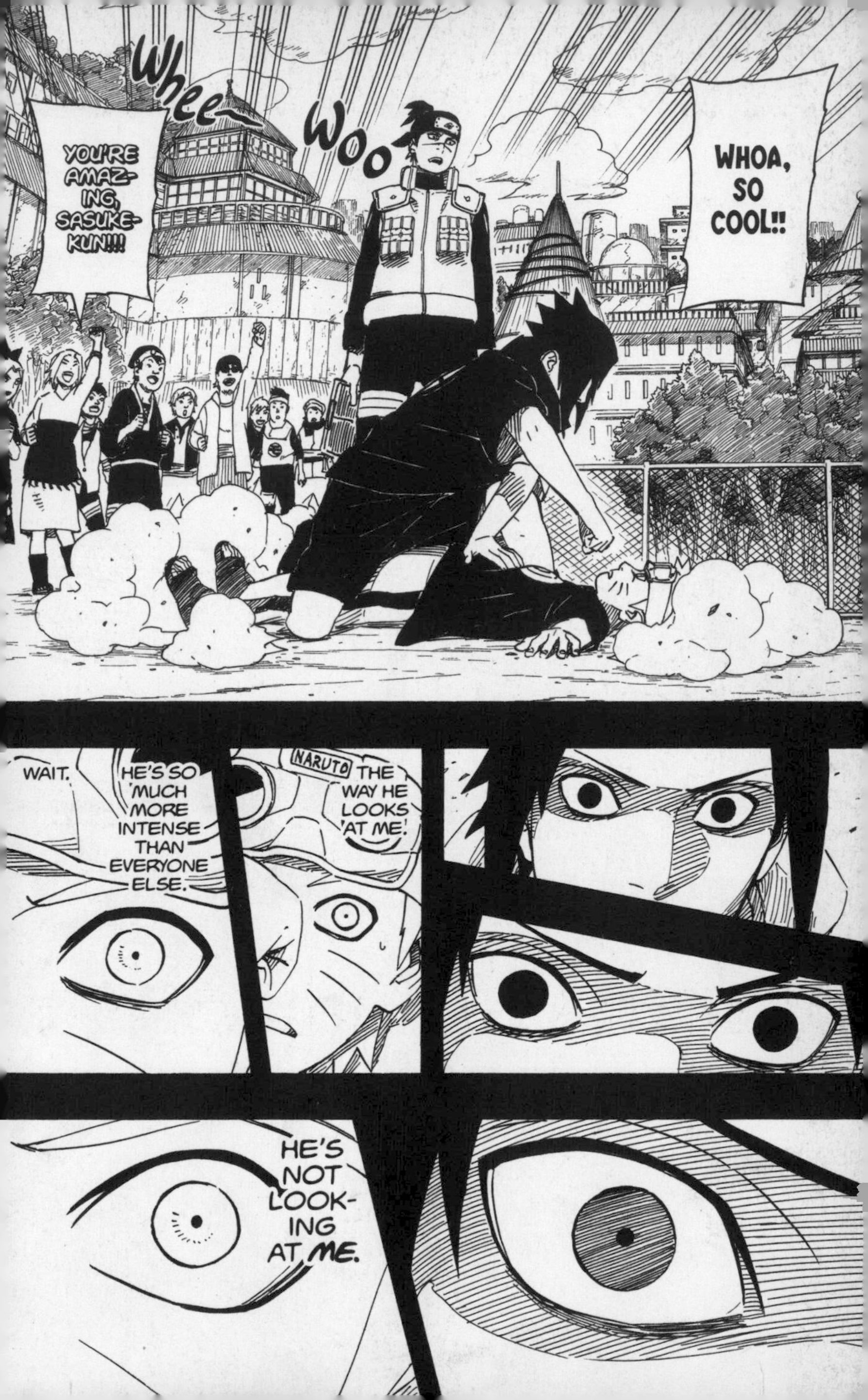
WHOA, SO COOL!!
Whee—Woo
YOU'RE AMAZ-ING, SASUKE-KUN!!!
THE WAY HE LOOKS AT ME.
NARUTO
HE'S SO MUCH MORE INTENSE THAN EVERYONE ELSE.
WAIT.
HE'S NOT LOOK-ING AT ME.

READ THIS WAY

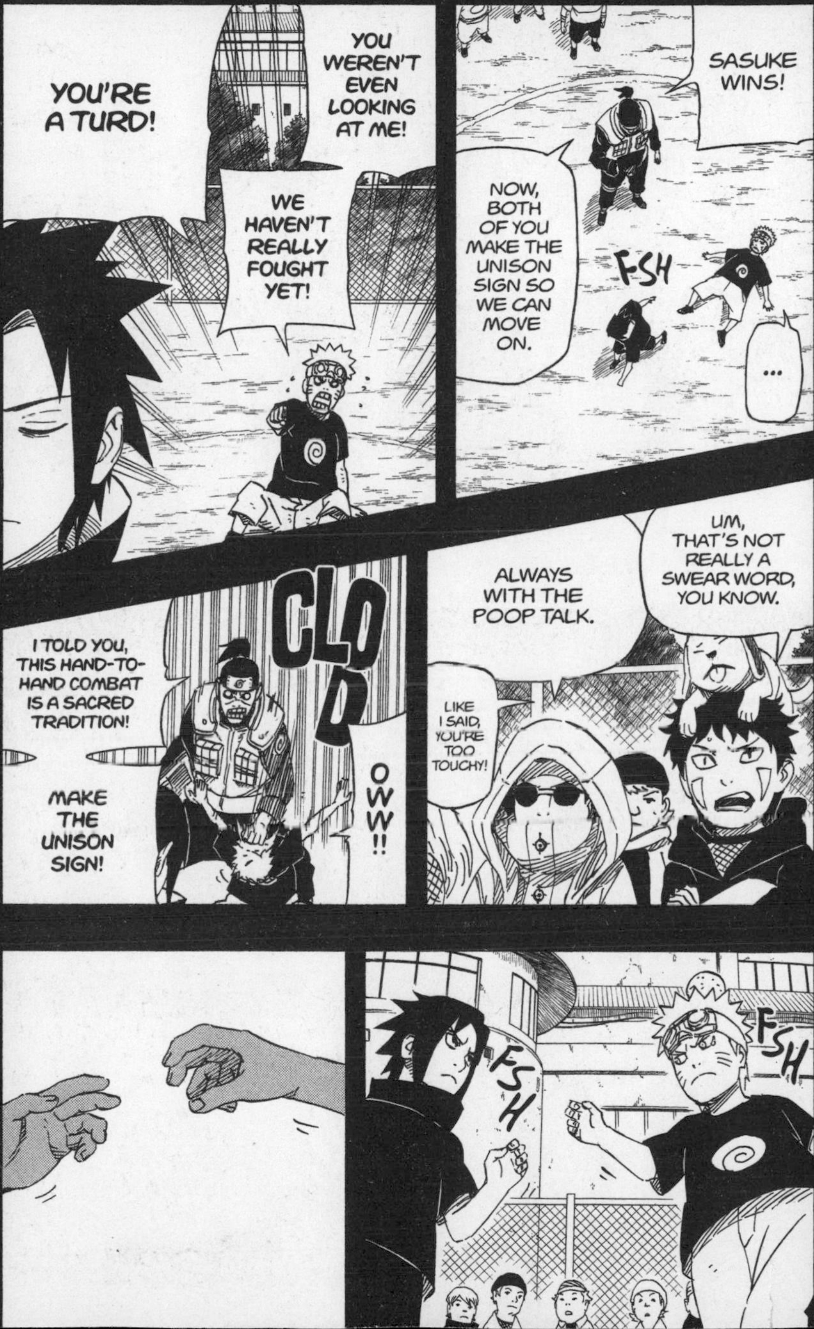
SASUKE WINS!
NOW, BOTH OF YOU MAKE THE UNISON SIGN SO WE CAN MOVE ON.
FSH
...
YOU WEREN'T EVEN LOOKING AT ME!
WE HAVEN'T REALLY FOUGHT YET!
YOU'RE A TURD!
UM, THAT'S NOT REALLY A SWEAR WORD, YOU KNOW.
ALWAYS WITH THE POOP TALK.
LIKE I SAID, YOU'RE TOO TOUCHY!
CLOD
OWW!!
I TOLD YOU, THIS HAND-TO-HAND COMBAT IS A SACRED TRADITION!
MAKE THE UNISON SIGN!
FSH
FSH

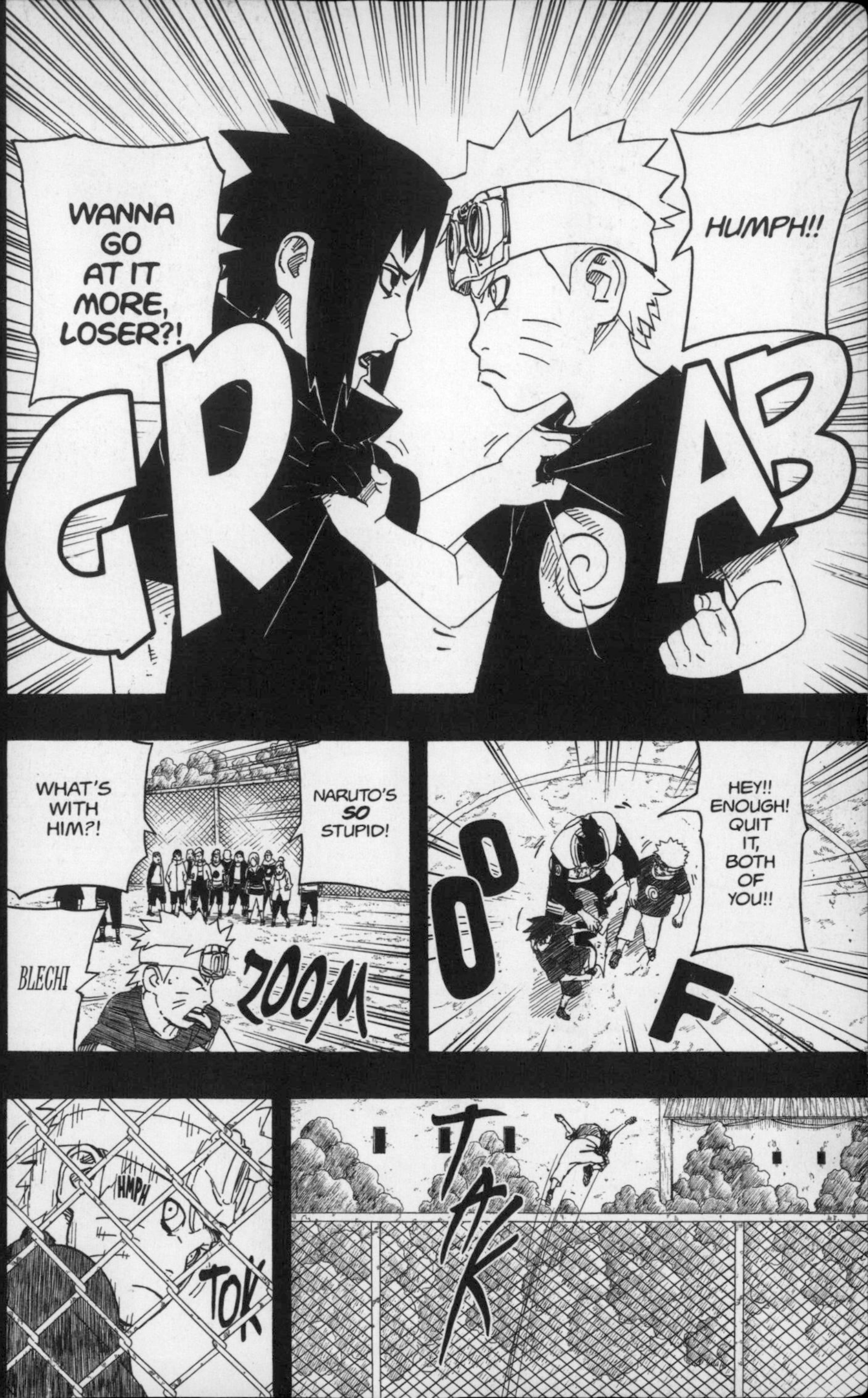
HUMPH!!
WANNA GO AT IT MORE, LOSER?!
GRAB
HEY!! ENOUGH! QUIT IT, BOTH OF YOU!!
OOF
NARUTO'S SO STUPID!
WHAT'S WITH HIM?!
ZOOM
BLECH!
TAK
HMPH
TOK

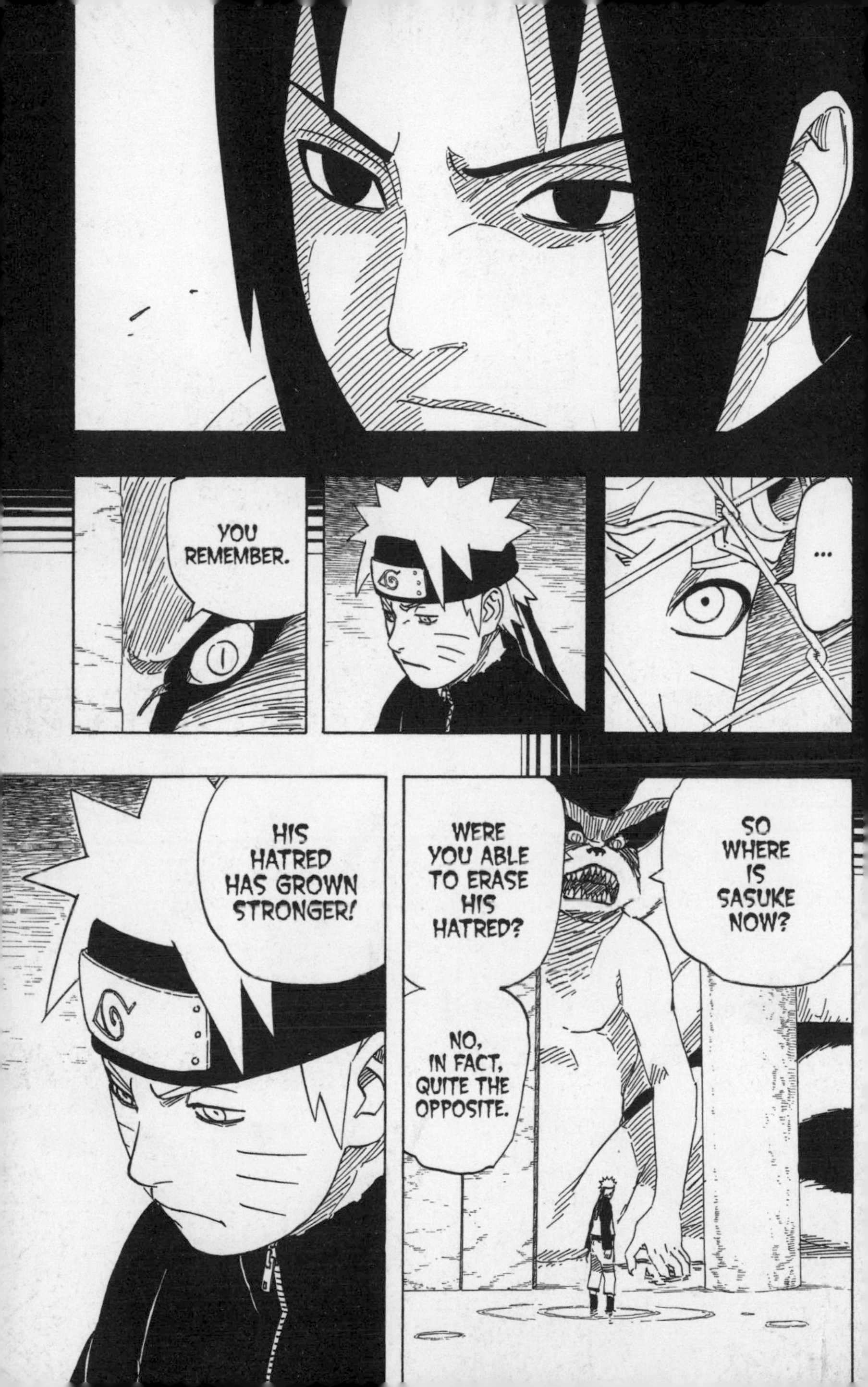
...
YOU REMEMBER.
SO WHERE IS SASUKE NOW?
WERE YOU ABLE TO ERASE HIS HATRED?
NO, IN FACT, QUITE THE OPPOSITE.
HIS HATRED HAS GROWN STRONGER!

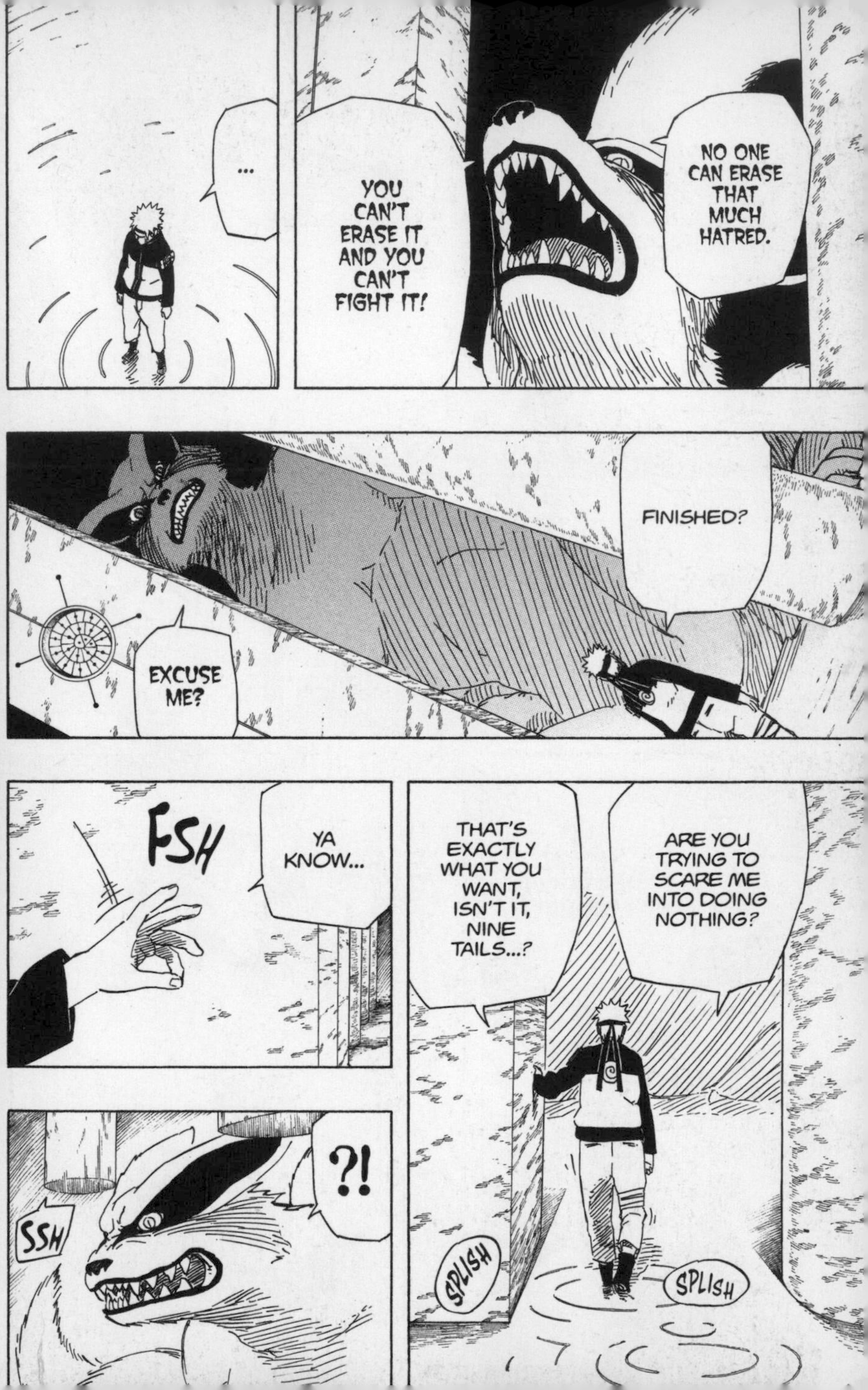
NO ONE CAN ERASE THAT MUCH HATRED.
YOU CAN'T ERASE IT AND YOU CAN'T FIGHT IT!
...
FINISHED?
EXCUSE ME?
ARE YOU TRYING TO SCARE ME INTO DOING NOTHING?
THAT'S EXACTLY WHAT YOU WANT, ISN'T IT, NINE TAILS...?
SPLISH
SPLISH
YA KNOW...
FSH
?!
SSH

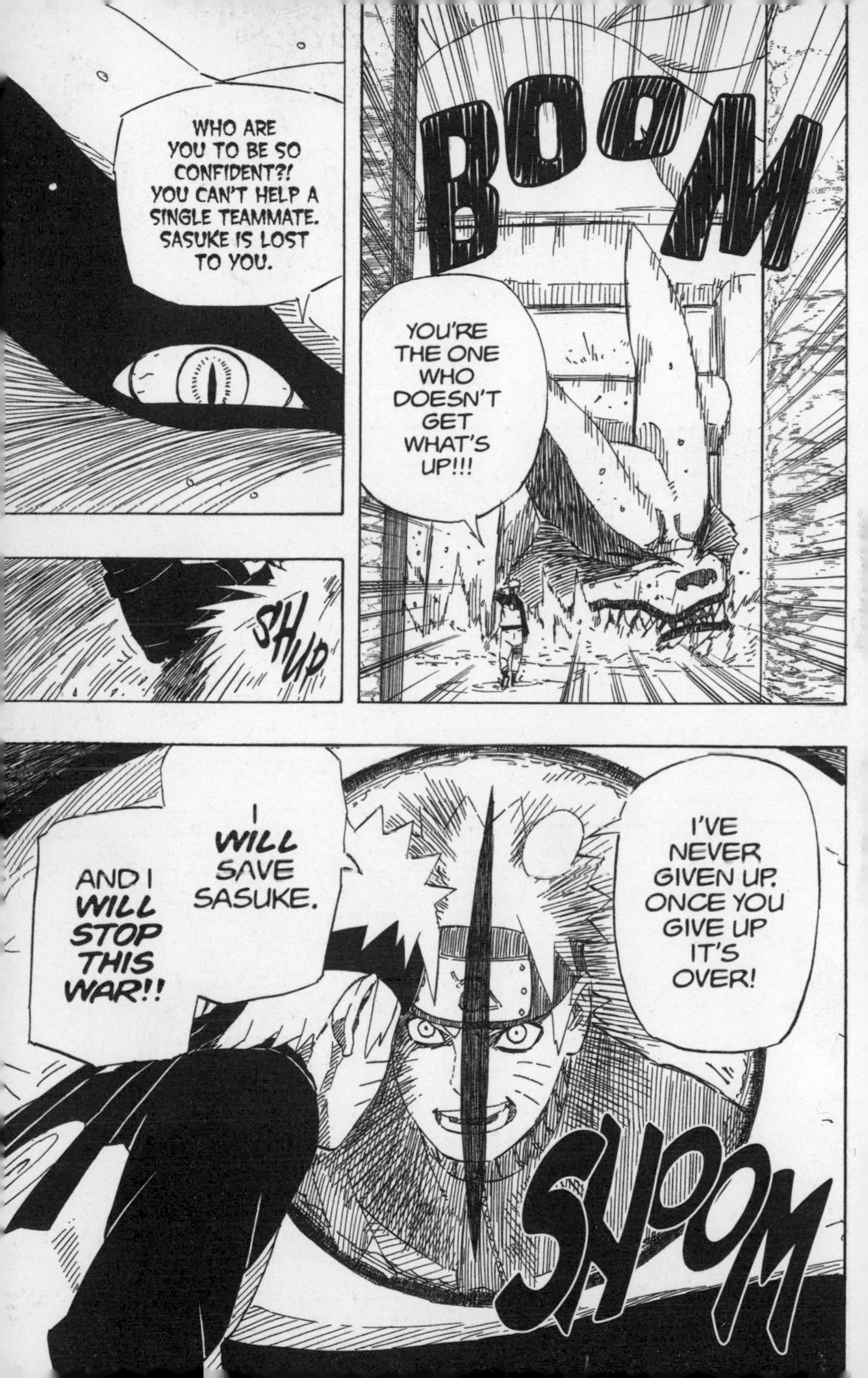
BOOM
YOU'RE THE ONE WHO DOESN'T GET WHAT'S UP!!!
WHO ARE YOU TO BE SO CONFIDENT?! YOU CAN'T HELP A SINGLE TEAMMATE. SASUKE IS LOST TO YOU.
SHUP
I'VE NEVER GIVEN UP. ONCE YOU GIVE UP IT'S OVER!
I ***WILL*** SAVE SASUKE.
AND I ***WILL*** STOP THIS WAR!!
SHOOM

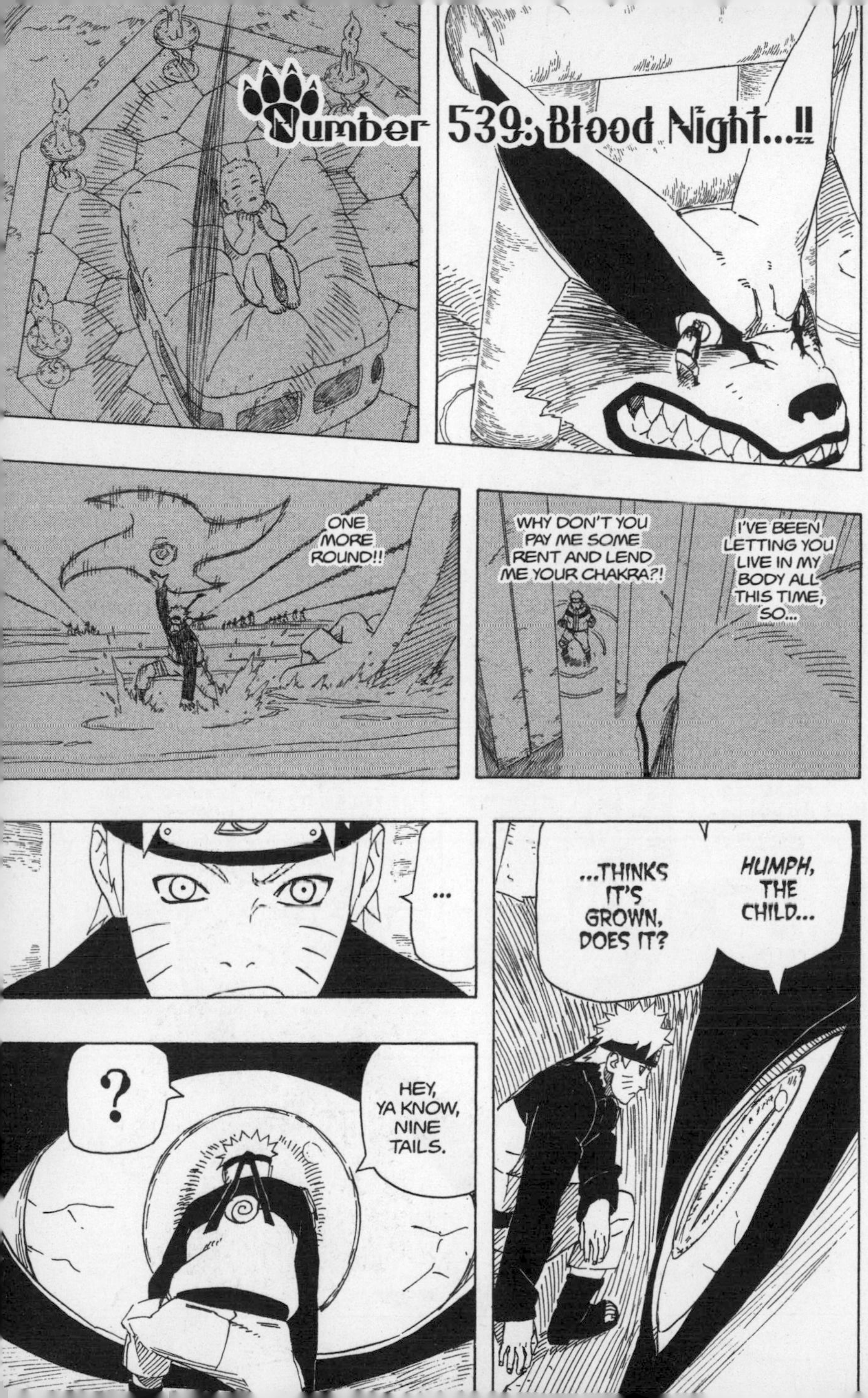
Number 539: Blood Night...!!
I'VE BEEN LETTING YOU LIVE IN MY BODY ALL THIS TIME, SO...
WHY DON'T YOU PAY ME SOME RENT AND LEND ME YOUR CHAKRA?!
ONE MORE ROUND!!
HUMPH, THE CHILD...
...THINKS IT'S GROWN, DOES IT?
...
HEY, YA KNOW, NINE TAILS.
?

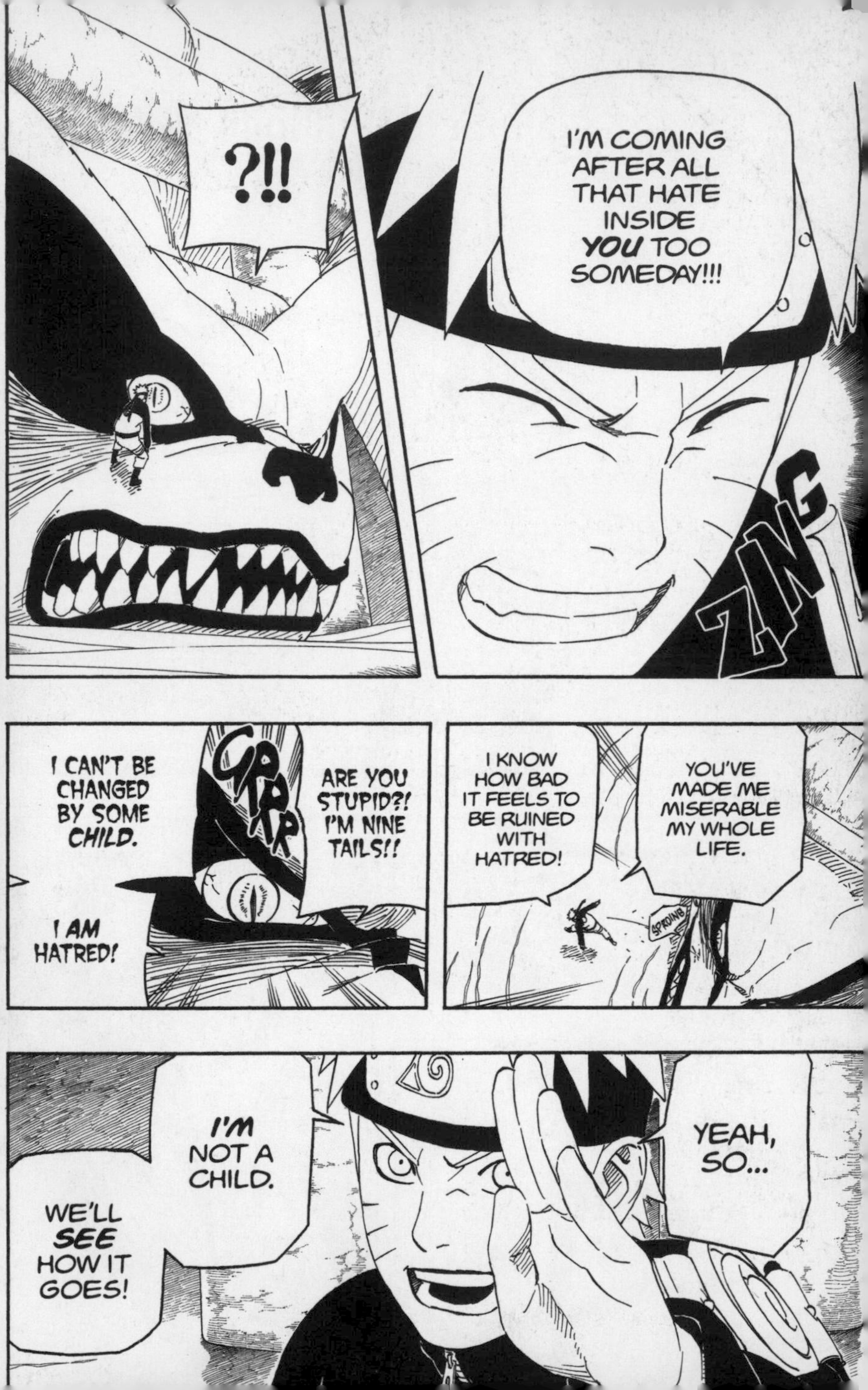
I'M COMING AFTER ALL THAT HATE INSIDE YOU TOO SOMEDAY!!!
ZING
?!!
YOU'VE MADE ME MISERABLE MY WHOLE LIFE.
I KNOW HOW BAD IT FEELS TO BE RUINED WITH HATRED!
SPROING
GRRR
ARE YOU STUPID?! I'M NINE TAILS!!
I CAN'T BE CHANGED BY SOME CHILD.
I AM HATRED!
YEAH, SO...
I'M NOT A CHILD.
WE'LL SEE HOW IT GOES!

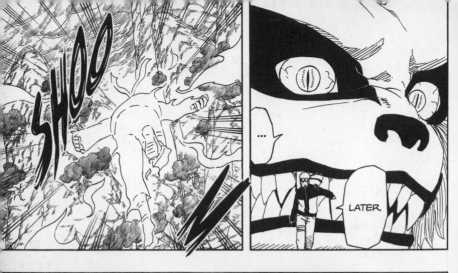

SHOO

...

LATER.

FOOSH

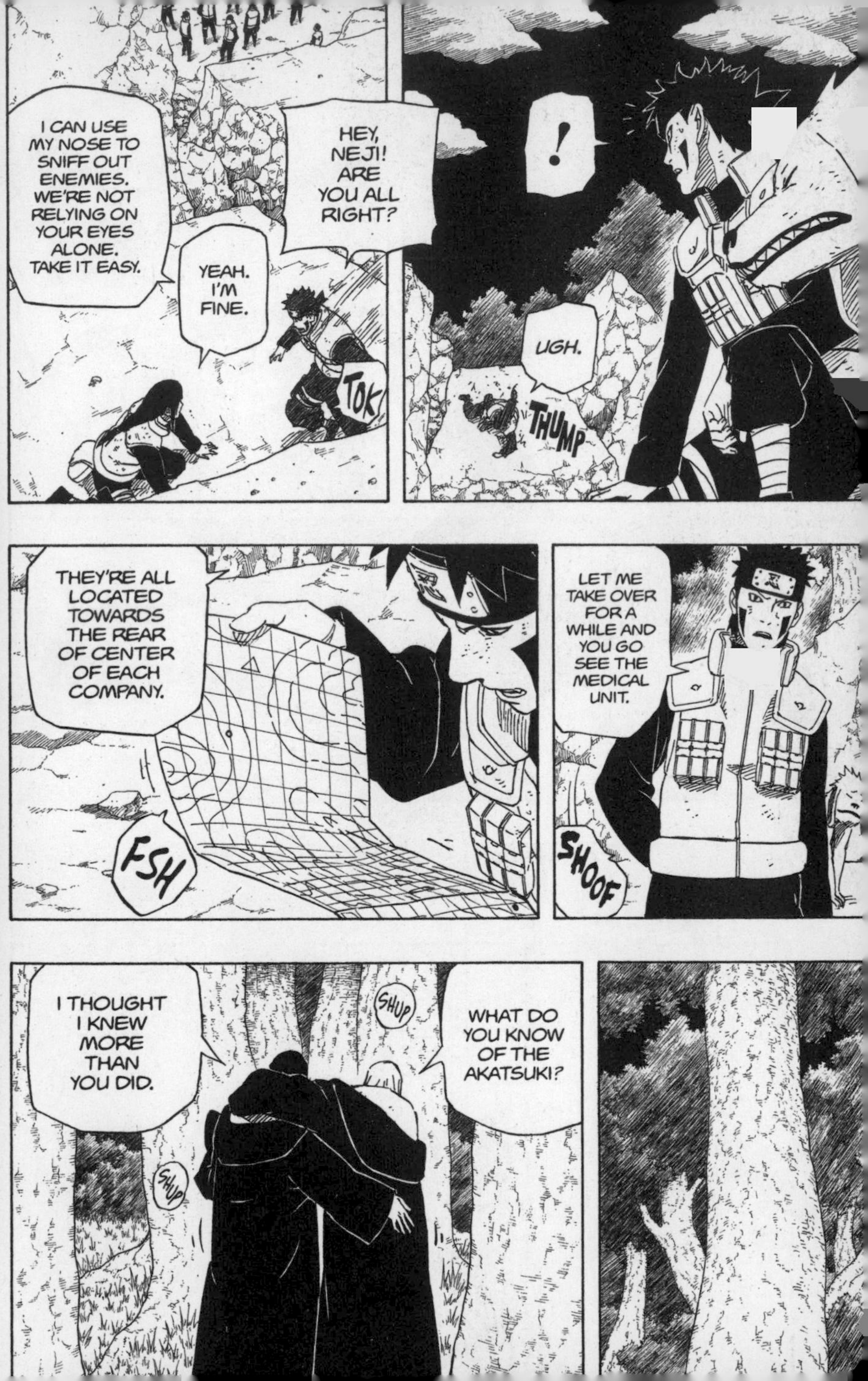
!
UGH.
THUMP
HEY, NEJI! ARE YOU ALL RIGHT?
YEAH. I'M FINE.
I CAN USE MY NOSE TO SNIFF OUT ENEMIES. WE'RE NOT RELYING ON YOUR EYES ALONE. TAKE IT EASY.
TOK
LET ME TAKE OVER FOR A WHILE AND YOU GO SEE THE MEDICAL UNIT.
SHOOF
THEY'RE ALL LOCATED TOWARDS THE REAR OF CENTER OF EACH COMPANY.
FSH
WHAT DO YOU KNOW OF THE AKATSUKI?
SHUP
I THOUGHT I KNEW MORE THAN YOU DID.
SHUP

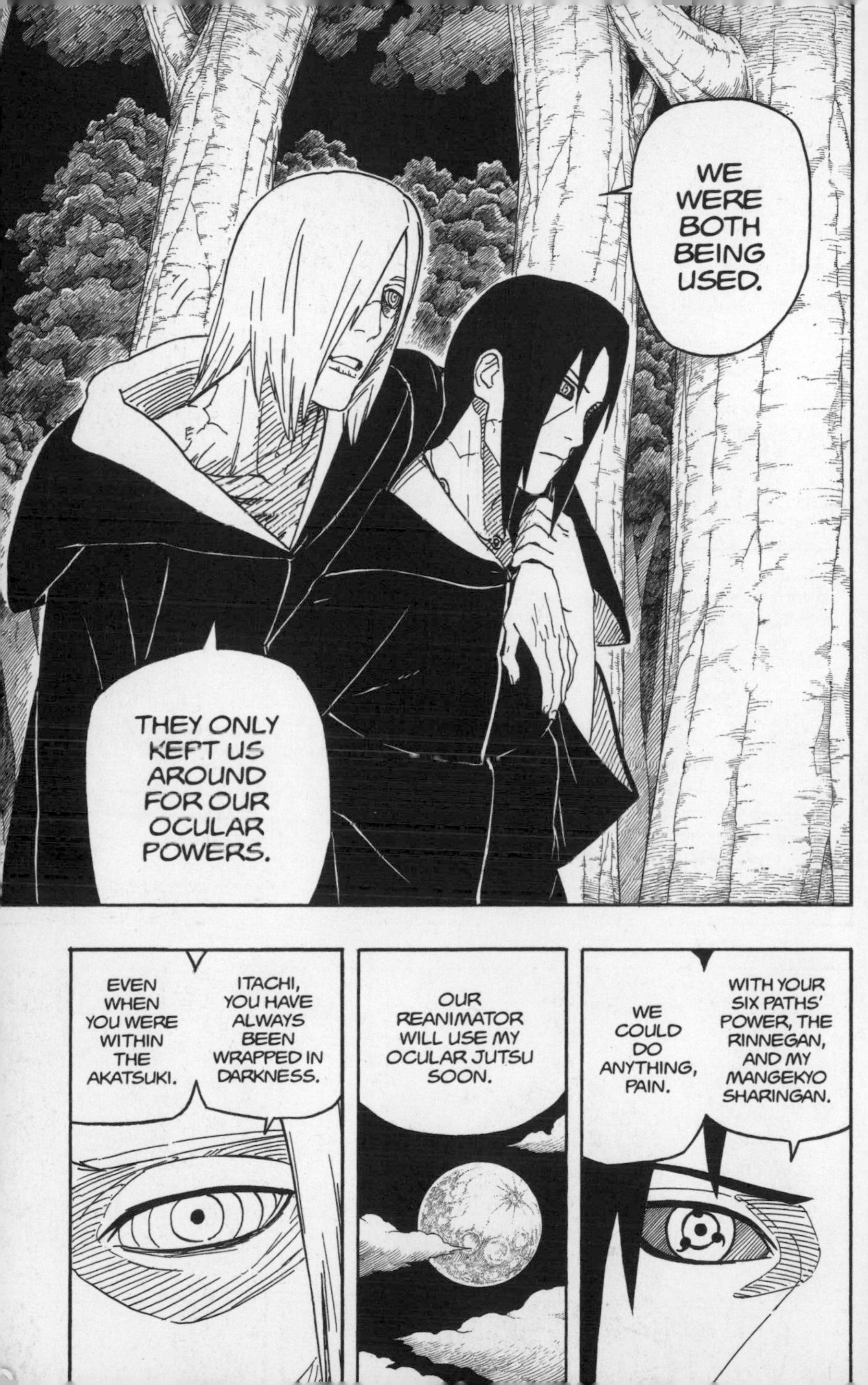
WE WERE BOTH BEING USED.
THEY ONLY KEPT US AROUND FOR OUR OCULAR POWERS.
WITH YOUR SIX PATHS' POWER, THE RINNEGAN, AND MY MANGEKYO SHARINGAN.
WE COULD DO ANYTHING, PAIN.
OUR REANIMATOR WILL USE MY OCULAR JUTSU SOON.
ITACHI, YOU HAVE ALWAYS BEEN WRAPPED IN DARKNESS.
EVEN WHEN YOU WERE WITHIN THE AKATSUKI.

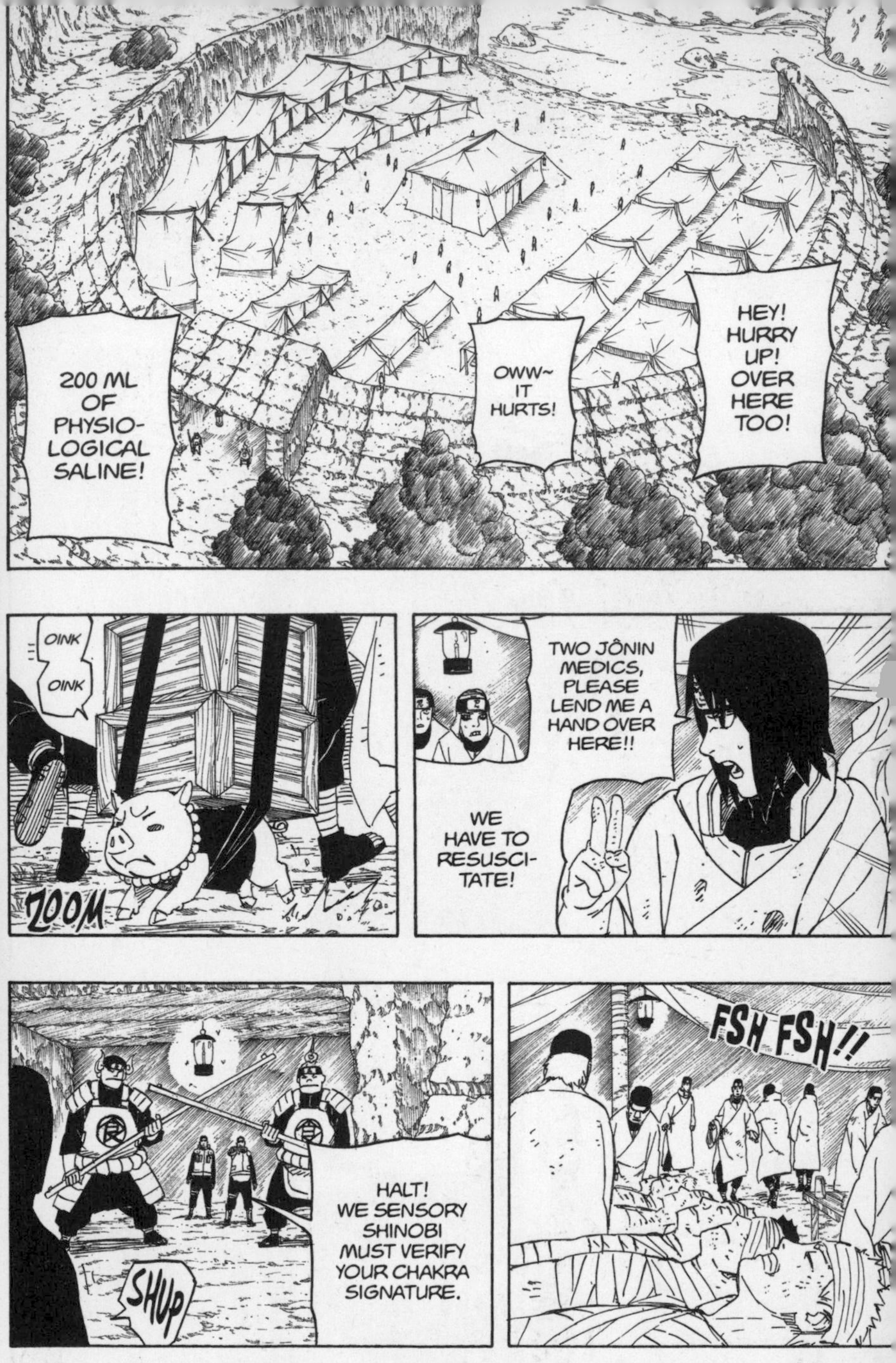
HEY! HURRY UP! OVER HERE TOO!
OWW~ IT HURTS!
200 ML OF PHYSIO-LOGICAL SALINE!
TWO JÔNIN MEDICS, PLEASE LEND ME A HAND OVER HERE!!
WE HAVE TO RESUSCI-TATE!
OINK
OINK
ZOOM
FSH FSH!!
HALT! WE SENSORY SHINOBI MUST VERIFY YOUR CHAKRA SIGNATURE.
SHUP

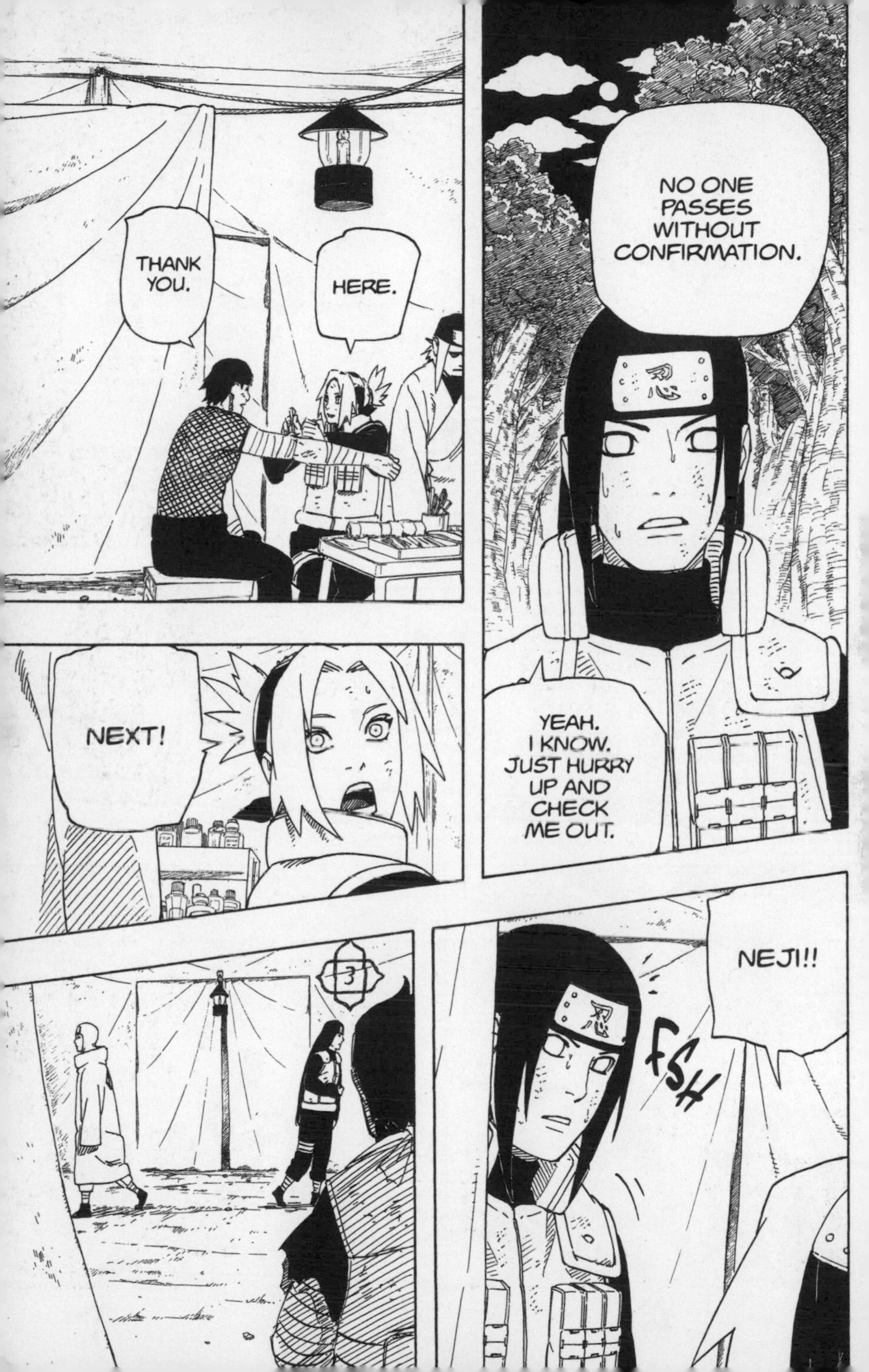
NO ONE PASSES WITHOUT CONFIRMATION.
YEAH. I KNOW. JUST HURRY UP AND CHECK ME OUT.
HERE.
THANK YOU.
NEXT!
NEJI!!
FSH
3

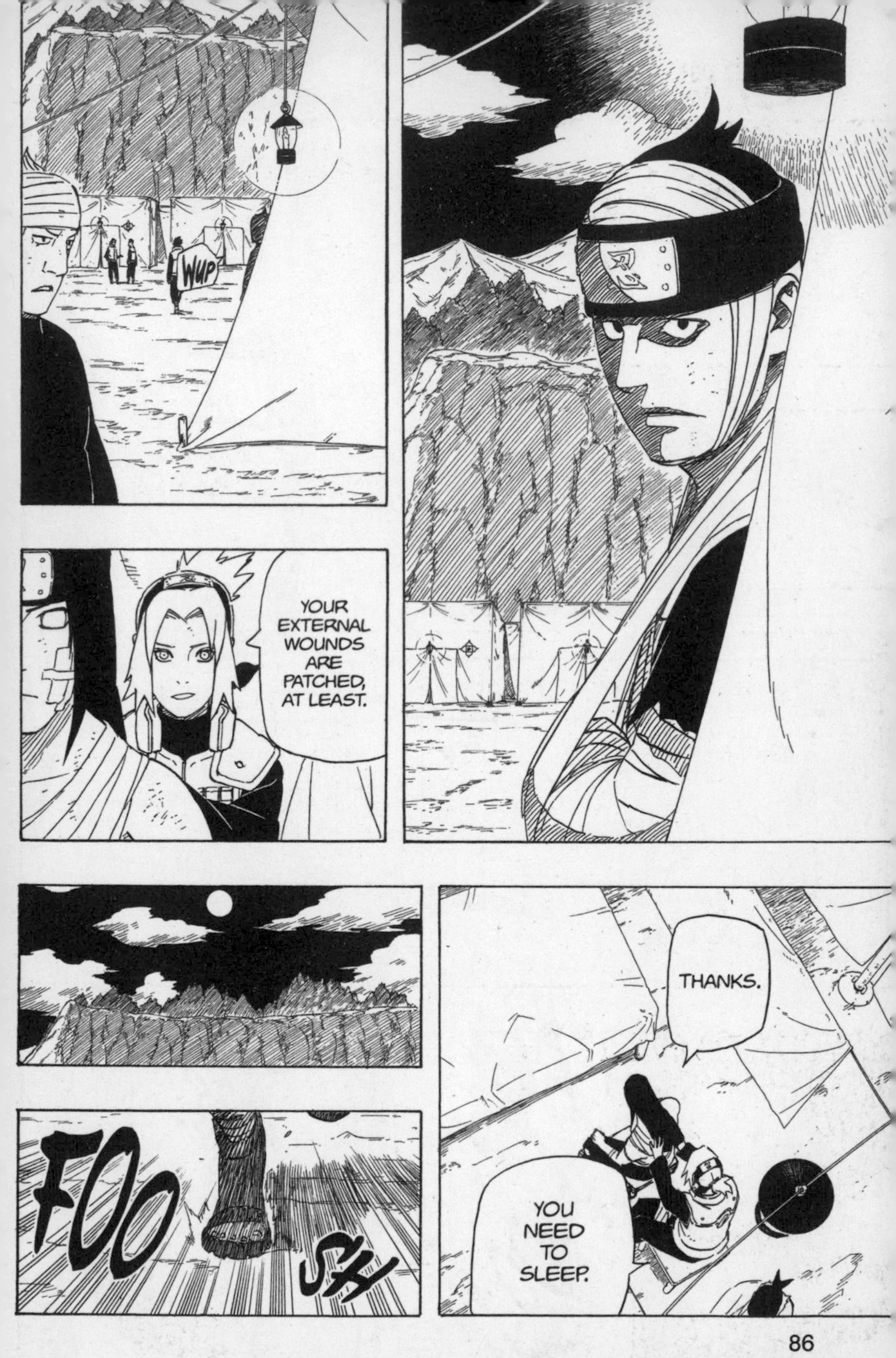
WUP
YOUR EXTERNAL WOUNDS ARE PATCHED, AT LEAST.
THANKS.
YOU NEED TO SLEEP.
FOOSH

READ THIS WAY

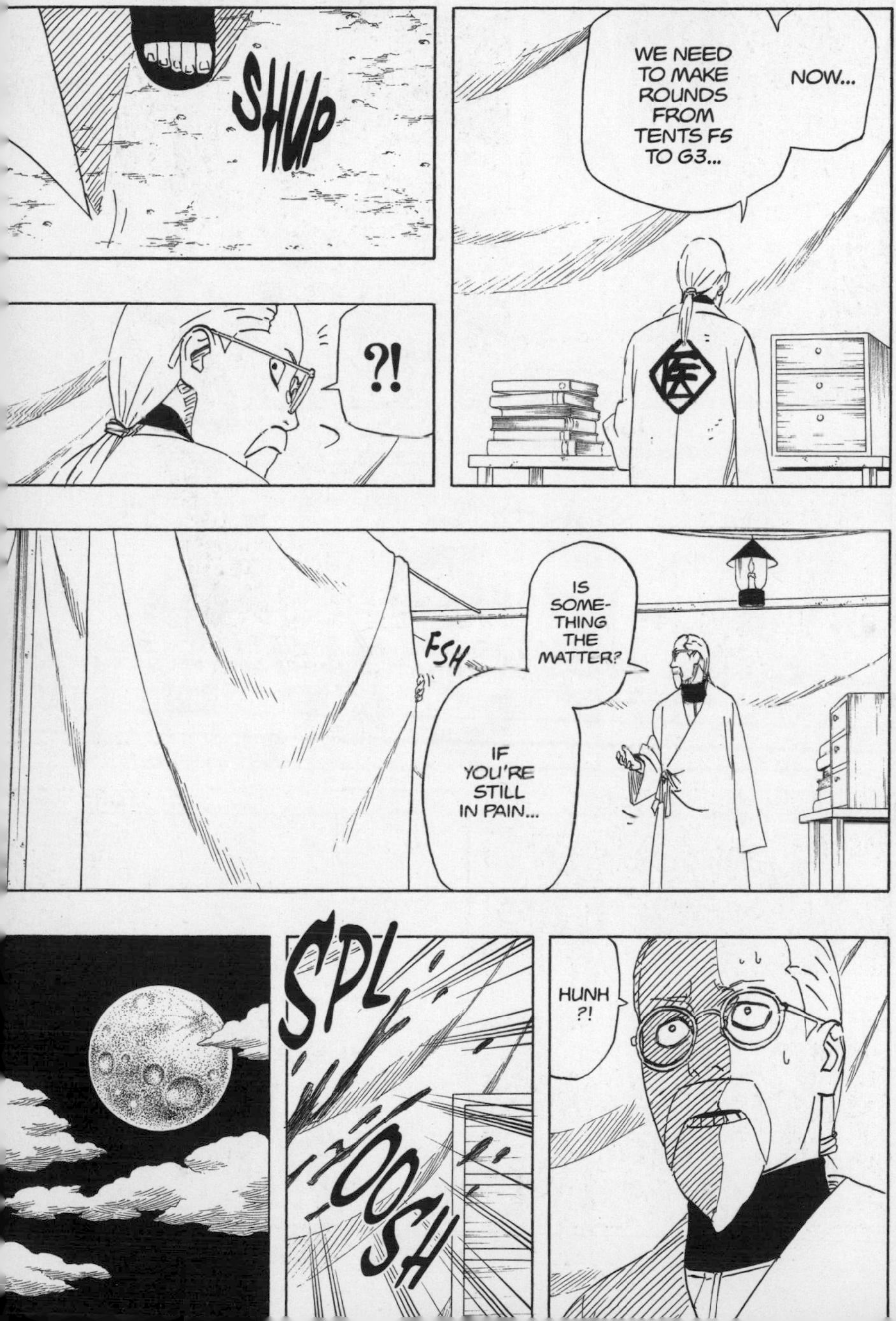

WE NEED TO MAKE ROUNDS FROM TENTS F5 TO G3...
NOW...
SHUP
?!
IS SOMETHING THE MATTER?
FSH
IF YOU'RE STILL IN PAIN...
HUNH ?!
SPL
WOOSH

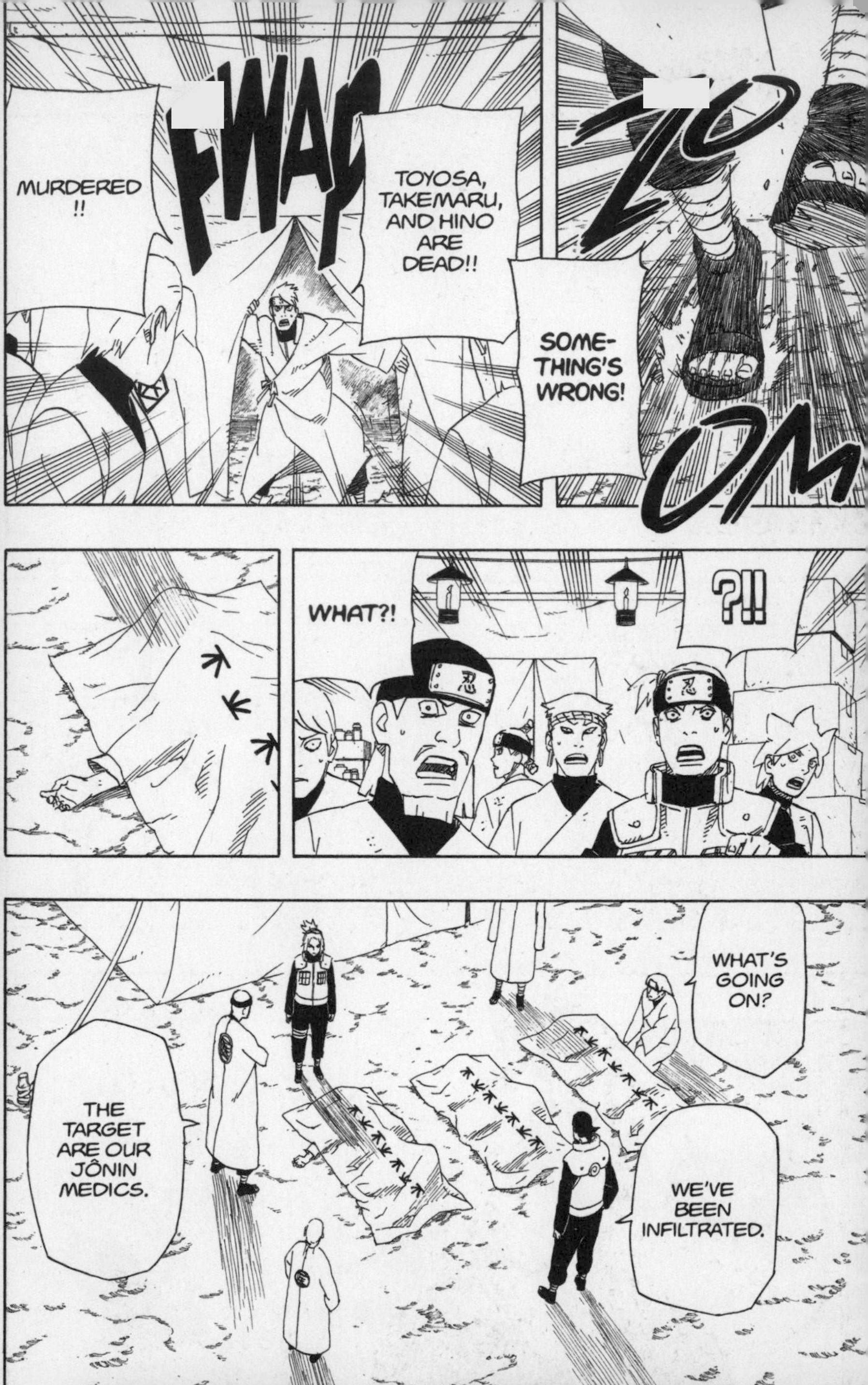
ZOOM
SOMETHING'S WRONG!
FWAP
TOYOSA, TAKEMARU, AND HINO ARE DEAD!!
MURDERED!!
?!!
WHAT?!
WHAT'S GOING ON?
WE'VE BEEN INFILTRATED.
THE TARGET ARE OUR JÔNIN MEDICS.

READ THIS WAY

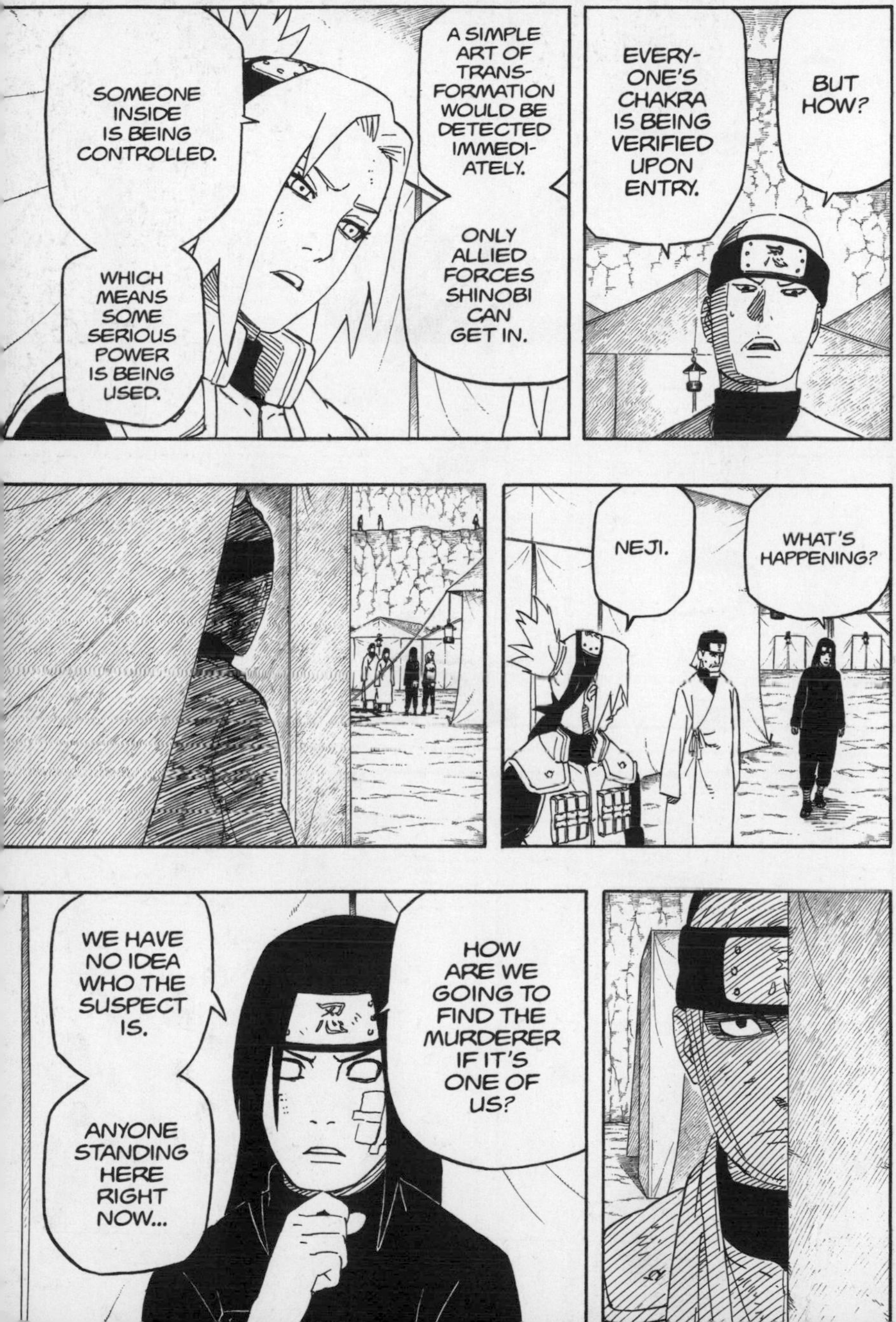
BUT HOW?
EVERYONE'S CHAKRA IS BEING VERIFIED UPON ENTRY.
A SIMPLE ART OF TRANSFORMATION WOULD BE DETECTED IMMEDIATELY.
ONLY ALLIED FORCES SHINOBI CAN GET IN.
SOMEONE INSIDE IS BEING CONTROLLED.
WHICH MEANS SOME SERIOUS POWER IS BEING USED.
WHAT'S HAPPENING?
NEJI.
HOW ARE WE GOING TO FIND THE MURDERER IF IT'S ONE OF US?
WE HAVE NO IDEA WHO THE SUSPECT IS.
ANYONE STANDING HERE RIGHT NOW...

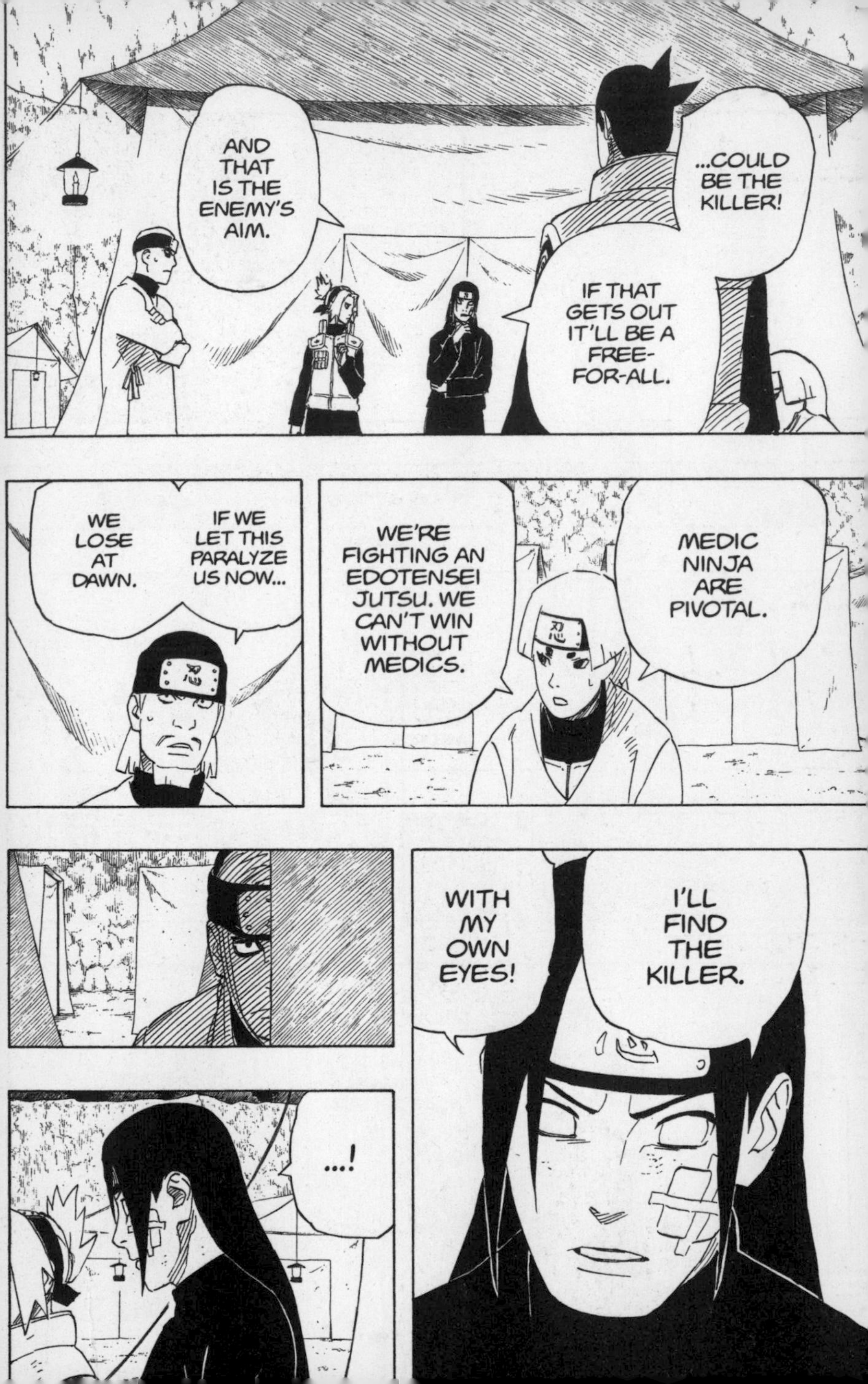
...COULD BE THE KILLER!
IF THAT GETS OUT IT'LL BE A FREE-FOR-ALL.
AND THAT IS THE ENEMY'S AIM.
MEDIC NINJA ARE PIVOTAL.
WE'RE FIGHTING AN EDOTENSEI JUTSU. WE CAN'T WIN WITHOUT MEDICS.
IF WE LET THIS PARALYZE US NOW...
WE LOSE AT DAWN.
I'LL FIND THE KILLER.
WITH MY OWN EYES!
...!

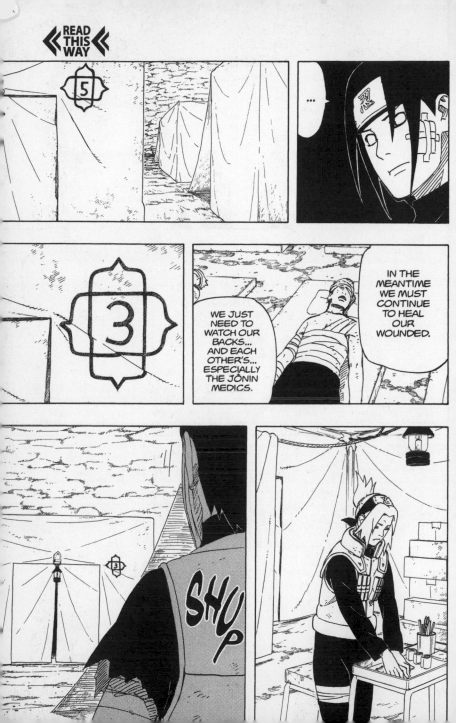

...

IN THE MEANTIME WE MUST CONTINUE TO HEAL OUR WOUNDED.

WE JUST NEED TO WATCH OUR BACKS... AND EACH OTHER'S... ESPECIALLY THE JÔNIN MEDICS.

SHUP

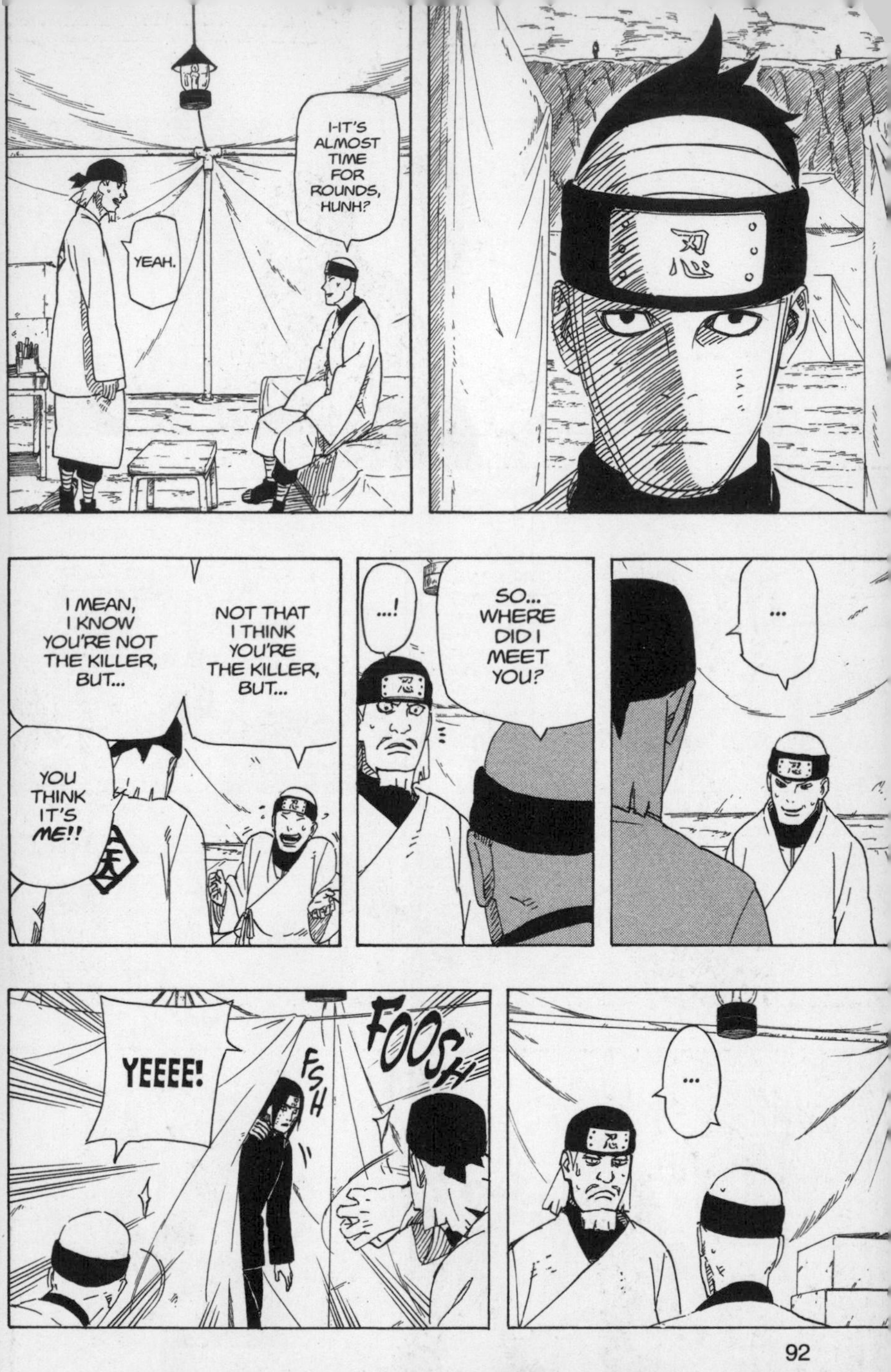
I-IT'S ALMOST TIME FOR ROUNDS, HUNH?
YEAH.
...
SO... WHERE DID I MEET YOU?
...!
NOT THAT I THINK YOU'RE THE KILLER, BUT...
I MEAN, I KNOW YOU'RE NOT THE KILLER, BUT...
YOU THINK IT'S *ME!!*
...
FOOSH
YEEEE!
FSH

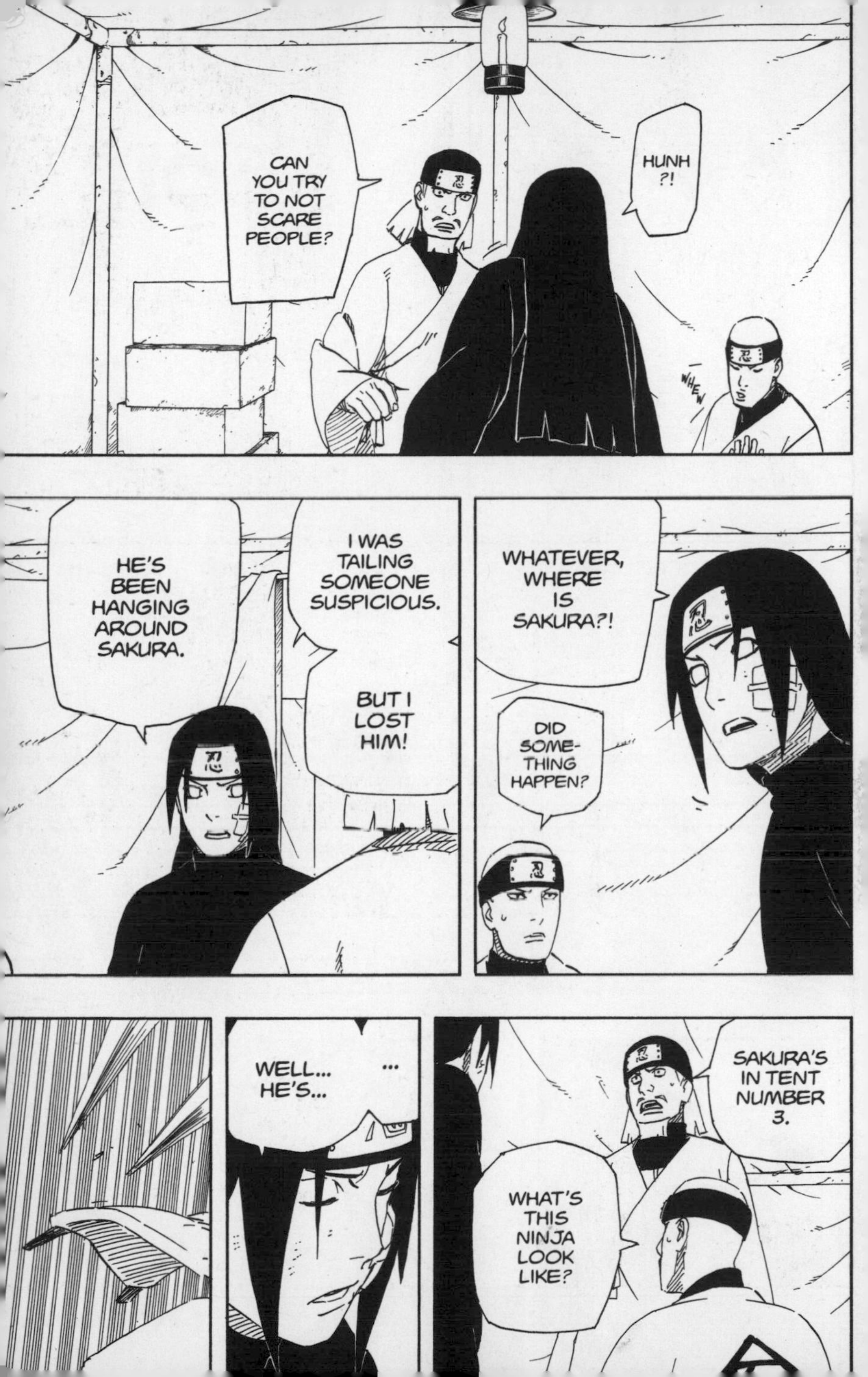
HUNH ?!
CAN YOU TRY TO NOT SCARE PEOPLE?
WHEW
WHATEVER, WHERE IS SAKURA?!
DID SOME-THING HAPPEN?
I WAS TAILING SOMEONE SUSPICIOUS.
BUT I LOST HIM!
HE'S BEEN HANGING AROUND SAKURA.
SAKURA'S IN TENT NUMBER 3.
WHAT'S THIS NINJA LOOK LIKE?
...
WELL... HE'S...

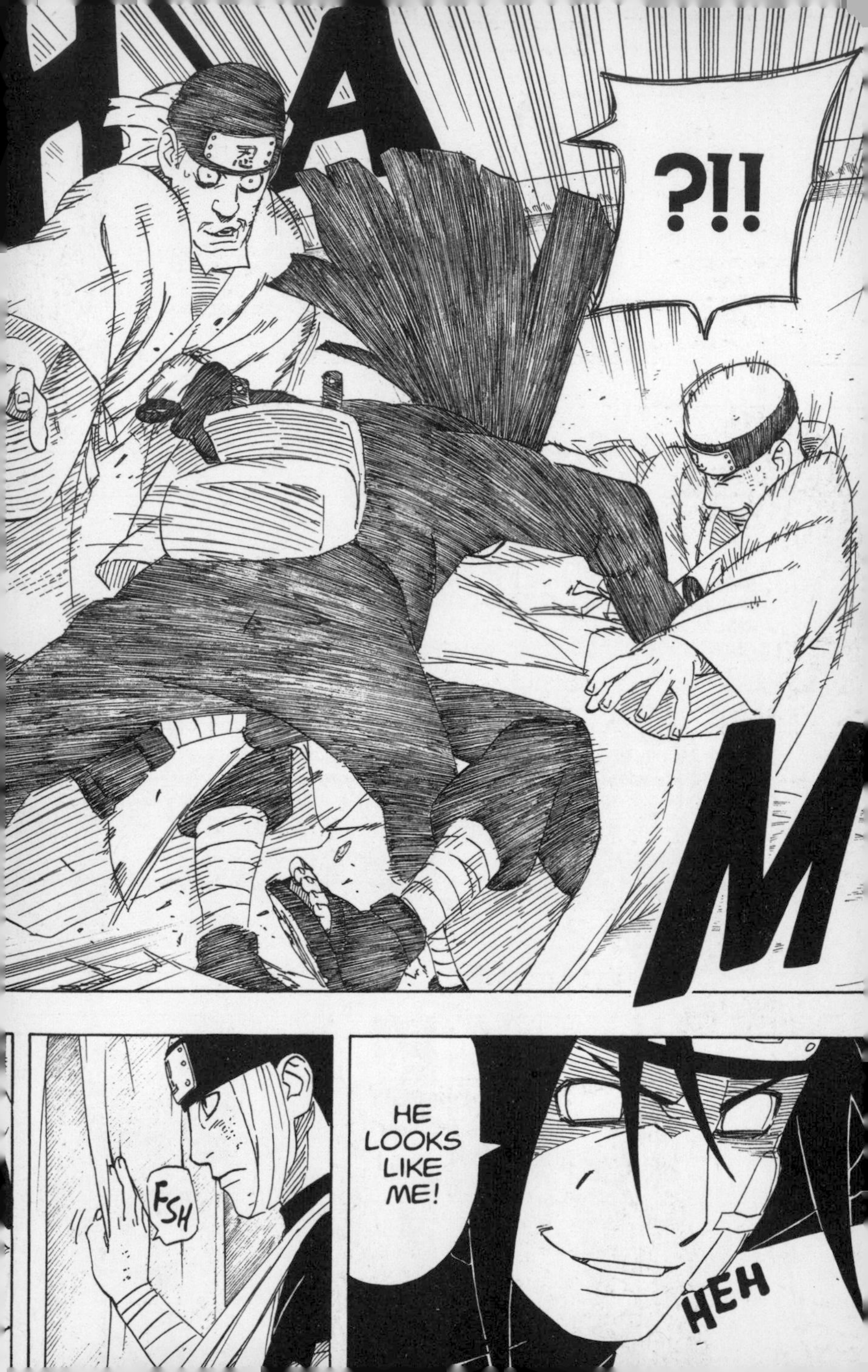
?!!
HE LOOKS LIKE ME!
HEH
FSH

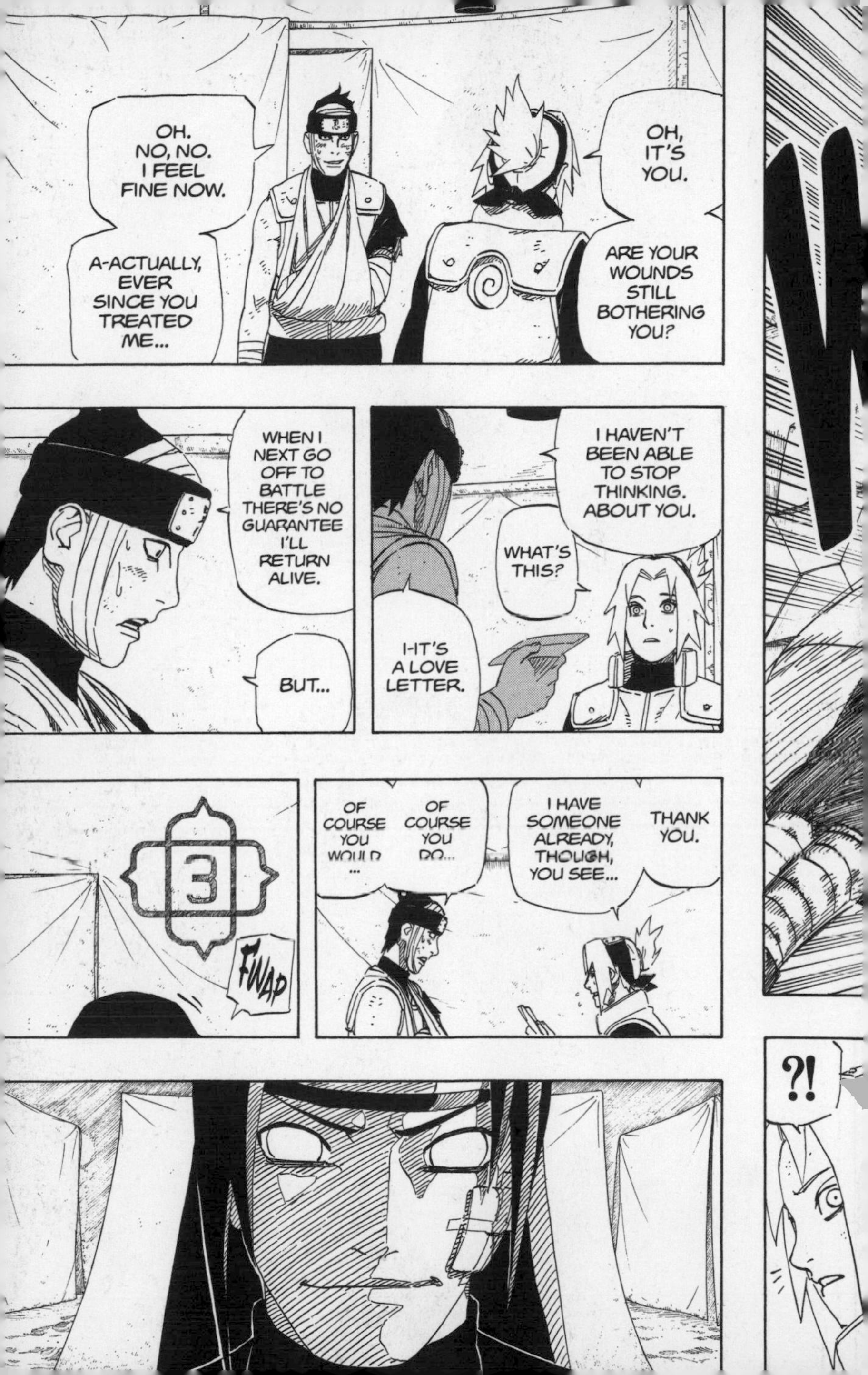
?!
OH, IT'S YOU.
ARE YOUR WOUNDS STILL BOTHERING YOU?
OH. NO, NO. I FEEL FINE NOW.
A-ACTUALLY, EVER SINCE YOU TREATED ME...
I HAVEN'T BEEN ABLE TO STOP THINKING. ABOUT YOU.
WHAT'S THIS?
I-IT'S A LOVE LETTER.
WHEN I NEXT GO OFF TO BATTLE THERE'S NO GUARANTEE I'LL RETURN ALIVE.
BUT...
THANK YOU.
I HAVE SOMEONE ALREADY, THOUGH, YOU SEE...
OF COURSE YOU DO...
OF COURSE YOU WOULD ...
3
FWAP

NARUTO

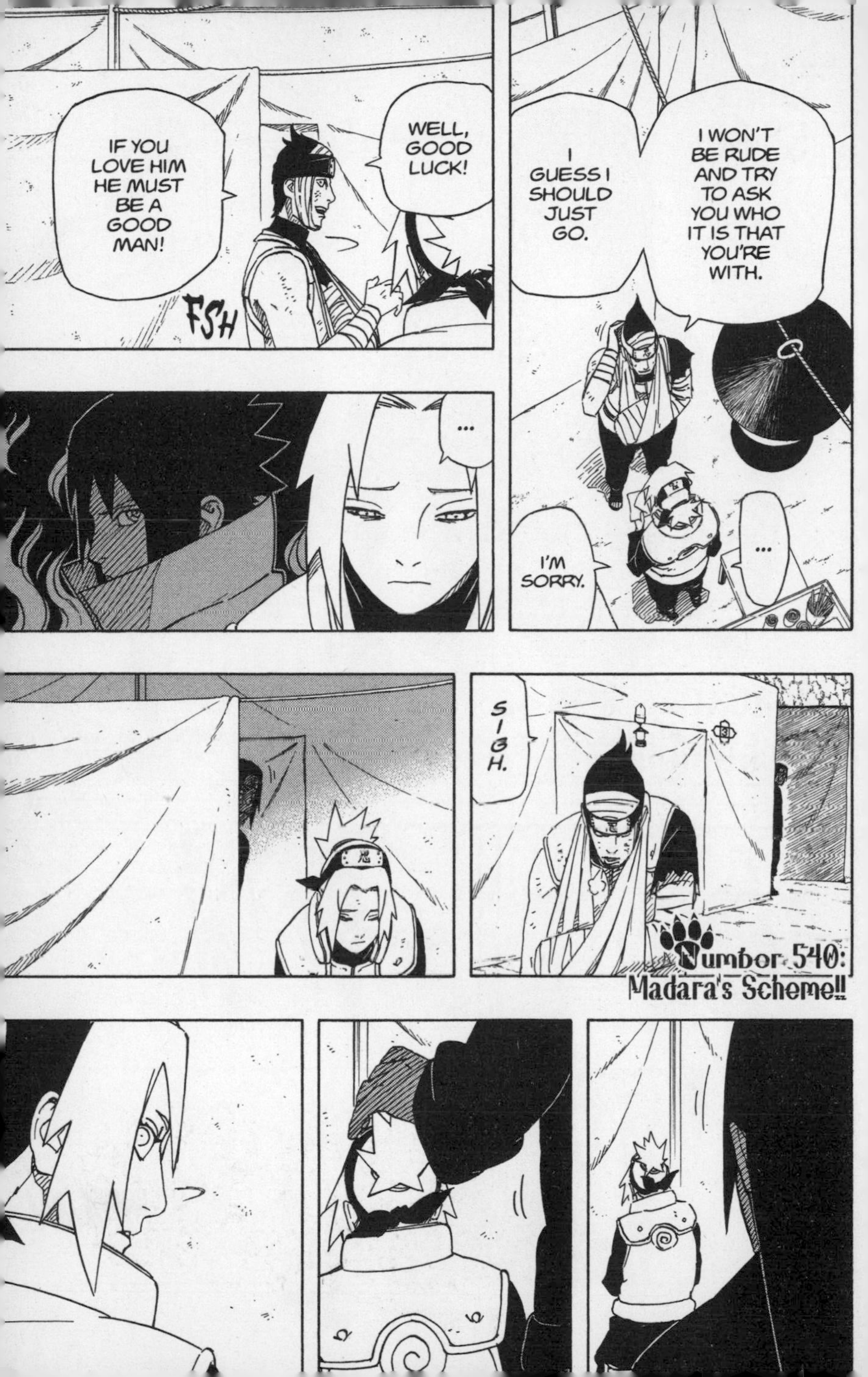
I WON'T BE RUDE AND TRY TO ASK YOU WHO IT IS THAT YOU'RE WITH.
I GUESS I SHOULD JUST GO.
...
I'M SORRY.
WELL, GOOD LUCK!
IF YOU LOVE HIM HE MUST BE A GOOD MAN!
FSH
...
SIGH.
Number 540: Madara's Scheme!!

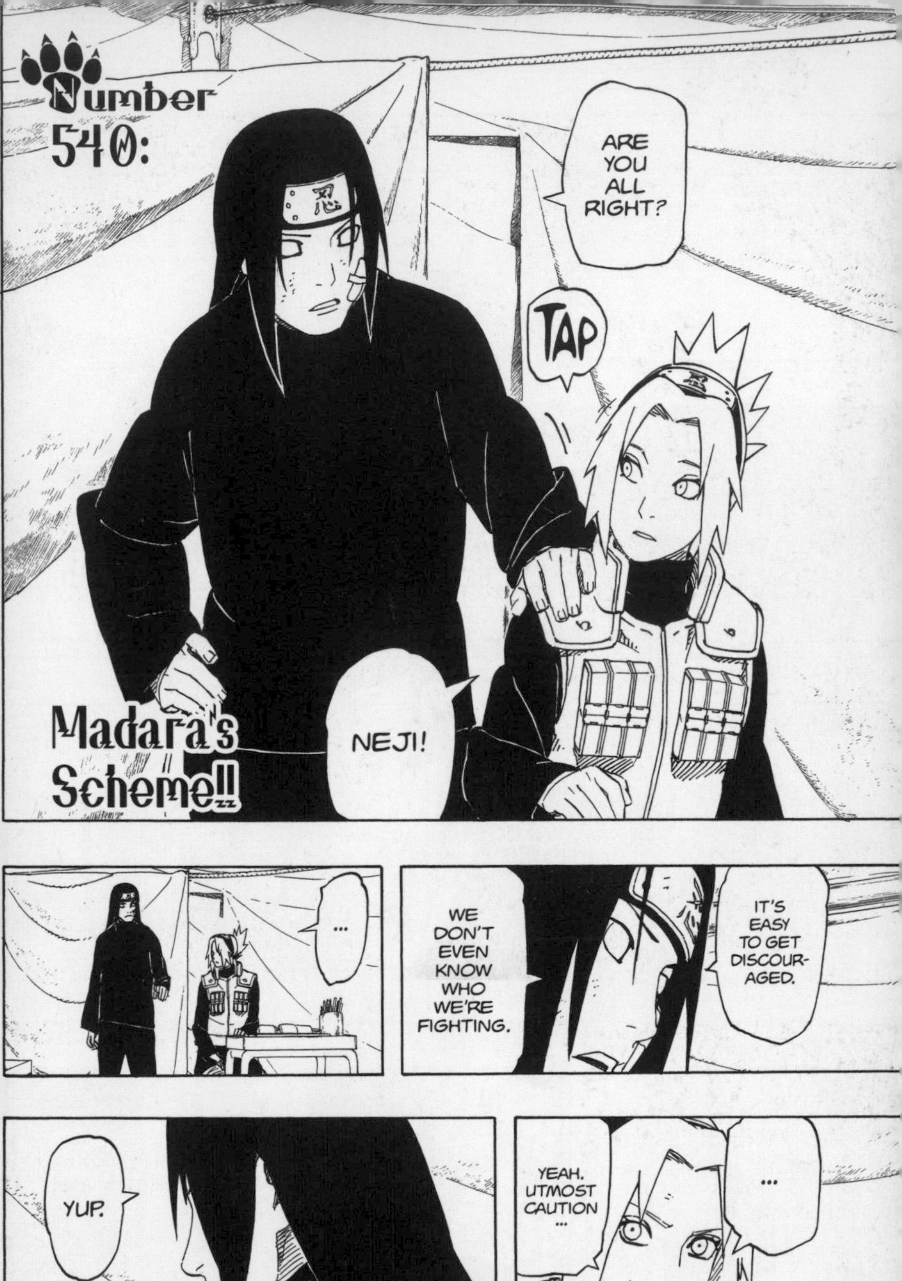
Number 540:
Madara's Scheme!!
ARE YOU ALL RIGHT?
TAP
NEJI!
IT'S EASY TO GET DISCOURAGED.
WE DON'T EVEN KNOW WHO WE'RE FIGHTING.
...
...
YEAH. UTMOST CAUTION ...
YUP.

READ THIS WAY

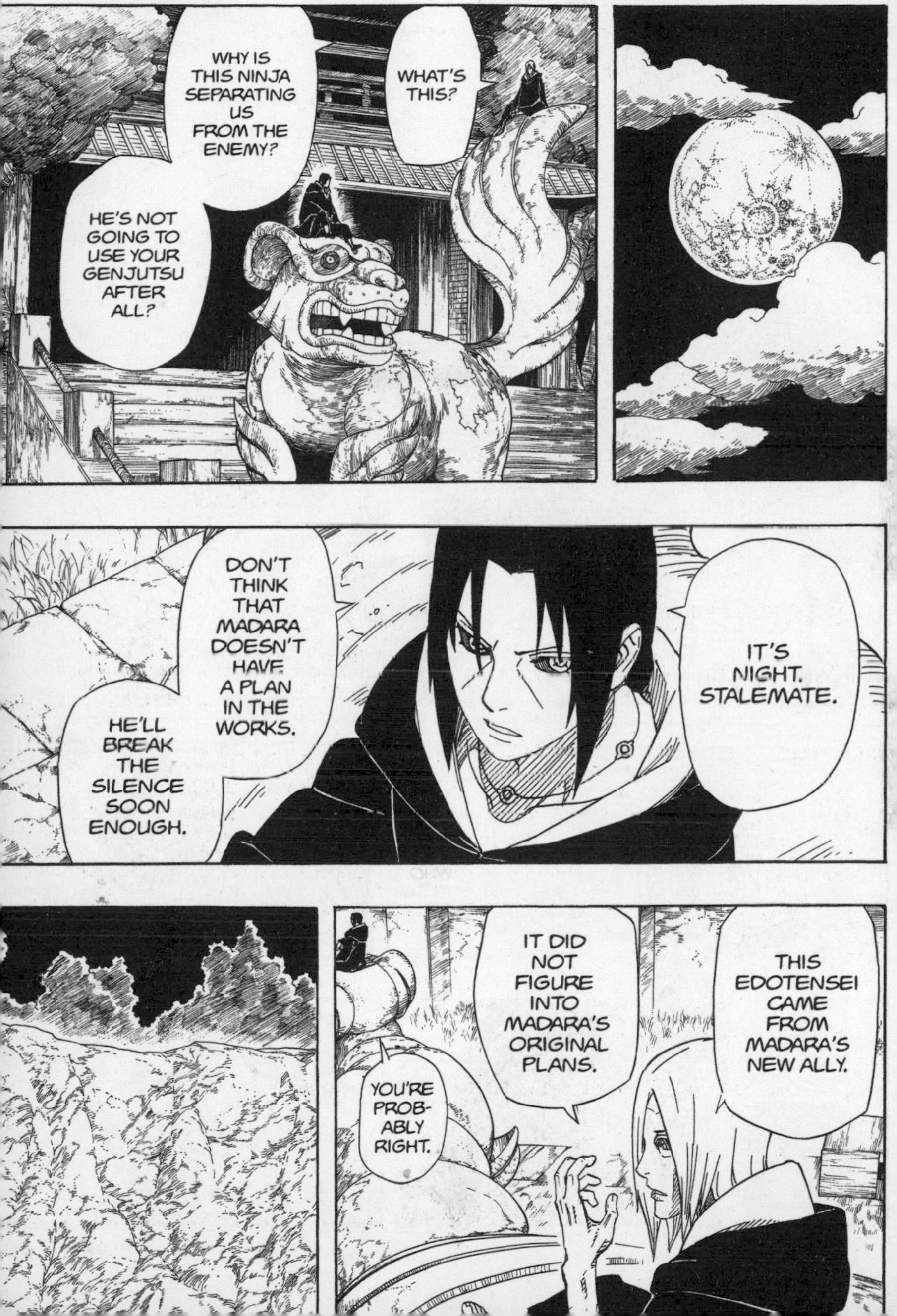
WHAT'S THIS?
WHY IS THIS NINJA SEPARATING US FROM THE ENEMY?
HE'S NOT GOING TO USE YOUR GENJUTSU AFTER ALL?
IT'S NIGHT. STALEMATE.
DON'T THINK THAT MADARA DOESN'T HAVE A PLAN IN THE WORKS.
HE'LL BREAK THE SILENCE SOON ENOUGH.
THIS EDOTENSEI CAME FROM MADARA'S NEW ALLY.
IT DID NOT FIGURE INTO MADARA'S ORIGINAL PLANS.
YOU'RE PROBABLY RIGHT.

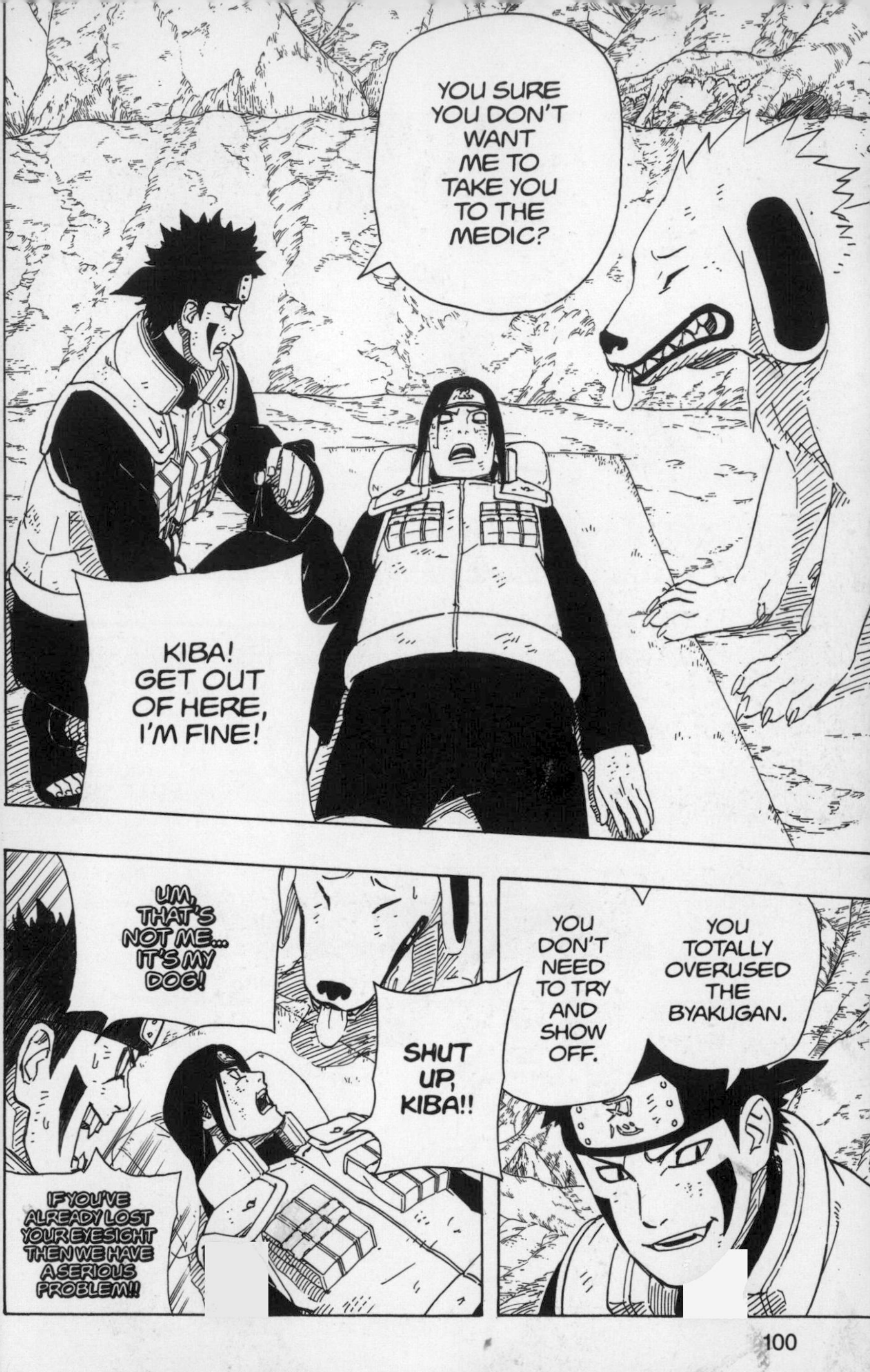
YOU SURE YOU DON'T WANT ME TO TAKE YOU TO THE MEDIC?
KIBA! GET OUT OF HERE, I'M FINE!
YOU TOTALLY OVERUSED THE BYAKUGAN.
YOU DON'T NEED TO TRY AND SHOW OFF.
SHUT UP, KIBA!!
UM, THAT'S NOT ME... IT'S MY DOG!
IF YOU'VE ALREADY LOST YOUR EYESIGHT THEN WE HAVE A SERIOUS PROBLEM!!

READ THIS WAY

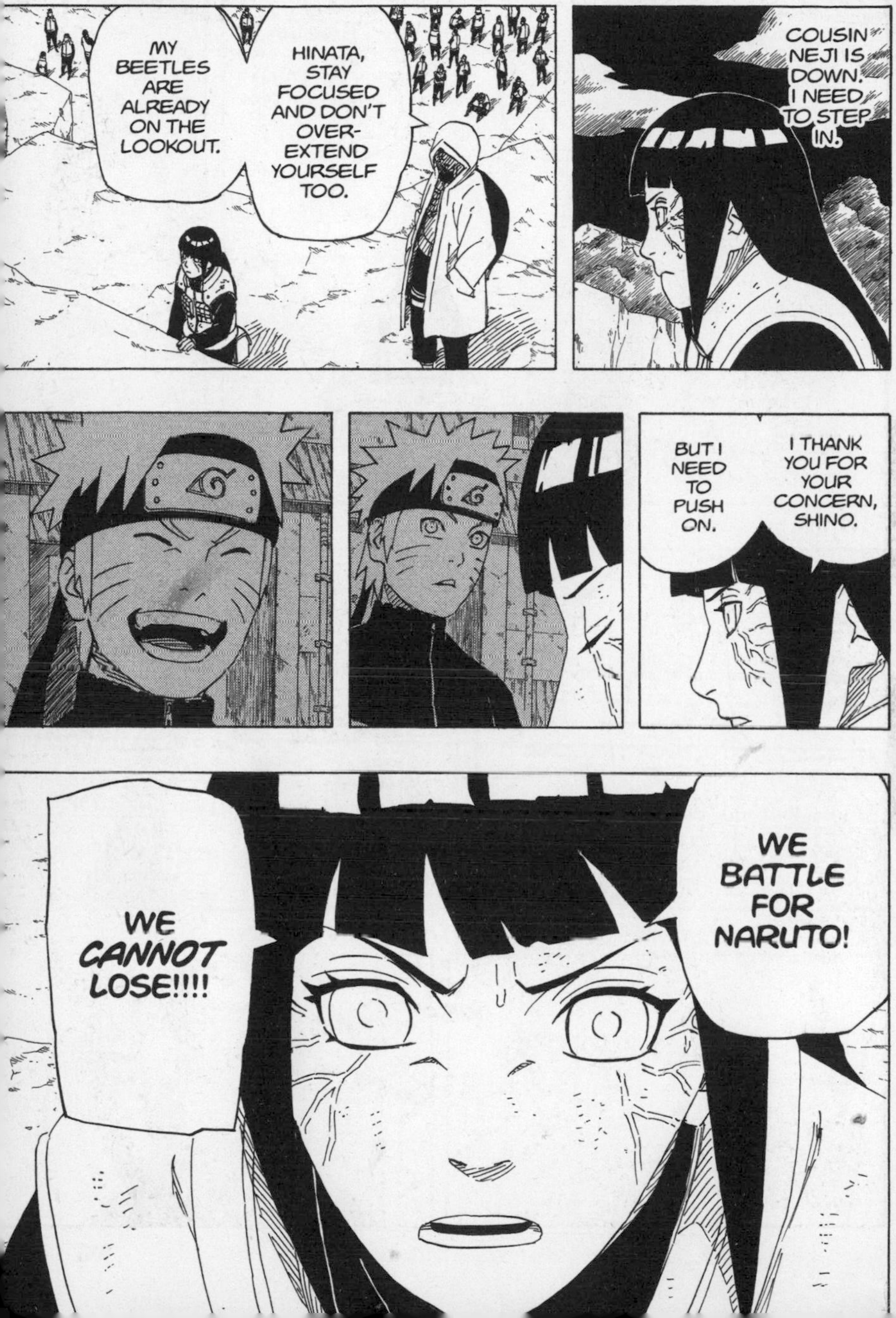
COUSIN NEJI IS DOWN. I NEED TO STEP IN.
HINATA, STAY FOCUSED AND DON'T OVER-EXTEND YOURSELF TOO.
MY BEETLES ARE ALREADY ON THE LOOKOUT.
I THANK YOU FOR YOUR CONCERN, SHINO.
BUT I NEED TO PUSH ON.
WE BATTLE FOR NARUTO!
WE CANNOT LOSE!!!!

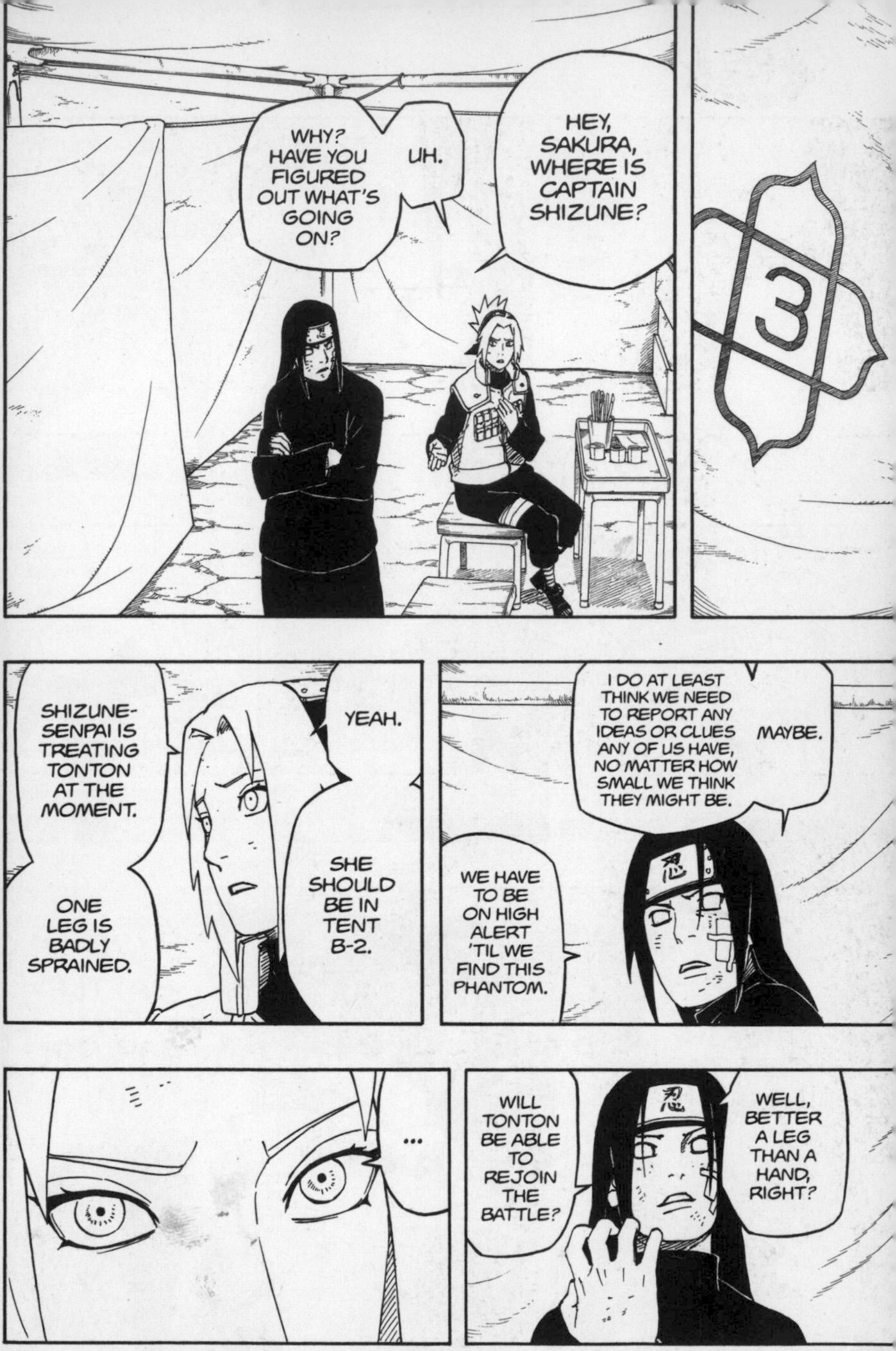
3
HEY, SAKURA, WHERE IS CAPTAIN SHIZUNE?
UH.
WHY? HAVE YOU FIGURED OUT WHAT'S GOING ON?
MAYBE.
I DO AT LEAST THINK WE NEED TO REPORT ANY IDEAS OR CLUES ANY OF US HAVE, NO MATTER HOW SMALL WE THINK THEY MIGHT BE.
WE HAVE TO BE ON HIGH ALERT 'TIL WE FIND THIS PHANTOM.
YEAH.
SHIZUNE-SENPAI IS TREATING TONTON AT THE MOMENT.
SHE SHOULD BE IN TENT B-2.
ONE LEG IS BADLY SPRAINED.
WELL, BETTER A LEG THAN A HAND, RIGHT?
WILL TONTON BE ABLE TO REJOIN THE BATTLE?
...

READ THIS WAY

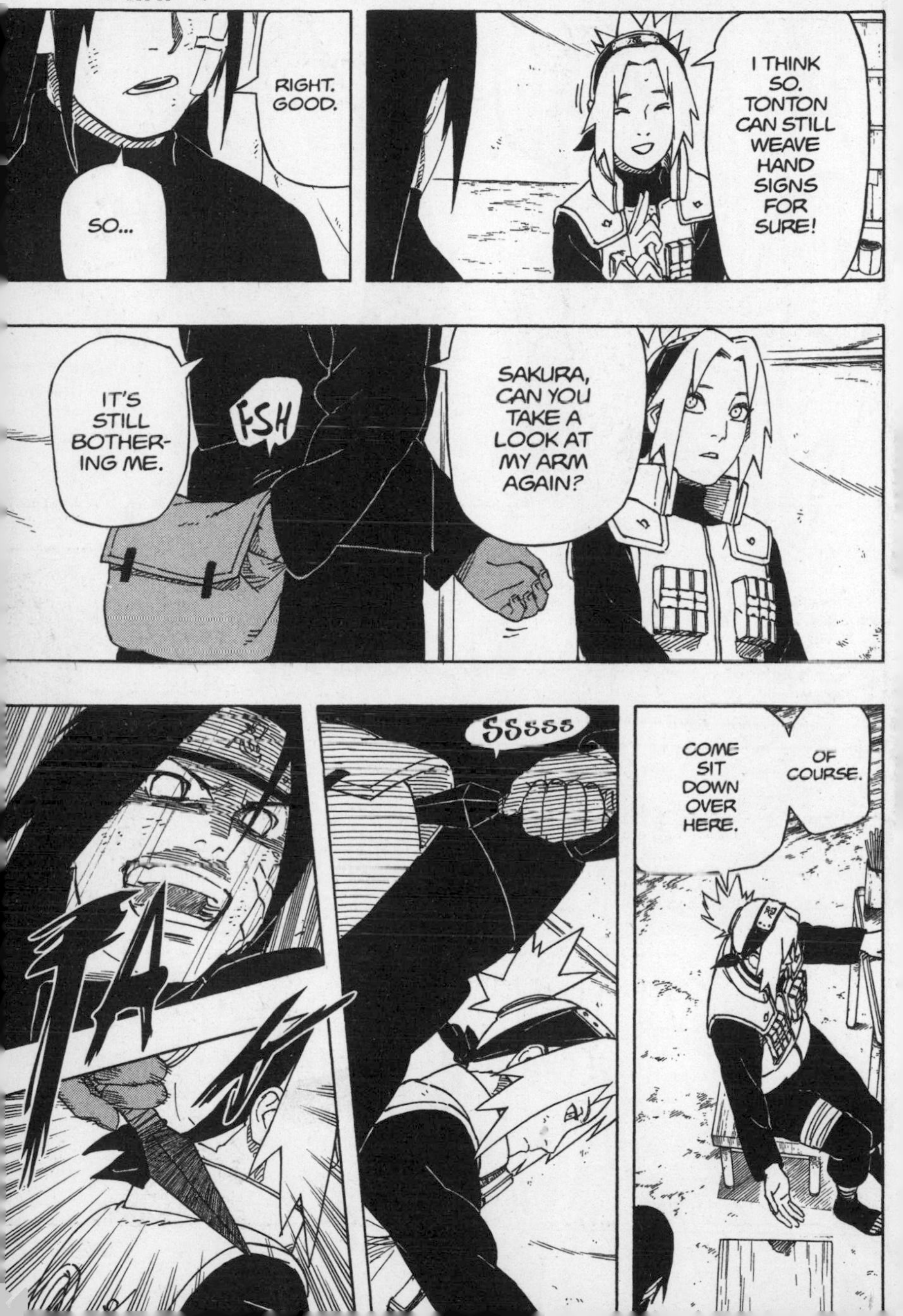
I THINK SO. TONTON CAN STILL WEAVE HAND SIGNS FOR SURE!
RIGHT. GOOD.
SO...
SAKURA, CAN YOU TAKE A LOOK AT MY ARM AGAIN?
FSH
IT'S STILL BOTHERING ME.
OF COURSE.
COME SIT DOWN OVER HERE.
SSSSS

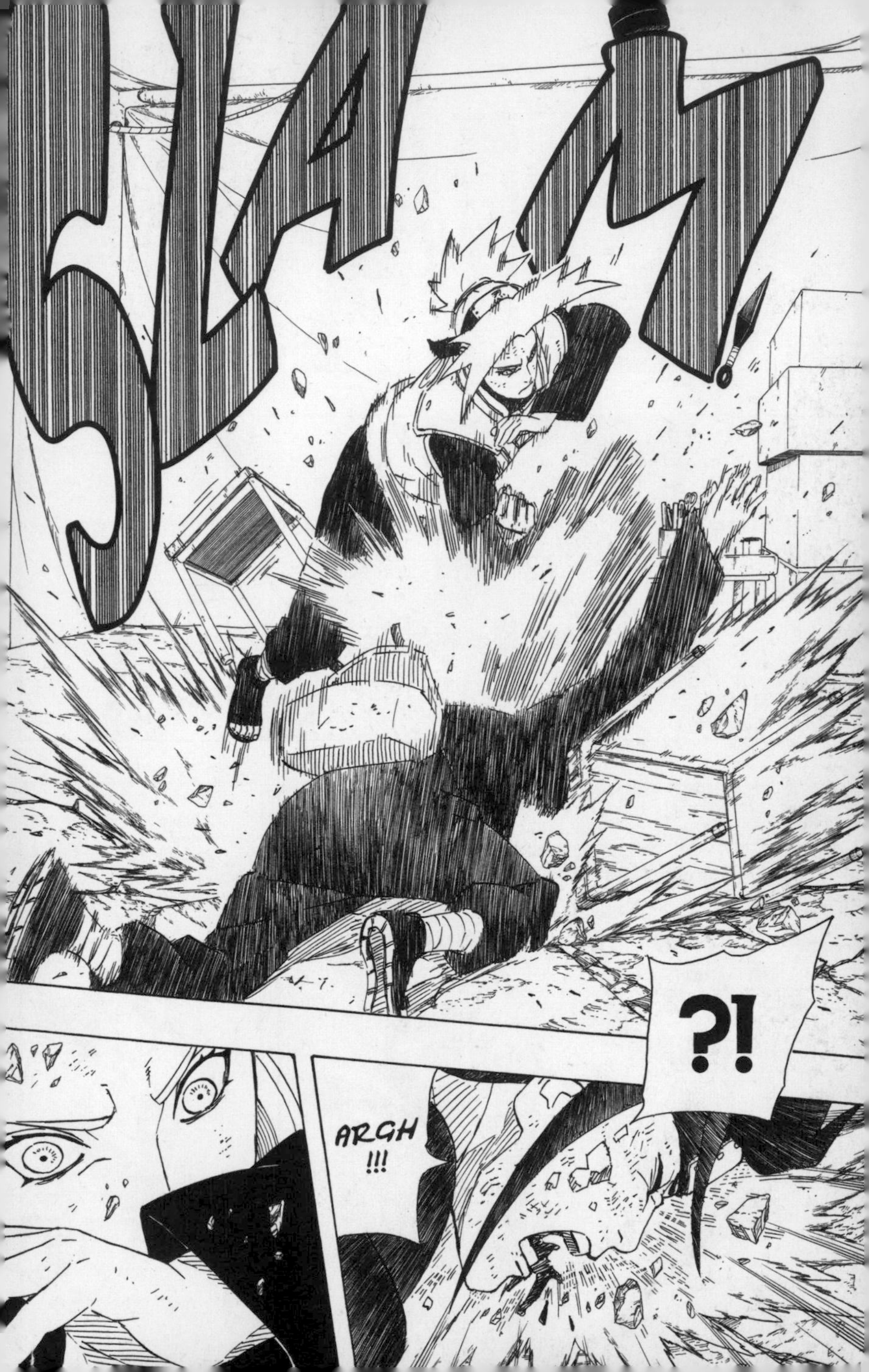
SLAM!
?!
ARGH !!!

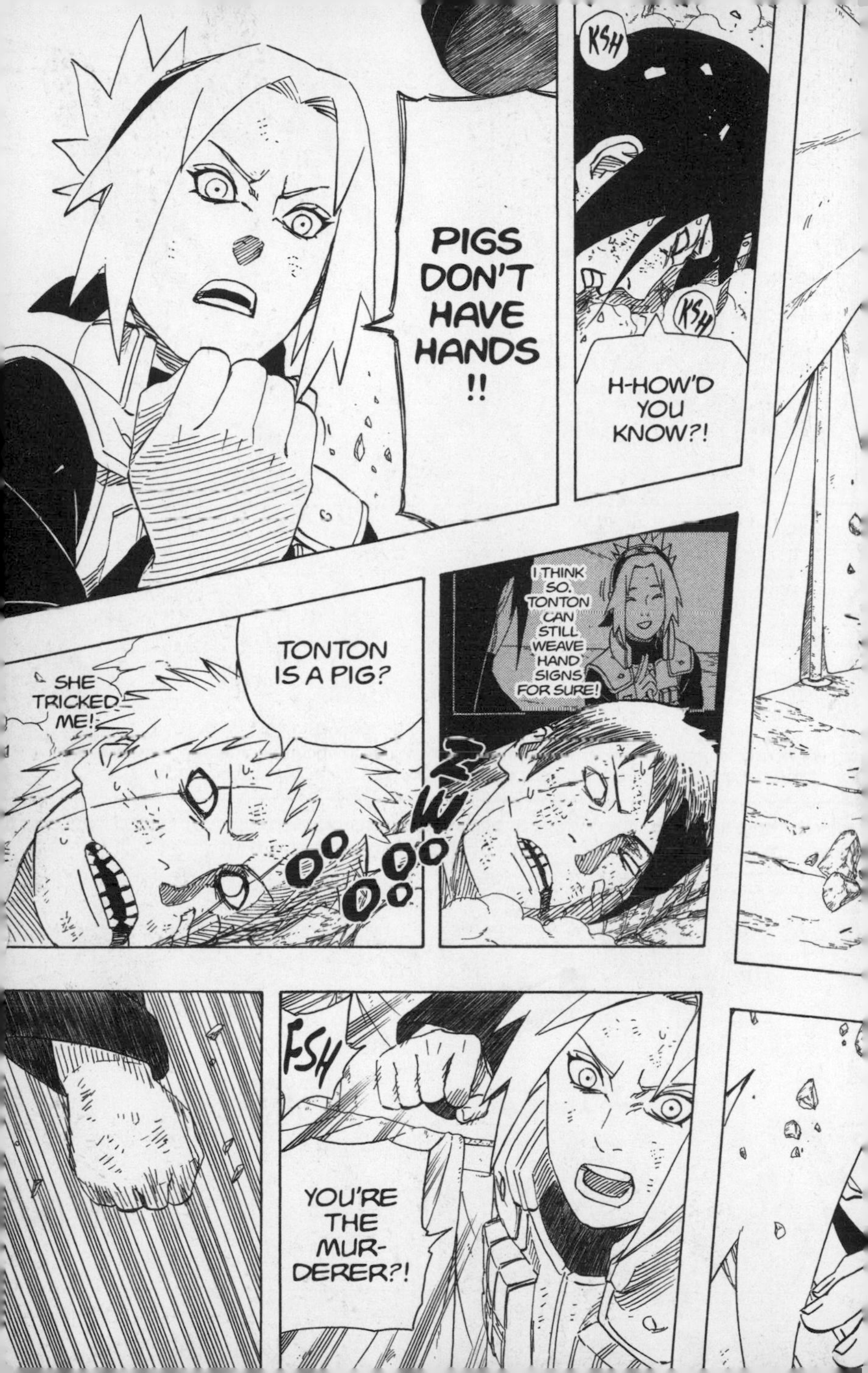
KSH
K'SH
H-HOW'D YOU KNOW?!
PIGS DON'T HAVE HANDS!!
I THINK SO. TONTON CAN STILL WEAVE HAND SIGNS FOR SURE!
TONTON IS A PIG?
SHE TRICKED ME!
FSH
YOU'RE THE MUR-DERER?!

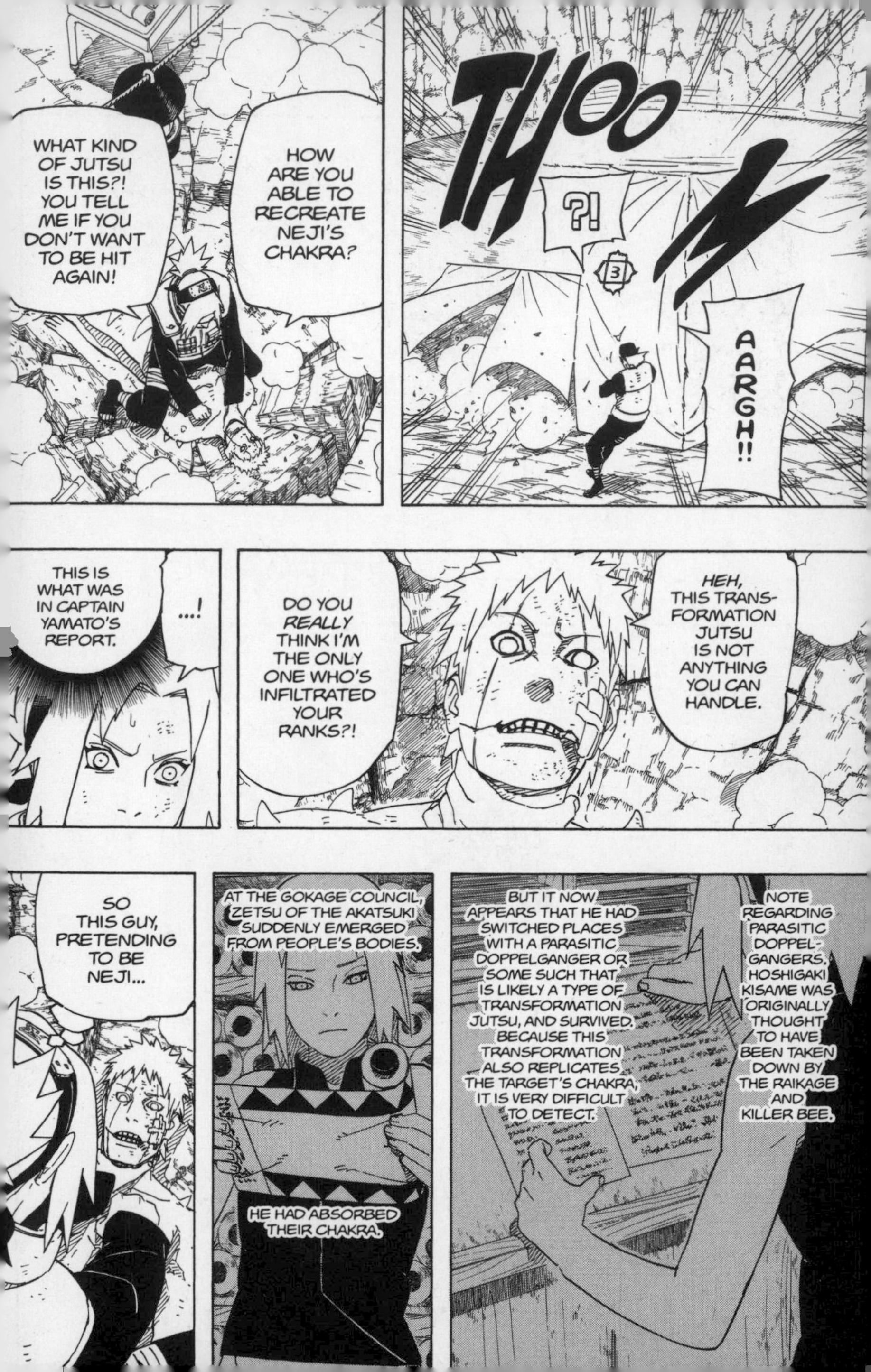
THOOM
?!
AARGH!!
HOW ARE YOU ABLE TO RECREATE NEJI'S CHAKRA?
WHAT KIND OF JUTSU IS THIS?! YOU TELL ME IF YOU DON'T WANT TO BE HIT AGAIN!
HEH, THIS TRANS-FORMATION JUTSU IS NOT ANYTHING YOU CAN HANDLE.
DO YOU *REALLY* THINK I'M THE ONLY ONE WHO'S INFILTRATED YOUR RANKS?!
...!
THIS IS WHAT WAS IN CAPTAIN YAMATO'S REPORT.
NOTE REGARDING PARASITIC DOPPEL-GANGERS. HOSHIGAKI KISAME WAS ORIGINALLY THOUGHT TO HAVE BEEN TAKEN DOWN BY THE RAIKAGE AND KILLER BEE.
BUT IT NOW APPEARS THAT HE HAD SWITCHED PLACES WITH A PARASITIC DOPPELGANGER OR SOME SUCH THAT IS LIKELY A TYPE OF TRANSFORMATION JUTSU, AND SURVIVED. BECAUSE THIS TRANSFORMATION ALSO REPLICATES THE TARGET'S CHAKRA, IT IS VERY DIFFICULT TO DETECT.
AT THE GOKAGE COUNCIL, ZETSU OF THE AKATSUKI SUDDENLY EMERGED FROM PEOPLE'S BODIES.
HE HAD ABSORBED THEIR CHAKRA.
SO THIS GUY, PRETENDING TO BE NEJI...

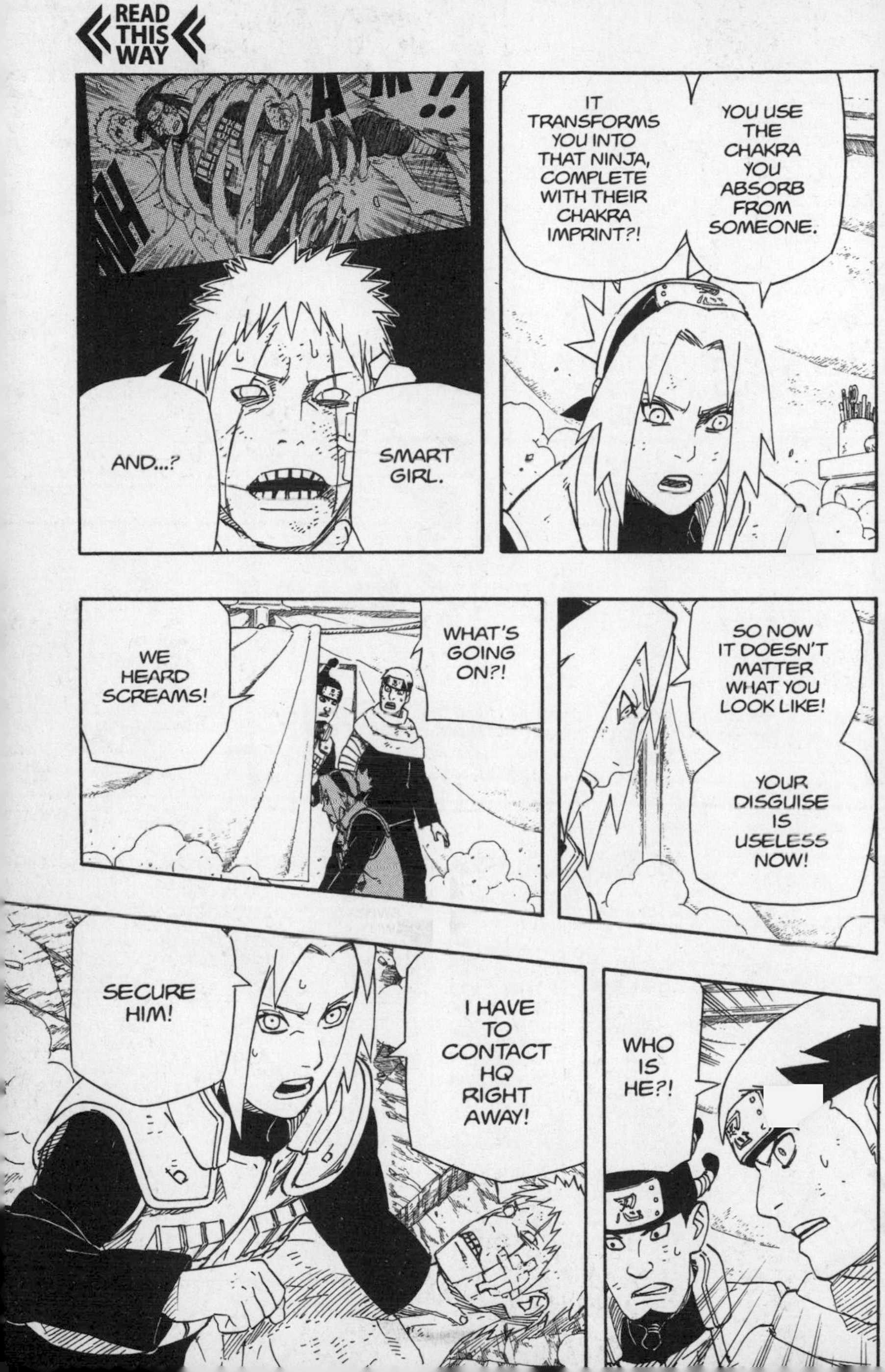
READ THIS WAY
YOU USE THE CHAKRA YOU ABSORB FROM SOMEONE.
IT TRANSFORMS YOU INTO THAT NINJA, COMPLETE WITH THEIR CHAKRA IMPRINT?!
SMART GIRL.
AND...?
SO NOW IT DOESN'T MATTER WHAT YOU LOOK LIKE!
YOUR DISGUISE IS USELESS NOW!
WHAT'S GOING ON?!
WE HEARD SCREAMS!
WHO IS HE?!
I HAVE TO CONTACT HQ RIGHT AWAY!
SECURE HIM!

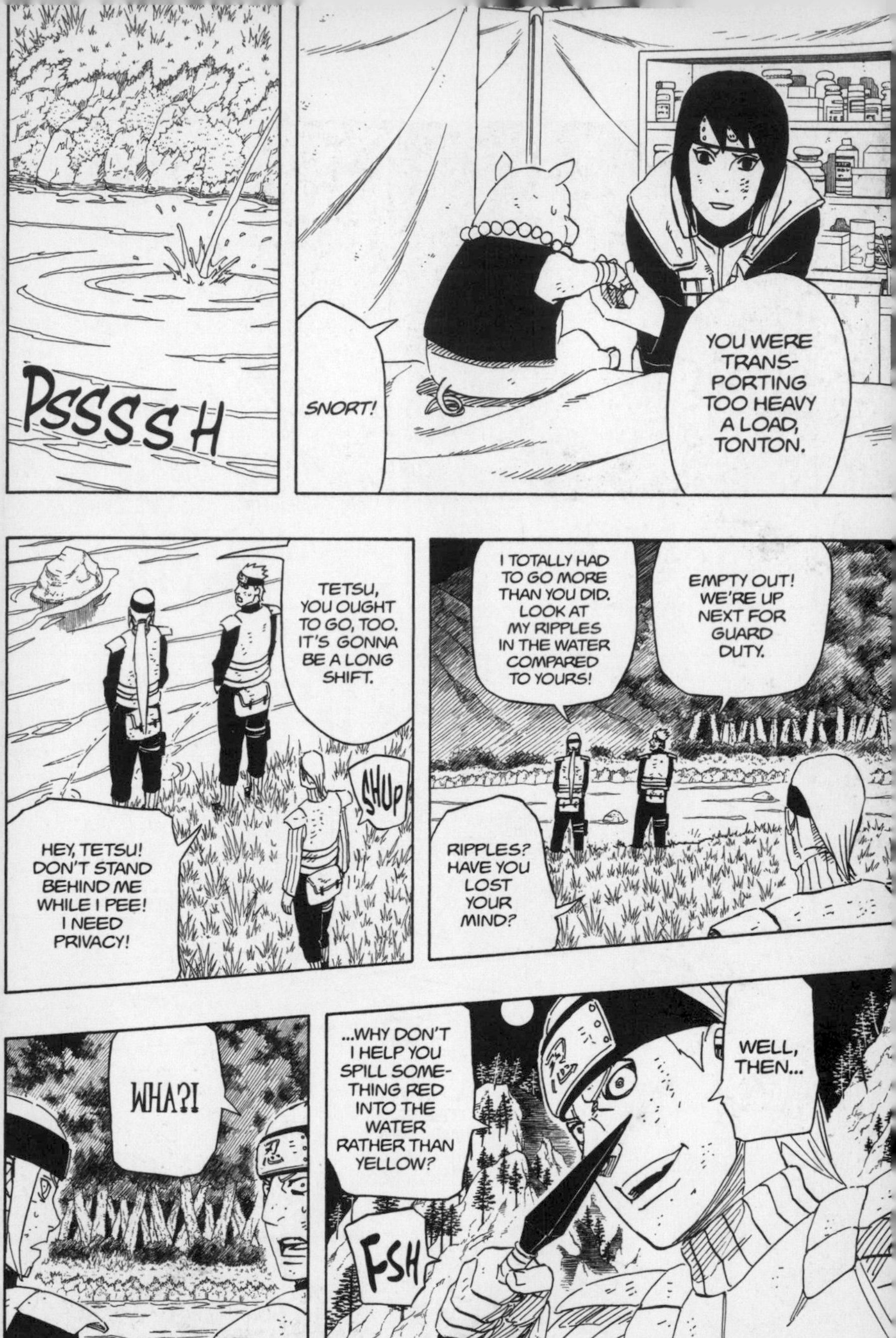
YOU WERE TRANS-PORTING TOO HEAVY A LOAD, TONTON.
SNORT!
PSSSSH
EMPTY OUT! WE'RE UP NEXT FOR GUARD DUTY.
I TOTALLY HAD TO GO MORE THAN YOU DID. LOOK AT MY RIPPLES IN THE WATER COMPARED TO YOURS!
RIPPLES? HAVE YOU LOST YOUR MIND?
TETSU, YOU OUGHT TO GO, TOO. IT'S GONNA BE A LONG SHIFT.
SHUP
HEY, TETSU! DON'T STAND BEHIND ME WHILE I PEE! I NEED PRIVACY!
WELL, THEN...
...WHY DON'T I HELP YOU SPILL SOME-THING RED INTO THE WATER RATHER THAN YELLOW?
FSH
WHA?!

READ THIS WAY

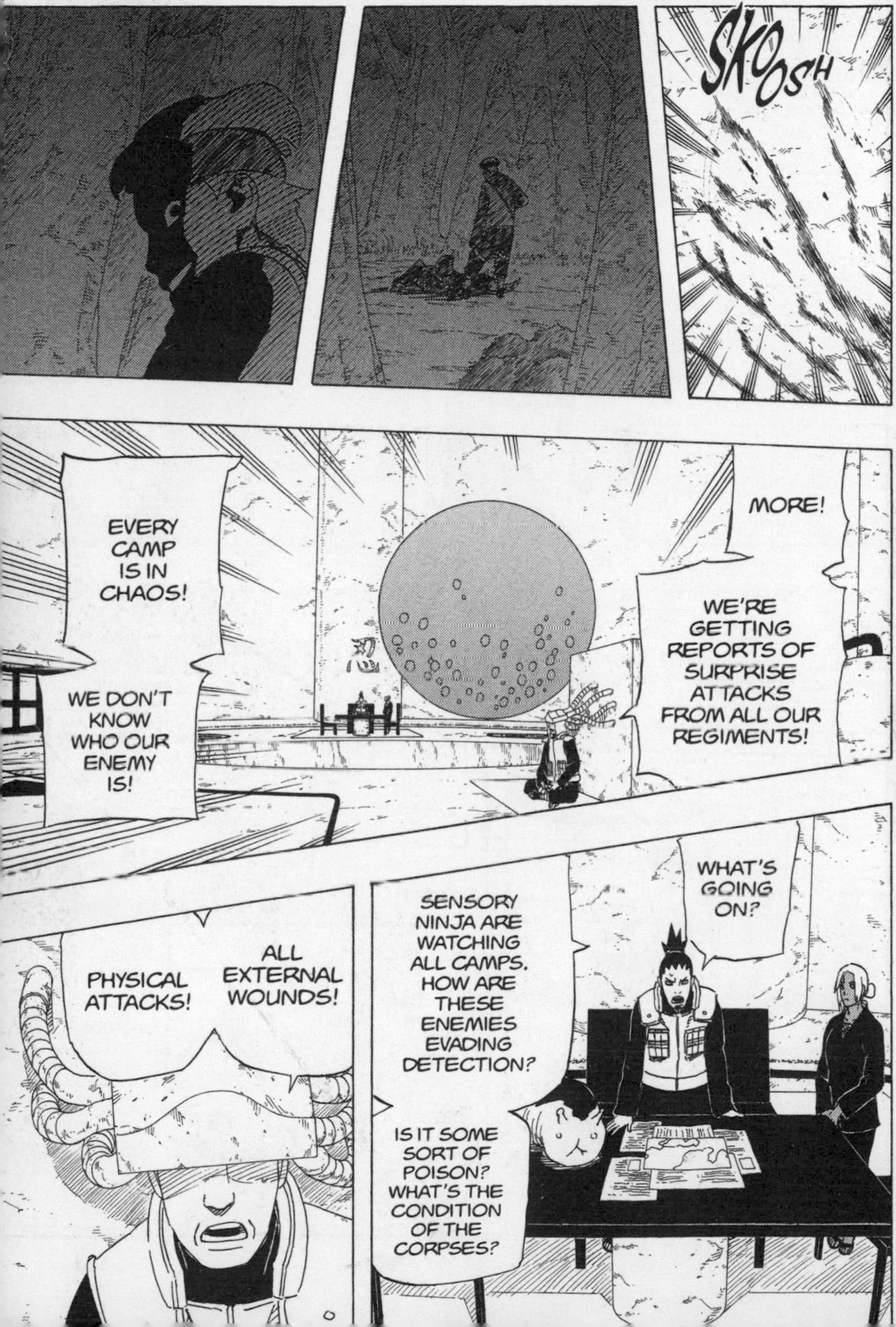
SKOOSH
MORE!
WE'RE GETTING REPORTS OF SURPRISE ATTACKS FROM ALL OUR REGIMENTS!
EVERY CAMP IS IN CHAOS!
WE DON'T KNOW WHO OUR ENEMY IS!
WHAT'S GOING ON?
SENSORY NINJA ARE WATCHING ALL CAMPS. HOW ARE THESE ENEMIES EVADING DETECTION?
IS IT SOME SORT OF POISON? WHAT'S THE CONDITION OF THE CORPSES?
ALL EXTERNAL WOUNDS!
PHYSICAL ATTACKS!

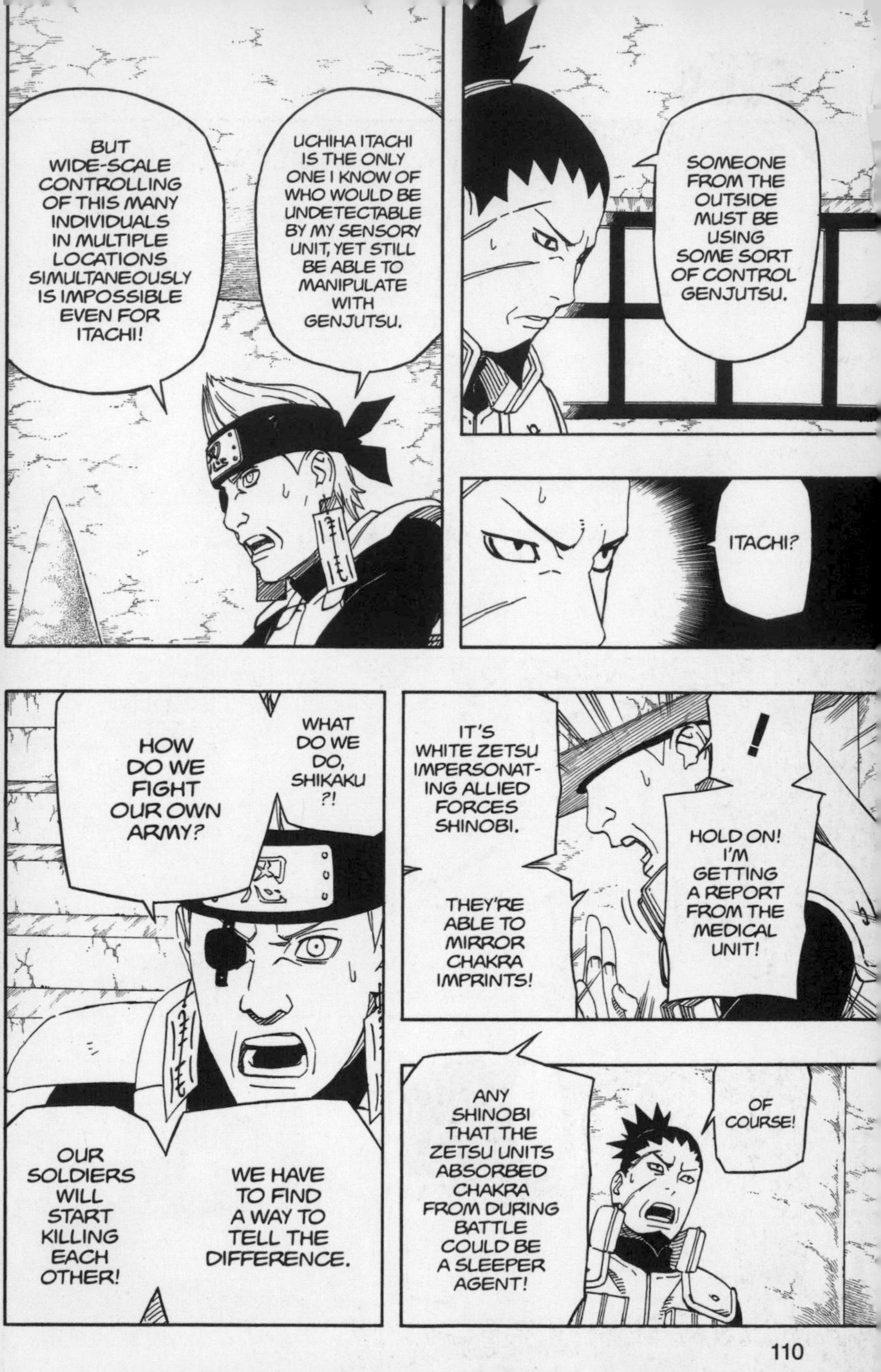
SOMEONE FROM THE OUTSIDE MUST BE USING SOME SORT OF CONTROL GENJUTSU.
ITACHI?
UCHIHA ITACHI IS THE ONLY ONE I KNOW OF WHO WOULD BE UNDETECTABLE BY MY SENSORY UNIT, YET STILL BE ABLE TO MANIPULATE WITH GENJUTSU.
BUT WIDE-SCALE CONTROLLING OF THIS MANY INDIVIDUALS IN MULTIPLE LOCATIONS SIMULTANEOUSLY IS IMPOSSIBLE EVEN FOR ITACHI!
!
HOLD ON! I'M GETTING A REPORT FROM THE MEDICAL UNIT!
IT'S WHITE ZETSU IMPERSONATING ALLIED FORCES SHINOBI.
THEY'RE ABLE TO MIRROR CHAKRA IMPRINTS!
OF COURSE!
ANY SHINOBI THAT THE ZETSU UNITS ABSORBED CHAKRA FROM DURING BATTLE COULD BE A SLEEPER AGENT!
WHAT DO WE DO, SHIKAKU?!
HOW DO WE FIGHT OUR OWN ARMY?
WE HAVE TO FIND A WAY TO TELL THE DIFFERENCE.
OUR SOLDIERS WILL START KILLING EACH OTHER!

READ THIS WAY

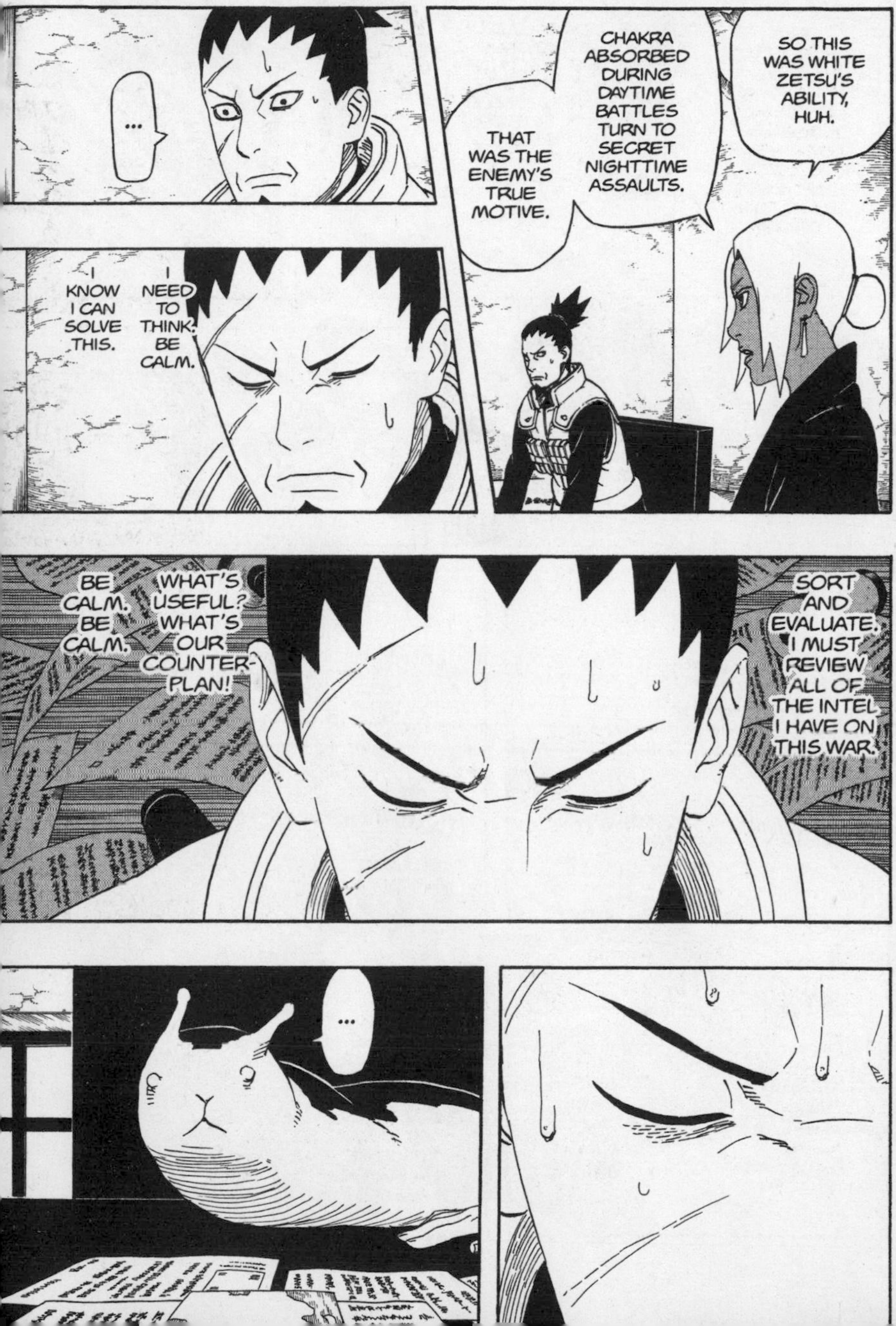
SO THIS WAS WHITE ZETSU'S ABILITY, HUH.
CHAKRA ABSORBED DURING DAYTIME BATTLES TURN TO SECRET NIGHTTIME ASSAULTS.
THAT WAS THE ENEMY'S TRUE MOTIVE.
...
I NEED TO THINK. BE CALM.
I KNOW I CAN SOLVE THIS.
SORT AND EVALUATE. I MUST REVIEW ALL OF THE INTEL I HAVE ON THIS WAR.
WHAT'S USEFUL? WHAT'S OUR COUNTER-PLAN!
BE CALM. BE CALM.
...

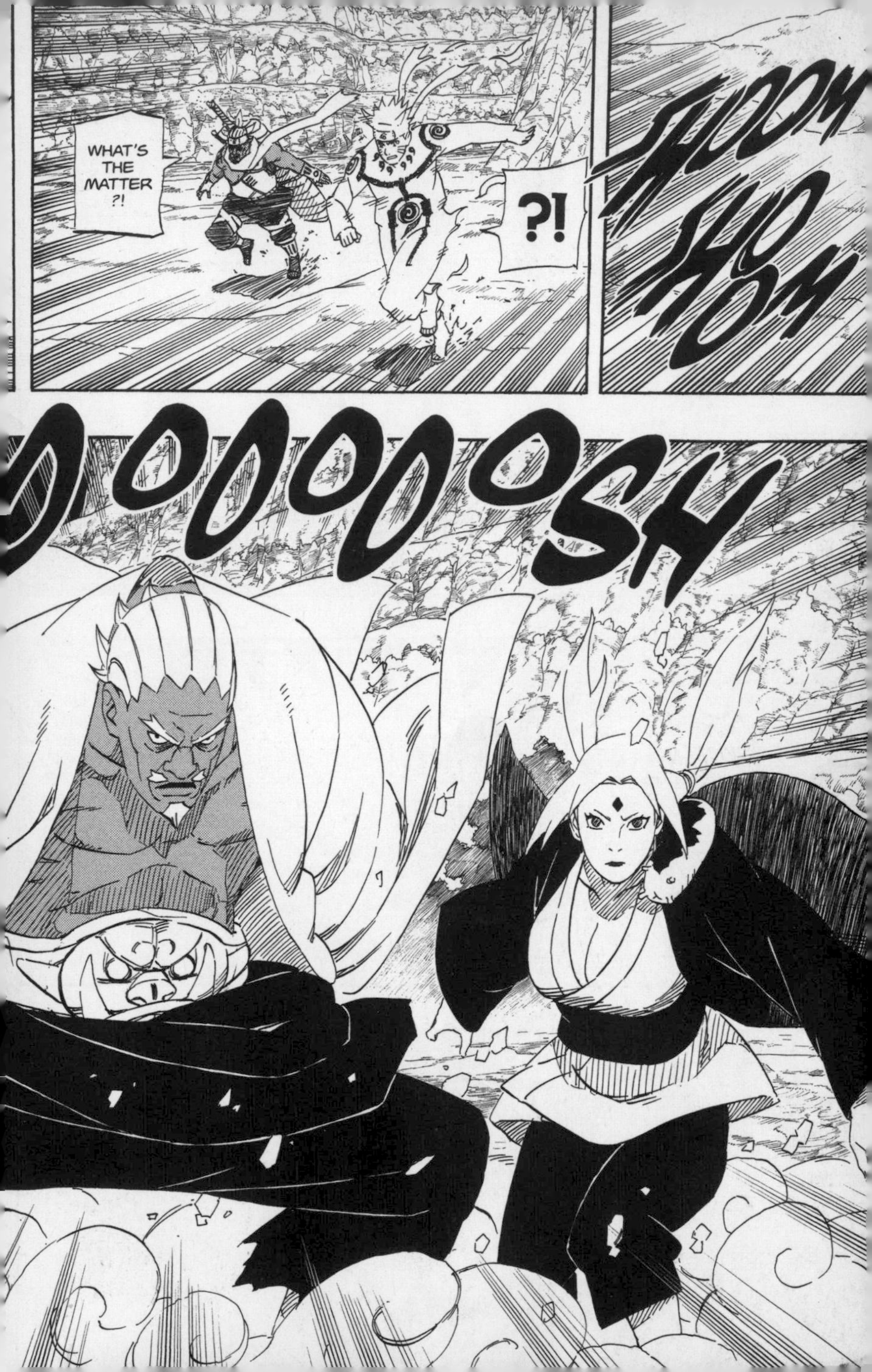
THOOM
?!
WHAT'S THE MATTER ?!
OOOOOOSH

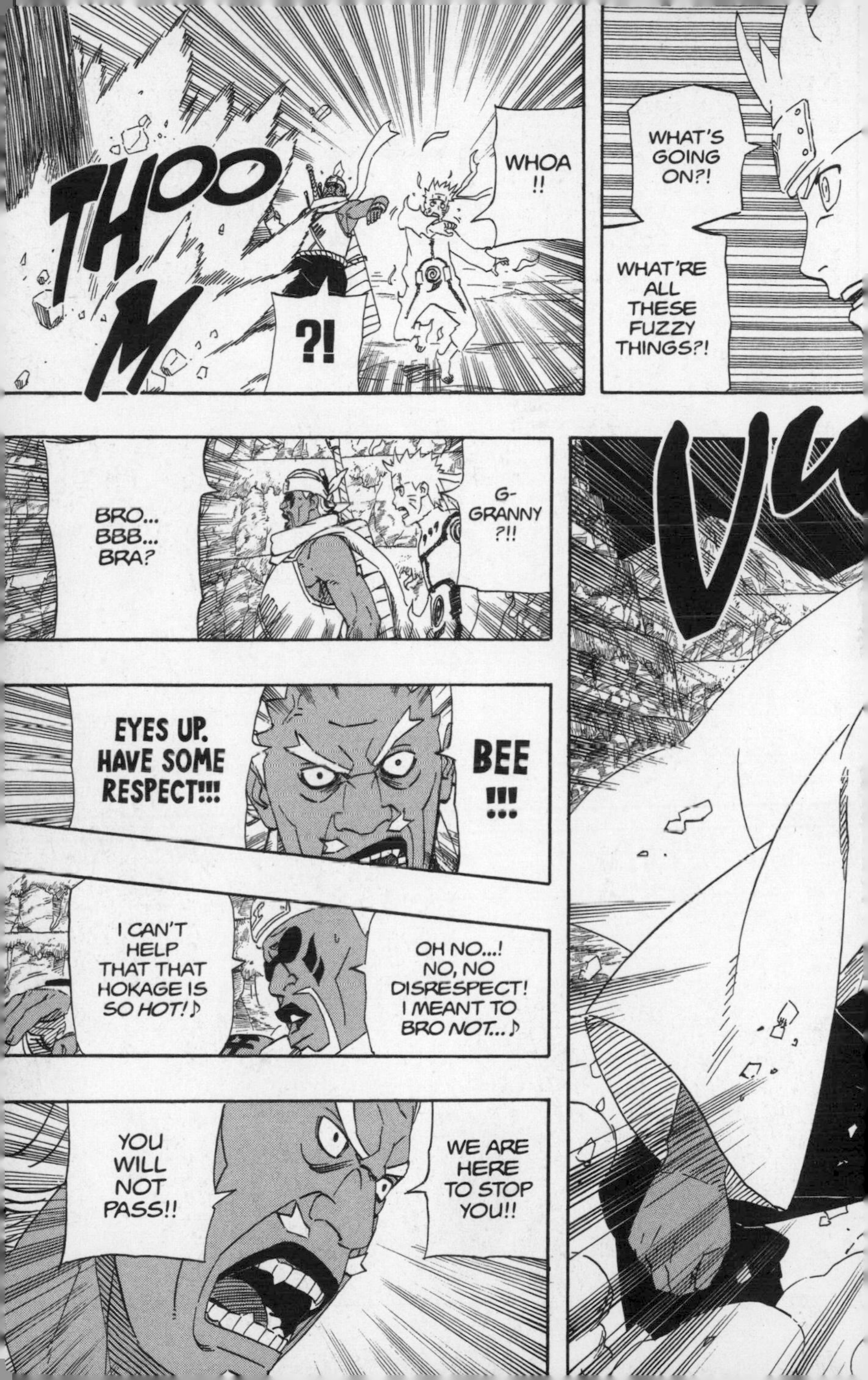

WHAT'S GOING ON?!
WHAT'RE ALL THESE FUZZY THINGS?!
WHOA!!
?!
THOOM
G-GRANNY?!!
BRO... BBB... BRA?
BEE!!!
EYES UP. HAVE SOME RESPECT!!!
OH NO...! NO, NO DISRESPECT! I MEANT TO BRO NOT...♪
I CAN'T HELP THAT THAT HOKAGE IS SO HOT!♪
WE ARE HERE TO STOP YOU!!
YOU WILL NOT PASS!!

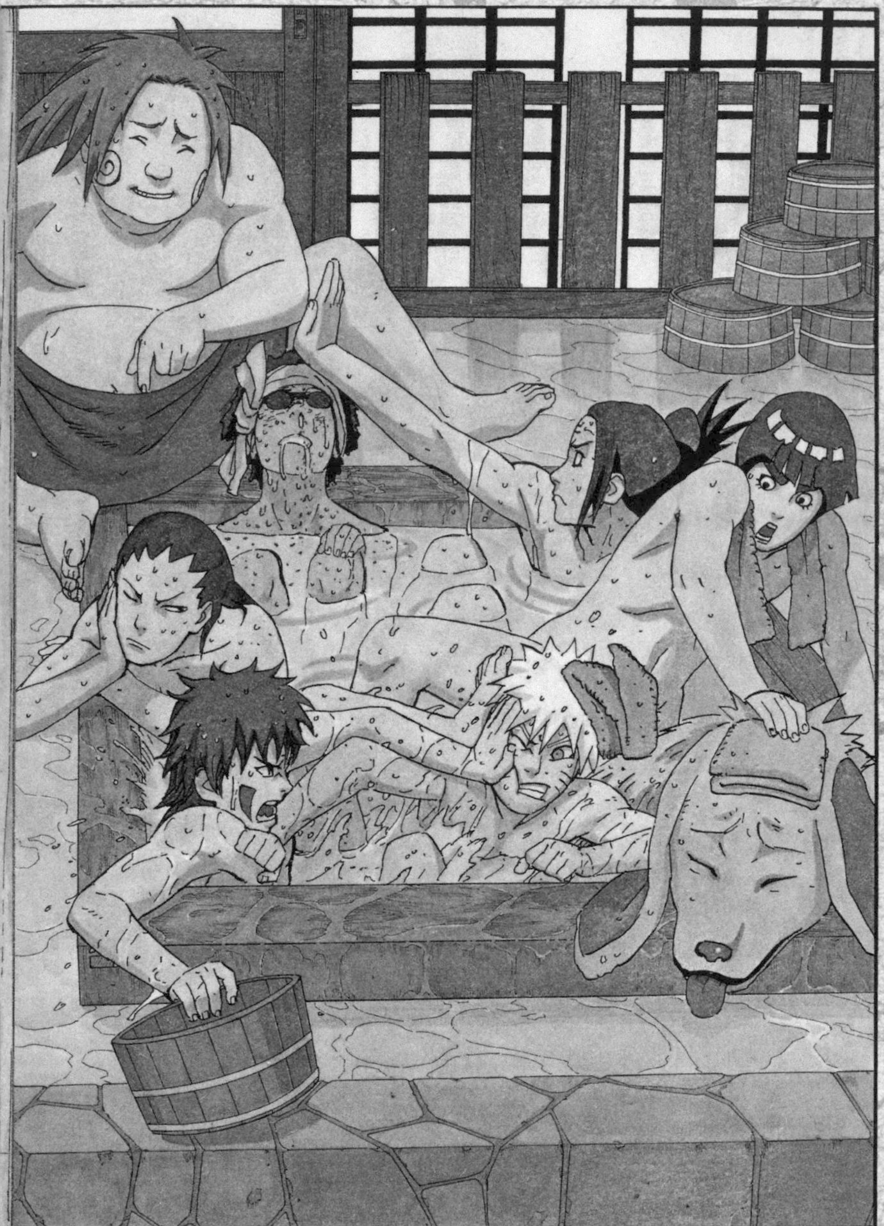

Number 541: Raikage vs. Naruto?!

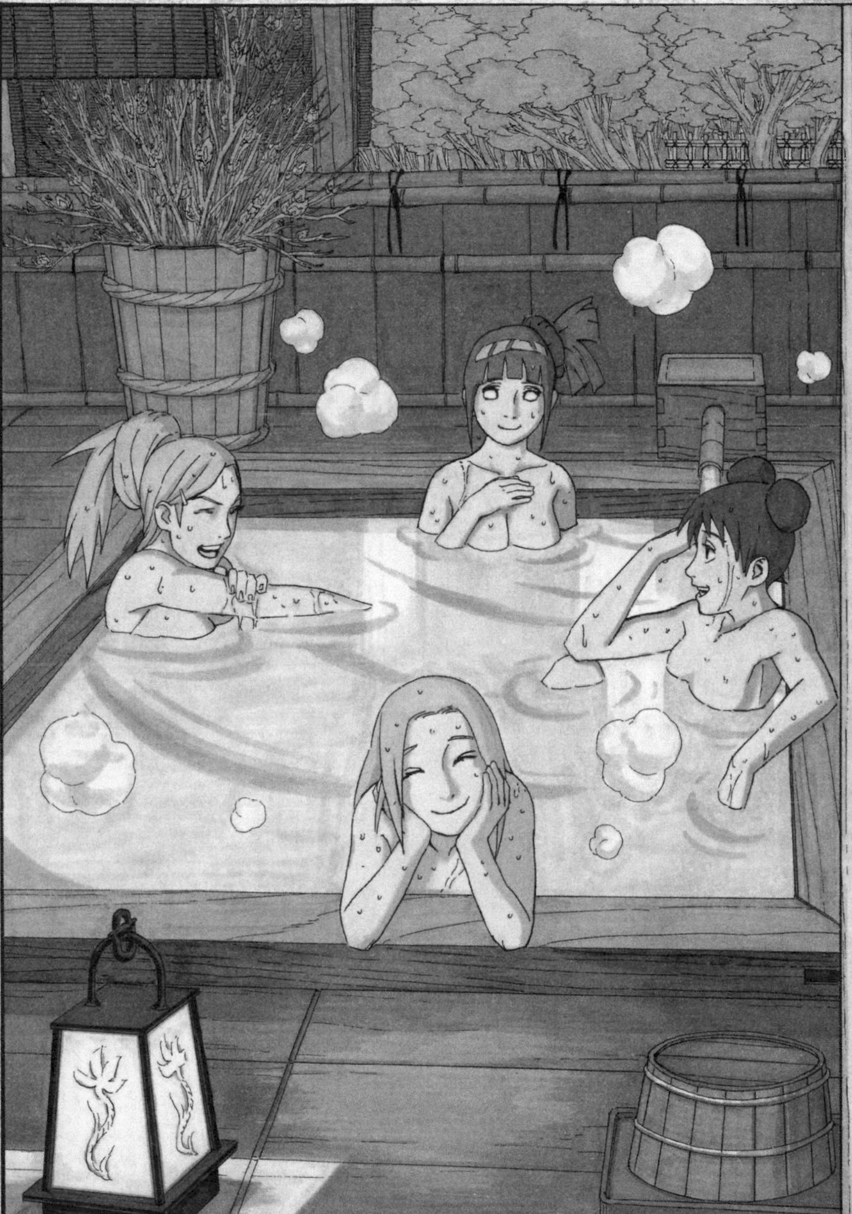

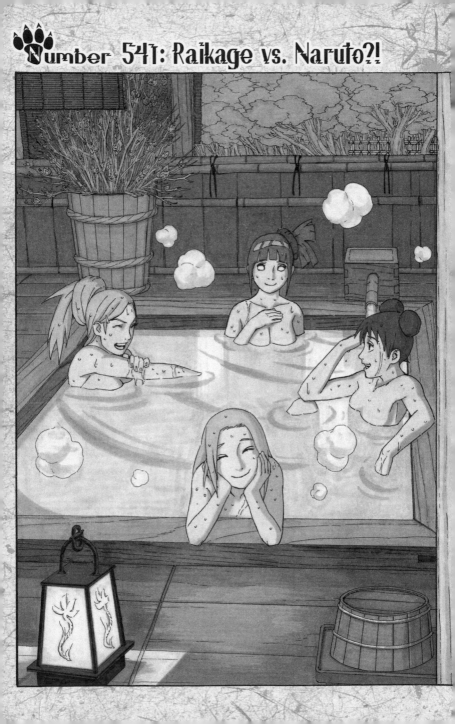

NARUTO

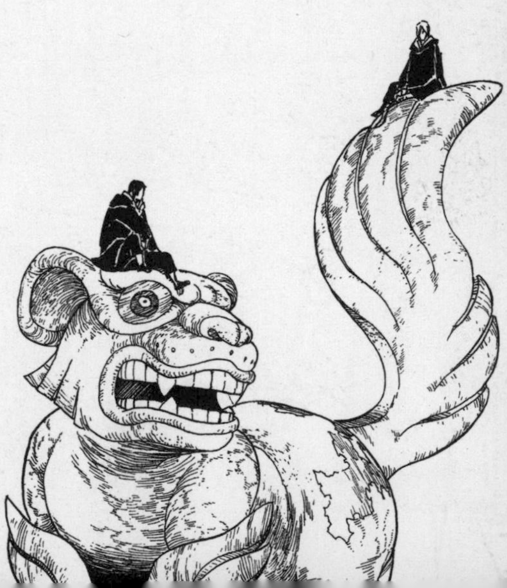

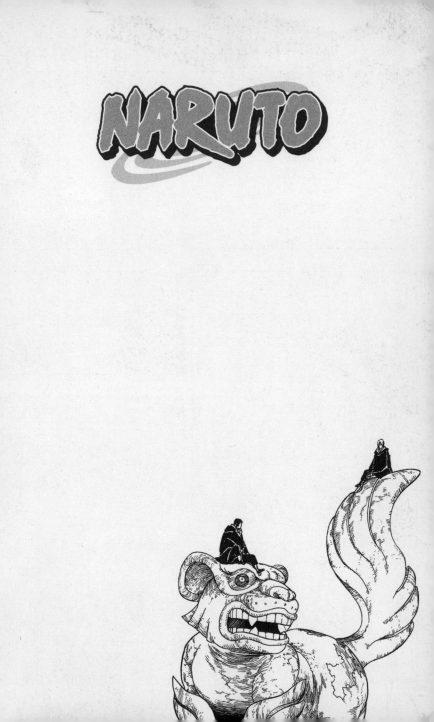

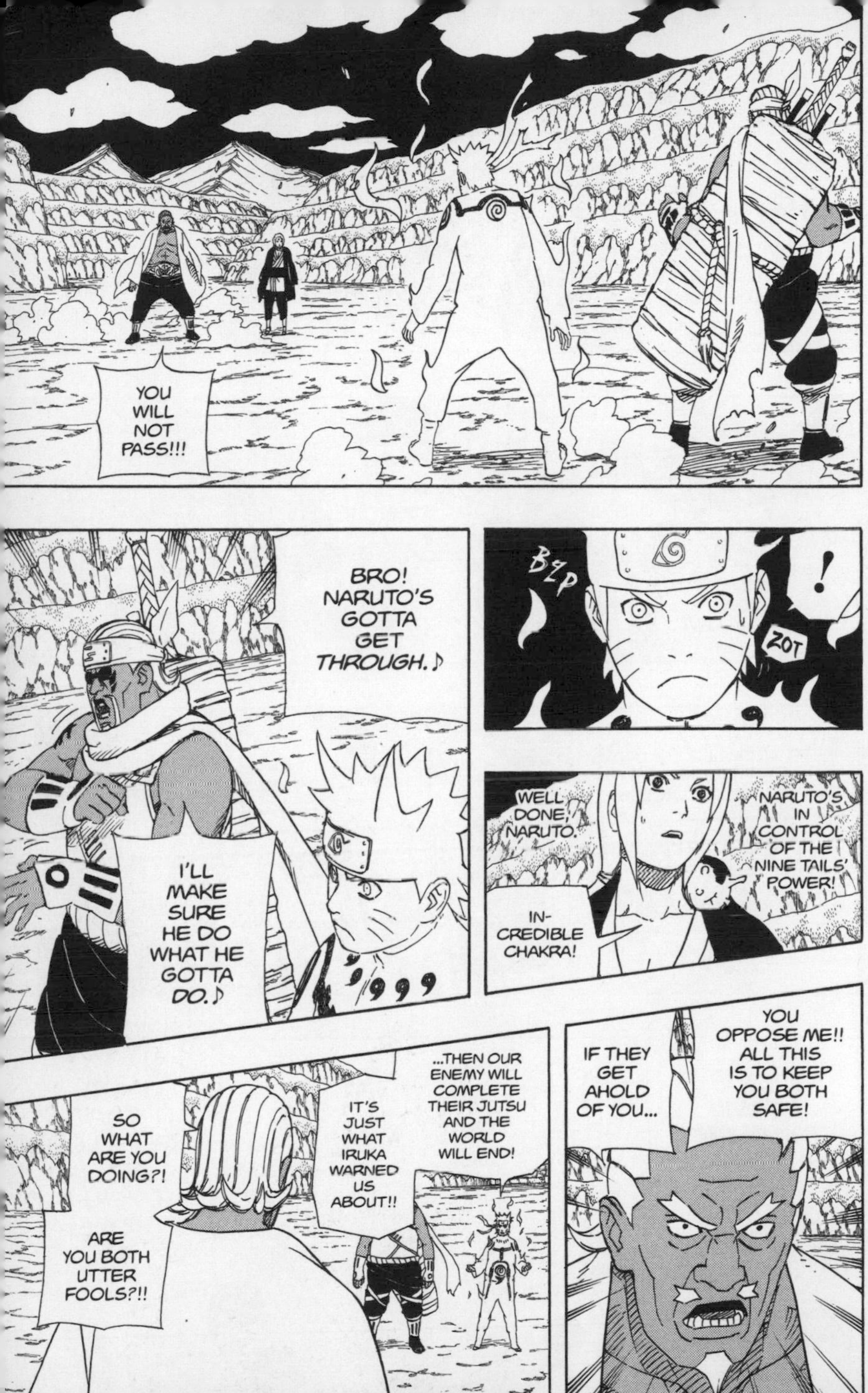
YOU WILL NOT PASS!!!
BZP
ZOT
!
NARUTO'S IN CONTROL OF THE NINE TAILS' POWER!
WELL DONE, NARUTO.
IN-CREDIBLE CHAKRA!
BRO! NARUTO'S GOTTA GET THROUGH.♪
I'LL MAKE SURE HE DO WHAT HE GOTTA DO.♪
YOU OPPOSE ME!! ALL THIS IS TO KEEP YOU BOTH SAFE!
IF THEY GET AHOLD OF YOU...
...THEN OUR ENEMY WILL COMPLETE THEIR JUTSU AND THE WORLD WILL END!
IT'S JUST WHAT IRUKA WARNED US ABOUT!!
SO WHAT ARE YOU DOING?!
ARE YOU BOTH UTTER FOOLS?!!

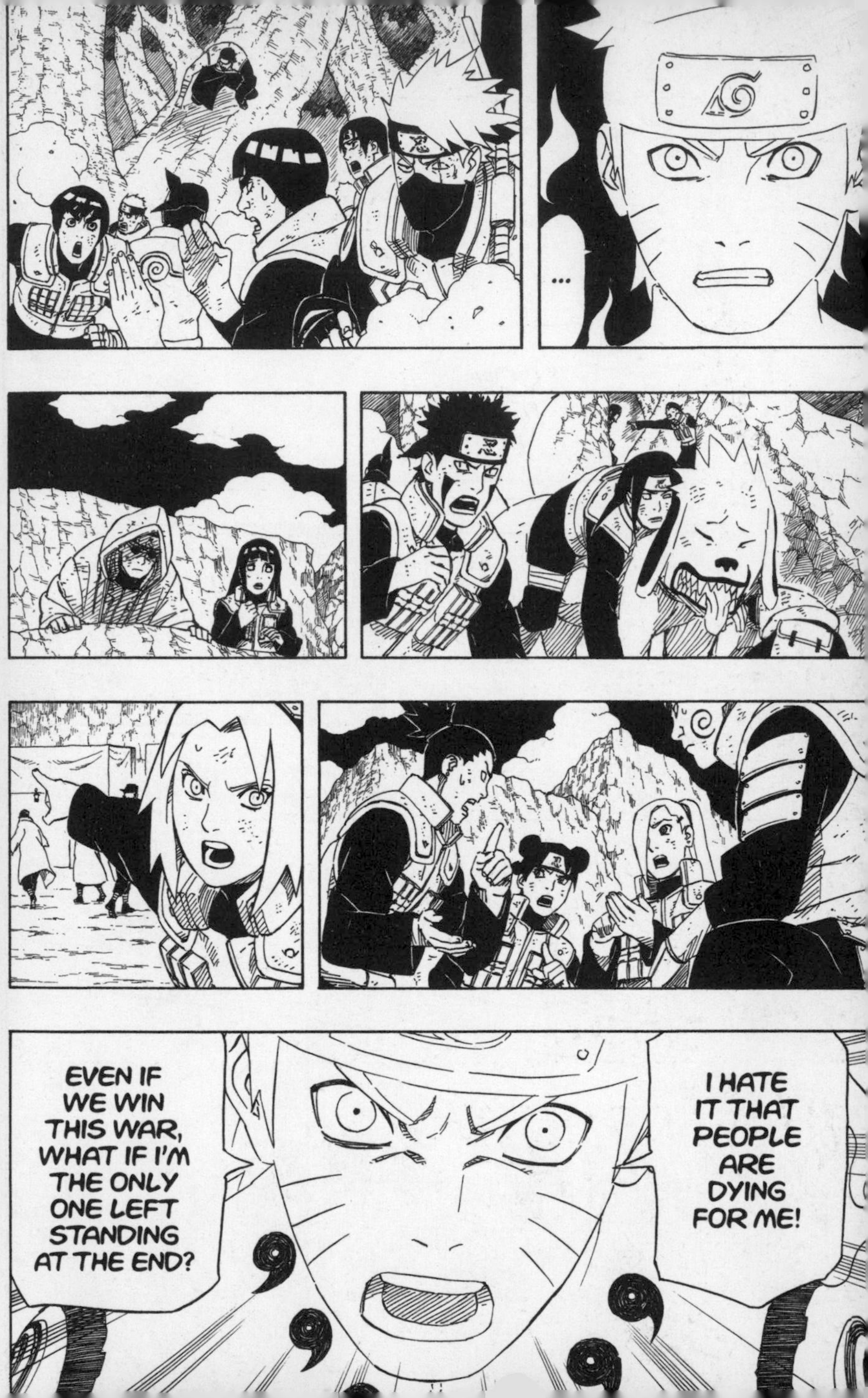
...
I HATE IT THAT PEOPLE ARE DYING FOR ME!
EVEN IF WE WIN THIS WAR, WHAT IF I'M THE ONLY ONE LEFT STANDING AT THE END?

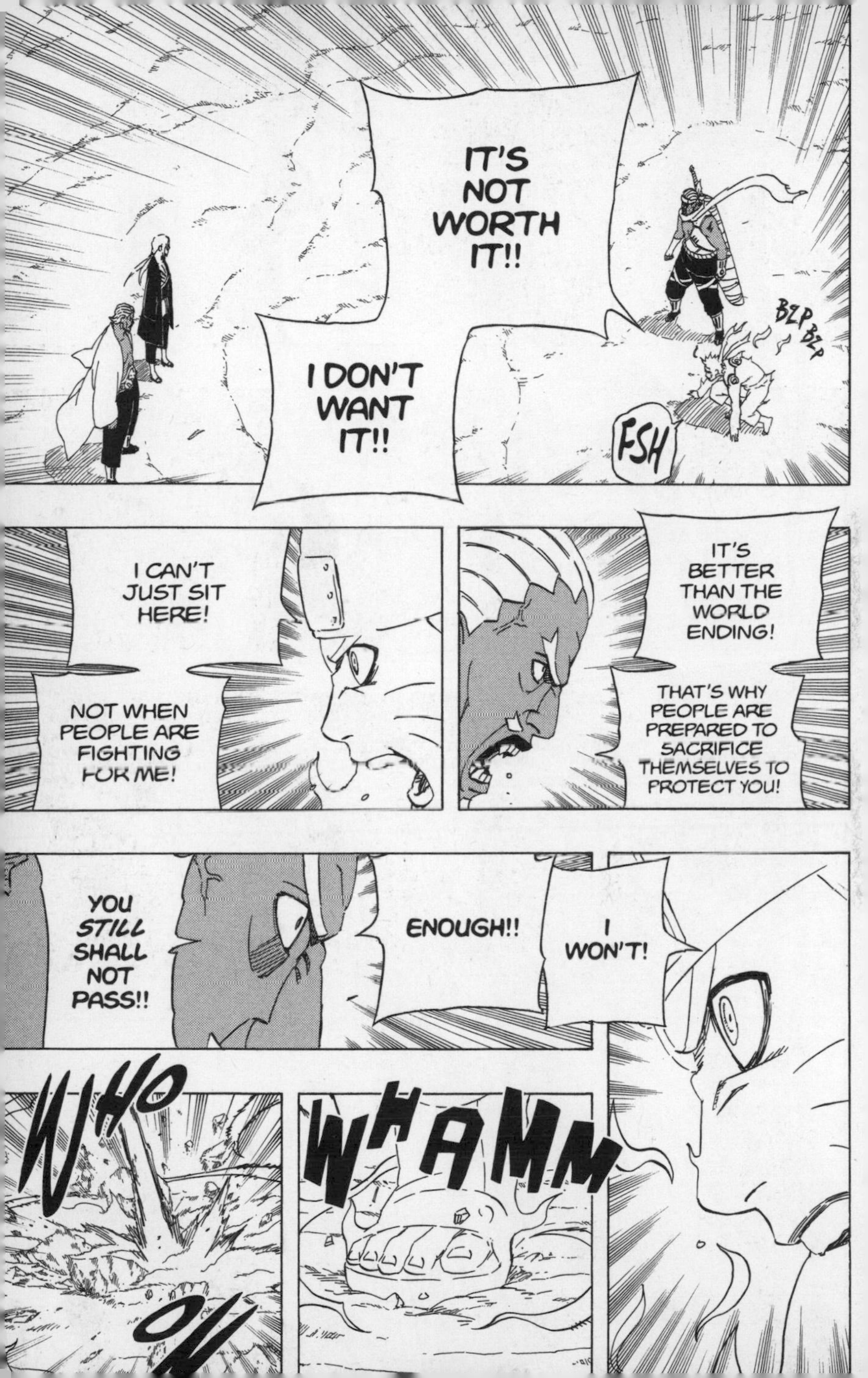
BZP BZP
IT'S NOT WORTH IT!!
FSH
I DON'T WANT IT!!
IT'S BETTER THAN THE WORLD ENDING!
THAT'S WHY PEOPLE ARE PREPARED TO SACRIFICE THEMSELVES TO PROTECT YOU!
I CAN'T JUST SIT HERE!
NOT WHEN PEOPLE ARE FIGHTING FOR ME!
I WON'T!
ENOUGH!!
YOU STILL SHALL NOT PASS!!
WHAMM
WHOOM

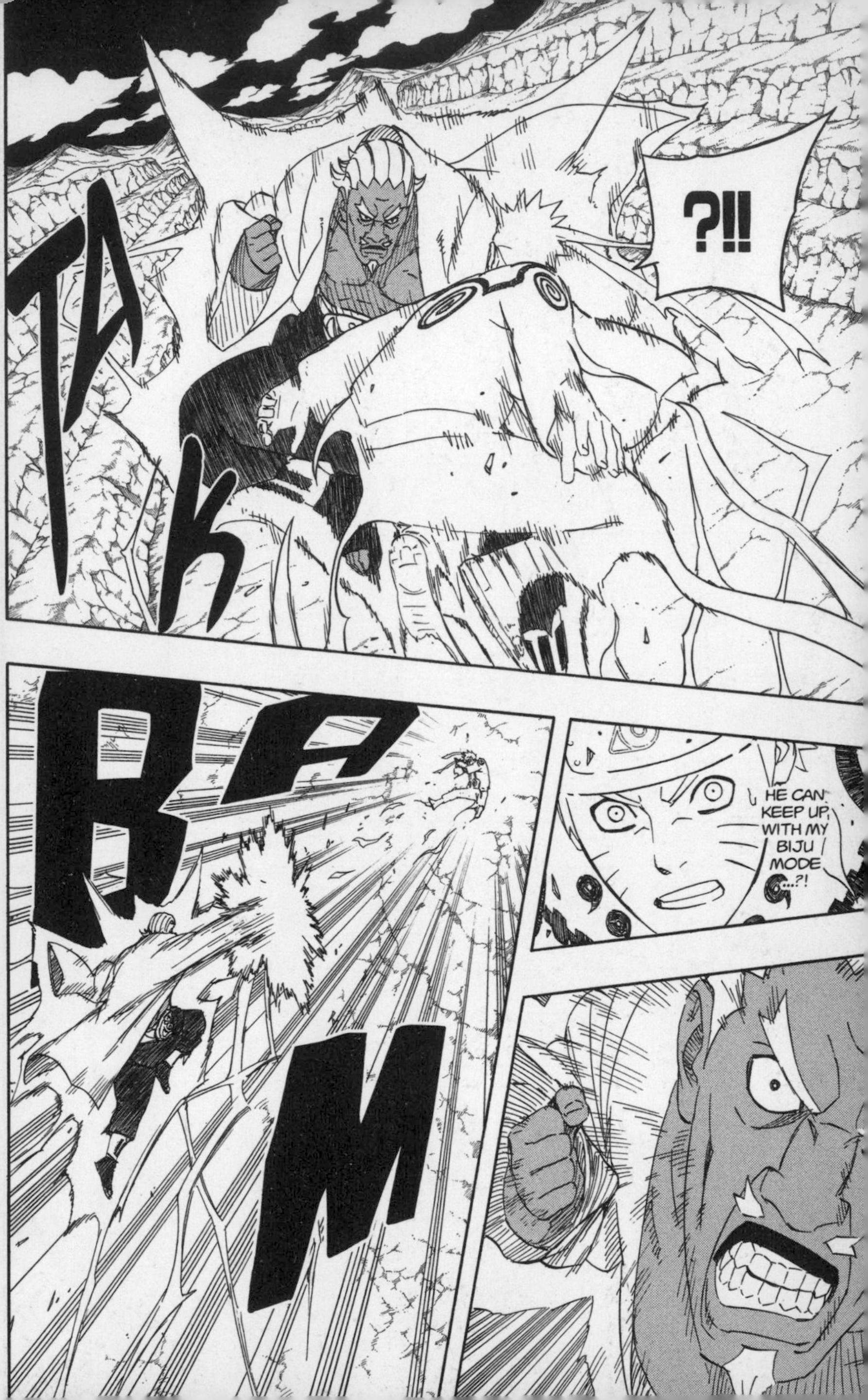
TAK
?!!
BAM
HE CAN KEEP UP WITH MY BIJU MODE...?!

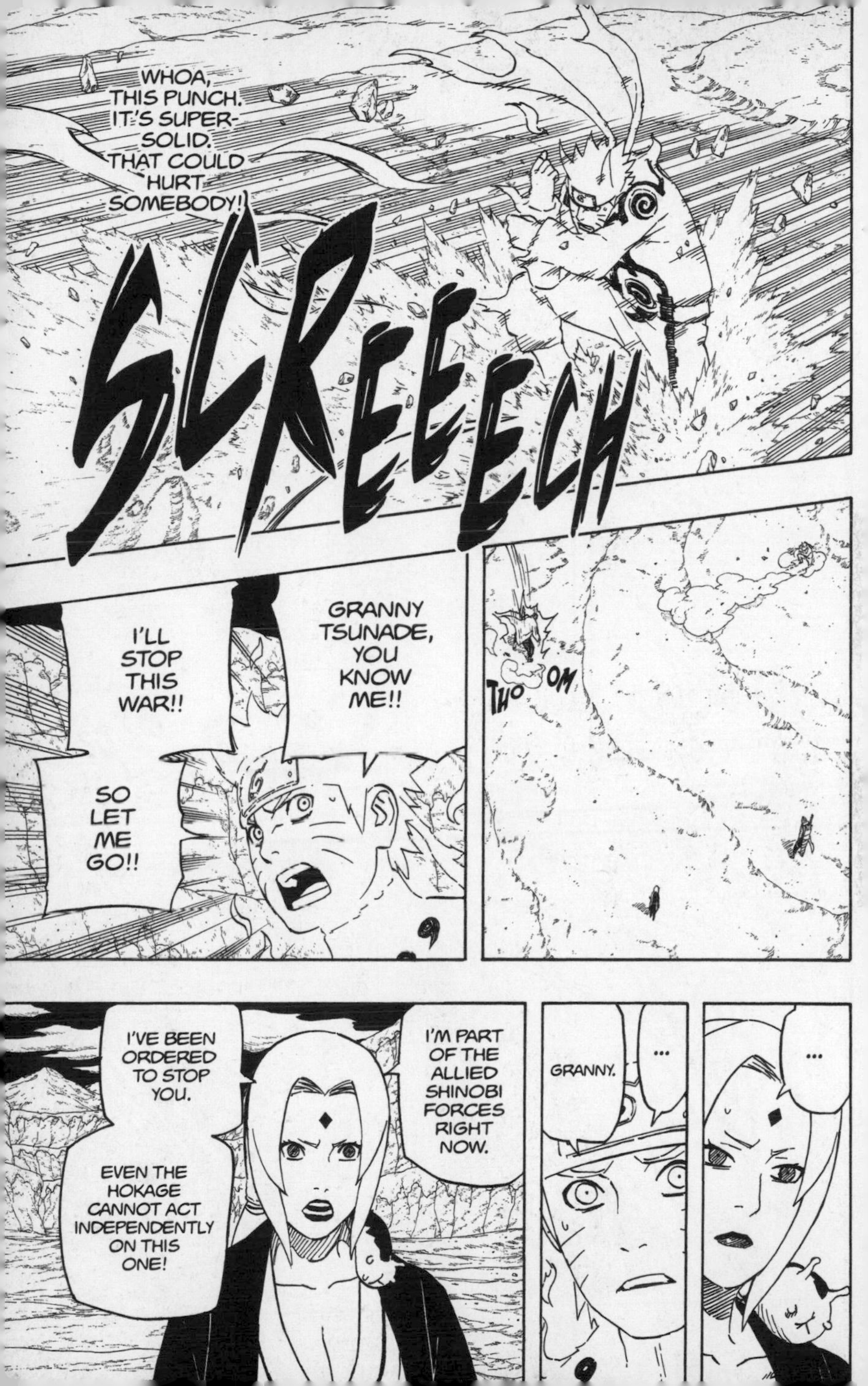
WHOA, THIS PUNCH. IT'S SUPER-SOLID. THAT COULD HURT SOMEBODY!
SCREEECH
THOOM
GRANNY TSUNADE, YOU KNOW ME!!
I'LL STOP THIS WAR!!
SO LET ME GO!!
...
...
GRANNY.
I'M PART OF THE ALLIED SHINOBI FORCES RIGHT NOW.
I'VE BEEN ORDERED TO STOP YOU.
EVEN THE HOKAGE CANNOT ACT INDEPENDENTLY ON THIS ONE!

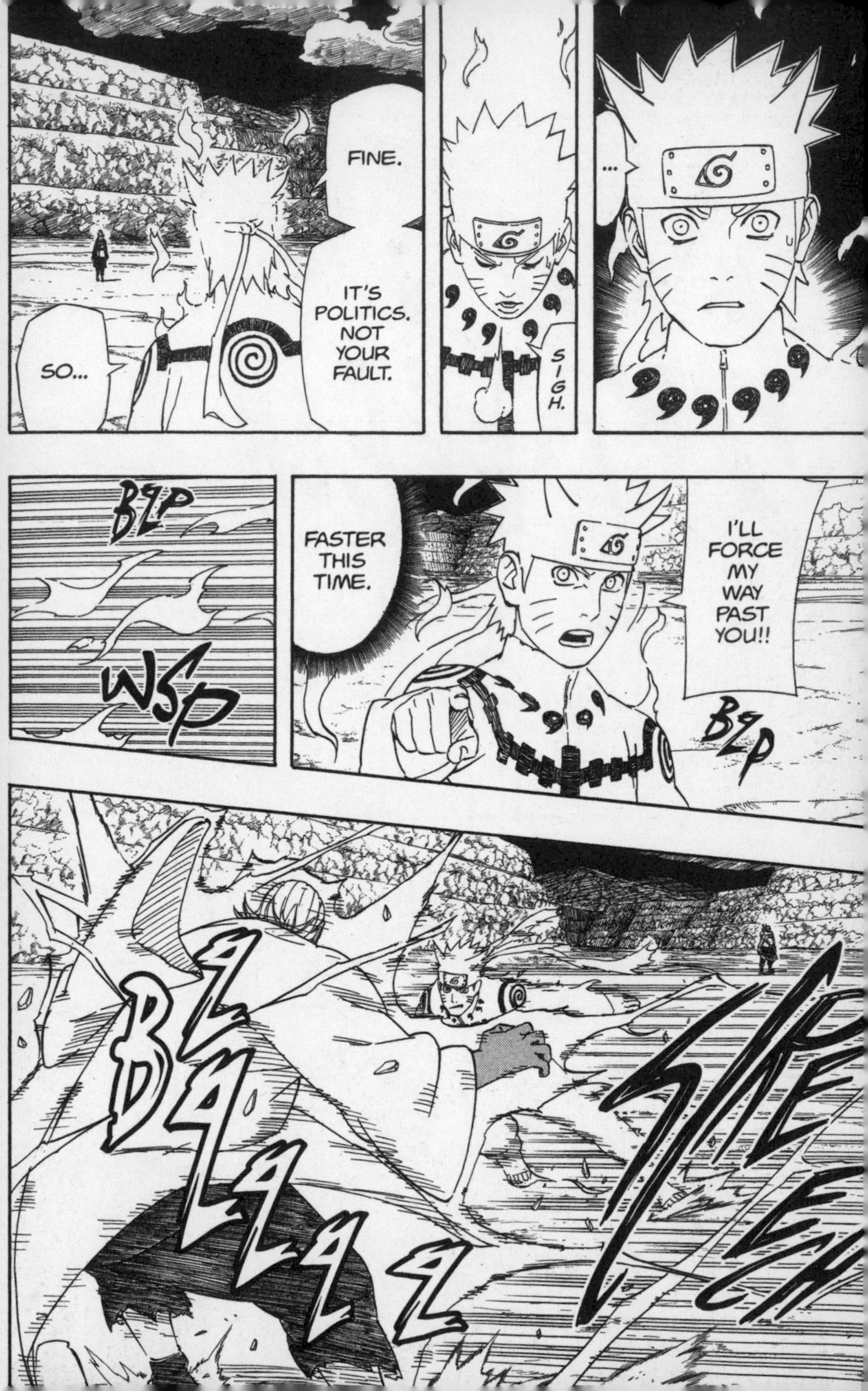
...
SIGH.
FINE.
IT'S POLITICS. NOT YOUR FAULT.
SO...
I'LL FORCE MY WAY PAST YOU!!
FASTER THIS TIME.
BZP
BZP
WSP
SKREECH
BZZZZZ

READ THIS WAY

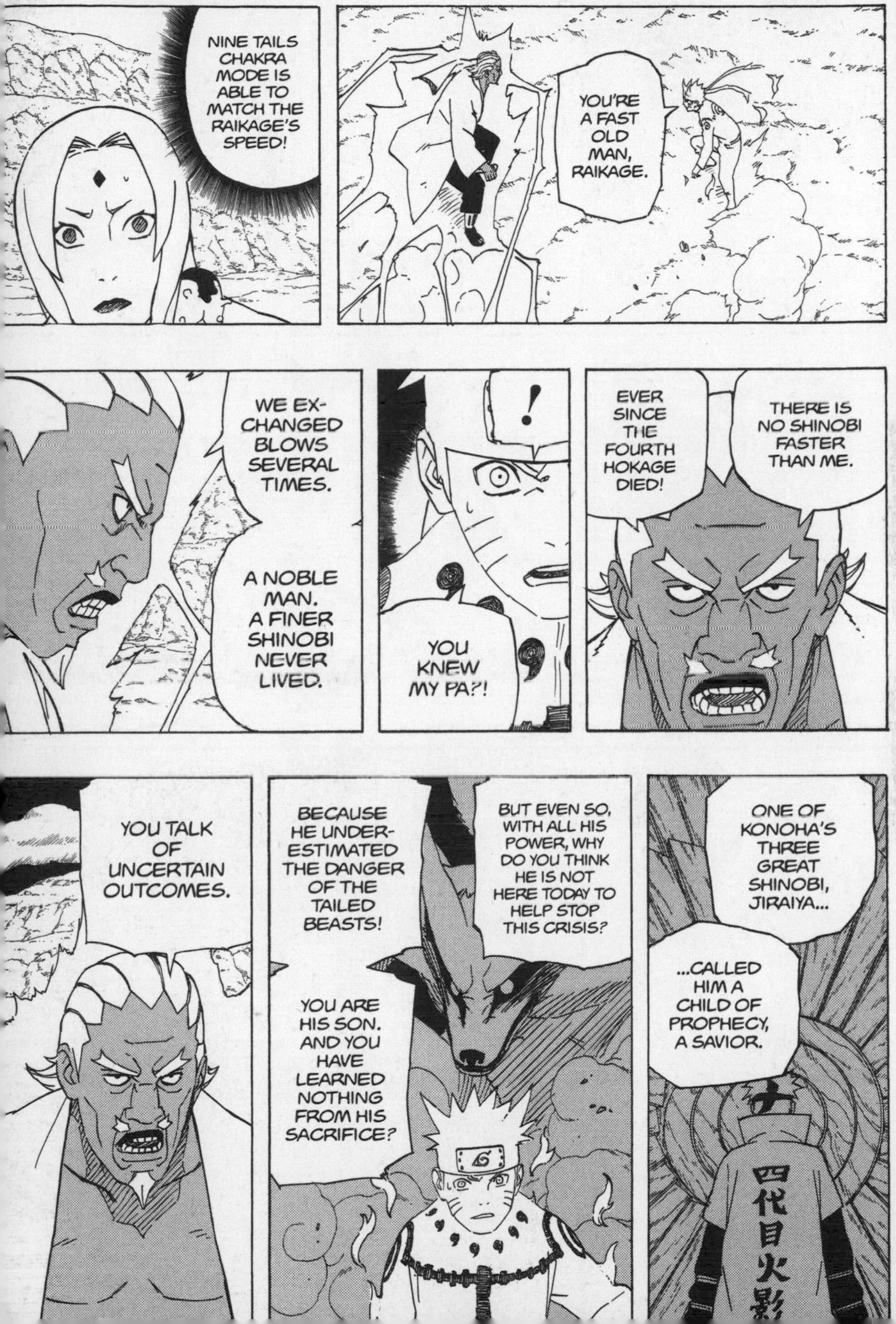
YOU'RE A FAST OLD MAN, RAIKAGE.
NINE TAILS CHAKRA MODE IS ABLE TO MATCH THE RAIKAGE'S SPEED!
THERE IS NO SHINOBI FASTER THAN ME.
EVER SINCE THE FOURTH HOKAGE DIED!
!
YOU KNEW MY PA?!
WE EX-CHANGED BLOWS SEVERAL TIMES.
A NOBLE MAN. A FINER SHINOBI NEVER LIVED.
ONE OF KONOHA'S THREE GREAT SHINOBI, JIRAIYA...
...CALLED HIM A CHILD OF PROPHECY, A SAVIOR.
四代目火影
BUT EVEN SO, WITH ALL HIS POWER, WHY DO YOU THINK HE IS NOT HERE TODAY TO HELP STOP THIS CRISIS?
BECAUSE HE UNDER-ESTIMATED THE DANGER OF THE TAILED BEASTS!
YOU ARE HIS SON. AND YOU HAVE LEARNED NOTHING FROM HIS SACRIFICE?
YOU TALK OF UNCERTAIN OUTCOMES.

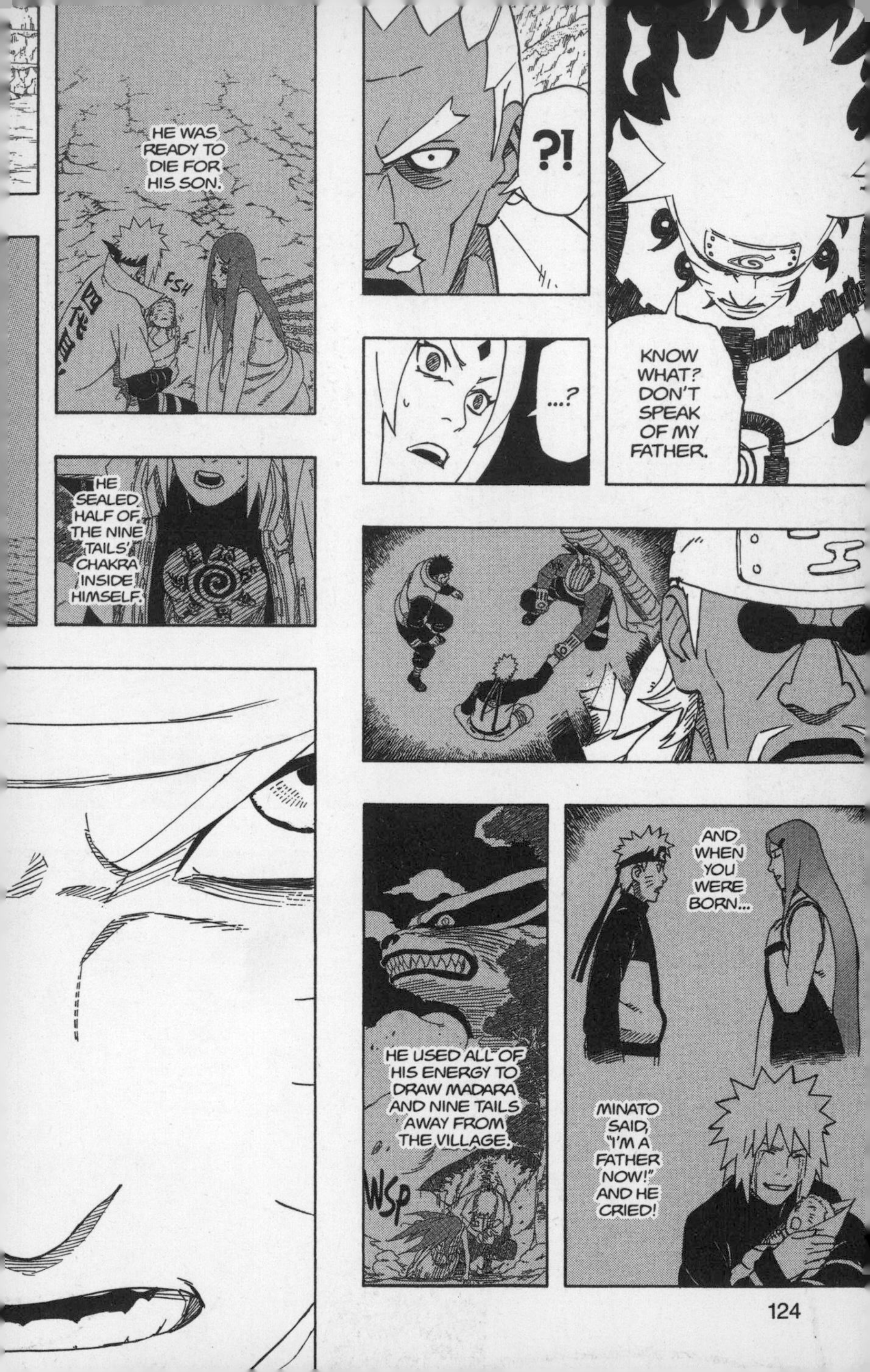
KNOW WHAT? DON'T SPEAK OF MY FATHER.
?!
...?
HE WAS READY TO DIE FOR HIS SON.
FSH
HE SEALED HALF OF THE NINE TAILS' CHAKRA INSIDE HIMSELF.
AND WHEN YOU WERE BORN...
MINATO SAID, "I'M A FATHER NOW!" AND HE CRIED!
HE USED ALL OF HIS ENERGY TO DRAW MADARA AND NINE TAILS AWAY FROM THE VILLAGE.
WSP

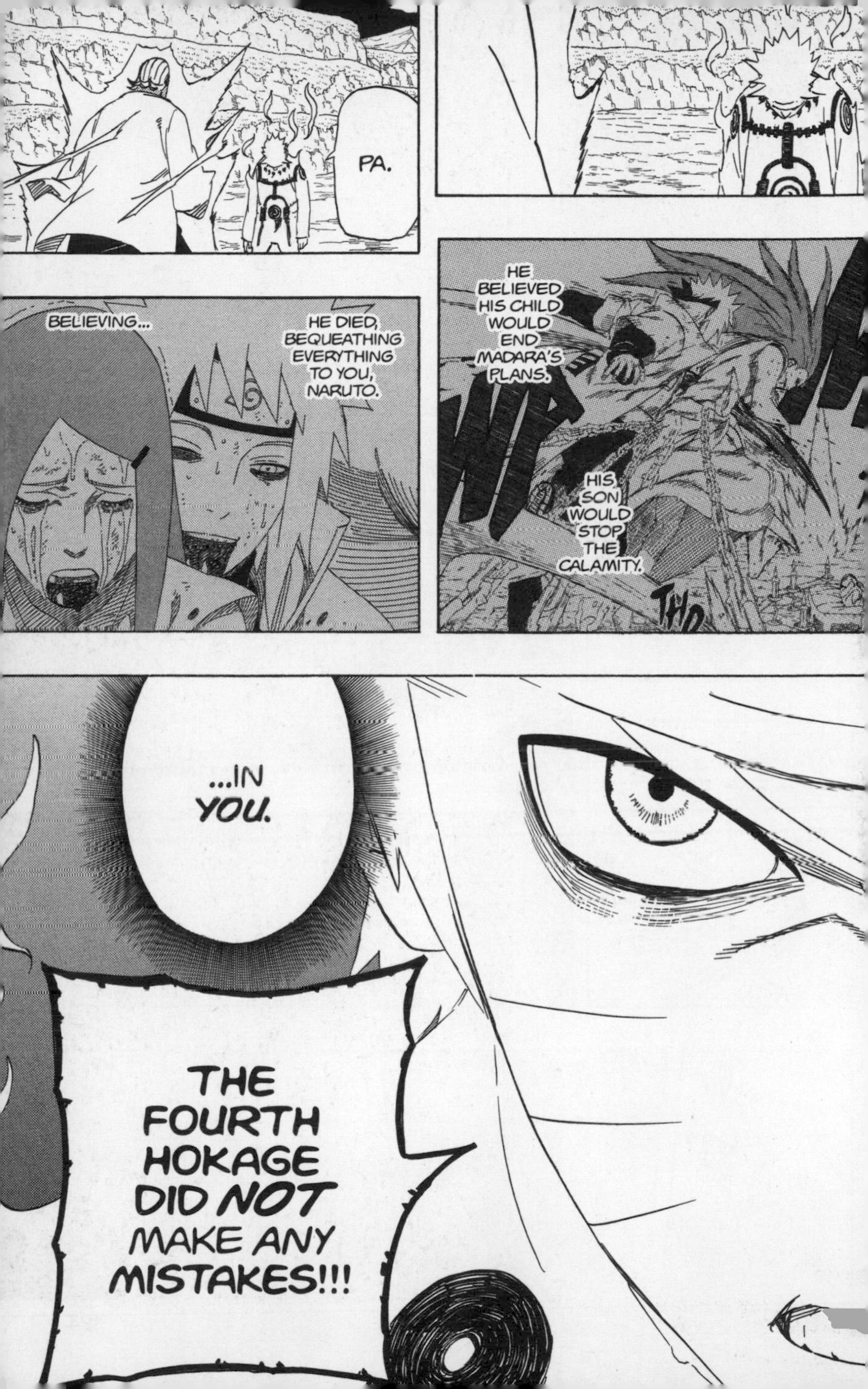
PA.
HE BELIEVED HIS CHILD WOULD END MADARA'S PLANS.
HIS SON WOULD STOP THE CALAMITY.
HE DIED, BEQUEATHING EVERYTHING TO YOU, NARUTO.
BELIEVING...
...IN YOU.
THE FOURTH HOKAGE DID NOT MAKE ANY MISTAKES!!!

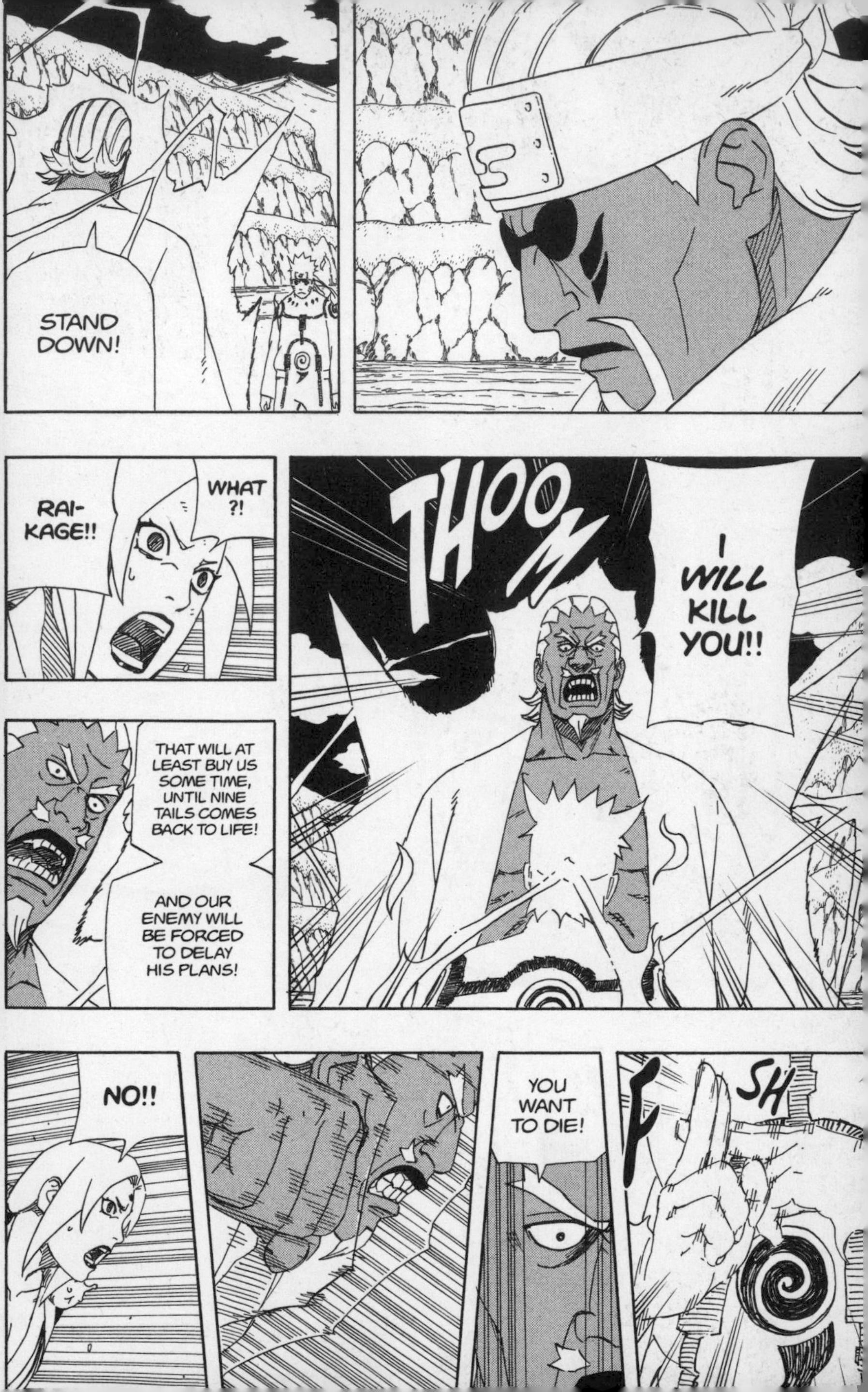
STAND DOWN!
THOOM
I WILL KILL YOU!!
WHAT ?!
RAI-KAGE!!
THAT WILL AT LEAST BUY US SOME TIME, UNTIL NINE TAILS COMES BACK TO LIFE!
AND OUR ENEMY WILL BE FORCED TO DELAY HIS PLANS!
F
SH
YOU WANT TO DIE!
NO!!

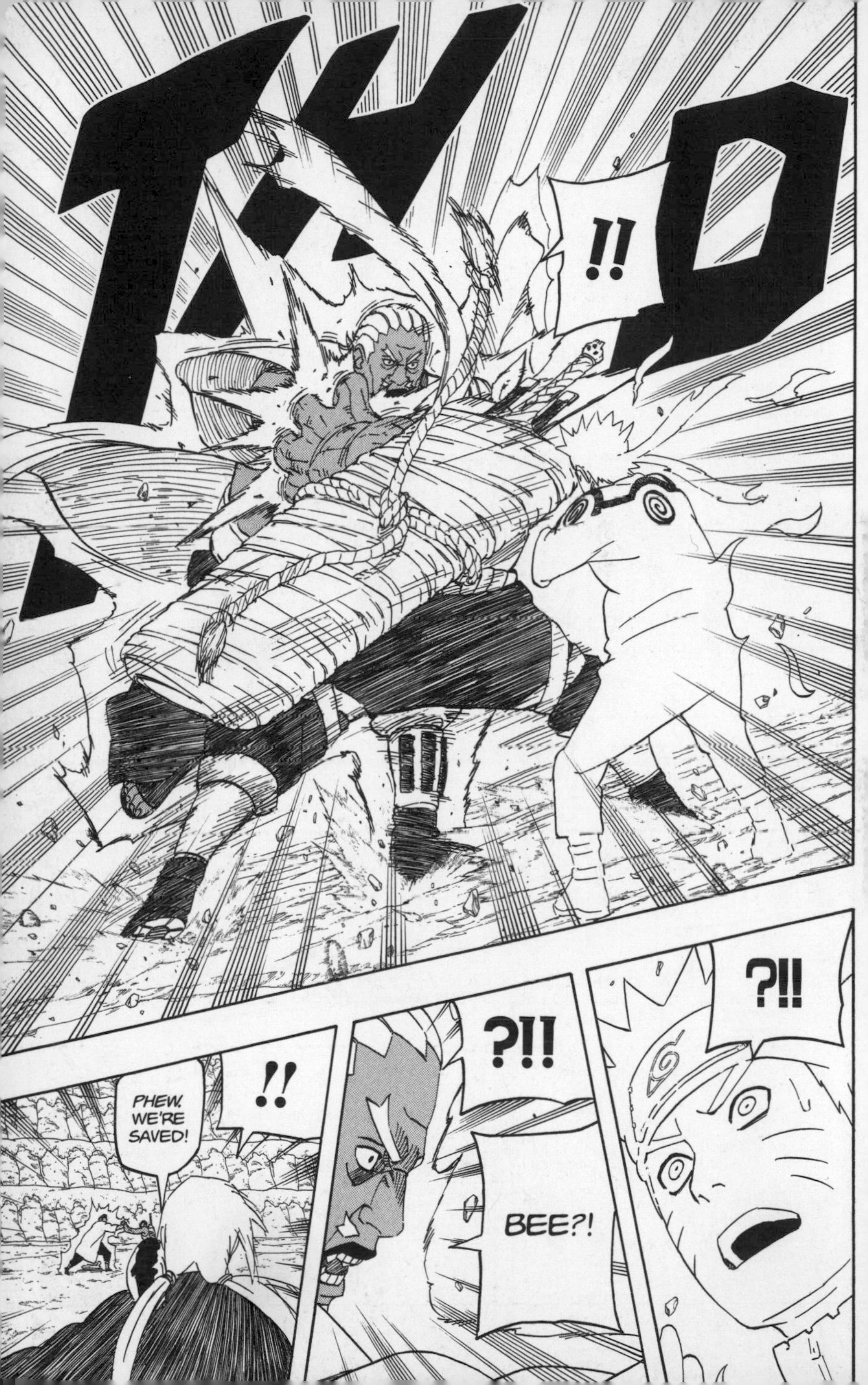

!!
?!!
?!!
BEE?!
!!
PHEW. WE'RE SAVED!

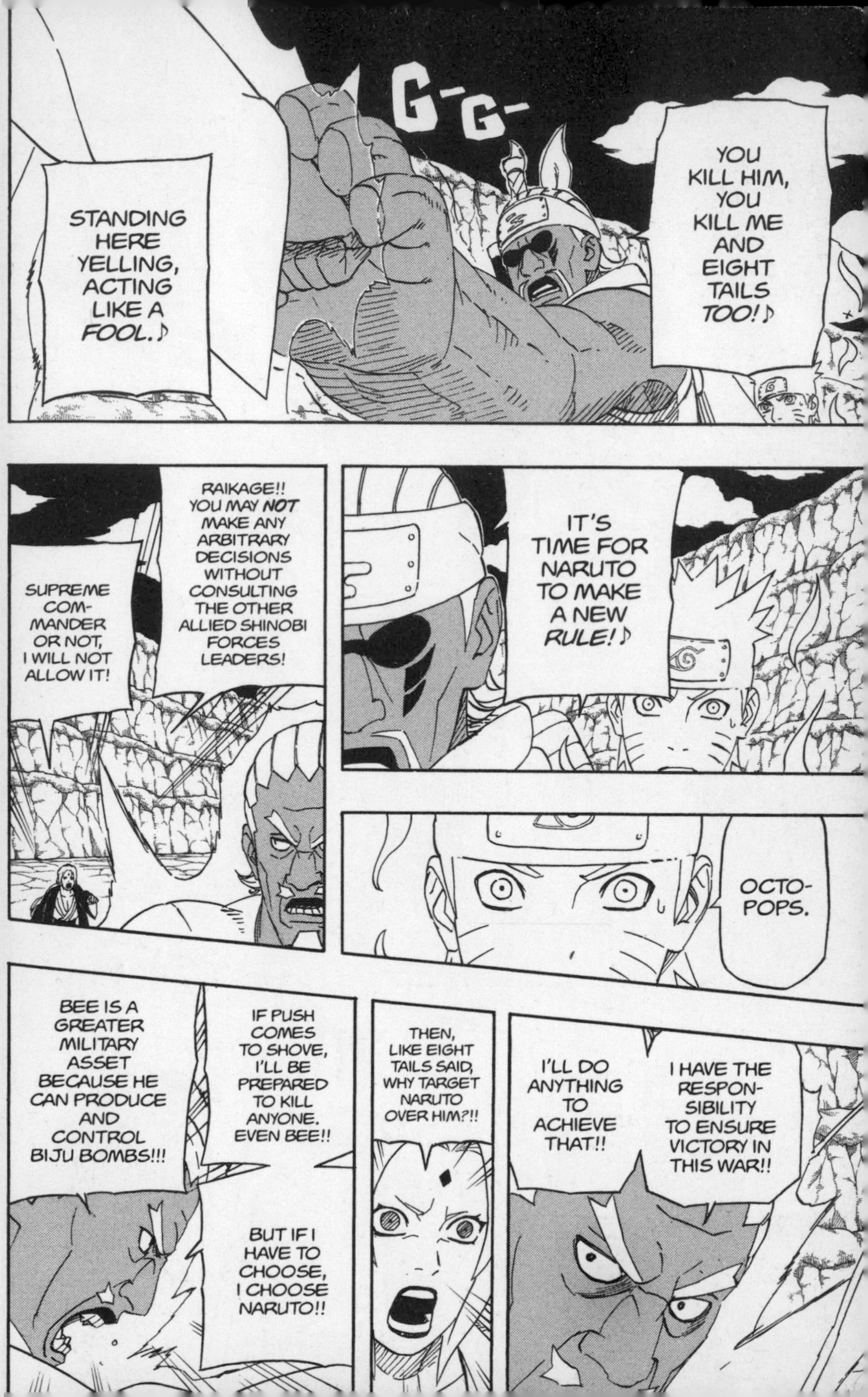
YOU KILL HIM, YOU KILL ME AND EIGHT TAILS TOO!♪
G-G-
STANDING HERE YELLING, ACTING LIKE A FOOL.♪
IT'S TIME FOR NARUTO TO MAKE A NEW RULE!♪
OCTOPOPS.
RAIKAGE!! YOU MAY NOT MAKE ANY ARBITRARY DECISIONS WITHOUT CONSULTING THE OTHER ALLIED SHINOBI FORCES LEADERS!
SUPREME COMMANDER OR NOT, I WILL NOT ALLOW IT!
I HAVE THE RESPONSIBILITY TO ENSURE VICTORY IN THIS WAR!!
I'LL DO ANYTHING TO ACHIEVE THAT!!
THEN, LIKE EIGHT TAILS SAID, WHY TARGET NARUTO OVER HIM?!!
IF PUSH COMES TO SHOVE, I'LL BE PREPARED TO KILL ANYONE. EVEN BEE!!
BEE IS A GREATER MILITARY ASSET BECAUSE HE CAN PRODUCE AND CONTROL BIJU BOMBS!!!
BUT IF I HAVE TO CHOOSE, I CHOOSE NARUTO!!

READ THIS WAY

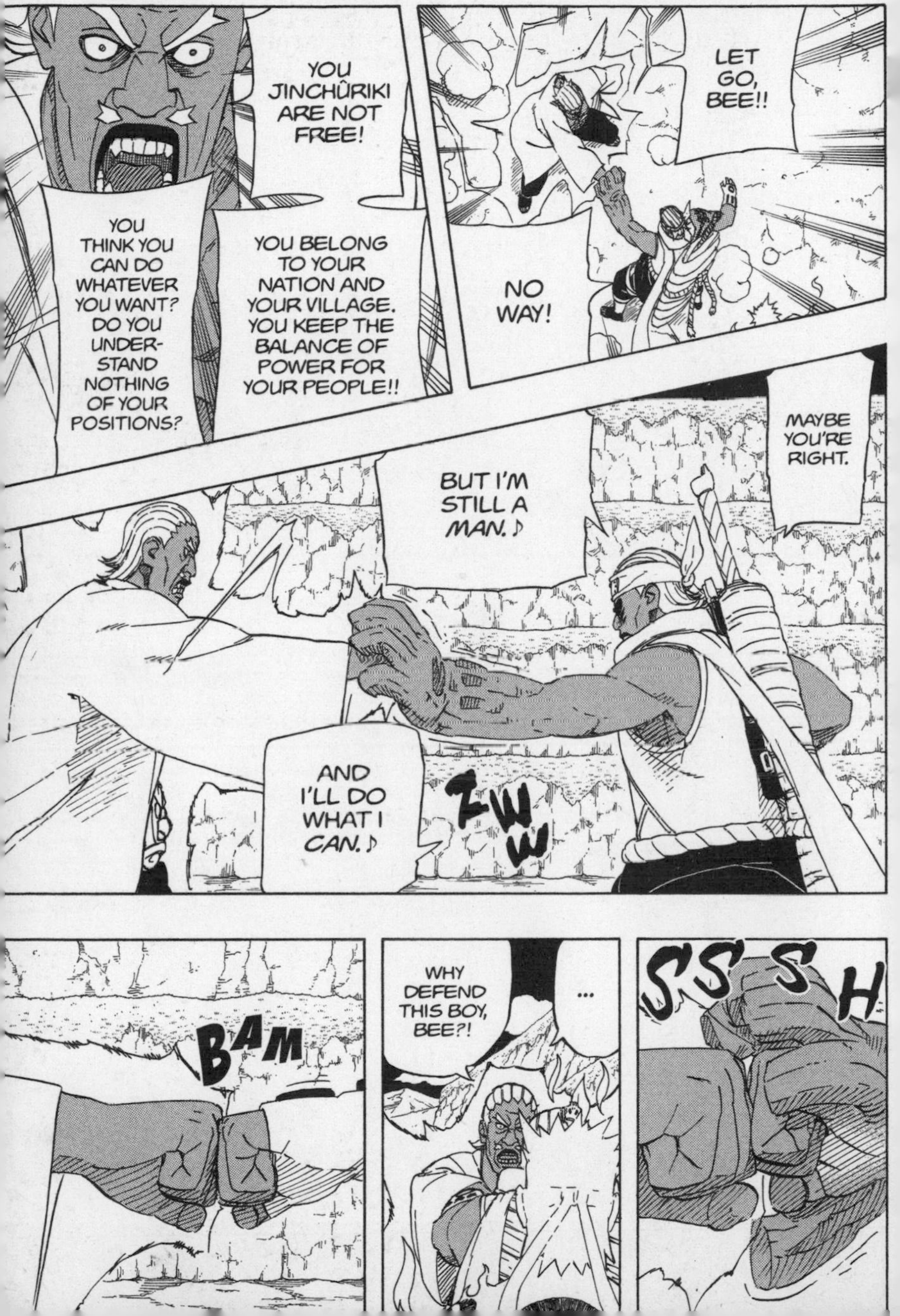
LET GO, BEE!!
NO WAY!
YOU JINCHŪRIKI ARE NOT FREE!
YOU BELONG TO YOUR NATION AND YOUR VILLAGE. YOU KEEP THE BALANCE OF POWER FOR YOUR PEOPLE!!
YOU THINK YOU CAN DO WHATEVER YOU WANT? DO YOU UNDER-STAND NOTHING OF YOUR POSITIONS?
MAYBE YOU'RE RIGHT.
BUT I'M STILL A MAN.♪
AND I'LL DO WHAT I CAN.♪
ZWW
SSSH
...
WHY DEFEND THIS BOY, BEE?!
BAM

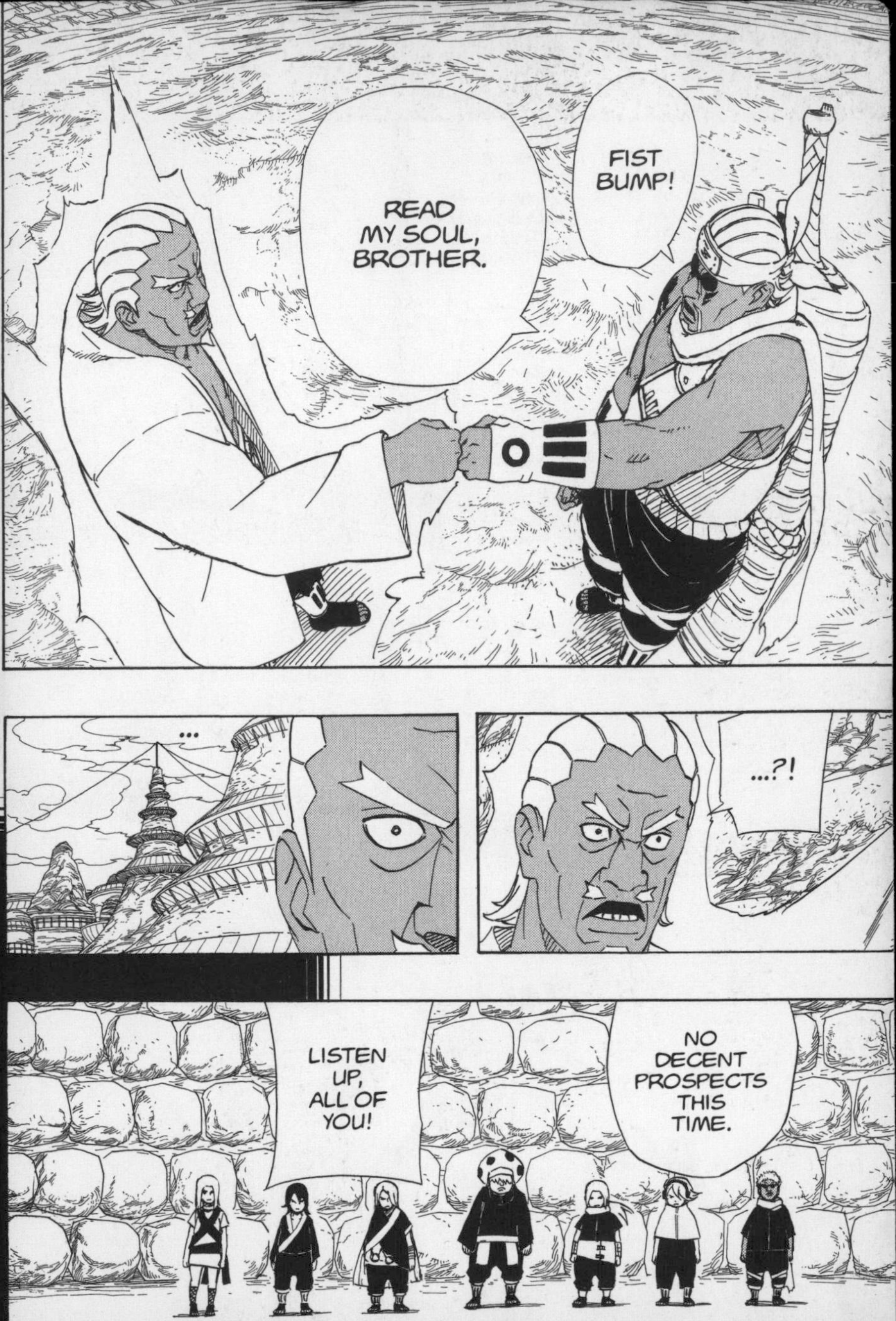
FIST BUMP!
READ MY SOUL, BROTHER.
...?!
...
NO DECENT PROSPECTS THIS TIME.
LISTEN UP, ALL OF YOU!

READ THIS WAY

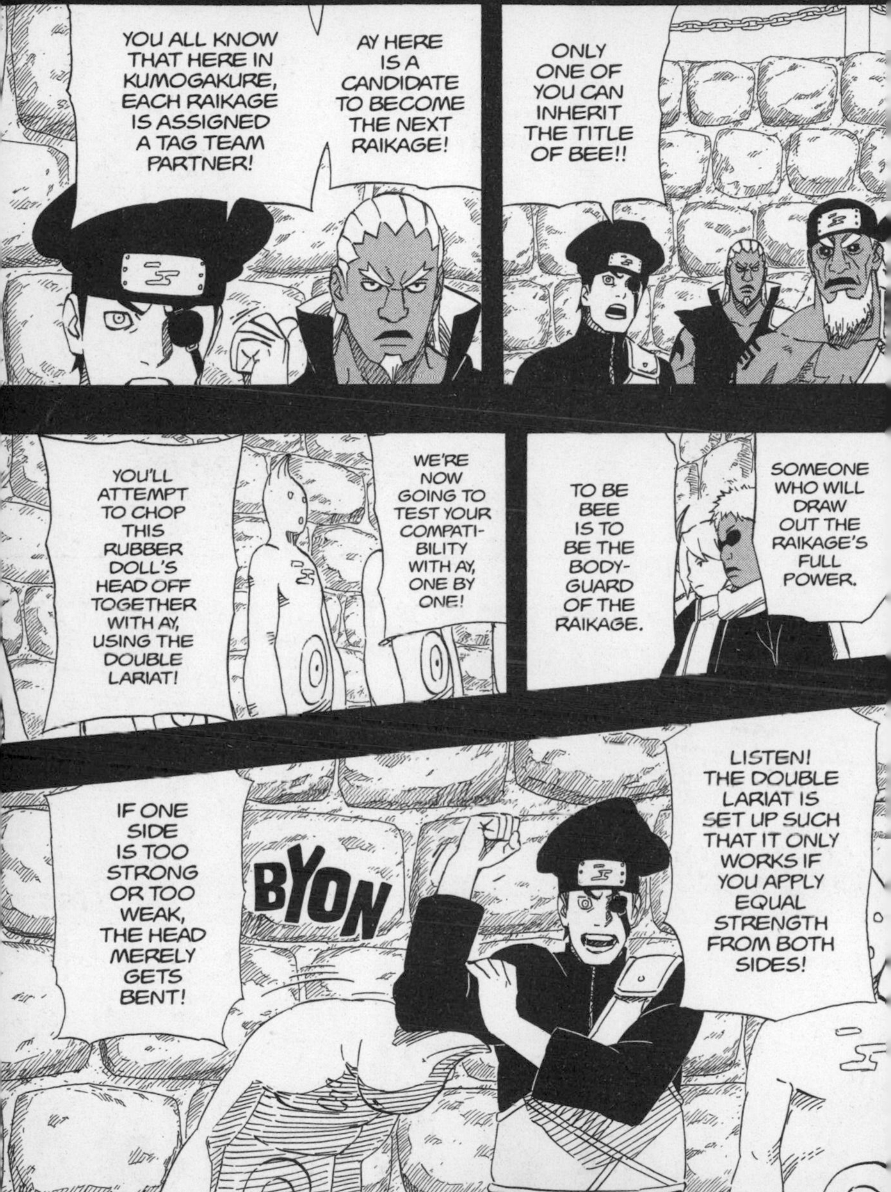
ONLY ONE OF YOU CAN INHERIT THE TITLE OF BEE!!
AY HERE IS A CANDIDATE TO BECOME THE NEXT RAIKAGE!
YOU ALL KNOW THAT HERE IN KUMOGAKURE, EACH RAIKAGE IS ASSIGNED A TAG TEAM PARTNER!
SOMEONE WHO WILL DRAW OUT THE RAIKAGE'S FULL POWER.
TO BE BEE IS TO BE THE BODY-GUARD OF THE RAIKAGE.
WE'RE NOW GOING TO TEST YOUR COMPATI-BILITY WITH AY, ONE BY ONE!
YOU'LL ATTEMPT TO CHOP THIS RUBBER DOLL'S HEAD OFF TOGETHER WITH AY, USING THE DOUBLE LARIAT!
LISTEN! THE DOUBLE LARIAT IS SET UP SUCH THAT IT ONLY WORKS IF YOU APPLY EQUAL STRENGTH FROM BOTH SIDES!
BYON
IF ONE SIDE IS TOO STRONG OR TOO WEAK, THE HEAD MERELY GETS BENT!

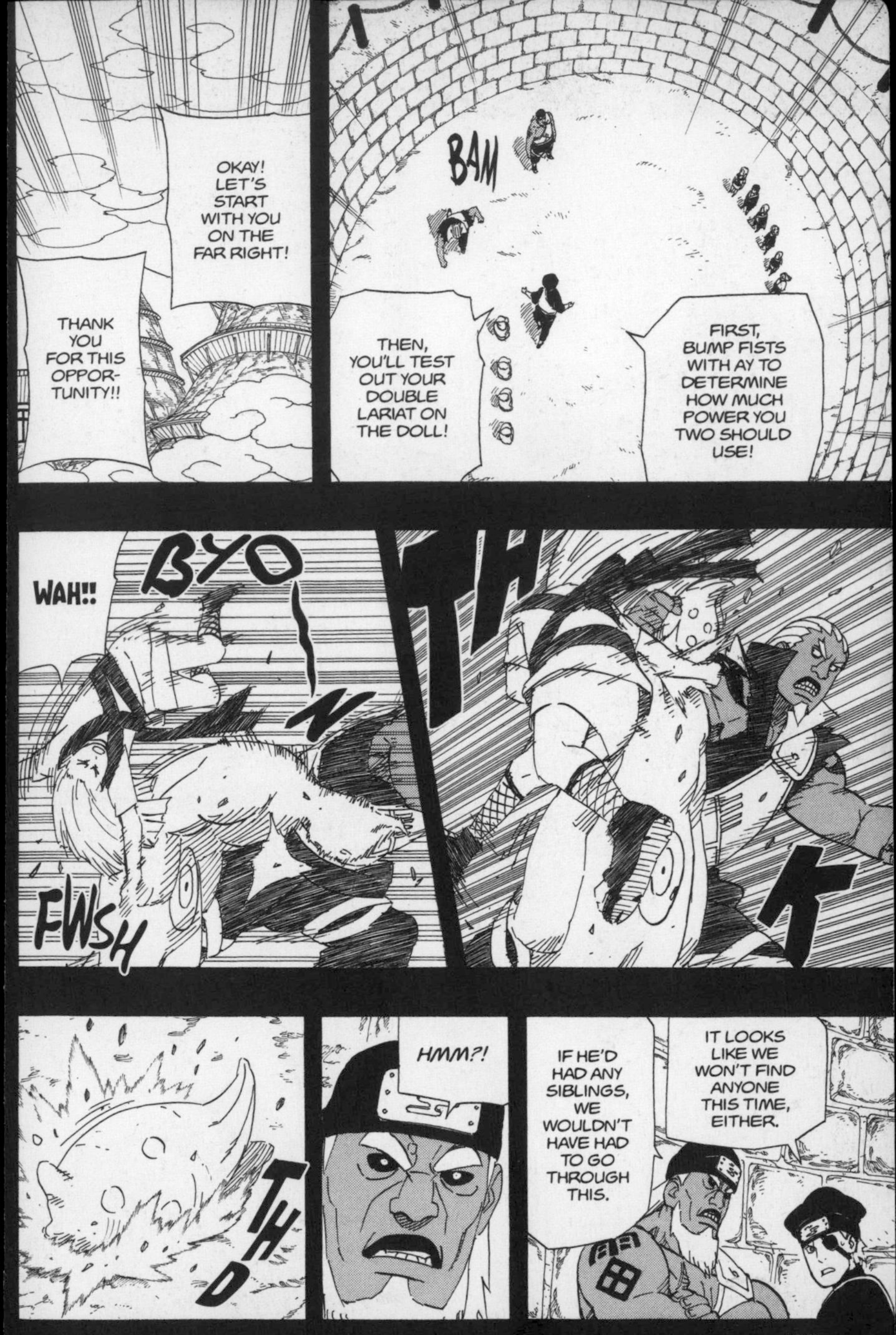

BAM
FIRST, BUMP FISTS WITH AY TO DETERMINE HOW MUCH POWER YOU TWO SHOULD USE!
THEN, YOU'LL TEST OUT YOUR DOUBLE LARIAT ON THE DOLL!
OKAY! LET'S START WITH YOU ON THE FAR RIGHT!
THANK YOU FOR THIS OPPOR-TUNITY!!
THK
BYO-N
WAH!!
FWSH
IT LOOKS LIKE WE WON'T FIND ANYONE THIS TIME, EITHER.
IF HE'D HAD ANY SIBLINGS, WE WOULDN'T HAVE HAD TO GO THROUGH THIS.
HMM?!
THD

READ THIS WAY

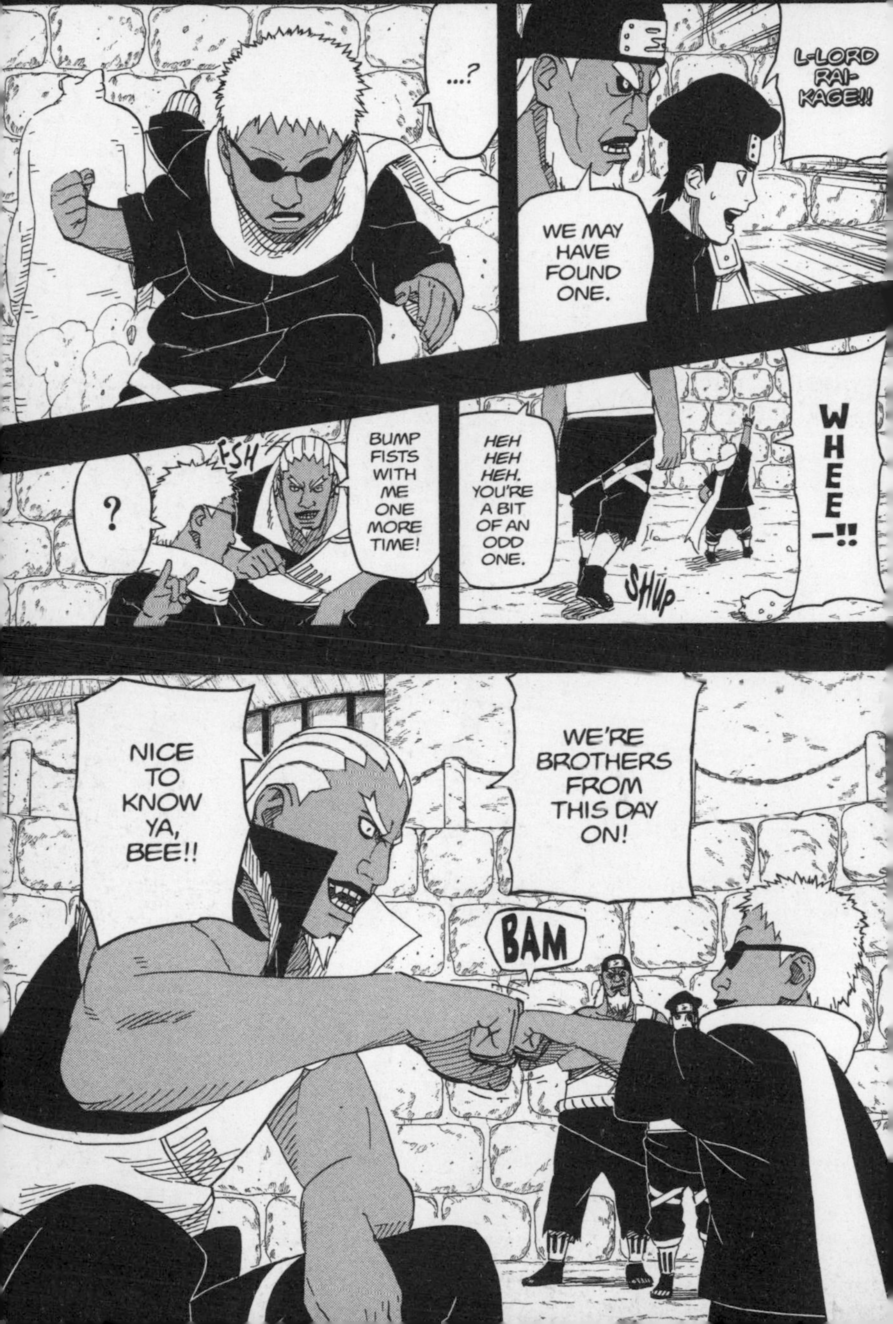
L-LORD RAI-KAGE!!
WE MAY HAVE FOUND ONE.
...?
WHEE—!!
HEH HEH HEH. YOU'RE A BIT OF AN ODD ONE.
SHUP
BUMP FISTS WITH ME ONE MORE TIME!
FSH
?
WE'RE BROTHERS FROM THIS DAY ON!
NICE TO KNOW YA, BEE!!
BAM

NARUTO

Number 542: The Secret Origin of the Ultimate Tag Team!!

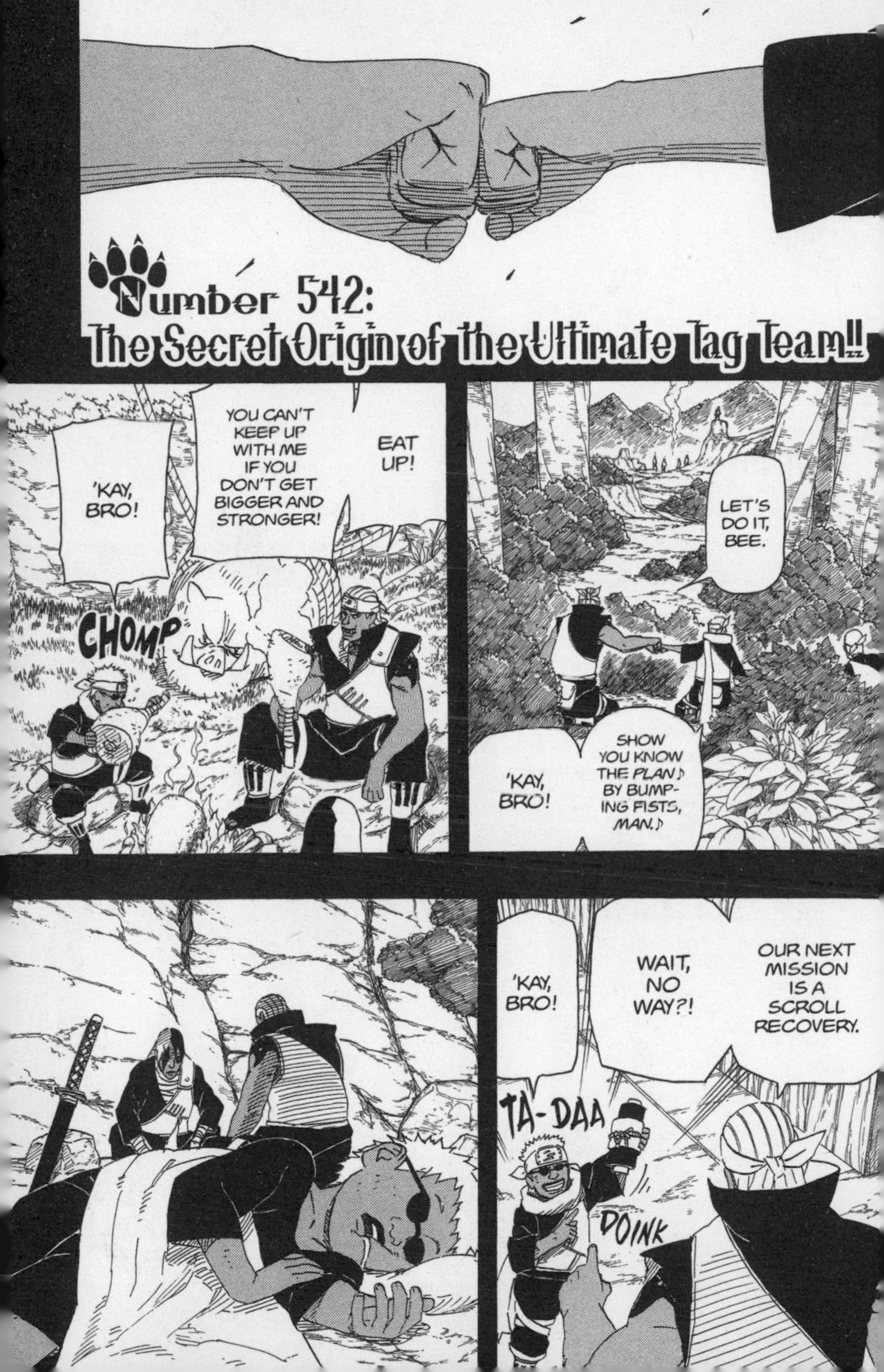
LET'S DO IT, BEE.
SHOW YOU KNOW THE *PLAN*♪ BY BUMPING FISTS, *MAN.*♪
'KAY, BRO!
EAT UP!
YOU CAN'T KEEP UP WITH ME IF YOU DON'T GET BIGGER AND STRONGER!
'KAY, BRO!
CHOMP
OUR NEXT MISSION IS A SCROLL RECOVERY.
WAIT, NO WAY?!
'KAY, BRO!
TA-DAA
DOINK

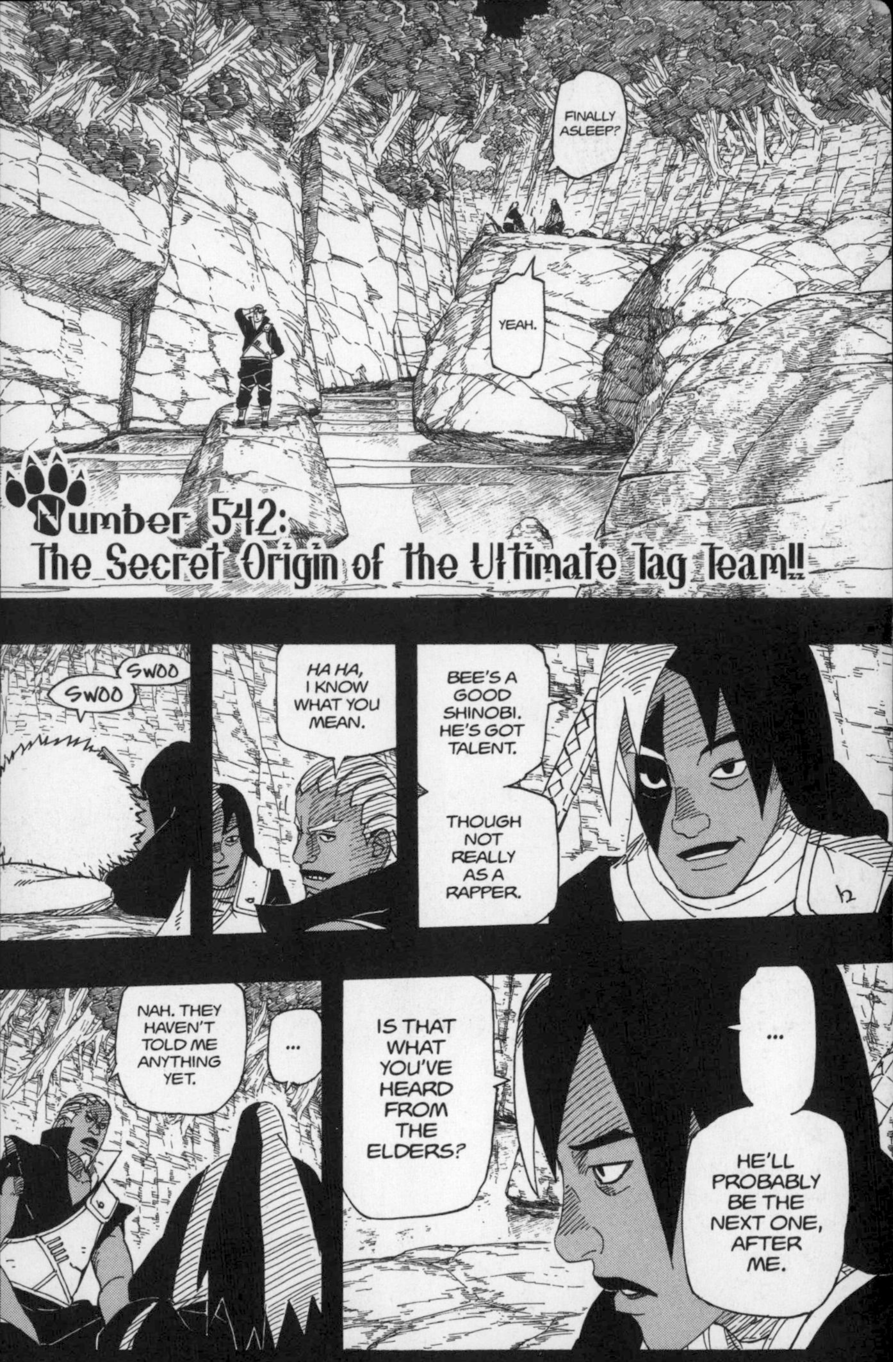
FINALLY ASLEEP?
YEAH.
Number 542: The Secret Origin of the Ultimate Tag Team!!
BEE'S A GOOD SHINOBI. HE'S GOT TALENT.
THOUGH NOT REALLY AS A RAPPER.
HA HA, I KNOW WHAT YOU MEAN.
SWOO
SWOO
...
HE'LL PROBABLY BE THE NEXT ONE, AFTER ME.
IS THAT WHAT YOU'VE HEARD FROM THE ELDERS?
...
NAH. THEY HAVEN'T TOLD ME ANYTHING YET.

READ THIS WAY

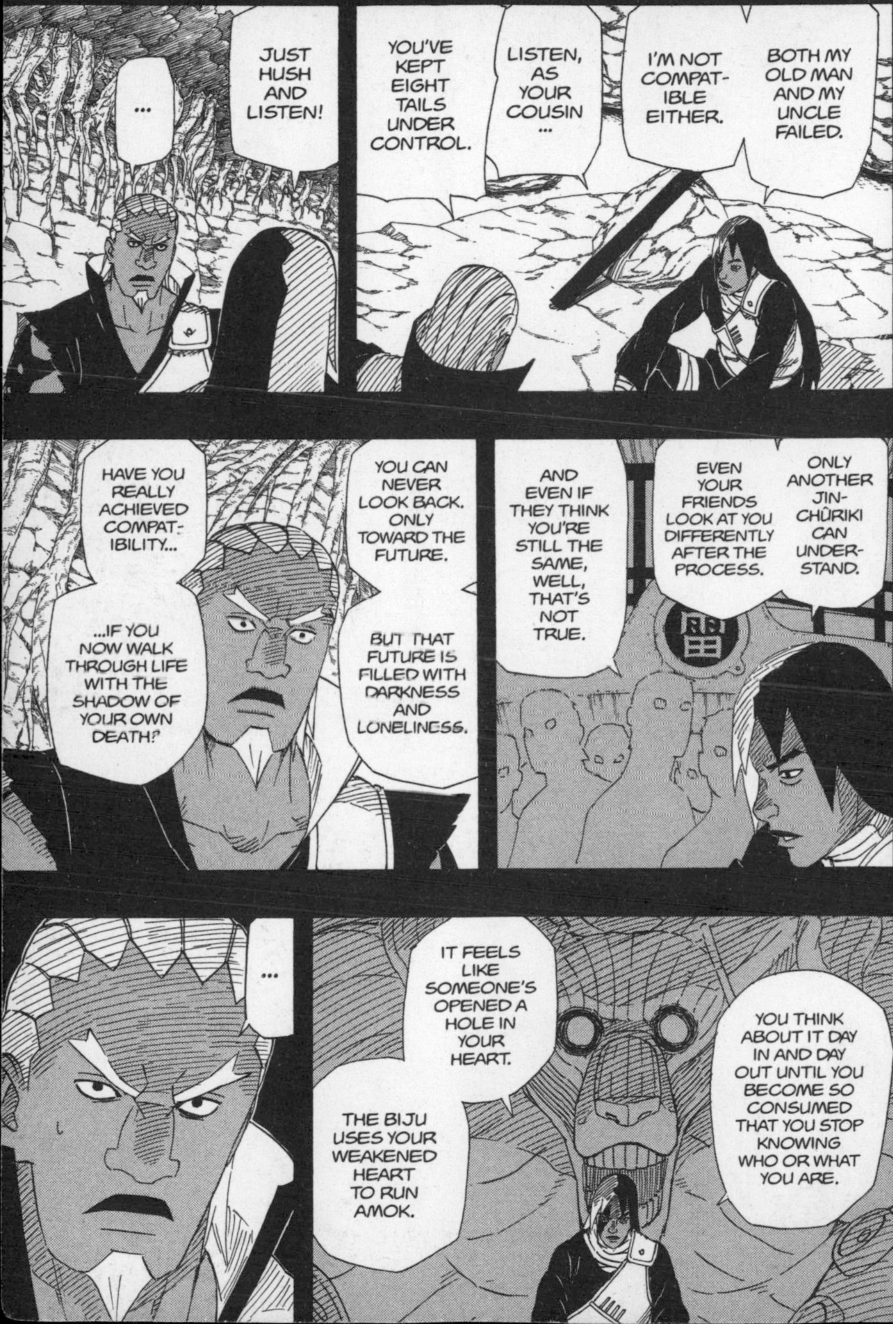
BOTH MY OLD MAN AND MY UNCLE FAILED.
I'M NOT COMPATIBLE EITHER.
LISTEN, AS YOUR COUSIN...
YOU'VE KEPT EIGHT TAILS UNDER CONTROL.
JUST HUSH AND LISTEN!
...
ONLY ANOTHER JINCHŪRIKI CAN UNDERSTAND.
EVEN YOUR FRIENDS LOOK AT YOU DIFFERENTLY AFTER THE PROCESS.
AND EVEN IF THEY THINK YOU'RE STILL THE SAME, WELL, THAT'S NOT TRUE.
YOU CAN NEVER LOOK BACK. ONLY TOWARD THE FUTURE.
BUT THAT FUTURE IS FILLED WITH DARKNESS AND LONELINESS.
HAVE YOU REALLY ACHIEVED COMPATIBILITY...
...IF YOU NOW WALK THROUGH LIFE WITH THE SHADOW OF YOUR OWN DEATH?
IT FEELS LIKE SOMEONE'S OPENED A HOLE IN YOUR HEART.
YOU THINK ABOUT IT DAY IN AND DAY OUT UNTIL YOU BECOME SO CONSUMED THAT YOU STOP KNOWING WHO OR WHAT YOU ARE.
THE BIJU USES YOUR WEAKENED HEART TO RUN AMOK.
...

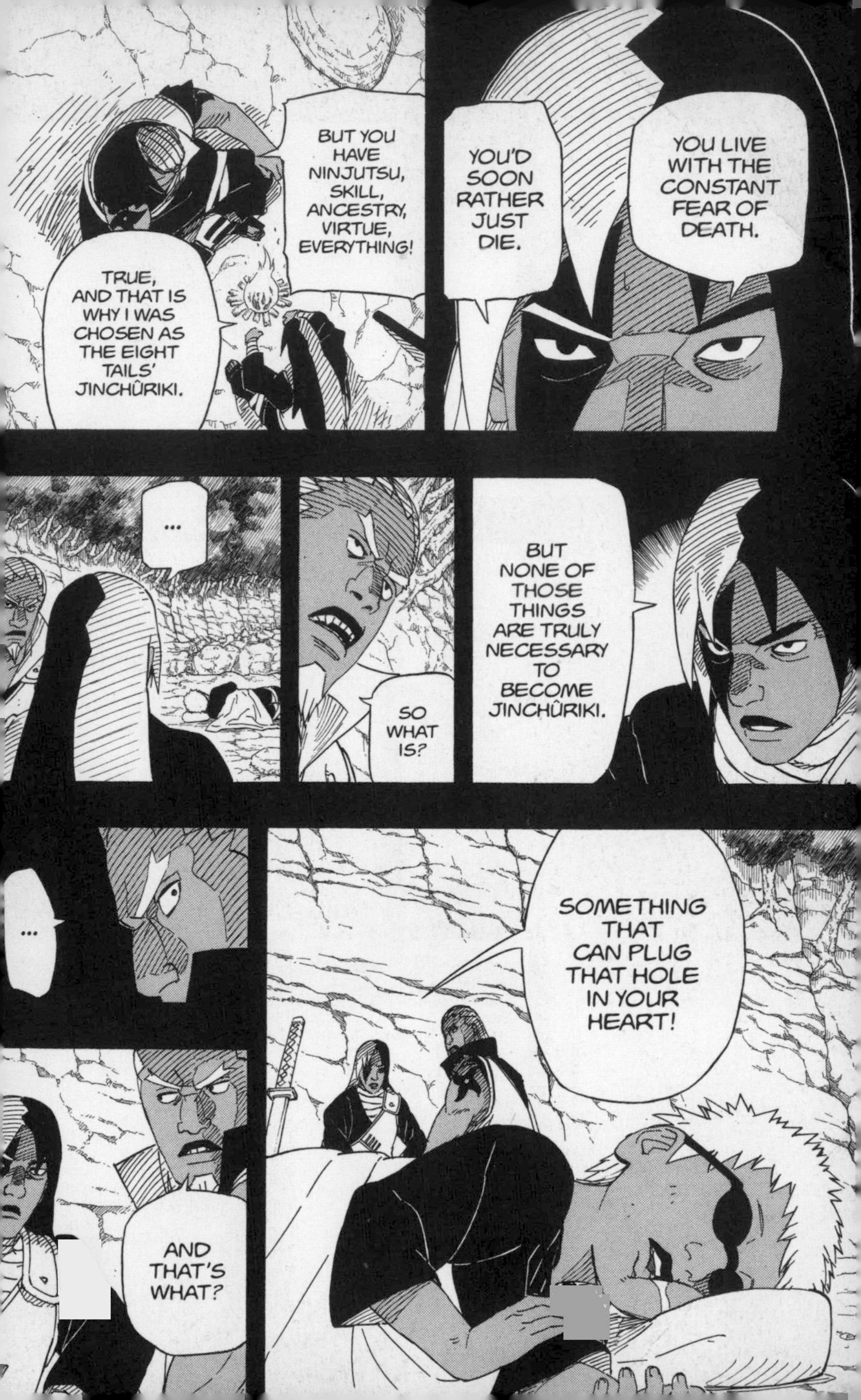
YOU LIVE WITH THE CONSTANT FEAR OF DEATH.
YOU'D SOON RATHER JUST DIE.
BUT YOU HAVE NINJUTSU, SKILL, ANCESTRY, VIRTUE, EVERYTHING!
TRUE, AND THAT IS WHY I WAS CHOSEN AS THE EIGHT TAILS' JINCHÛRIKI.
BUT NONE OF THOSE THINGS ARE TRULY NECESSARY TO BECOME JINCHÛRIKI.
SO WHAT IS?
...
SOMETHING THAT CAN PLUG THAT HOLE IN YOUR HEART!
...
AND THAT'S WHAT?

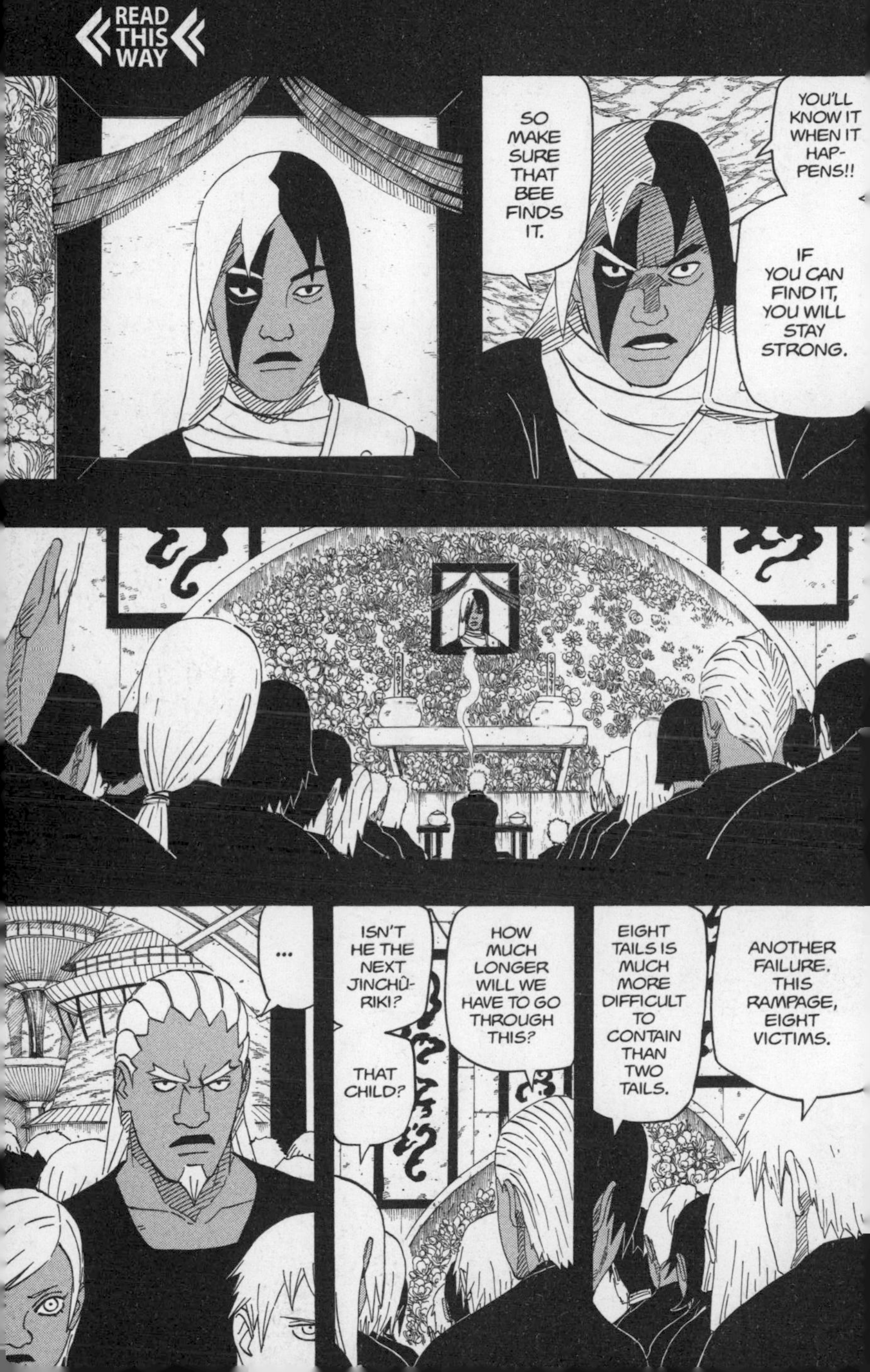
READ THIS WAY
YOU'LL KNOW IT WHEN IT HAP-PENS!!
SO MAKE SURE THAT BEE FINDS IT.
IF YOU CAN FIND IT, YOU WILL STAY STRONG.
ANOTHER FAILURE. THIS RAMPAGE, EIGHT VICTIMS.
EIGHT TAILS IS MUCH MORE DIFFICULT TO CONTAIN THAN TWO TAILS.
HOW MUCH LONGER WILL WE HAVE TO GO THROUGH THIS?
ISN'T HE THE NEXT JINCHÛ-RIKI?
THAT CHILD?
...

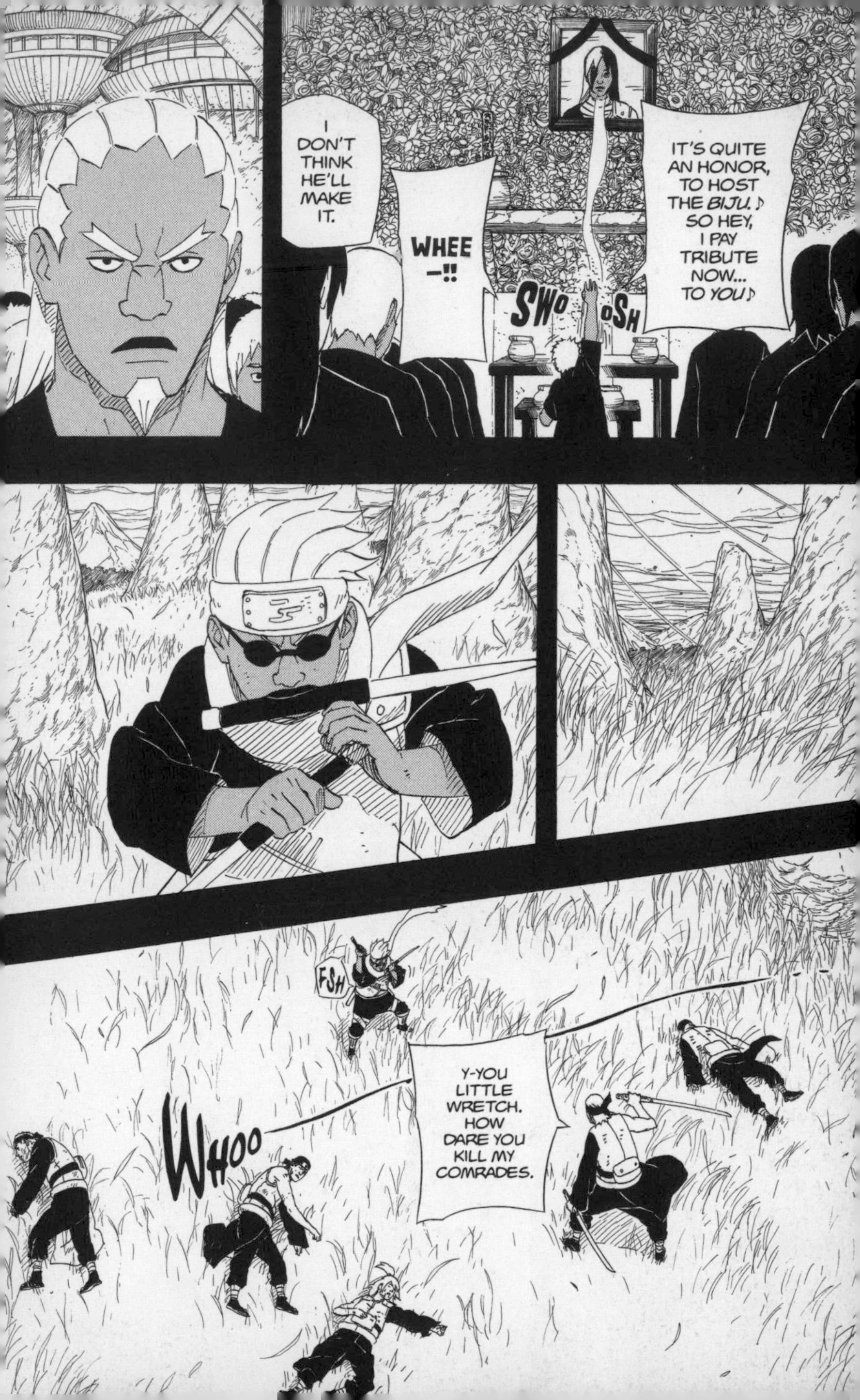
IT'S QUITE AN HONOR, TO HOST THE BIJU.♪ SO HEY, I PAY TRIBUTE NOW... TO YOU♪
SWOOSH
I DON'T THINK HE'LL MAKE IT.
WHEE—!!
FSH
Y-YOU LITTLE WRETCH. HOW DARE YOU KILL MY COMRADES.
WHOO

READ THIS WAY

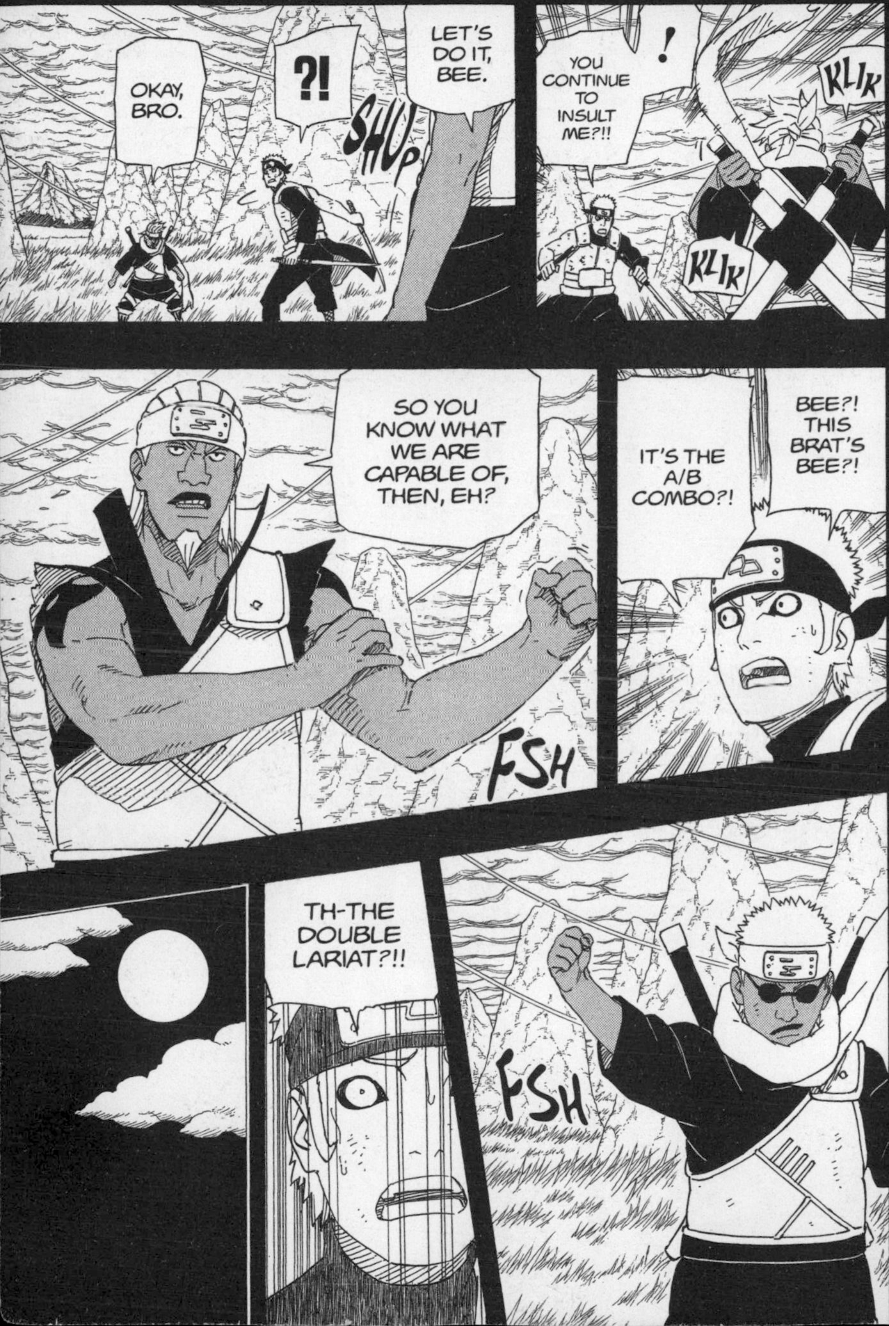
KLIK
!
YOU CONTINUE TO INSULT ME?!!
KLIK
LET'S DO IT, BEE.
?!
SHUP
OKAY, BRO.
BEE?! THIS BRAT'S BEE?!
IT'S THE A/B COMBO?!
SO YOU KNOW WHAT WE ARE CAPABLE OF, THEN, EH?
FSH
FSH
TH-THE DOUBLE LARIAT?!!

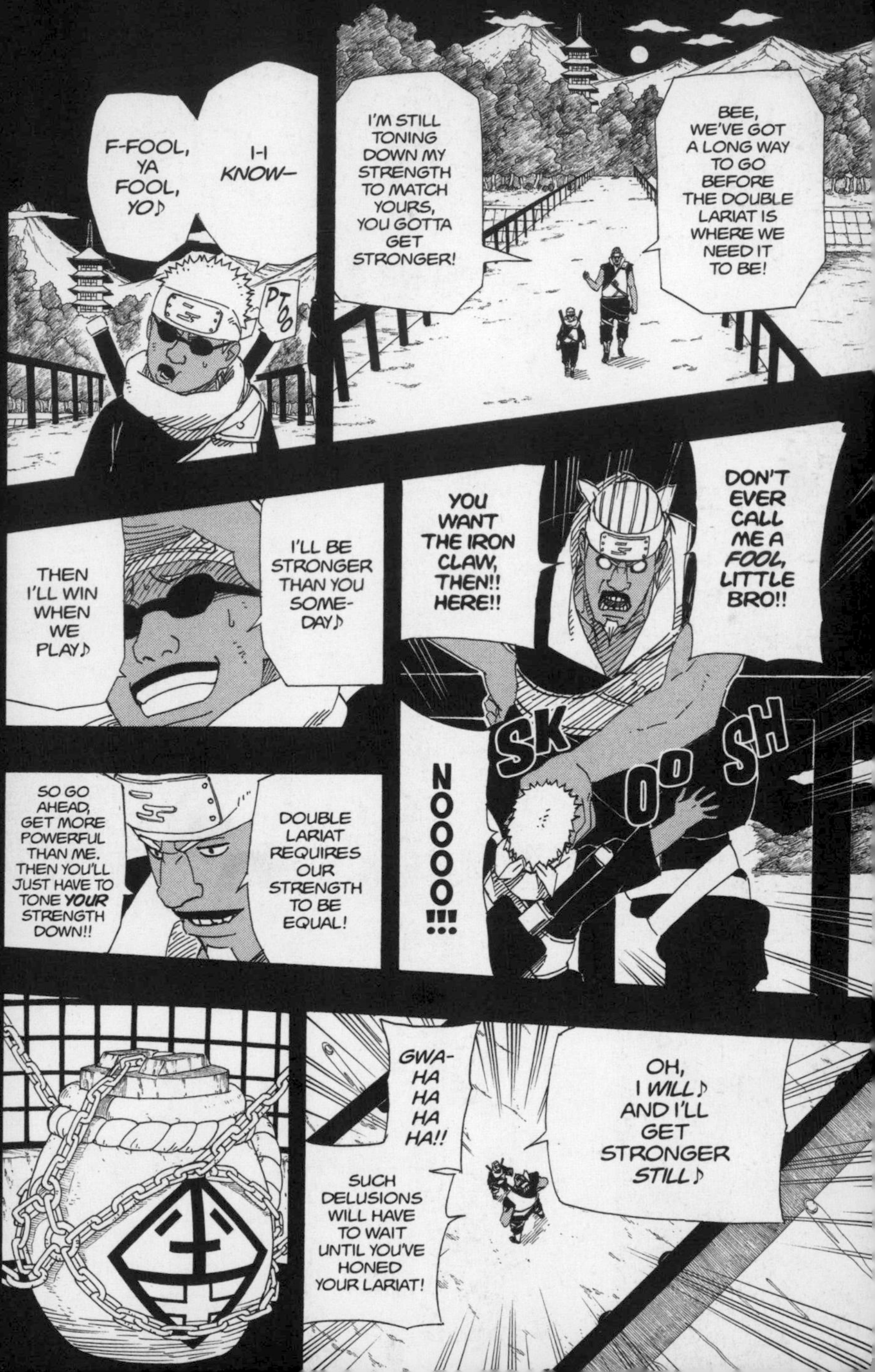
BEE, WE'VE GOT A LONG WAY TO GO BEFORE THE DOUBLE LARIAT IS WHERE WE NEED IT TO BE!
I'M STILL TONING DOWN MY STRENGTH TO MATCH YOURS, YOU GOTTA GET STRONGER!
I-I KNOW–
F-FOOL, YA FOOL, YO♪
PTOO
DON'T EVER CALL ME A *FOOL*, LITTLE BRO!!
YOU WANT THE IRON CLAW, THEN!! HERE!!
SKOOSH
NOOOO!!!
I'LL BE STRONGER THAN YOU SOME-DAY♪
THEN I'LL WIN WHEN WE PLAY♪
DOUBLE LARIAT REQUIRES OUR STRENGTH TO BE EQUAL!
SO GO AHEAD, GET MORE POWERFUL THAN ME. THEN YOU'LL JUST HAVE TO TONE *YOUR* STRENGTH DOWN!!
OH, I WILL♪ AND I'LL GET STRONGER *STILL*♪
GWA-HA HA HA HA!!
SUCH DELUSIONS WILL HAVE TO WAIT UNTIL YOU'VE HONED YOUR LARIAT!

READ THIS WAY

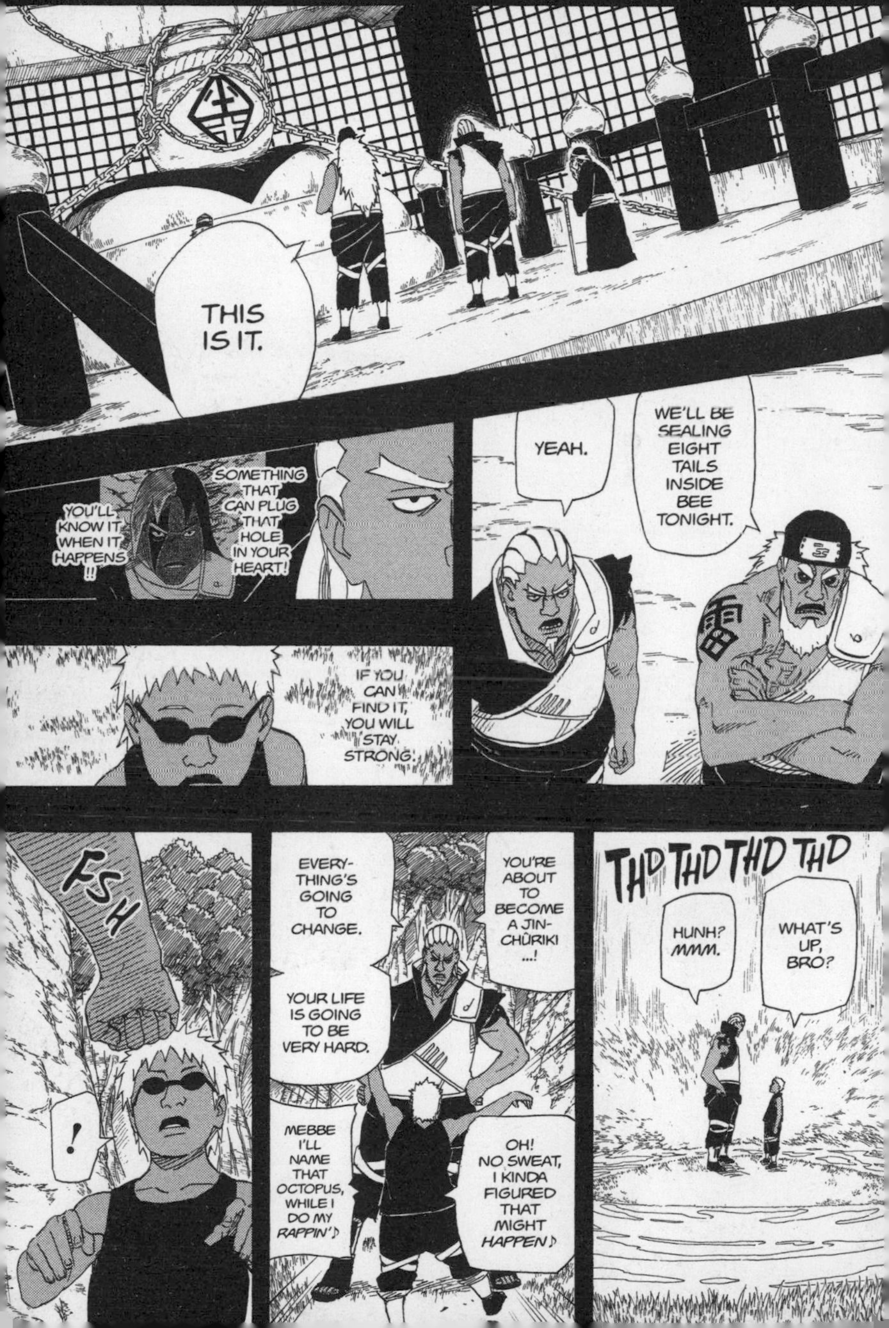

THIS IS IT.
WE'LL BE SEALING EIGHT TAILS INSIDE BEE TONIGHT.
YEAH.
SOMETHING THAT CAN PLUG THAT HOLE IN YOUR HEART!
YOU'LL KNOW IT WHEN IT HAPPENS!!
IF YOU CAN FIND IT, YOU WILL STAY STRONG.
THD THD THD THD
WHAT'S UP, BRO?
HUNH? MMM.
YOU'RE ABOUT TO BECOME A JINCHŪRIKI ...!
EVERY-THING'S GOING TO CHANGE.
YOUR LIFE IS GOING TO BE VERY HARD.
OH! NO SWEAT, I KINDA FIGURED THAT MIGHT HAPPEN♪
MEBBE I'LL NAME THAT OCTOPUS, WHILE I DO MY RAPPIN'♪
FSH
!

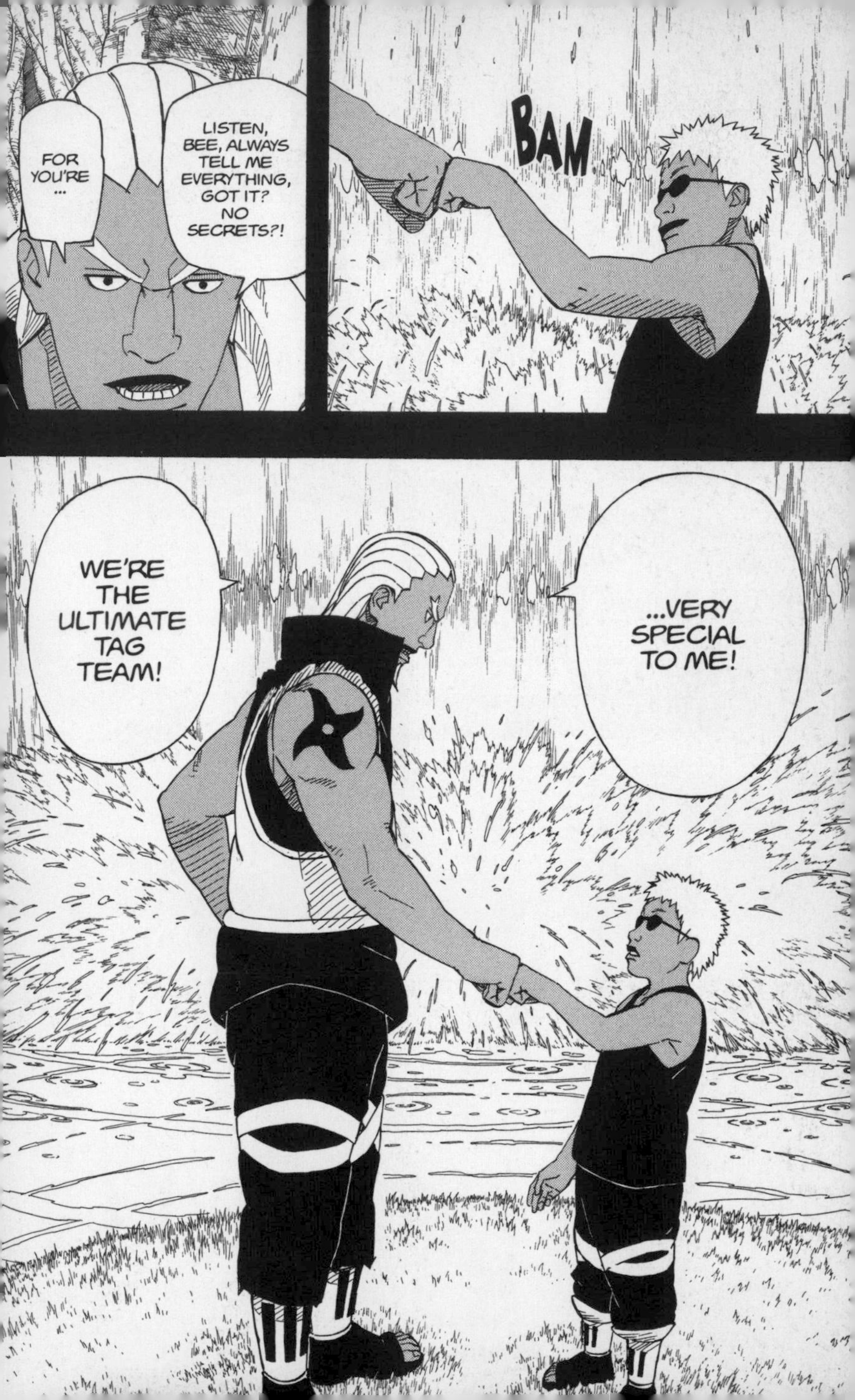
BAM
LISTEN, BEE, ALWAYS TELL ME EVERYTHING, GOT IT? NO SECRETS?!
FOR YOU'RE ...
...VERY SPECIAL TO ME!
WE'RE THE ULTIMATE TAG TEAM!

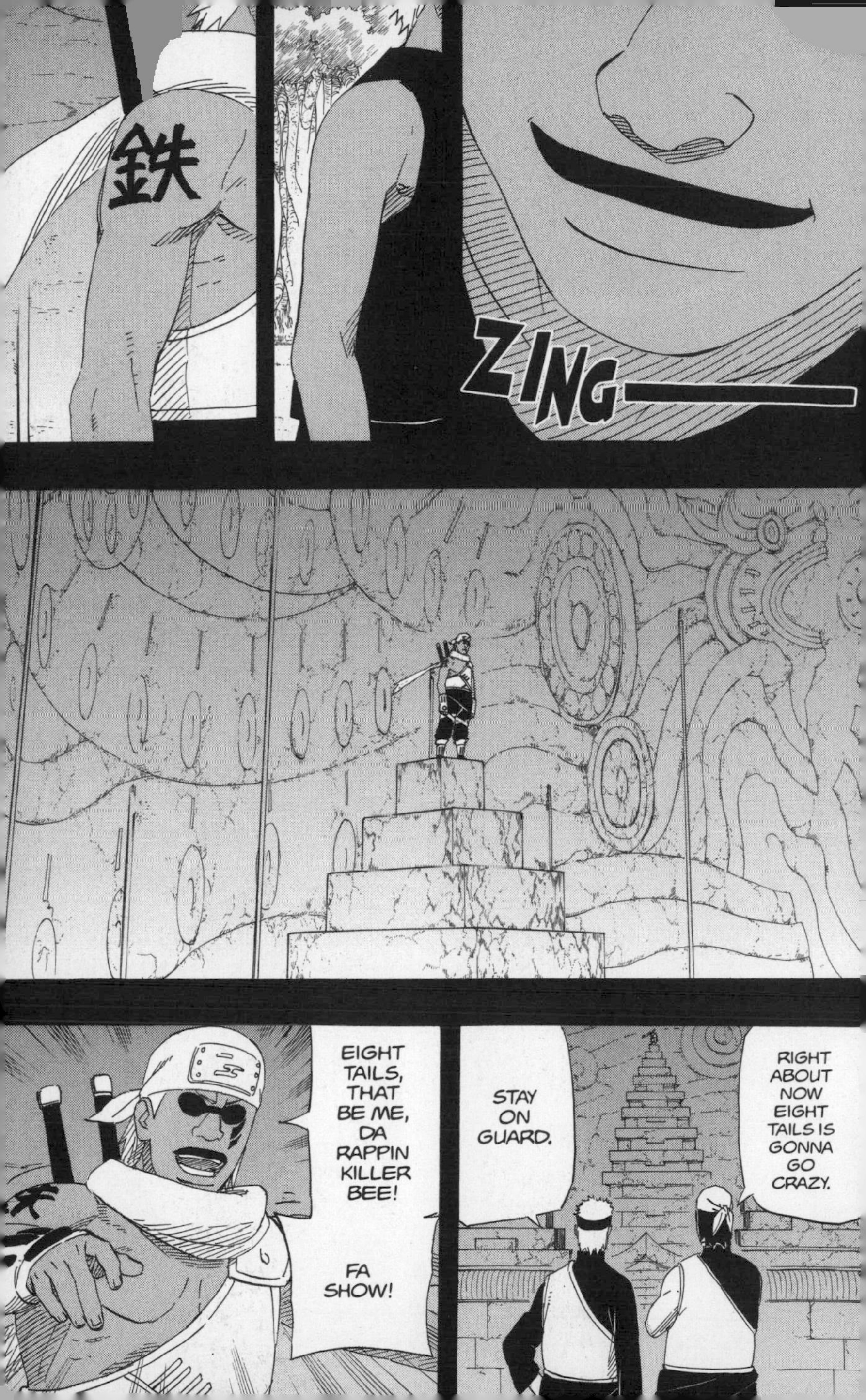
ZING
鉄
RIGHT ABOUT NOW EIGHT TAILS IS GONNA GO CRAZY.
STAY ON GUARD.
EIGHT TAILS, THAT BE ME, DA RAPPIN KILLER BEE!
FA SHOW!

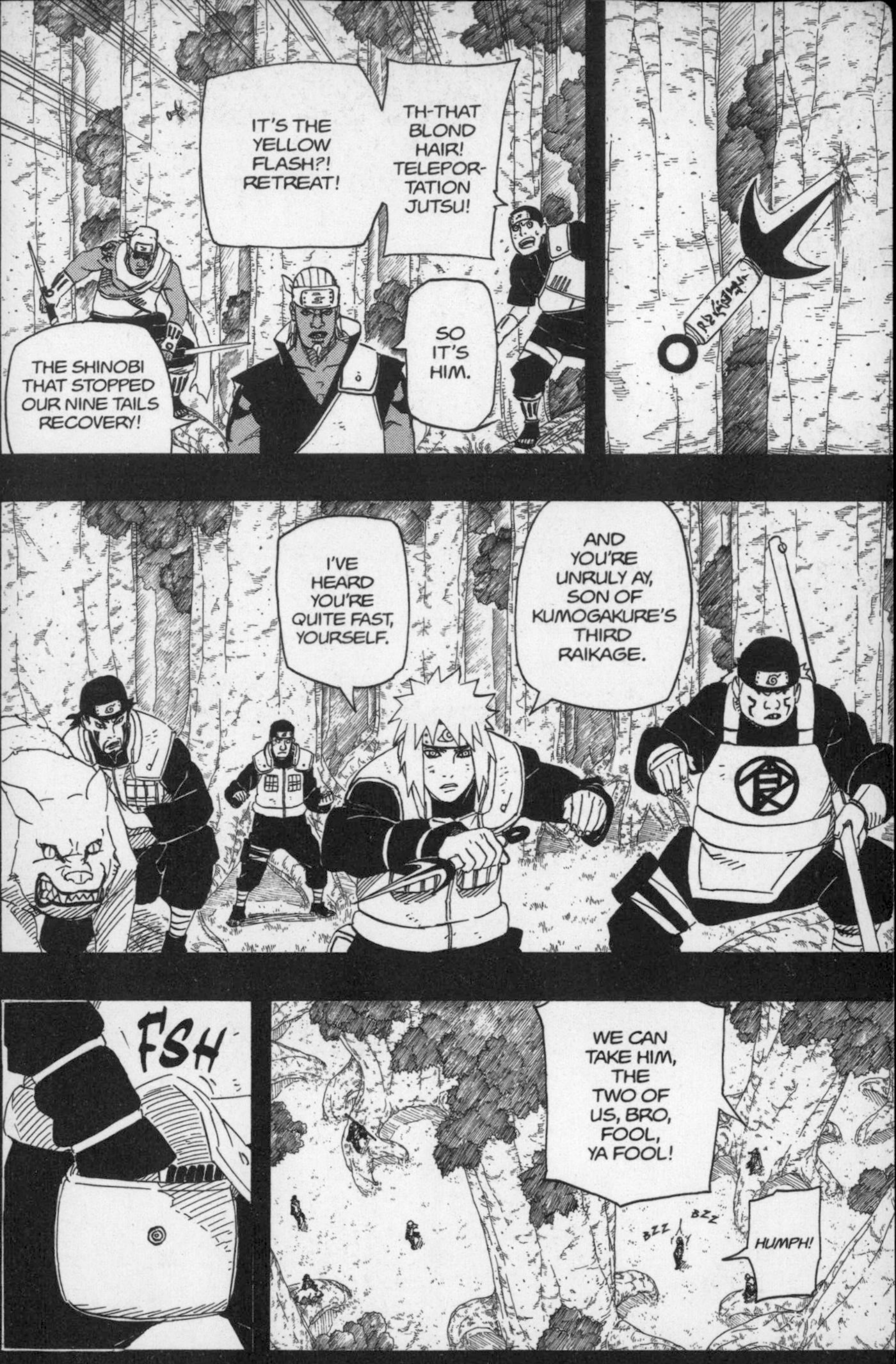
TH-THAT BLOND HAIR! TELEPOR-TATION JUTSU!
IT'S THE YELLOW FLASH?! RETREAT!
SO IT'S HIM.
THE SHINOBI THAT STOPPED OUR NINE TAILS RECOVERY!
AND YOU'RE UNRULY AY, SON OF KUMOGAKURE'S THIRD RAIKAGE.
I'VE HEARD YOU'RE QUITE FAST, YOURSELF.
WE CAN TAKE HIM, THE TWO OF US, BRO, FOOL, YA FOOL!
BZZ
BZZ
HUMPH!
FSH

READ THIS WAY

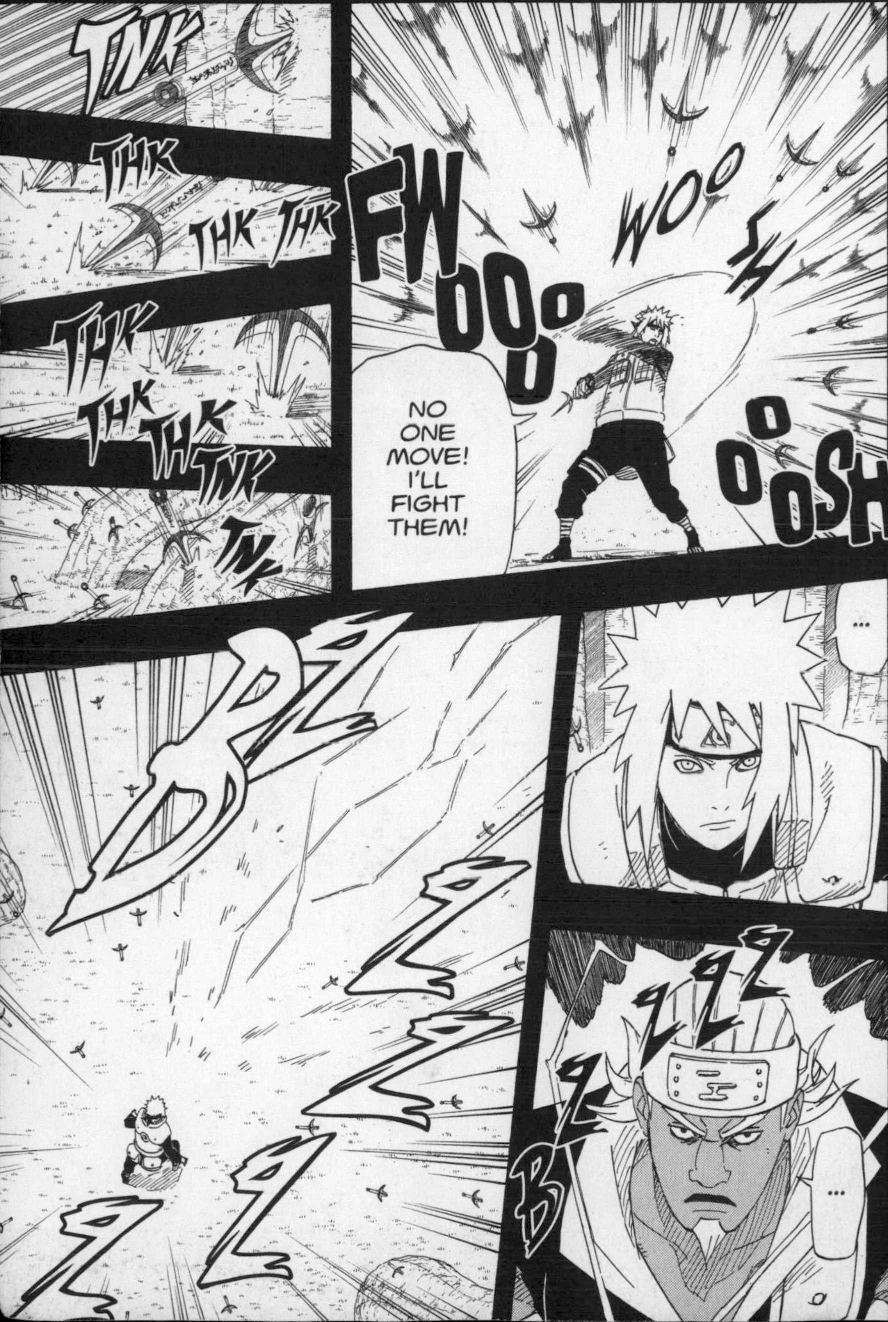
FWOOOO
WOOSH
OOOSH
NO ONE MOVE! I'LL FIGHT THEM!
TNK
THK
THK THK
THK
THK THK
TNK
TNK
...
...

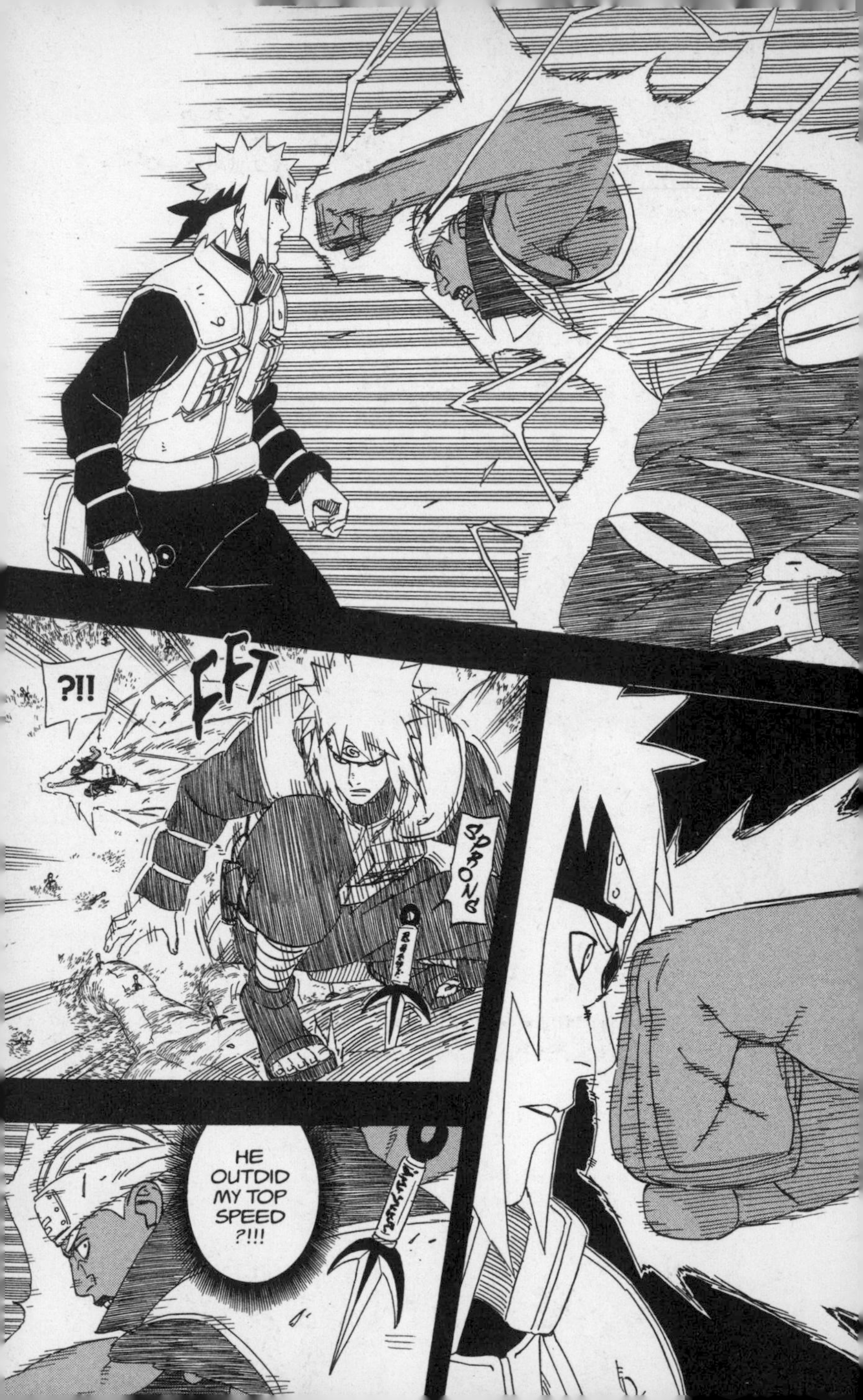
SPRONG
EFT
?!!
HE OUTDID MY TOP SPEED ?!!!

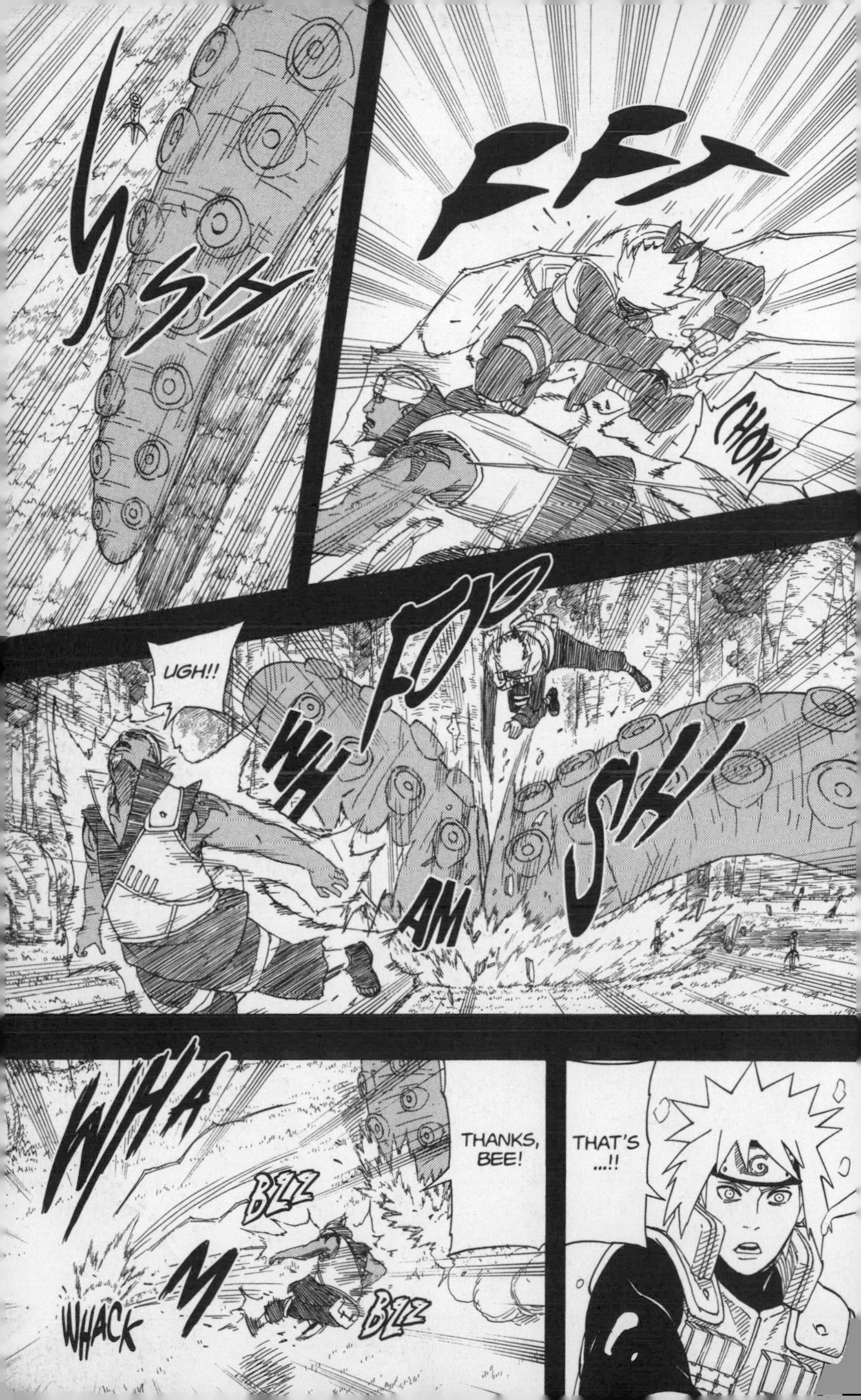

FFT
CHOK
UGH!!
WHAM
THAT'S ...!!
THANKS, BEE!
WHAM
BZZ
BZZ
WHACK

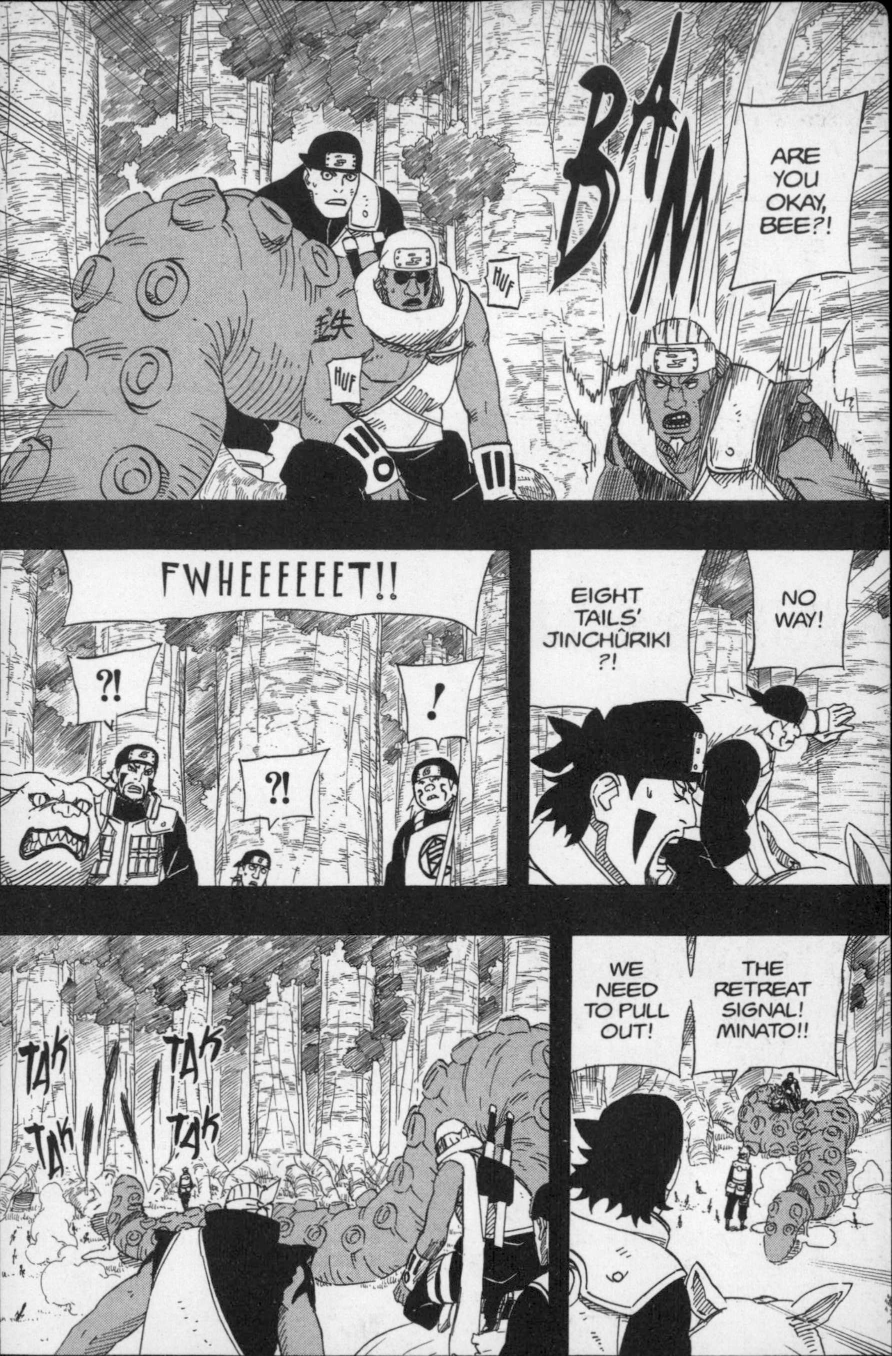
ARE YOU OKAY, BEE?!
BAM
HUF
HUF
NO WAY!
EIGHT TAILS' JINCHÛRIKI ?!
FWHEEEEEET!!
!
?!
?!
THE RETREAT SIGNAL! MINATO!!
WE NEED TO PULL OUT!
TAK
TAK
TAK
TAK

READ THIS WAY

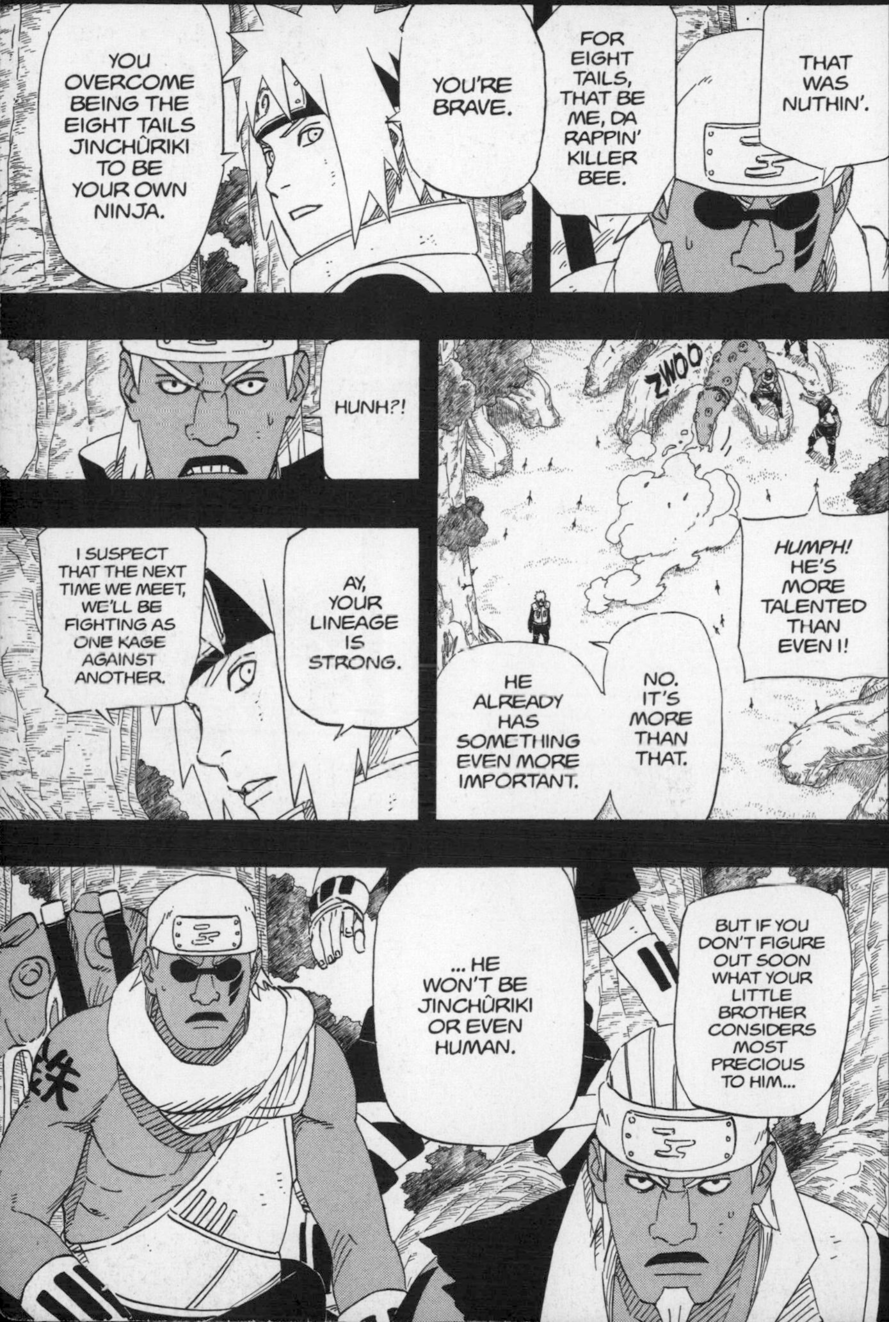
THAT WAS NUTHIN'.
FOR EIGHT TAILS, THAT BE ME, DA RAPPIN' KILLER BEE.
YOU'RE BRAVE.
YOU OVERCOME BEING THE EIGHT TAILS JINCHÛRIKI TO BE YOUR OWN NINJA.
ZWOO
HUMPH! HE'S MORE TALENTED THAN EVEN I!
NO. IT'S MORE THAN THAT.
HE ALREADY HAS SOMETHING EVEN MORE IMPORTANT.
HUNH?!
AY, YOUR LINEAGE IS STRONG.
I SUSPECT THAT THE NEXT TIME WE MEET, WE'LL BE FIGHTING AS ONE KAGE AGAINST ANOTHER.
BUT IF YOU DON'T FIGURE OUT SOON WHAT YOUR LITTLE BROTHER CONSIDERS MOST PRECIOUS TO HIM...
... HE WON'T BE JINCHÛRIKI OR EVEN HUMAN.

NARUTO

Number 543: Truer Words

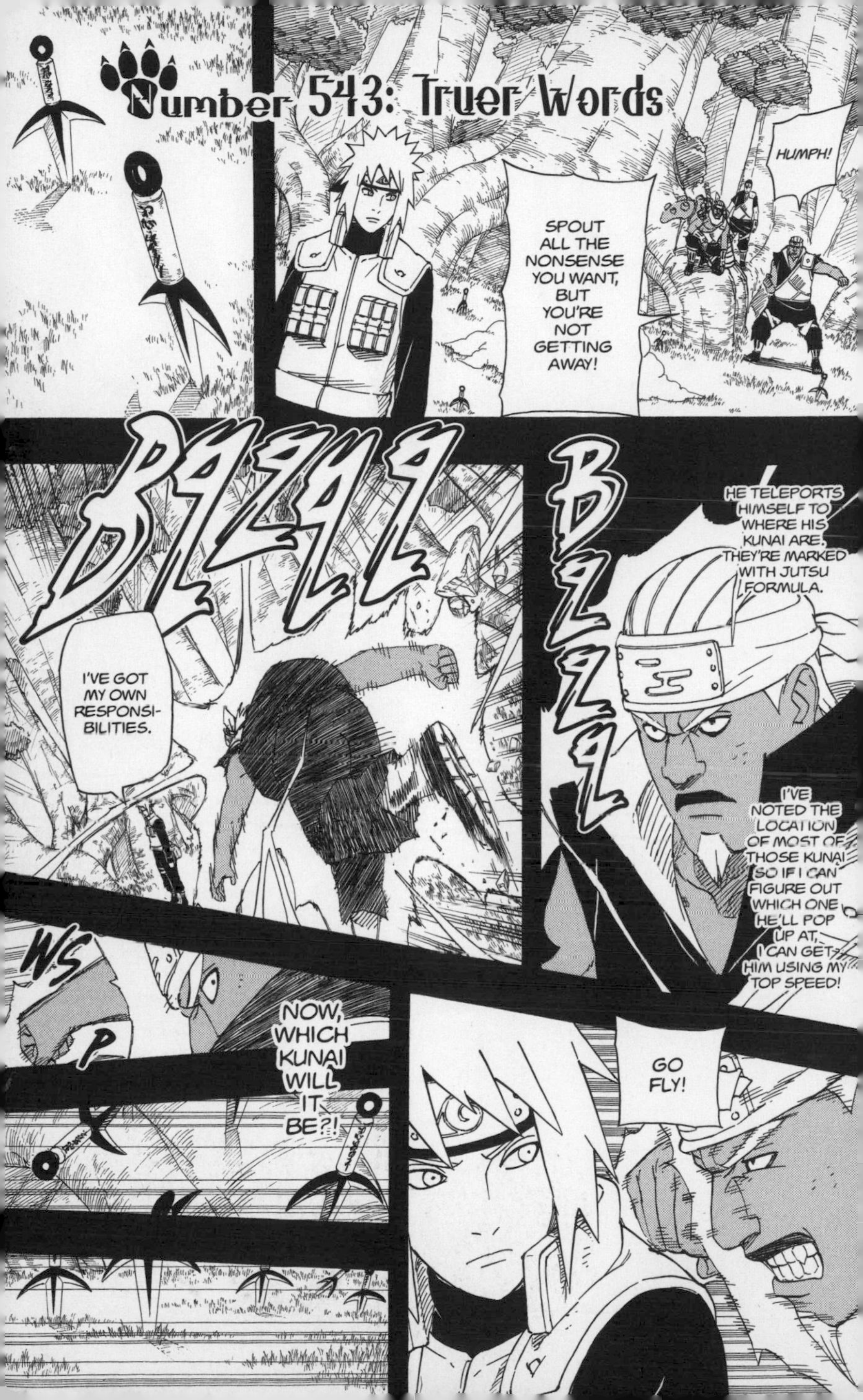
HUMPH!
SPOUT ALL THE NONSENSE YOU WANT, BUT YOU'RE NOT GETTING AWAY!
HE TELEPORTS HIMSELF TO WHERE HIS KUNAI ARE. THEY'RE MARKED WITH JUTSU FORMULA.
I'VE NOTED THE LOCATION OF MOST OF THOSE KUNAI SO IF I CAN FIGURE OUT WHICH ONE HE'LL POP UP AT, I CAN GET HIM USING MY TOP SPEED!
I'VE GOT MY OWN RESPONSI-BILITIES.
GO FLY!
NOW, WHICH KUNAI WILL IT BE?!

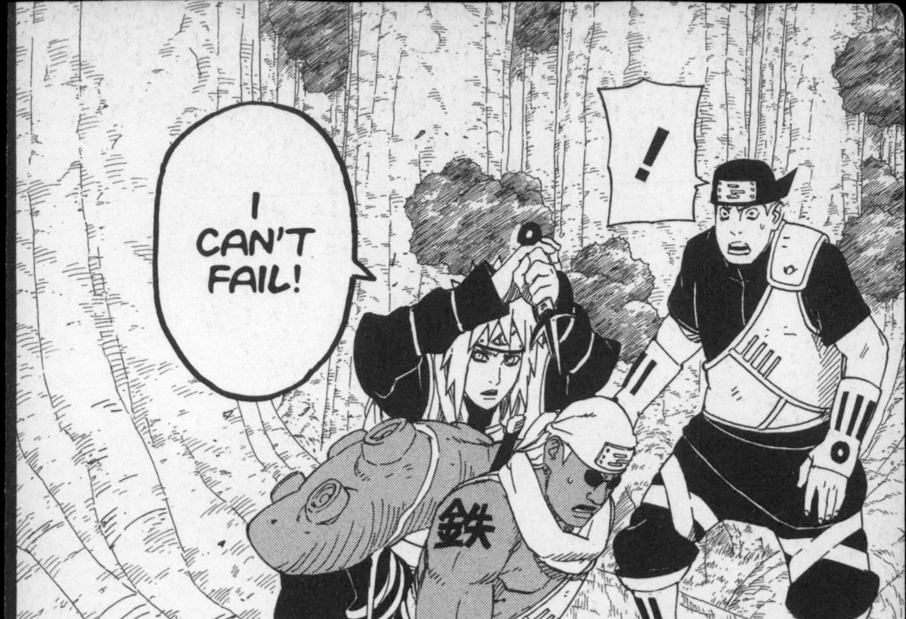
!
I CAN'T FAIL!

Number 543: Truer Words

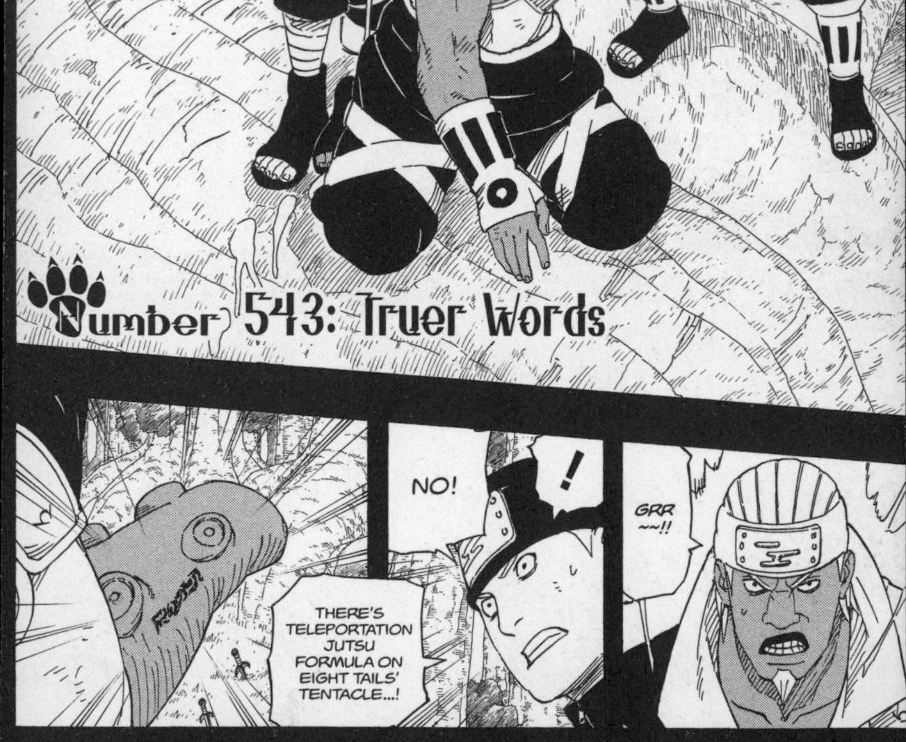
GRR ~~!!
!
NO!
THERE'S TELEPORTATION JUTSU FORMULA ON EIGHT TAILS' TENTACLE...!

READ THIS WAY

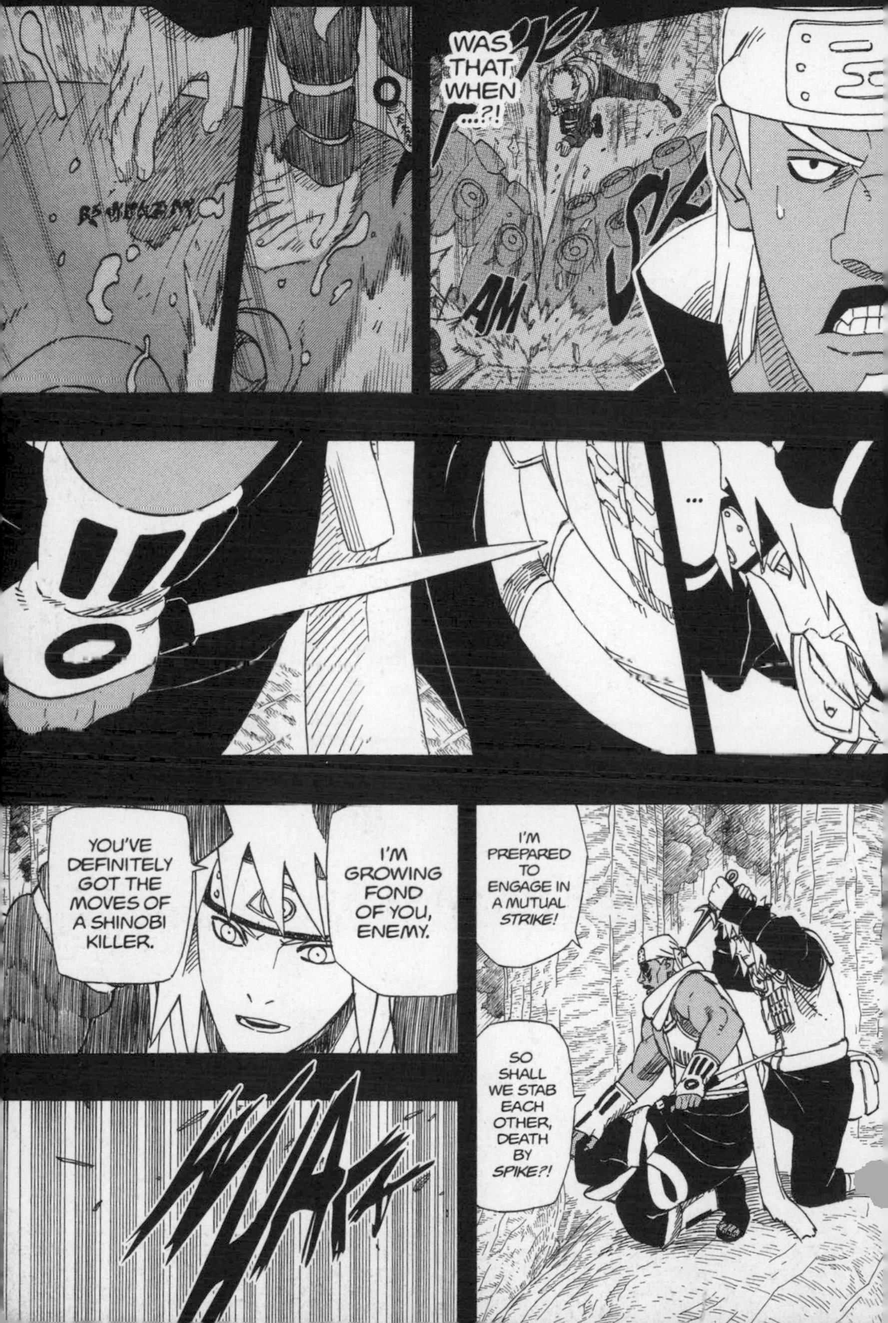
WAS THAT WHEN ...?!
...
I'M PREPARED TO ENGAGE IN A MUTUAL STRIKE!
SO SHALL WE STAB EACH OTHER, DEATH BY SPIKE?!
I'M GROWING FOND OF YOU, ENEMY.
YOU'VE DEFINITELY GOT THE MOVES OF A SHINOBI KILLER.

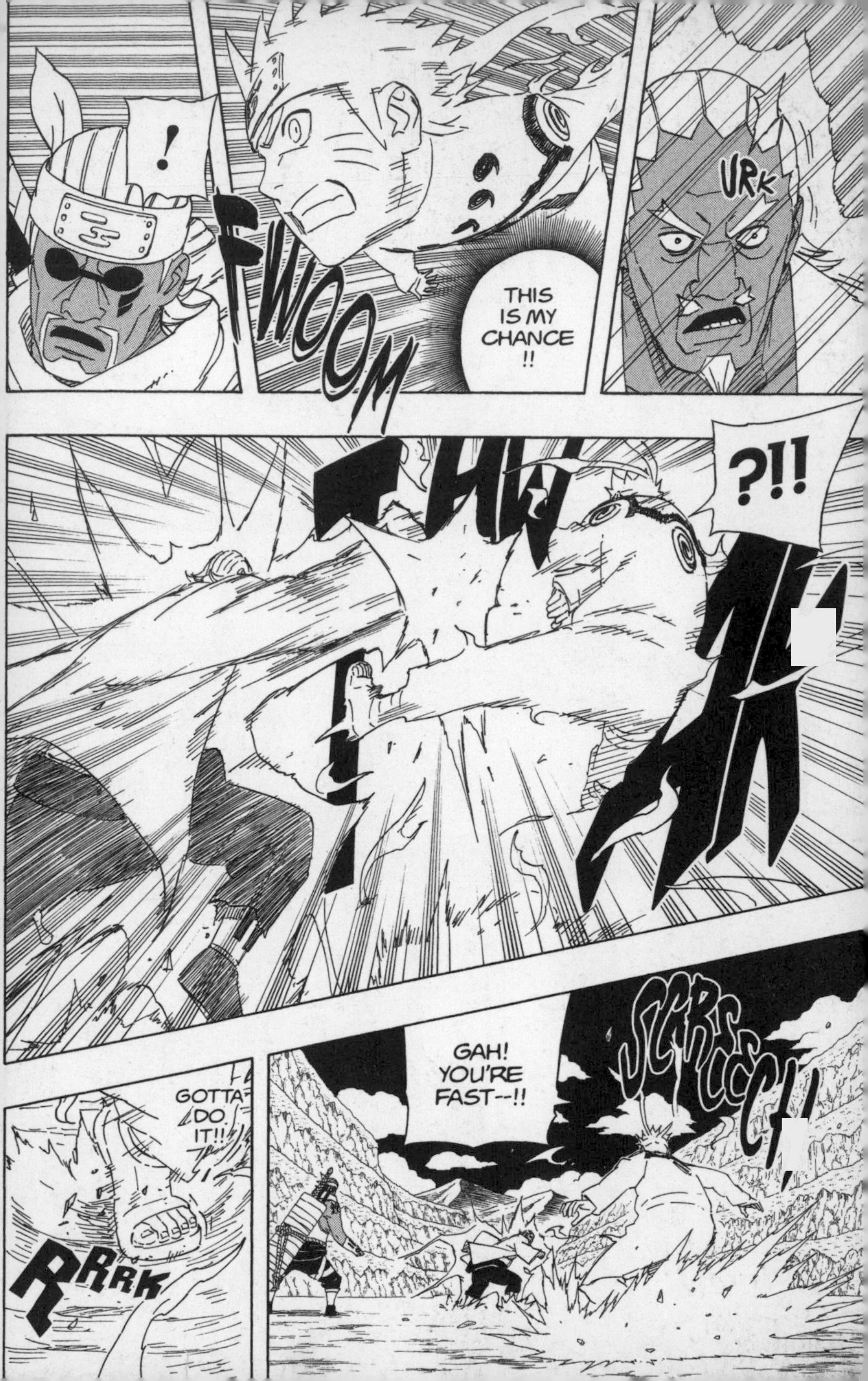
URK
THIS IS MY CHANCE !!
FWOOM
!
?!!
GAH! YOU'RE FAST--!!
SCREECH
GOTTA DO IT!!
RRRK

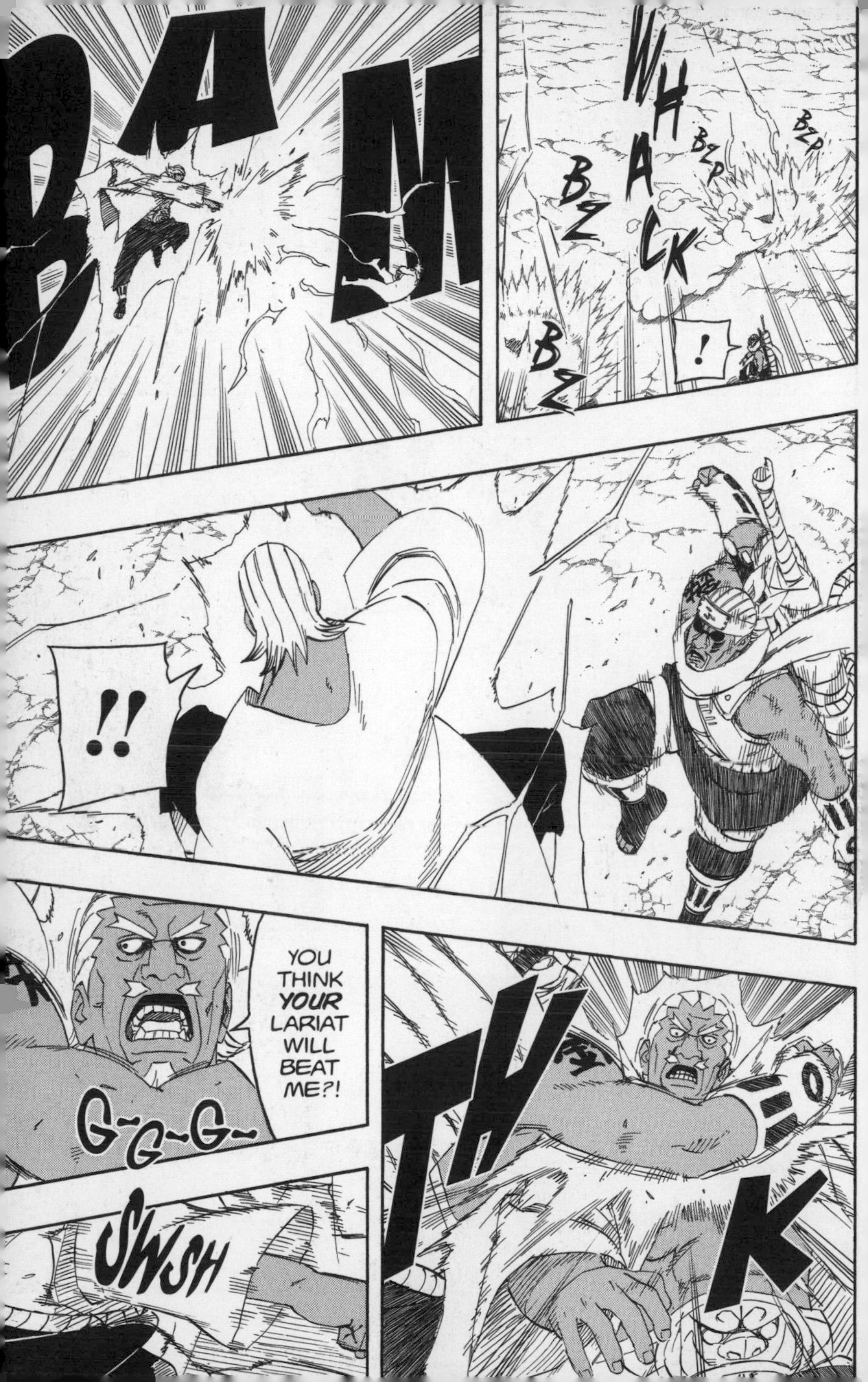
WHACK
BZP
BZP
BZ
BZ
!
BAM
!!
THK
YOU THINK YOUR LARIAT WILL BEAT ME?!
G-G-G-
SWSH

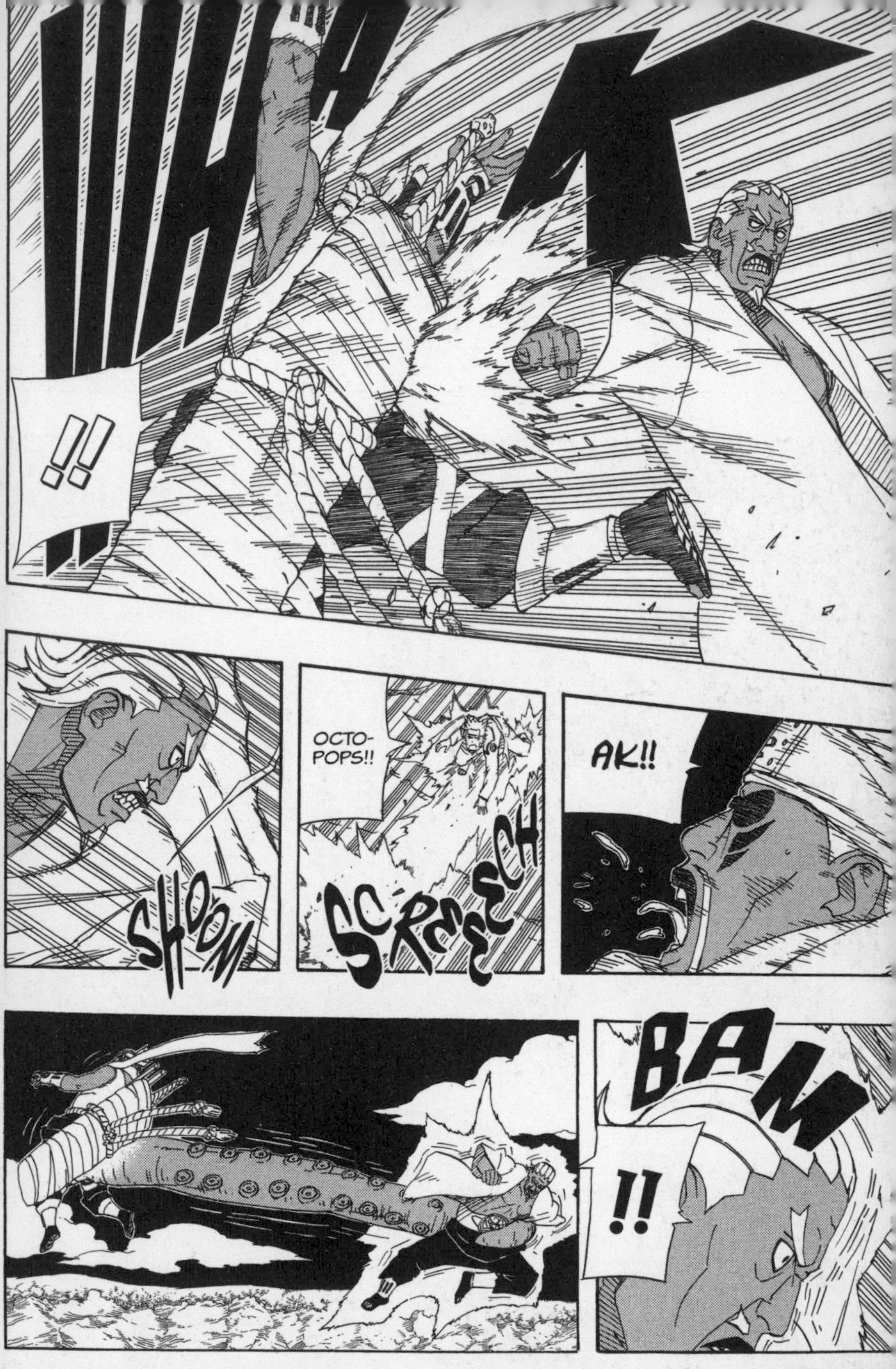
WHAK
!!
AK!!
OCTO-POPS!!
SCREEECH
SHOOM
BAM
!!

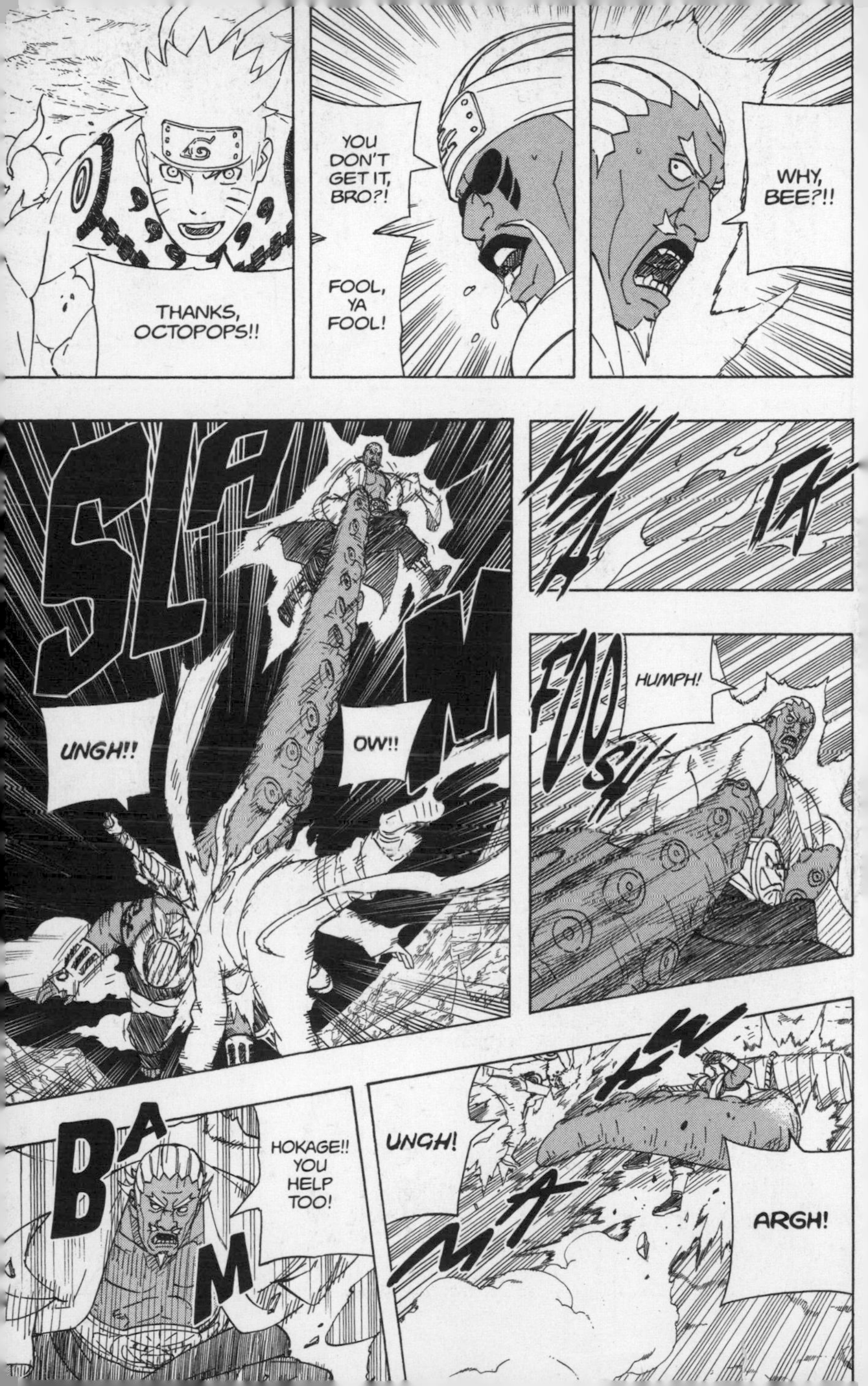
WHY, BEE?!!
YOU DON'T GET IT, BRO?!
FOOL, YA FOOL!
THANKS, OCTOPOPS!!
FOOSH
HUMPH!
SLAM
OW!!
UNGH!!
ARGH!
UNGH!
BAM
HOKAGE!! YOU HELP TOO!

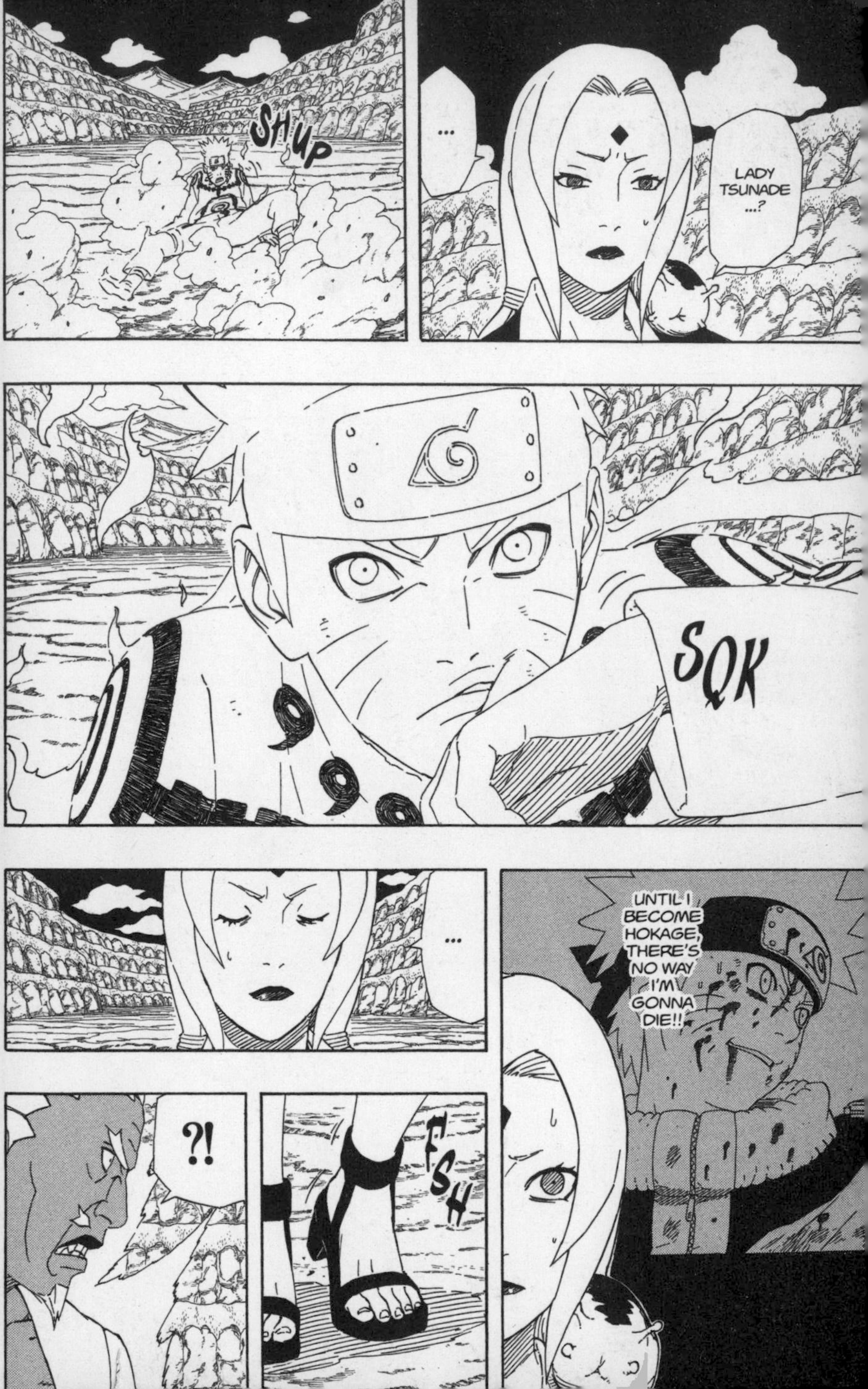
LADY TSUNADE ...?
...
SHUP
SQK
UNTIL I BECOME HOKAGE, THERE'S NO WAY I'M GONNA DIE!!
...
FSH
?!

READ THIS WAY

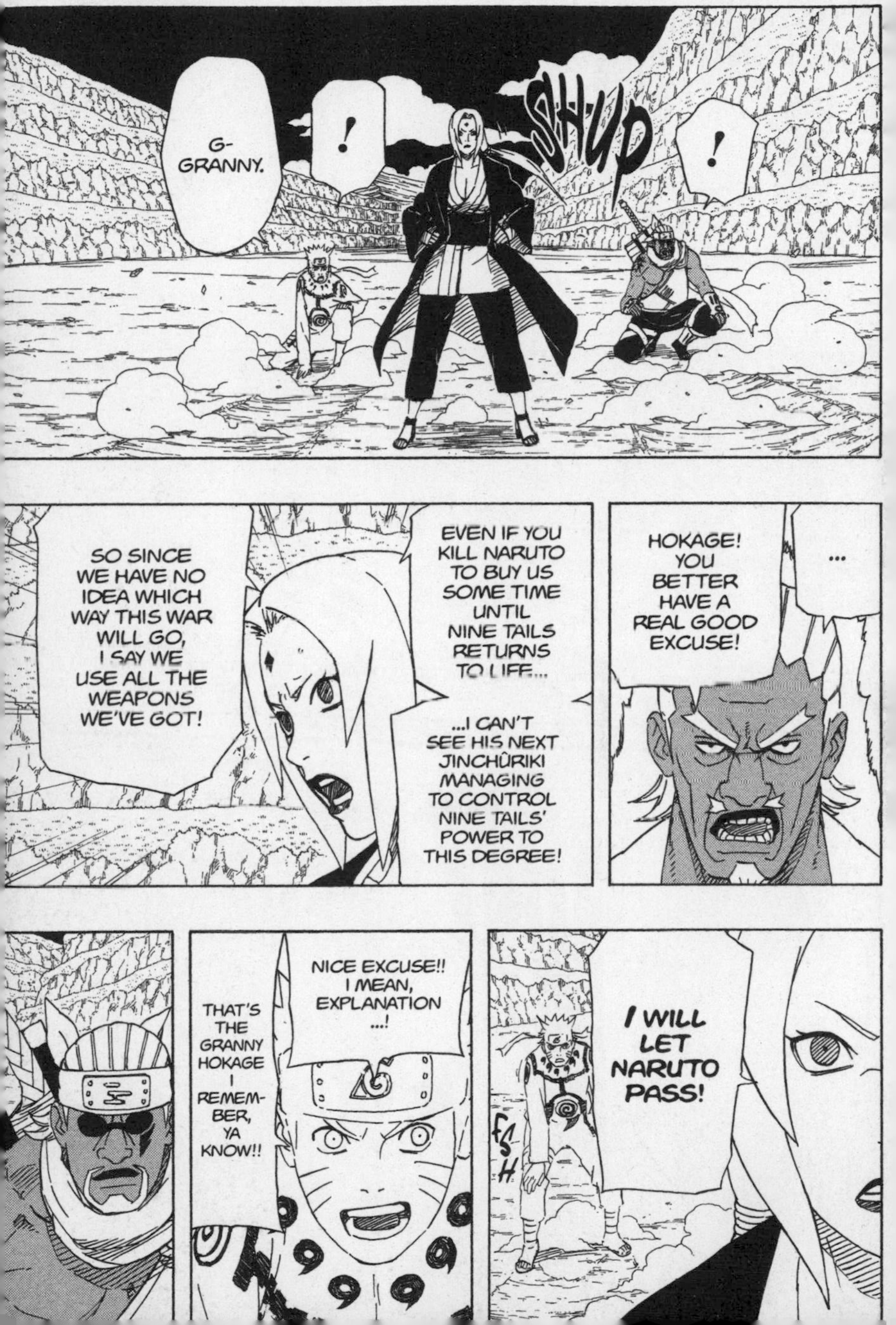
!
SHUP
!
G-GRANNY.
...
HOKAGE! YOU BETTER HAVE A REAL GOOD EXCUSE!
EVEN IF YOU KILL NARUTO TO BUY US SOME TIME UNTIL NINE TAILS RETURNS TO LIFE...
...I CAN'T SEE HIS NEXT JINCHÛRIKI MANAGING TO CONTROL NINE TAILS' POWER TO THIS DEGREE!
SO SINCE WE HAVE NO IDEA WHICH WAY THIS WAR WILL GO, I SAY WE USE ALL THE WEAPONS WE'VE GOT!
I WILL LET NARUTO PASS!
FSH
NICE EXCUSE!! I MEAN, EXPLANATION ...!
THAT'S THE GRANNY HOKAGE I REMEMBER, YA KNOW!!

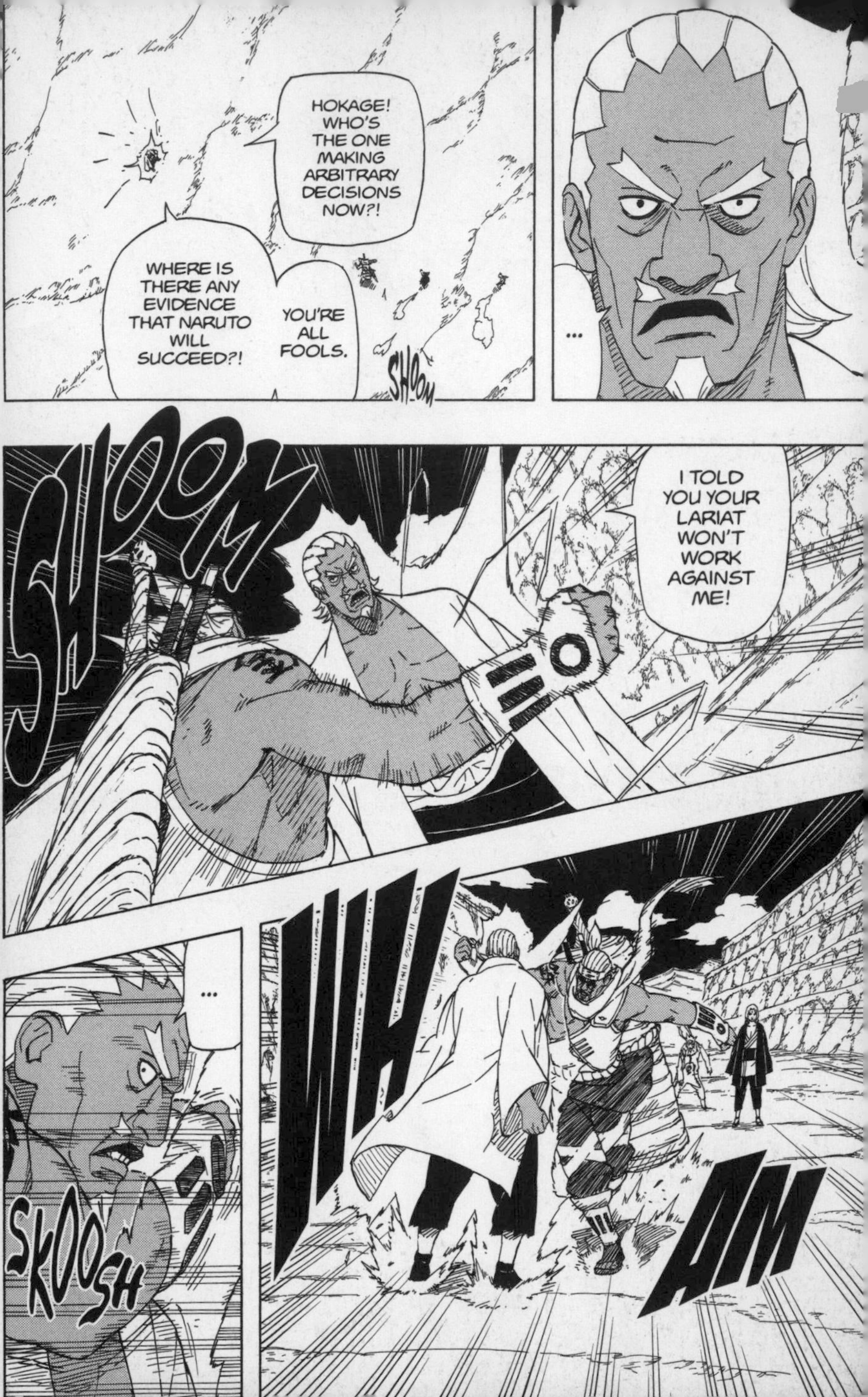
...
HOKAGE! WHO'S THE ONE MAKING ARBITRARY DECISIONS NOW?!
WHERE IS THERE ANY EVIDENCE THAT NARUTO WILL SUCCEED?!
YOU'RE ALL FOOLS.
SHOOM
I TOLD YOU YOUR LARIAT WON'T WORK AGAINST ME!
SHOOM
WHAM
...
SKOOSH

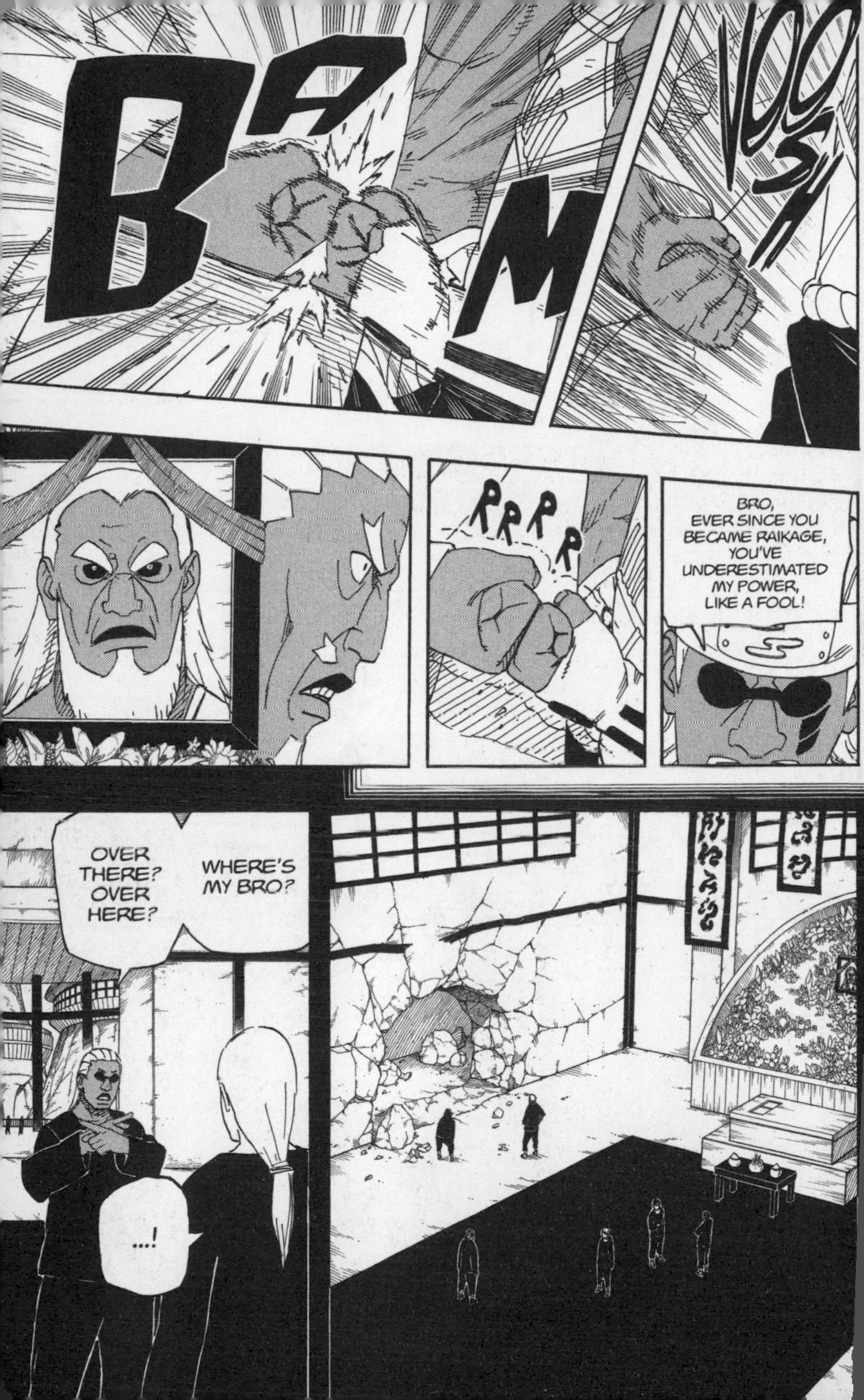
VOOSH
BAM
BRO, EVER SINCE YOU BECAME RAIKAGE, YOU'VE UNDERESTIMATED MY POWER, LIKE A FOOL!
RRRR
WHERE'S MY BRO?
OVER THERE? OVER HERE?
...!

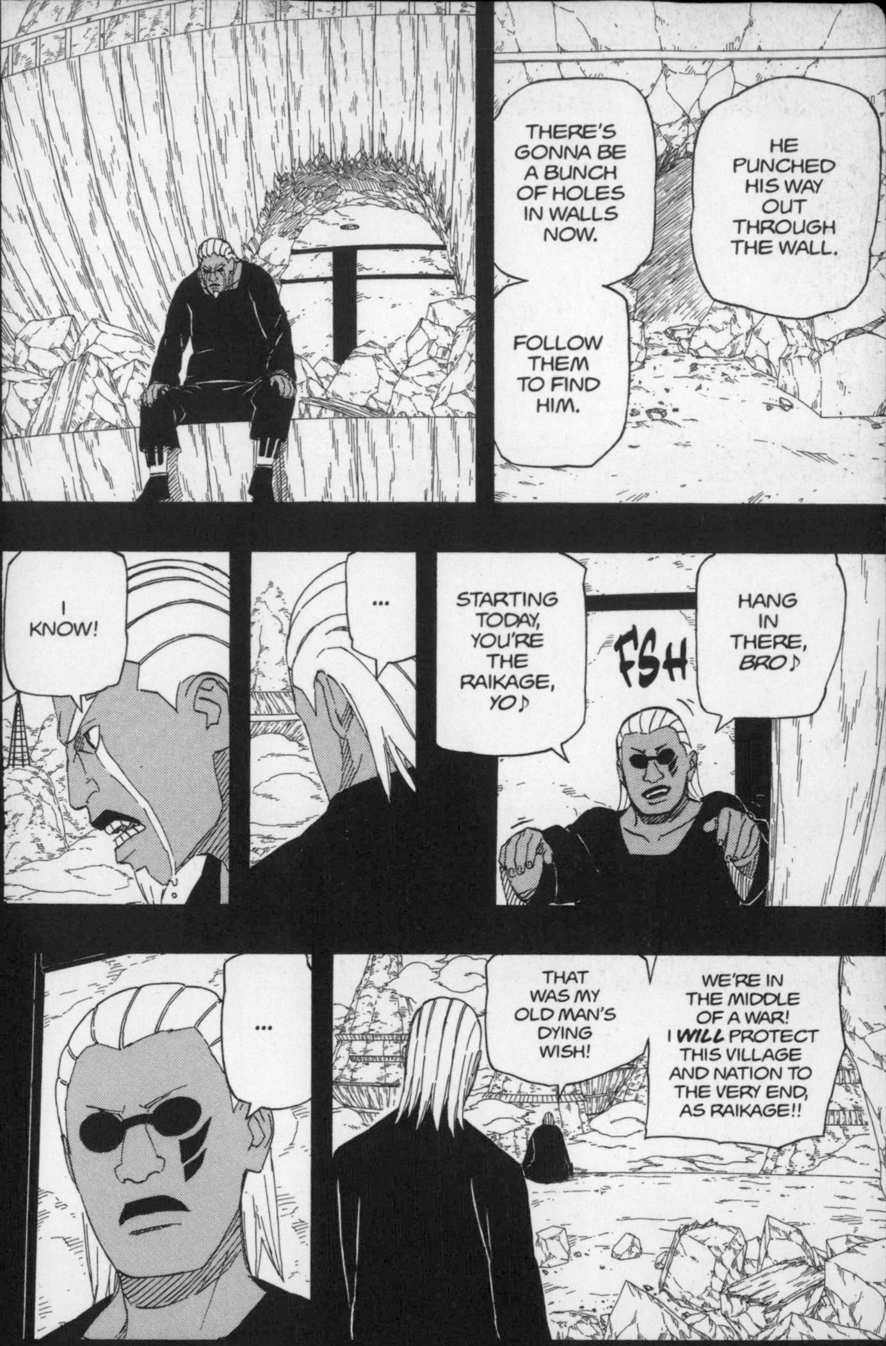
HE PUNCHED HIS WAY OUT THROUGH THE WALL.
THERE'S GONNA BE A BUNCH OF HOLES IN WALLS NOW.
FOLLOW THEM TO FIND HIM.
HANG IN THERE, BRO♪
FSH
STARTING TODAY, YOU'RE THE RAIKAGE, YO♪
...
I KNOW!
WE'RE IN THE MIDDLE OF A WAR! I WILL PROTECT THIS VILLAGE AND NATION TO THE VERY END, AS RAIKAGE!!
THAT WAS MY OLD MAN'S DYING WISH!
...

READ THIS WAY

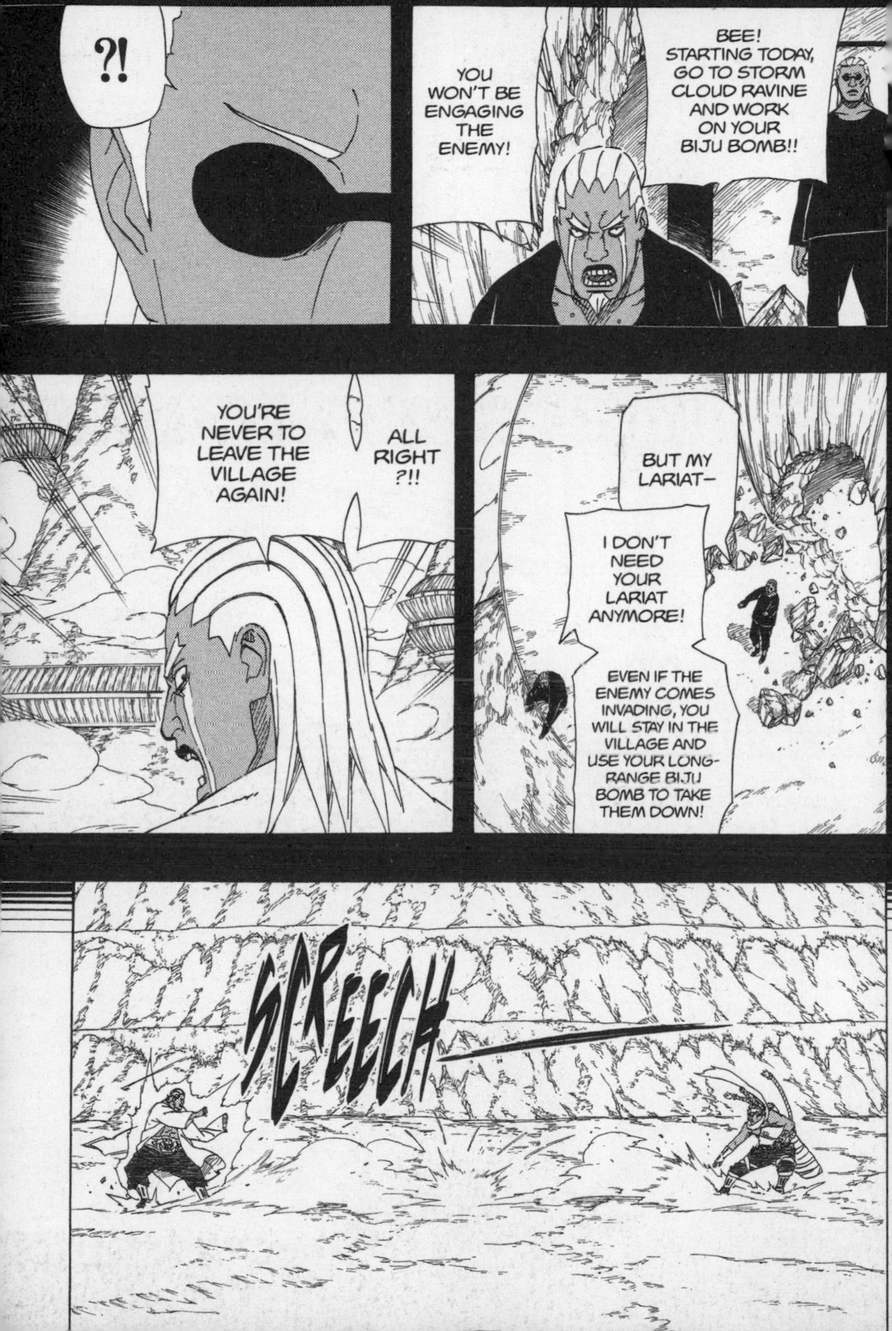
BEE! STARTING TODAY, GO TO STORM CLOUD RAVINE AND WORK ON YOUR BIJU BOMB!!
YOU WON'T BE ENGAGING THE ENEMY!
?!
BUT MY LARIAT—
I DON'T NEED YOUR LARIAT ANYMORE!
EVEN IF THE ENEMY COMES INVADING, YOU WILL STAY IN THE VILLAGE AND USE YOUR LONG-RANGE BIJU BOMB TO TAKE THEM DOWN!
YOU'RE NEVER TO LEAVE THE VILLAGE AGAIN!
ALL RIGHT ?!!
SCREECH

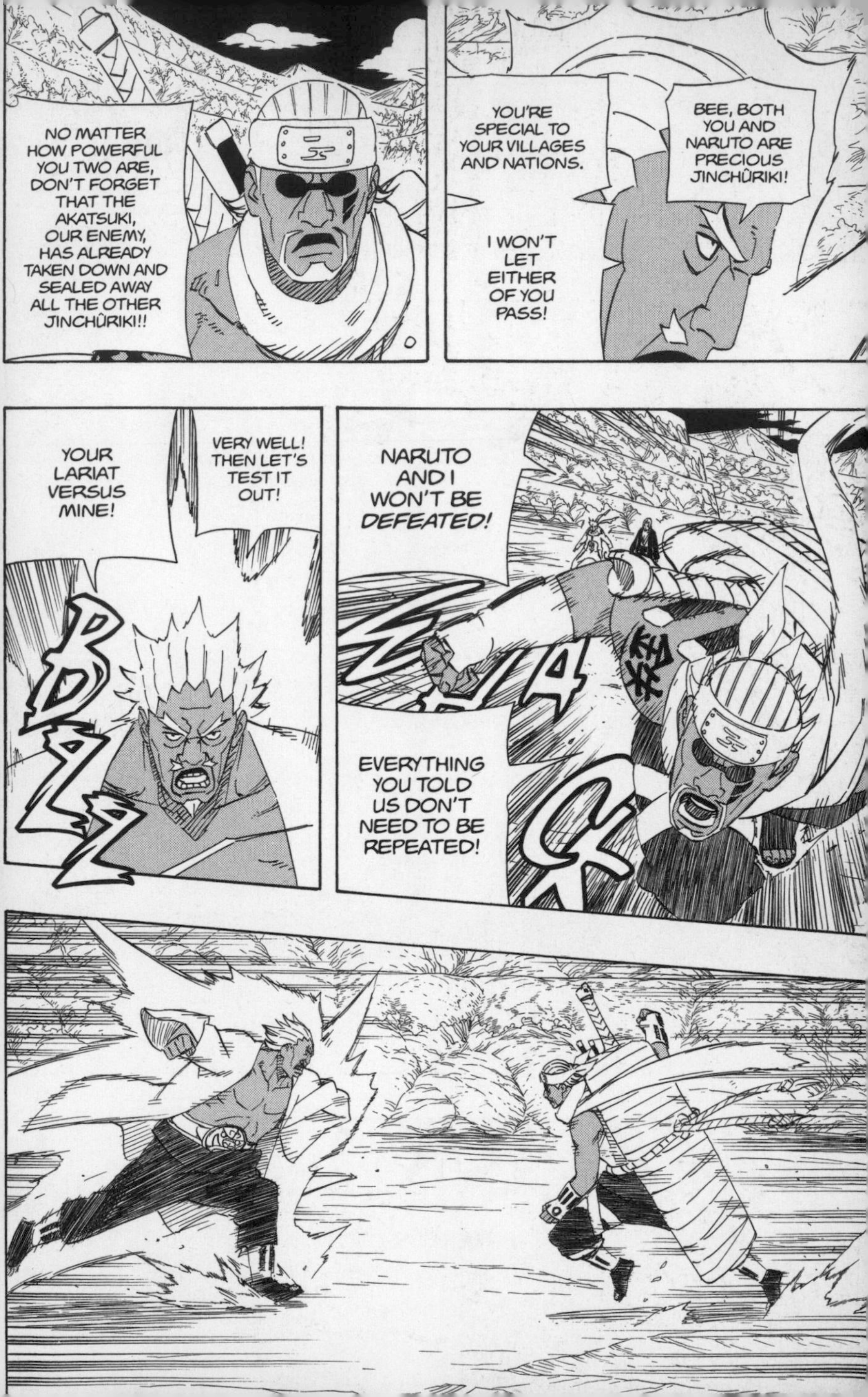
BEE, BOTH YOU AND NARUTO ARE PRECIOUS JINCHÛRIKI!
YOU'RE SPECIAL TO YOUR VILLAGES AND NATIONS.
I WON'T LET EITHER OF YOU PASS!
NO MATTER HOW POWERFUL YOU TWO ARE, DON'T FORGET THAT THE AKATSUKI, OUR ENEMY, HAS ALREADY TAKEN DOWN AND SEALED AWAY ALL THE OTHER JINCHÛRIKI!!
NARUTO AND I WON'T BE *DEFEATED!*
EVERYTHING YOU TOLD US DON'T NEED TO BE REPEATED!
VERY WELL! THEN LET'S TEST IT OUT!
YOUR LARIAT VERSUS MINE!

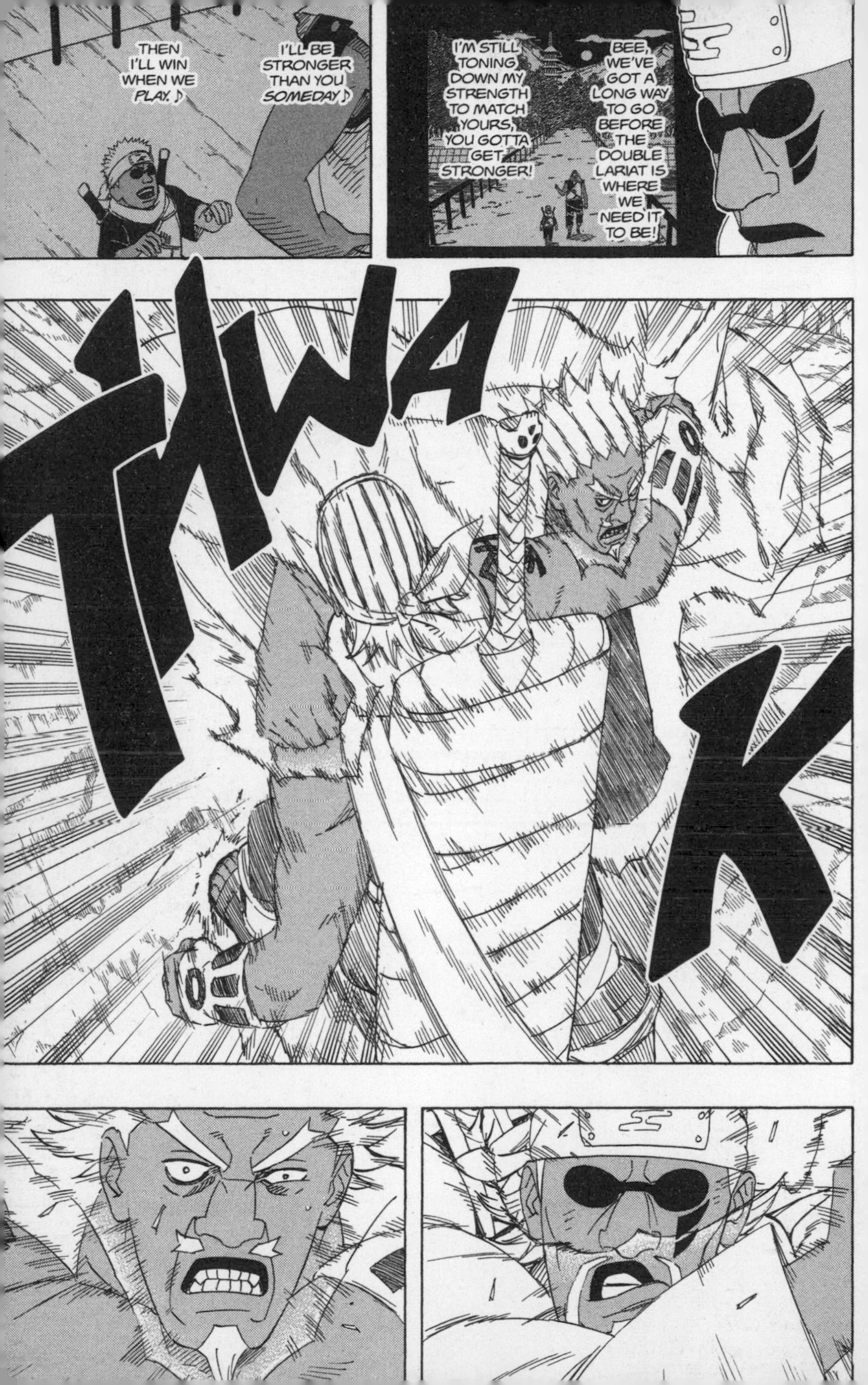
BEE, WE'VE GOT A LONG WAY TO GO BEFORE THE DOUBLE LARIAT IS WHERE WE NEED IT TO BE!
I'M STILL TONING DOWN MY STRENGTH TO MATCH YOURS, YOU GOTTA GET STRONGER!
I'LL BE STRONGER THAN YOU *SOMEDAY*♪
THEN I'LL WIN WHEN WE *PLAY*.♪
THWAK

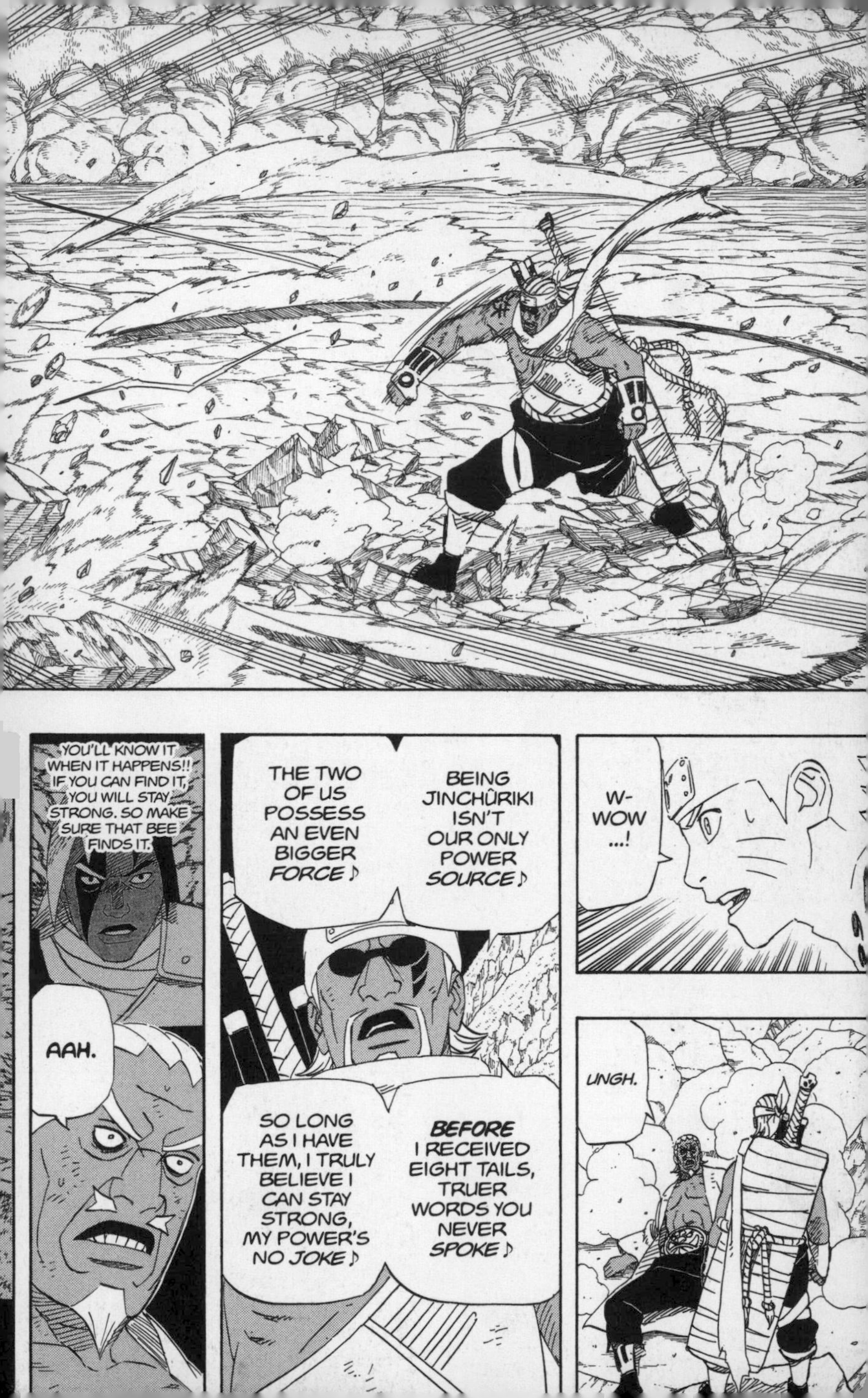
W-WOW...!
UNGH.
BEING JINCHÛRIKI ISN'T OUR ONLY POWER SOURCE♪
THE TWO OF US POSSESS AN EVEN BIGGER FORCE♪
BEFORE I RECEIVED EIGHT TAILS, TRUER WORDS YOU NEVER SPOKE♪
SO LONG AS I HAVE THEM, I TRULY BELIEVE I CAN STAY STRONG, MY POWER'S NO JOKE♪
YOU'LL KNOW IT WHEN IT HAPPENS!! IF YOU CAN FIND IT, YOU WILL STAY STRONG. SO MAKE SURE THAT BEE FINDS IT.
AAH.

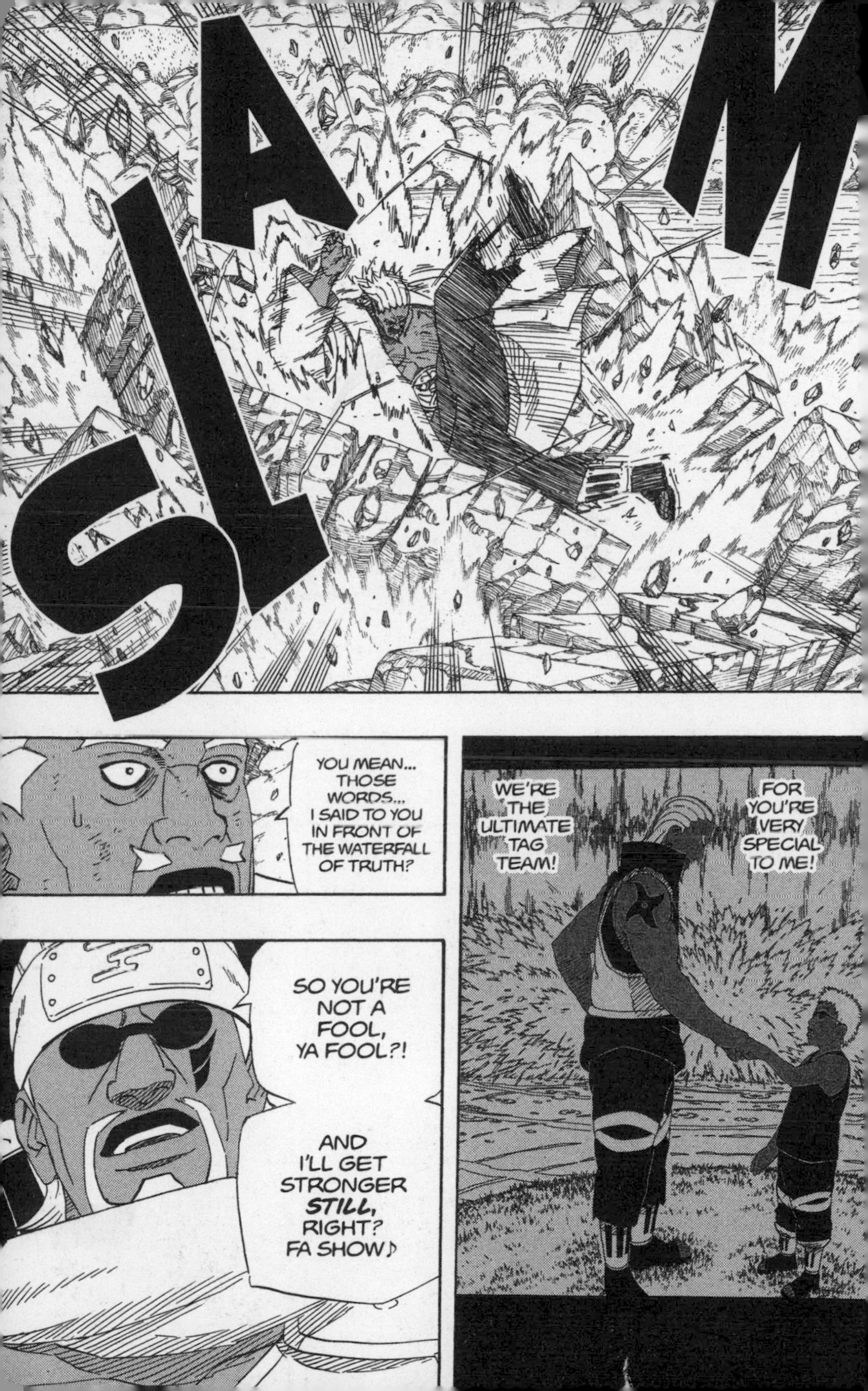
SLAM
FOR YOU'RE VERY SPECIAL TO ME!
WE'RE THE ULTIMATE TAG TEAM!
YOU MEAN... THOSE WORDS... I SAID TO YOU IN FRONT OF THE WATERFALL OF TRUTH?
SO YOU'RE NOT A FOOL, YA FOOL?!
AND I'LL GET STRONGER *STILL*, RIGHT? FA SHOW♪

NARUTO

Number 544: Two Suns!!

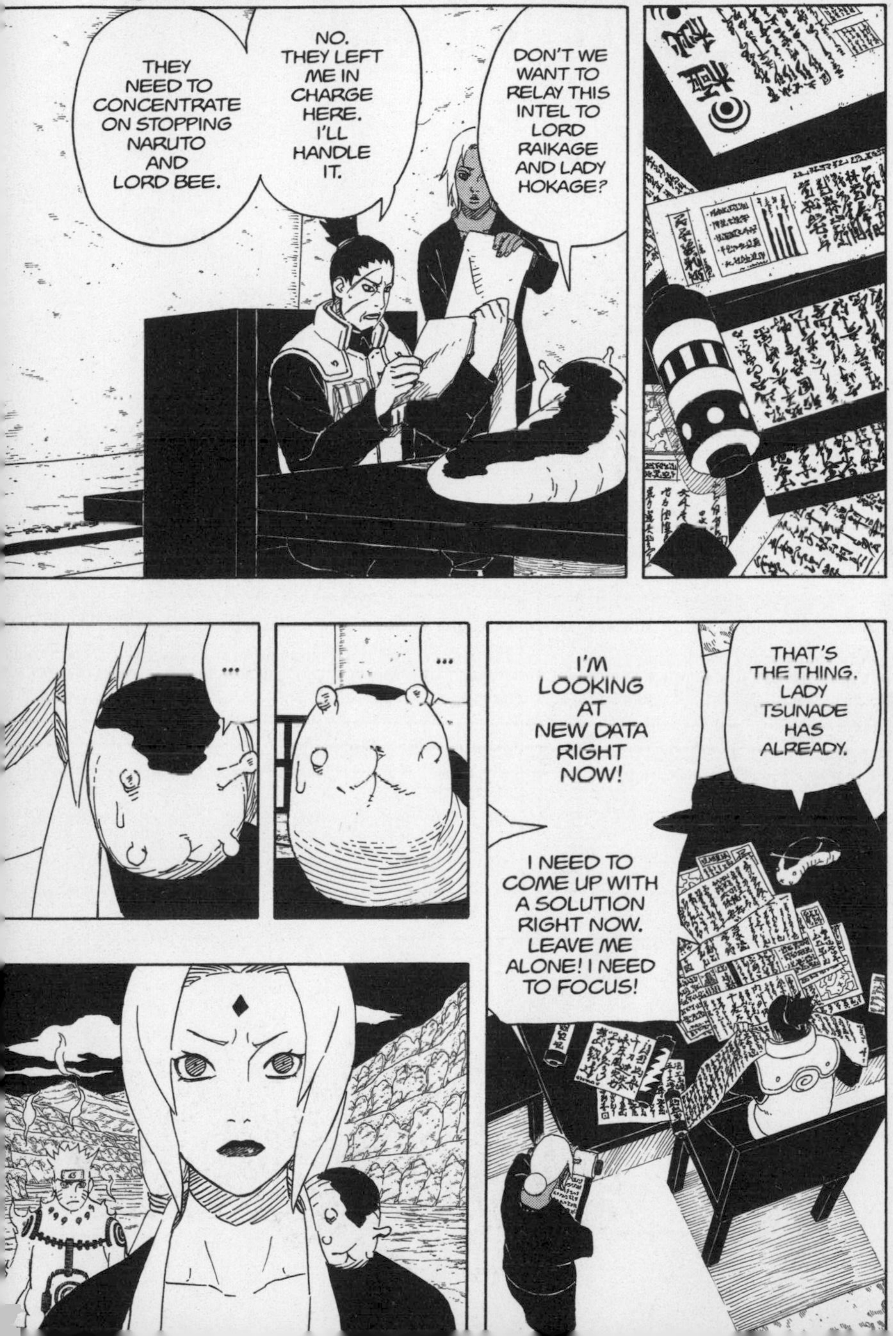

DON'T WE WANT TO RELAY THIS INTEL TO LORD RAIKAGE AND LADY HOKAGE?
NO. THEY LEFT ME IN CHARGE HERE. I'LL HANDLE IT.
THEY NEED TO CONCENTRATE ON STOPPING NARUTO AND LORD BEE.
THAT'S THE THING. LADY TSUNADE HAS ALREADY.
I'M LOOKING AT NEW DATA RIGHT NOW!
I NEED TO COME UP WITH A SOLUTION RIGHT NOW. LEAVE ME ALONE! I NEED TO FOCUS!
...
...

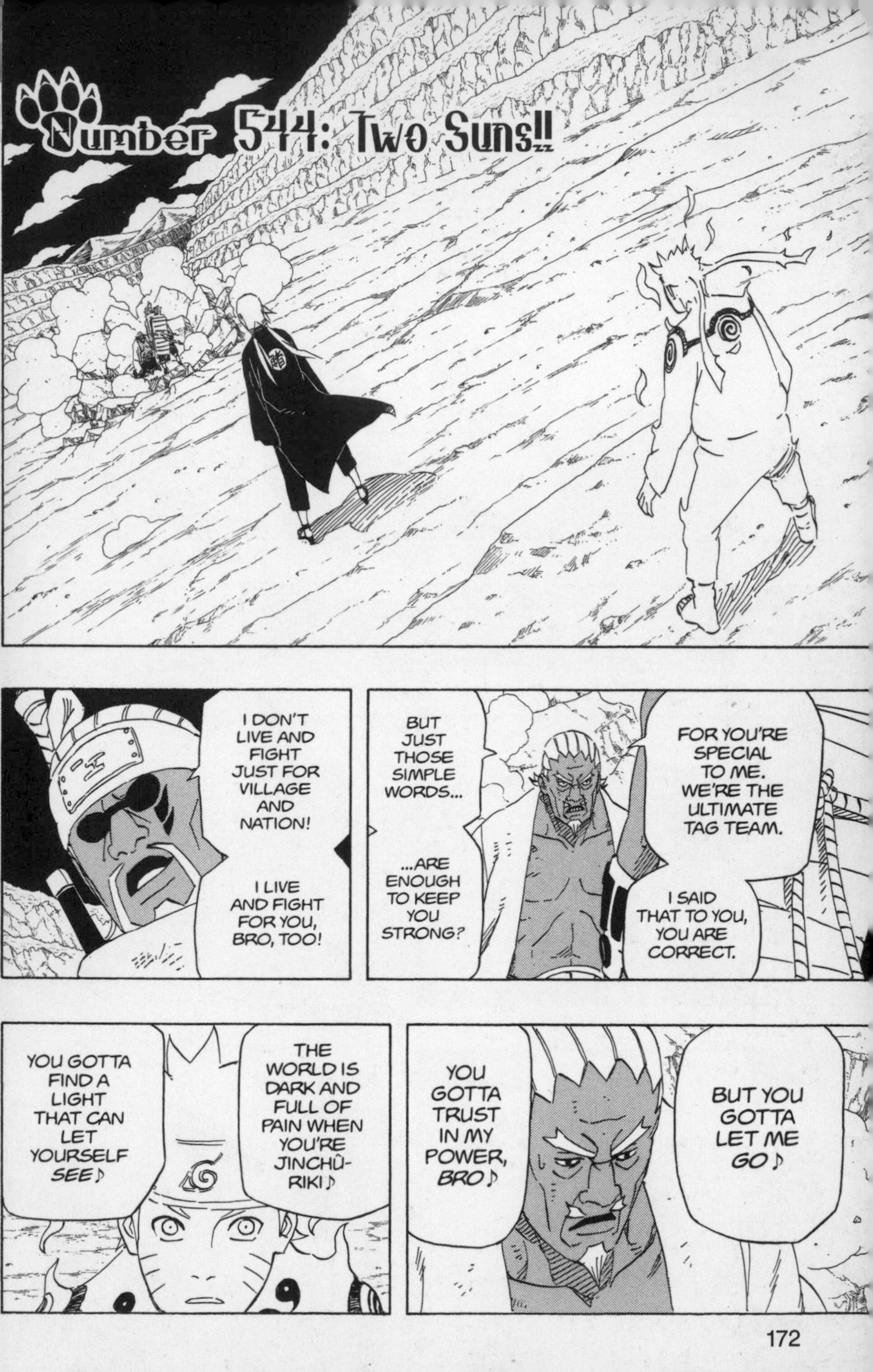
Number 544: Two Suns!!
FOR YOU'RE SPECIAL TO ME. WE'RE THE ULTIMATE TAG TEAM.
I SAID THAT TO YOU, YOU ARE CORRECT.
BUT JUST THOSE SIMPLE WORDS...
...ARE ENOUGH TO KEEP YOU STRONG?
I DON'T LIVE AND FIGHT JUST FOR VILLAGE AND NATION!
I LIVE AND FIGHT FOR YOU, BRO, TOO!
BUT YOU GOTTA LET ME *GO*♪
YOU GOTTA TRUST IN MY POWER, *BRO*♪
THE WORLD IS DARK AND FULL OF PAIN WHEN YOU'RE JINCHÛ-RIKI♪
YOU GOTTA FIND A LIGHT THAT CAN LET YOURSELF *SEE*♪

READ THIS WAY

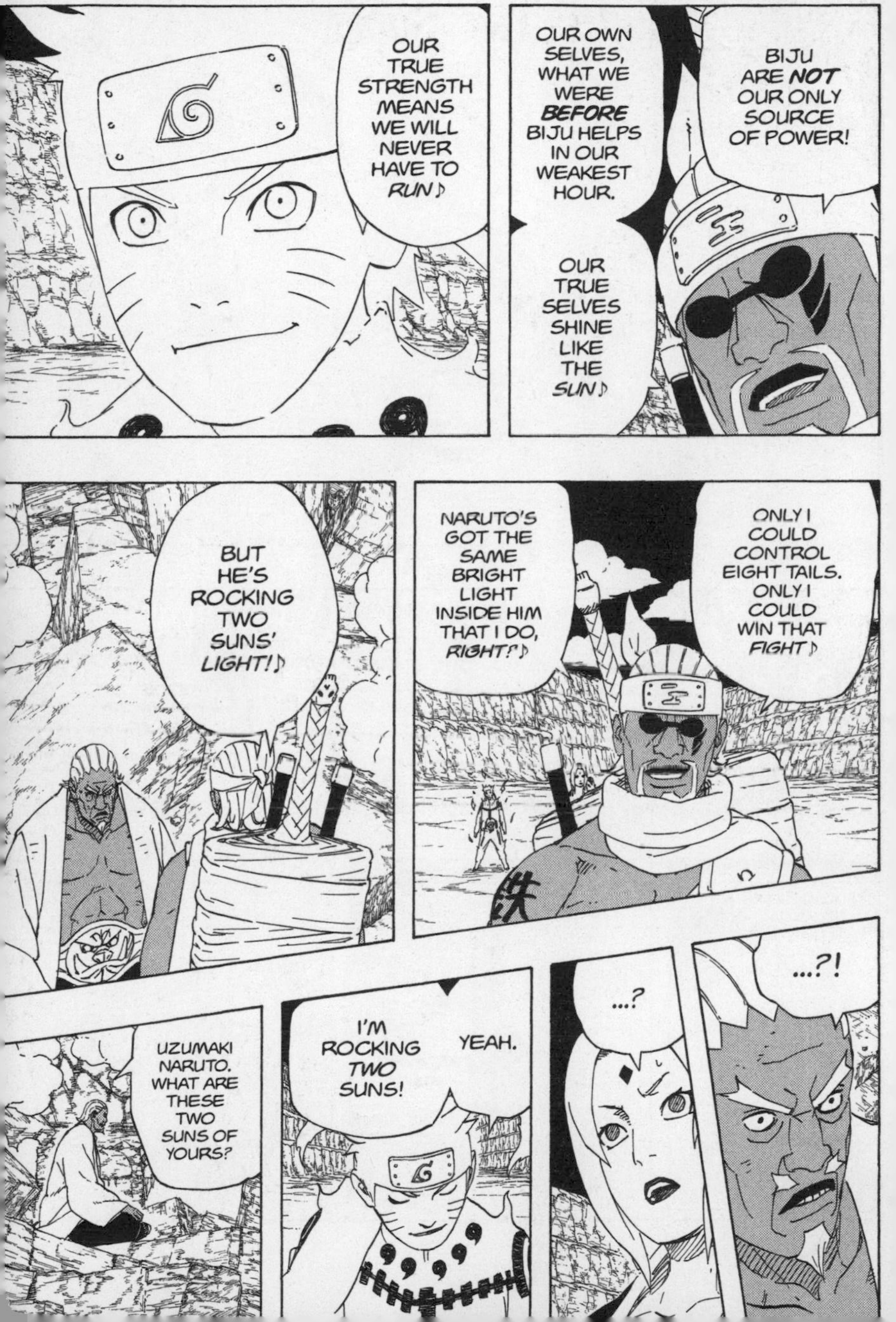
BIJU ARE NOT OUR ONLY SOURCE OF POWER!
OUR OWN SELVES, WHAT WE WERE BEFORE BIJU HELPS IN OUR WEAKEST HOUR.
OUR TRUE SELVES SHINE LIKE THE SUN♪
OUR TRUE STRENGTH MEANS WE WILL NEVER HAVE TO RUN♪
ONLY I COULD CONTROL EIGHT TAILS. ONLY I COULD WIN THAT FIGHT♪
NARUTO'S GOT THE SAME BRIGHT LIGHT INSIDE HIM THAT I DO, RIGHT?♪
BUT HE'S ROCKING TWO SUNS' LIGHT!♪
...?!
...?
YEAH.
I'M ROCKING TWO SUNS!
UZUMAKI NARUTO. WHAT ARE THESE TWO SUNS OF YOURS?

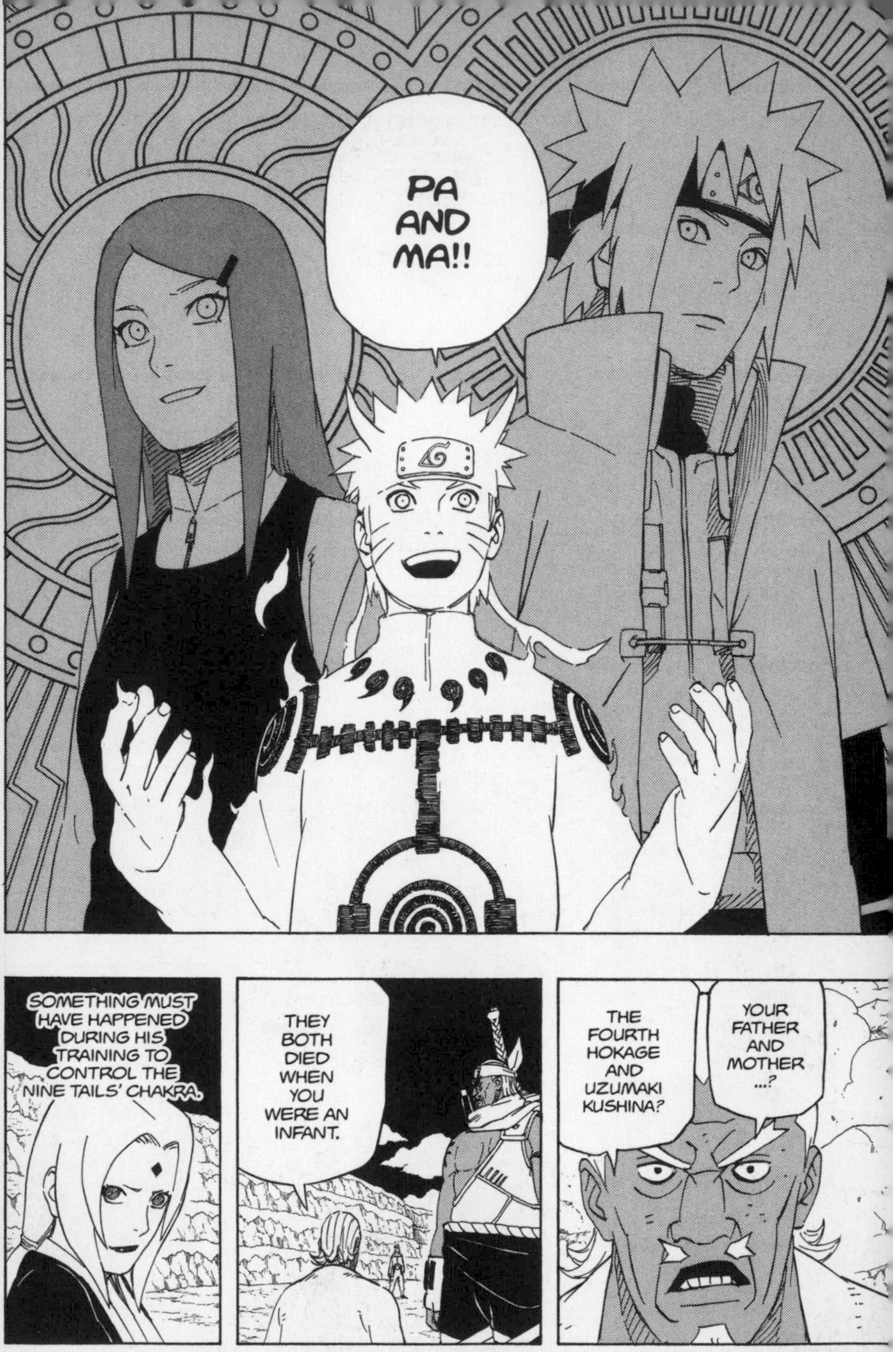
PA AND MA!!
YOUR FATHER AND MOTHER ...?
THE FOURTH HOKAGE AND UZUMAKI KUSHINA?
THEY BOTH DIED WHEN YOU WERE AN INFANT.
SOMETHING MUST HAVE HAPPENED DURING HIS TRAINING TO CONTROL THE NINE TAILS' CHAKRA.

READ THIS WAY

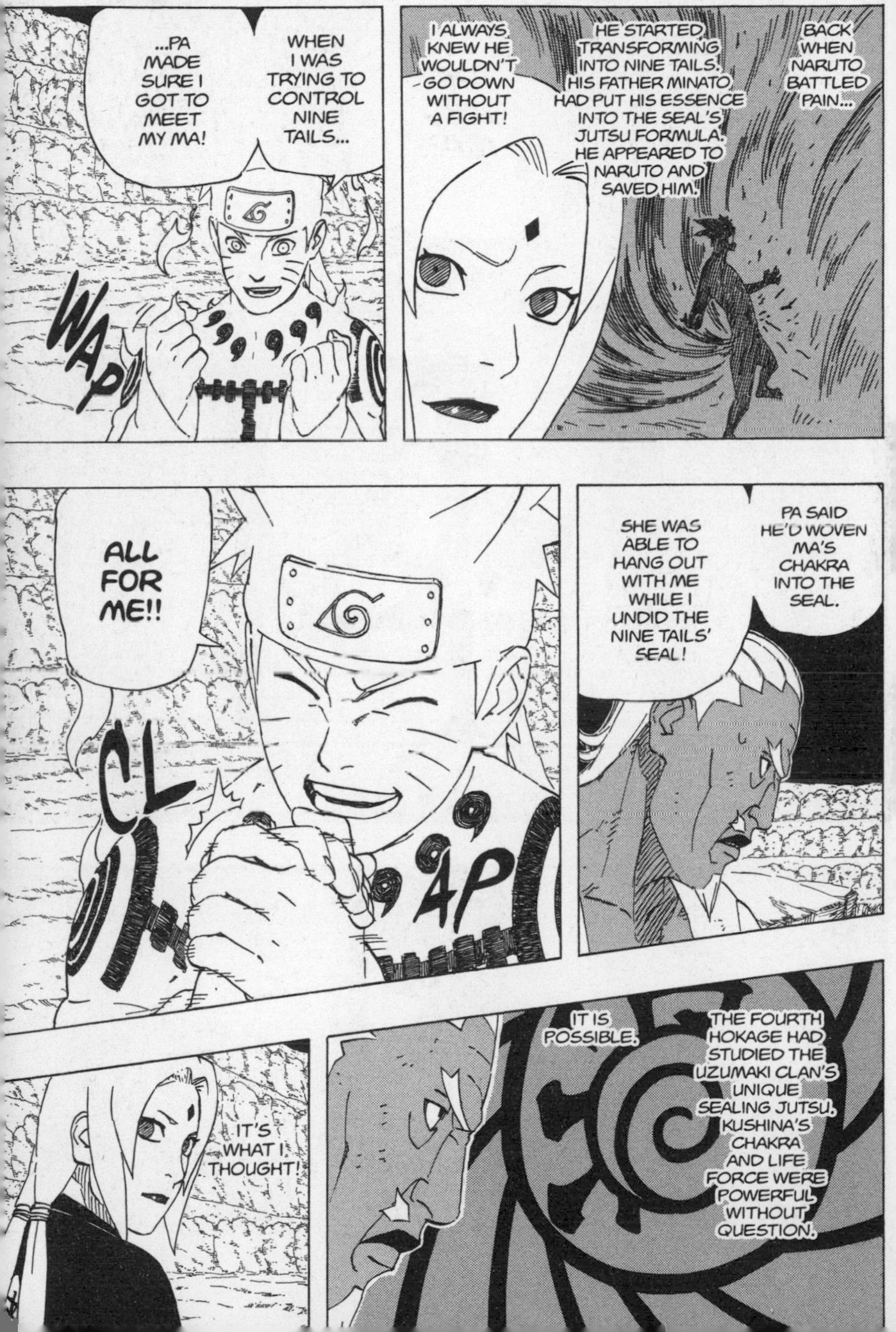
BACK WHEN NARUTO BATTLED PAIN...
HE STARTED TRANSFORMING INTO NINE TAILS. HIS FATHER MINATO HAD PUT HIS ESSENCE INTO THE SEAL'S JUTSU FORMULA. HE APPEARED TO NARUTO AND SAVED HIM.
I ALWAYS KNEW HE WOULDN'T GO DOWN WITHOUT A FIGHT!
WHEN I WAS TRYING TO CONTROL NINE TAILS...
...PA MADE SURE I GOT TO MEET MY MA!
WAP
PA SAID HE'D WOVEN MA'S CHAKRA INTO THE SEAL.
SHE WAS ABLE TO HANG OUT WITH ME WHILE I UNDID THE NINE TAILS' SEAL!
ALL FOR ME!!
CLAP
THE FOURTH HOKAGE HAD STUDIED THE UZUMAKI CLAN'S UNIQUE SEALING JUTSU. KUSHINA'S CHAKRA AND LIFE FORCE WERE POWERFUL WITHOUT QUESTION.
IT IS POSSIBLE.
IT'S WHAT I THOUGHT!

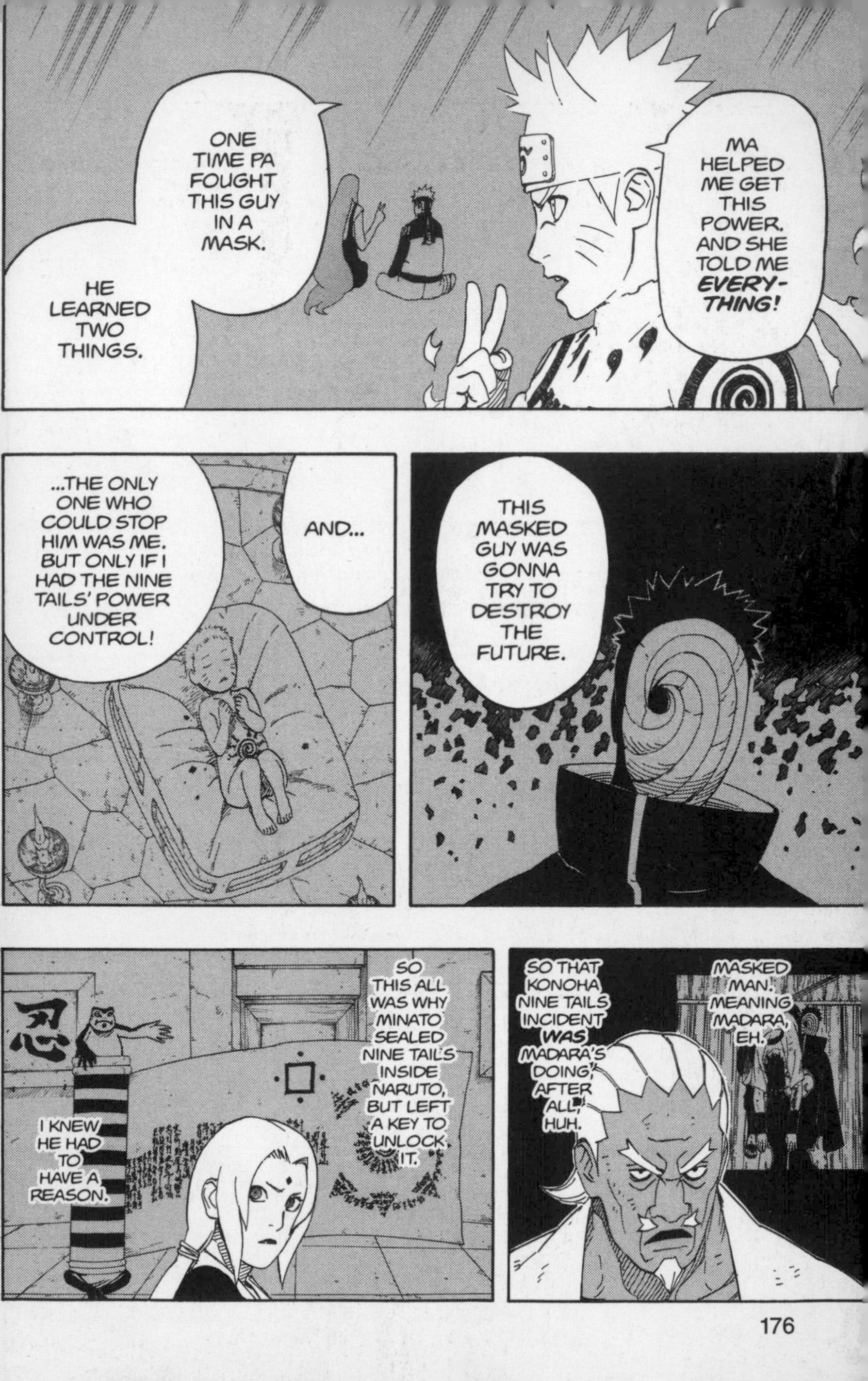
MA HELPED ME GET THIS POWER. AND SHE TOLD ME **EVERYTHING!**
ONE TIME PA FOUGHT THIS GUY IN A MASK.
HE LEARNED TWO THINGS.
THIS MASKED GUY WAS GONNA TRY TO DESTROY THE FUTURE.
AND...
...THE ONLY ONE WHO COULD STOP HIM WAS ME. BUT ONLY IF I HAD THE NINE TAILS' POWER UNDER CONTROL!
MASKED MAN. MEANING MADARA, EH.
SO THAT KONOHA NINE TAILS INCIDENT **WAS** MADARA'S DOING, AFTER ALL, HUH.
SO THIS ALL WAS WHY MINATO SEALED NINE TAILS INSIDE NARUTO, BUT LEFT A KEY TO UNLOCK IT.
忍
I KNEW HE HAD TO HAVE A REASON.

READ THIS WAY

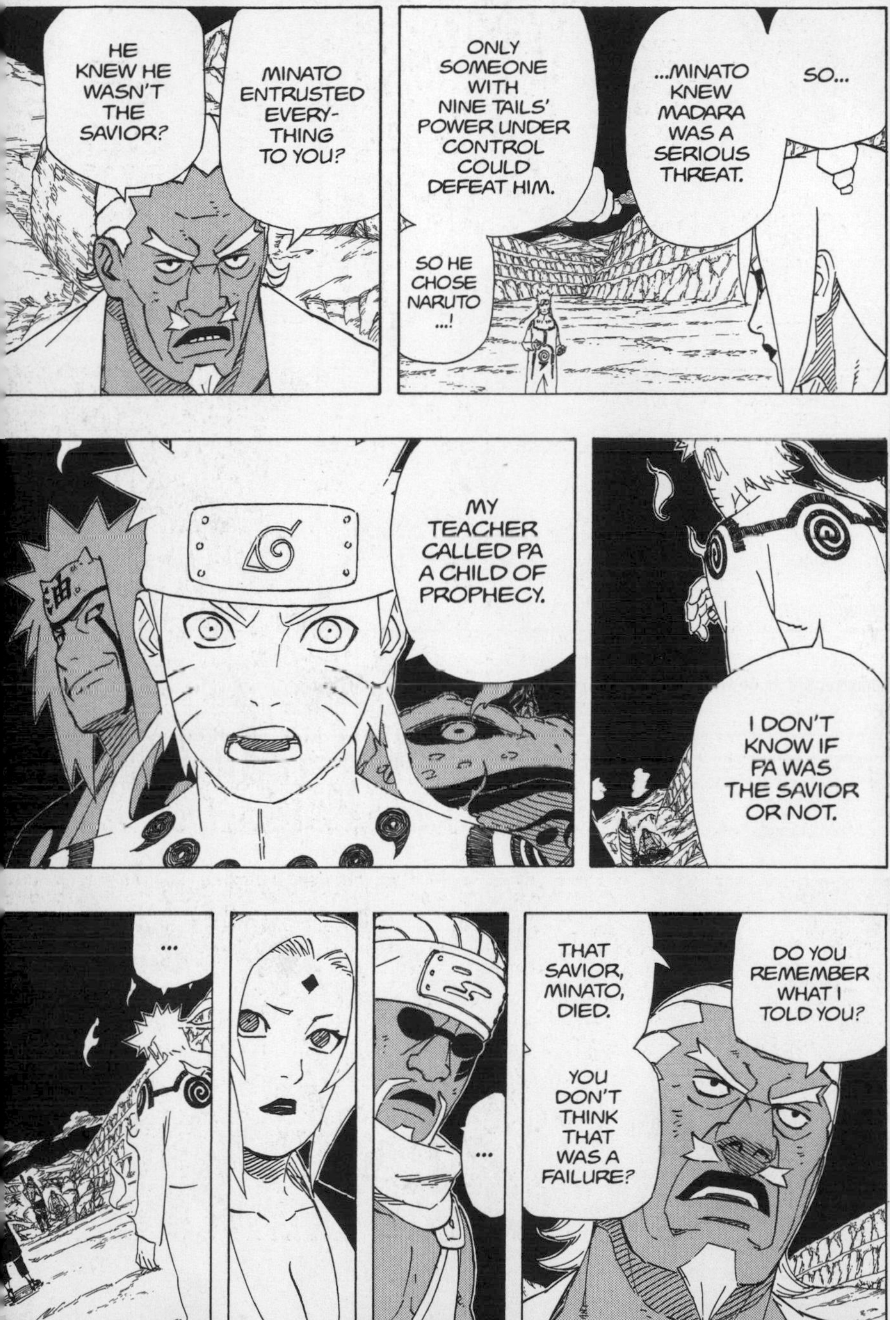
SO...
...MINATO KNEW MADARA WAS A SERIOUS THREAT.
ONLY SOMEONE WITH NINE TAILS' POWER UNDER CONTROL COULD DEFEAT HIM.
SO HE CHOSE NARUTO ...!
MINATO ENTRUSTED EVERYTHING TO YOU?
HE KNEW HE WASN'T THE SAVIOR?
I DON'T KNOW IF PA WAS THE SAVIOR OR NOT.
MY TEACHER CALLED PA A CHILD OF PROPHECY.
DO YOU REMEMBER WHAT I TOLD YOU?
THAT SAVIOR, MINATO, DIED.
YOU DON'T THINK THAT WAS A FAILURE?
...
...

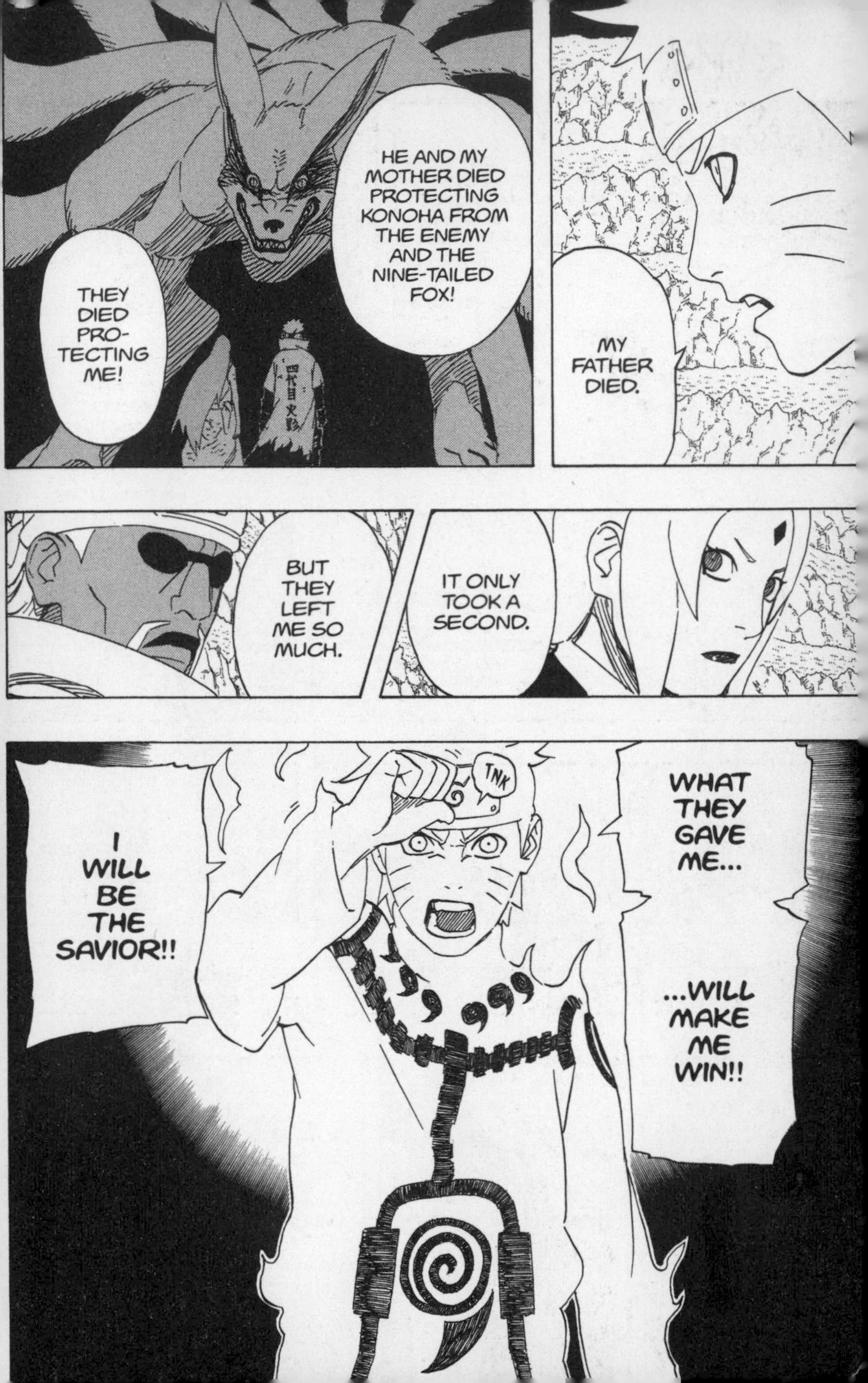

MY FATHER DIED.
HE AND MY MOTHER DIED PROTECTING KONOHA FROM THE ENEMY AND THE NINE-TAILED FOX!
THEY DIED PRO-TECTING ME!
IT ONLY TOOK A SECOND.
BUT THEY LEFT ME SO MUCH.
WHAT THEY GAVE ME...
TNK
...WILL MAKE ME WIN!!
I WILL BE THE SAVIOR!!

READ THIS WAY

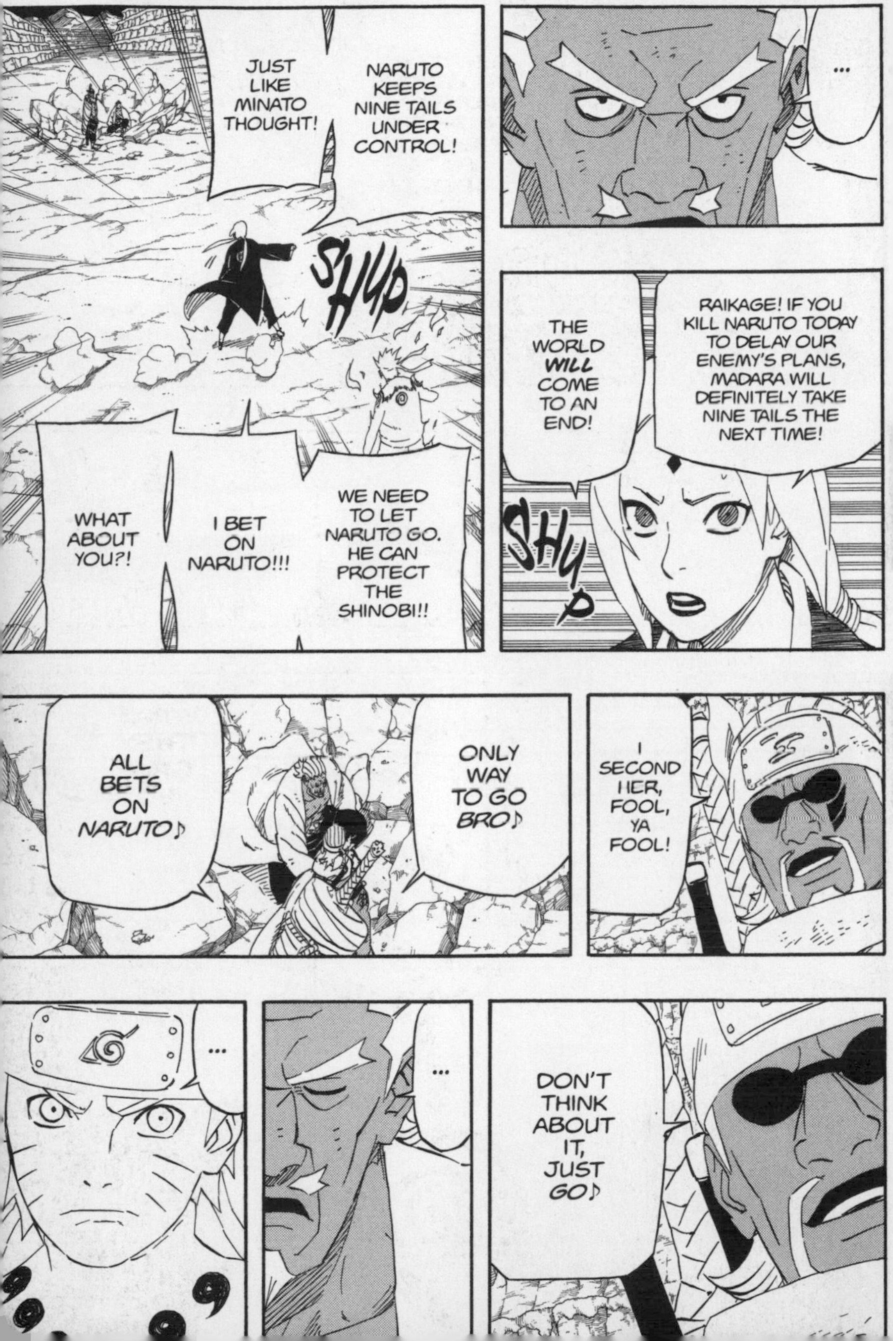
...
RAIKAGE! IF YOU KILL NARUTO TODAY TO DELAY OUR ENEMY'S PLANS, MADARA WILL DEFINITELY TAKE NINE TAILS THE NEXT TIME!
THE WORLD **WILL** COME TO AN END!
SHUP
NARUTO KEEPS NINE TAILS UNDER CONTROL!
JUST LIKE MINATO THOUGHT!
SHUP
WE NEED TO LET NARUTO GO. HE CAN PROTECT THE SHINOBI!!
I BET ON NARUTO!!!
WHAT ABOUT YOU?!
I SECOND HER, FOOL, YA FOOL!
ONLY WAY TO GO *BRO*♪
ALL BETS ON *NARUTO*♪
DON'T THINK ABOUT IT, JUST *GO*♪
...
...

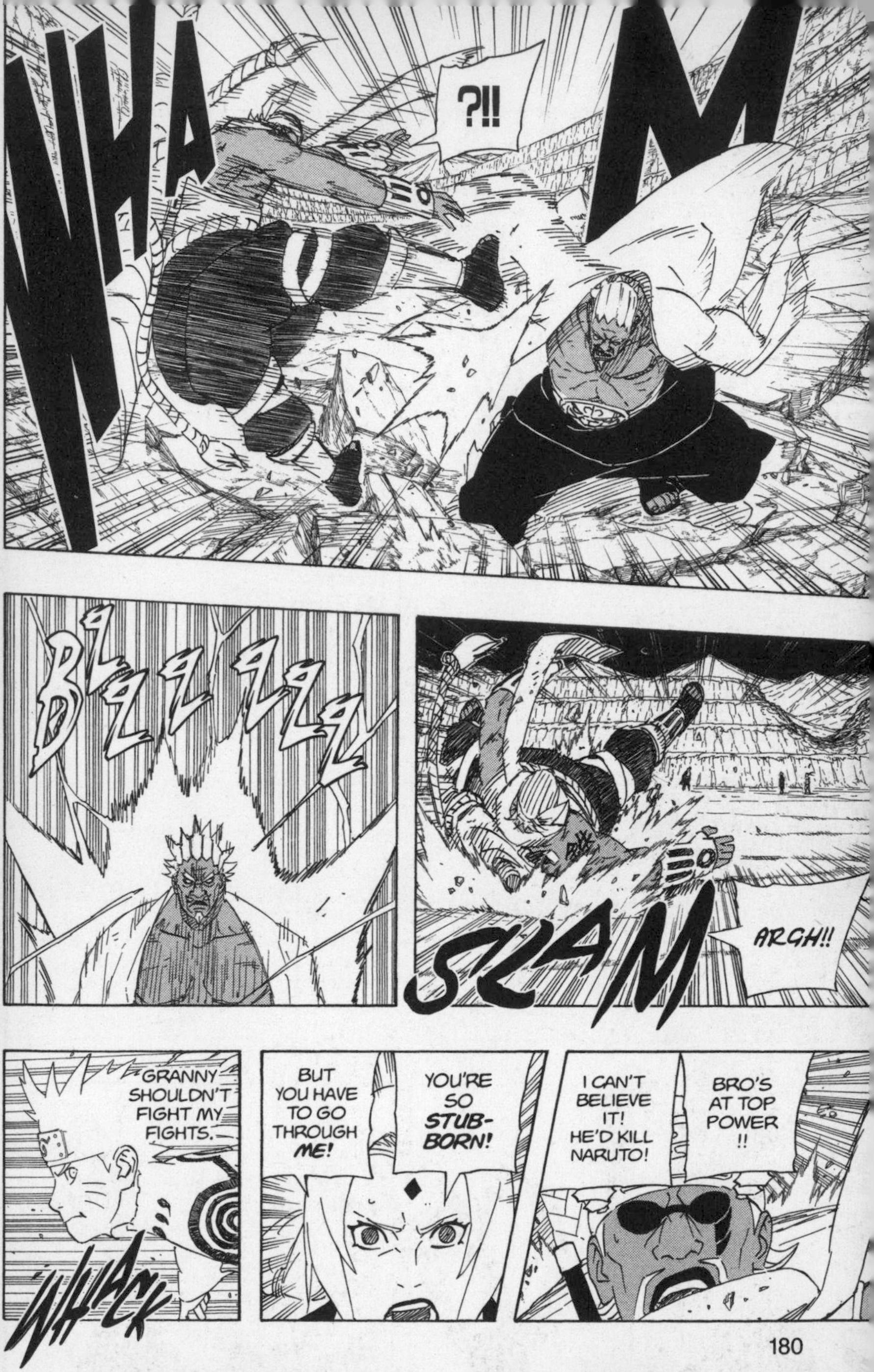
WHAM
?!!
SLAM
ARGH!!
BZZZZZ
BRO'S AT TOP POWER !!
I CAN'T BELIEVE IT! HE'D KILL NARUTO!
YOU'RE SO *STUB-BORN!*
BUT YOU HAVE TO GO THROUGH *ME!*
GRANNY SHOULDN'T FIGHT MY FIGHTS.
WHACK

READ THIS WAY

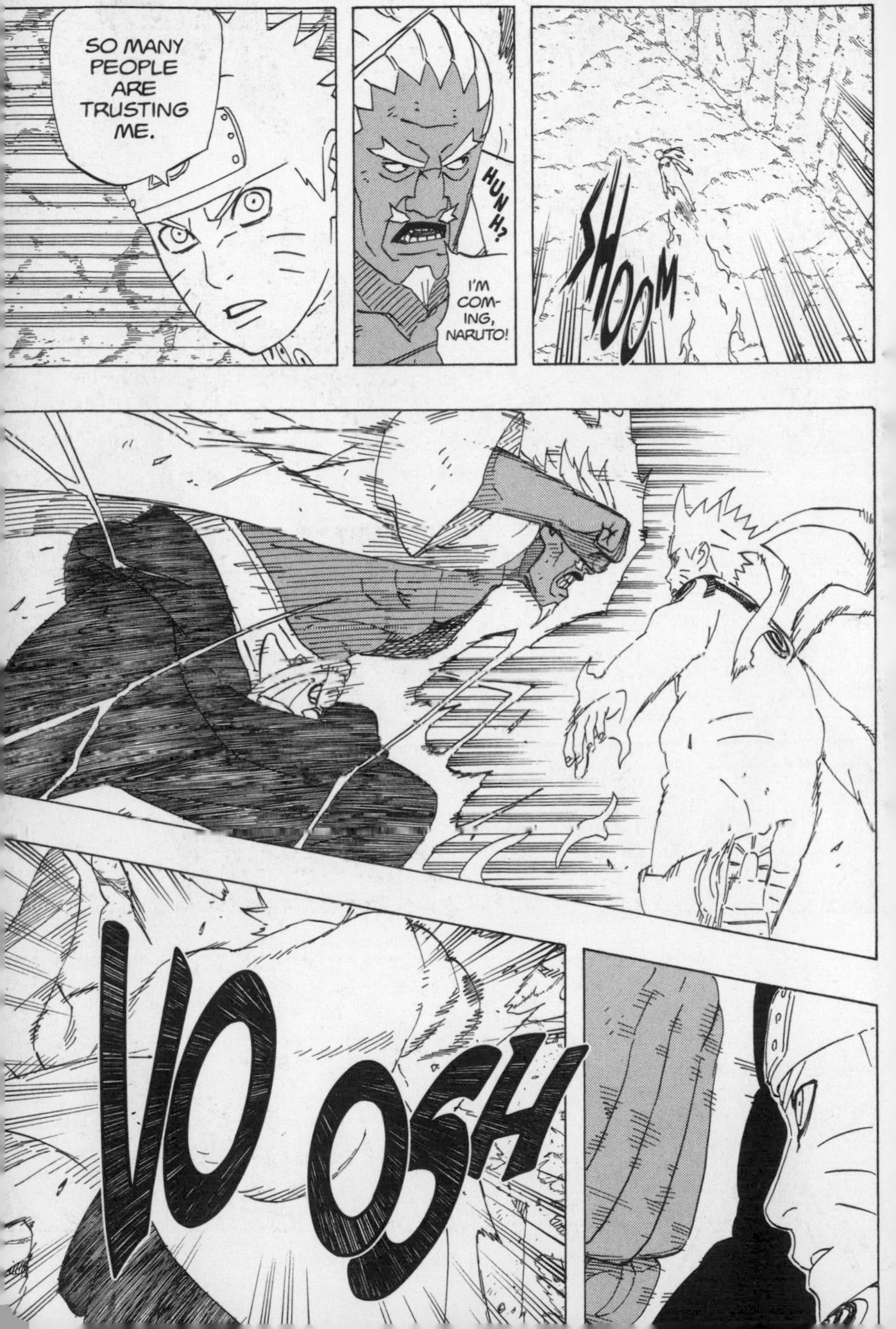
SHOOM
HUNH?
I'M COMING, NARUTO!
SO MANY PEOPLE ARE TRUSTING ME.
VOOSH

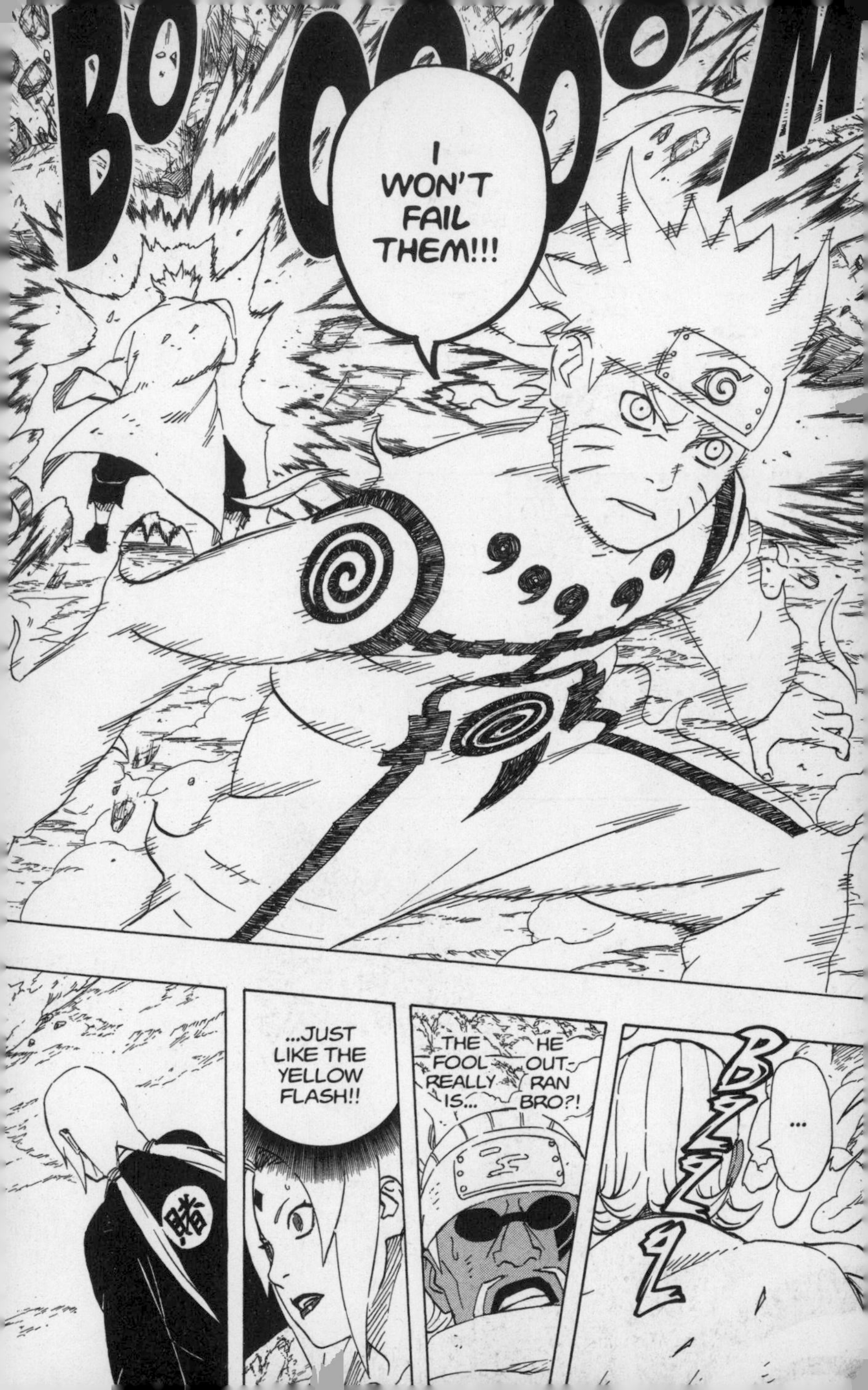

BOOOOM
I WON'T FAIL THEM!!!
...
HE OUT-RAN BRO?!
THE FOOL REALLY IS...
...JUST LIKE THE YELLOW FLASH!!

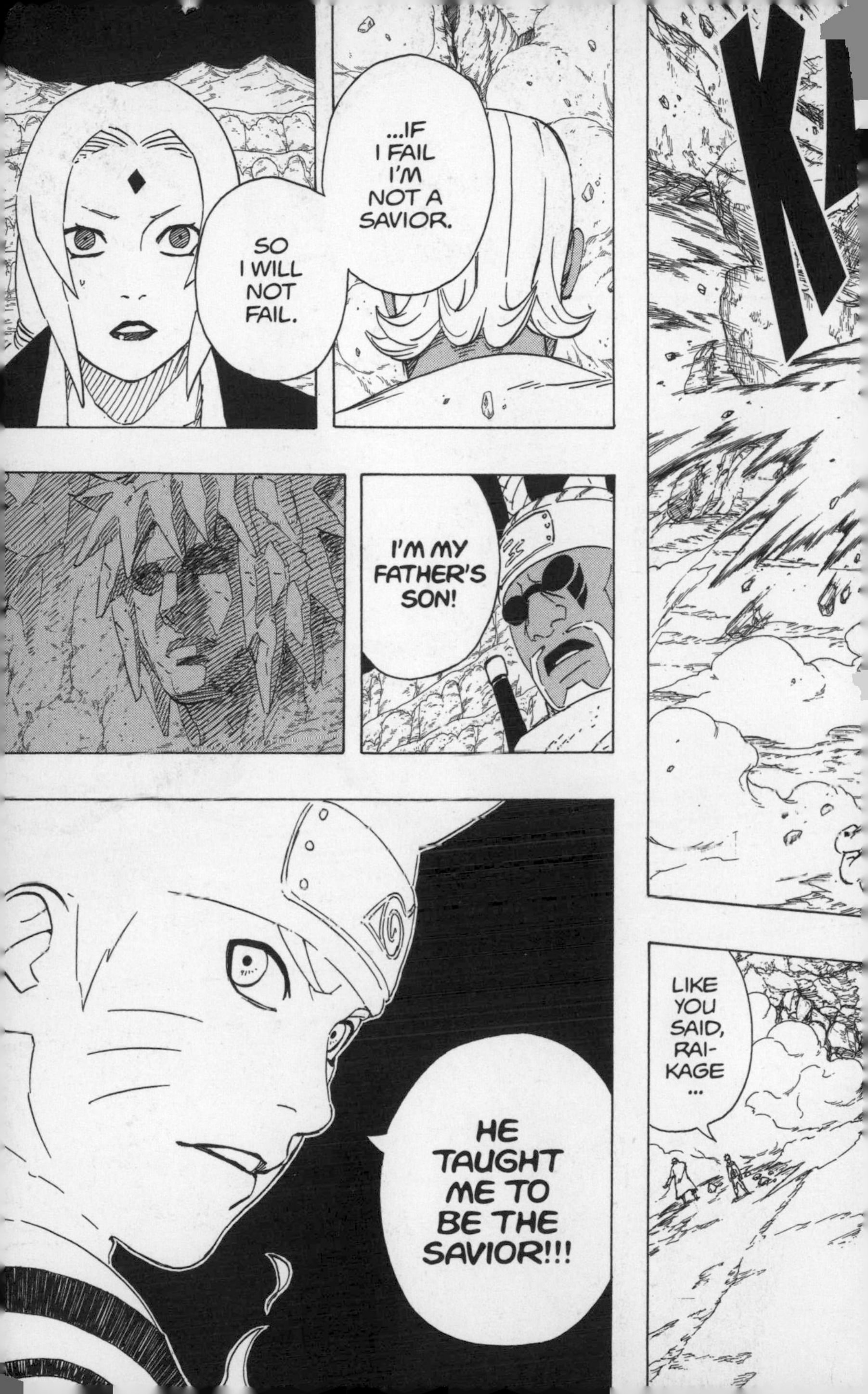

LIKE YOU SAID, RAI-KAGE...
...IF I FAIL I'M NOT A SAVIOR.
SO I WILL NOT FAIL.
I'M MY FATHER'S SON!
HE TAUGHT ME TO BE THE SAVIOR!!!

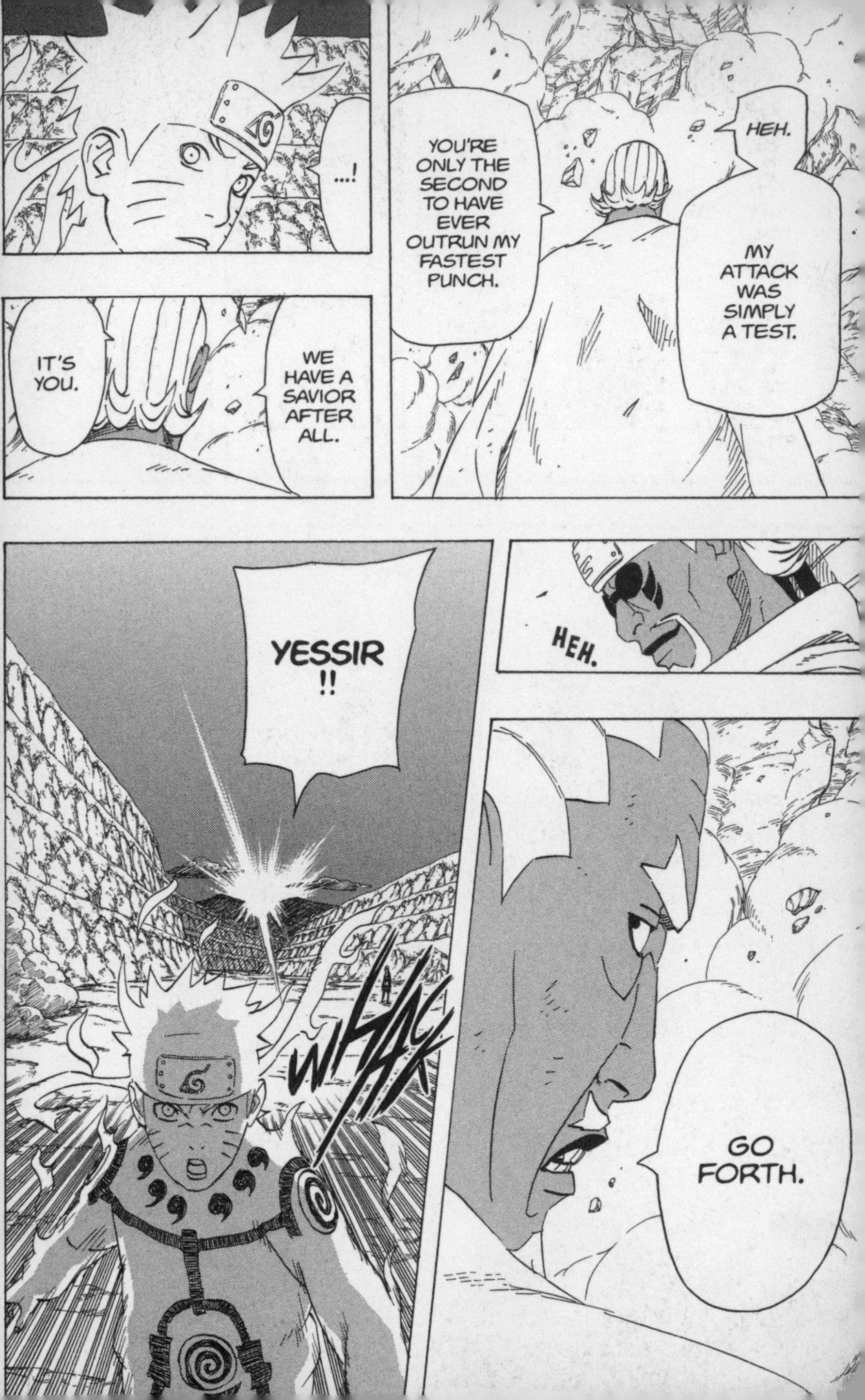
HEH.
MY ATTACK WAS SIMPLY A TEST.
YOU'RE ONLY THE SECOND TO HAVE EVER OUTRUN MY FASTEST PUNCH.
...!
WE HAVE A SAVIOR AFTER ALL.
IT'S YOU.
HEH.
GO FORTH.
YESSIR !!

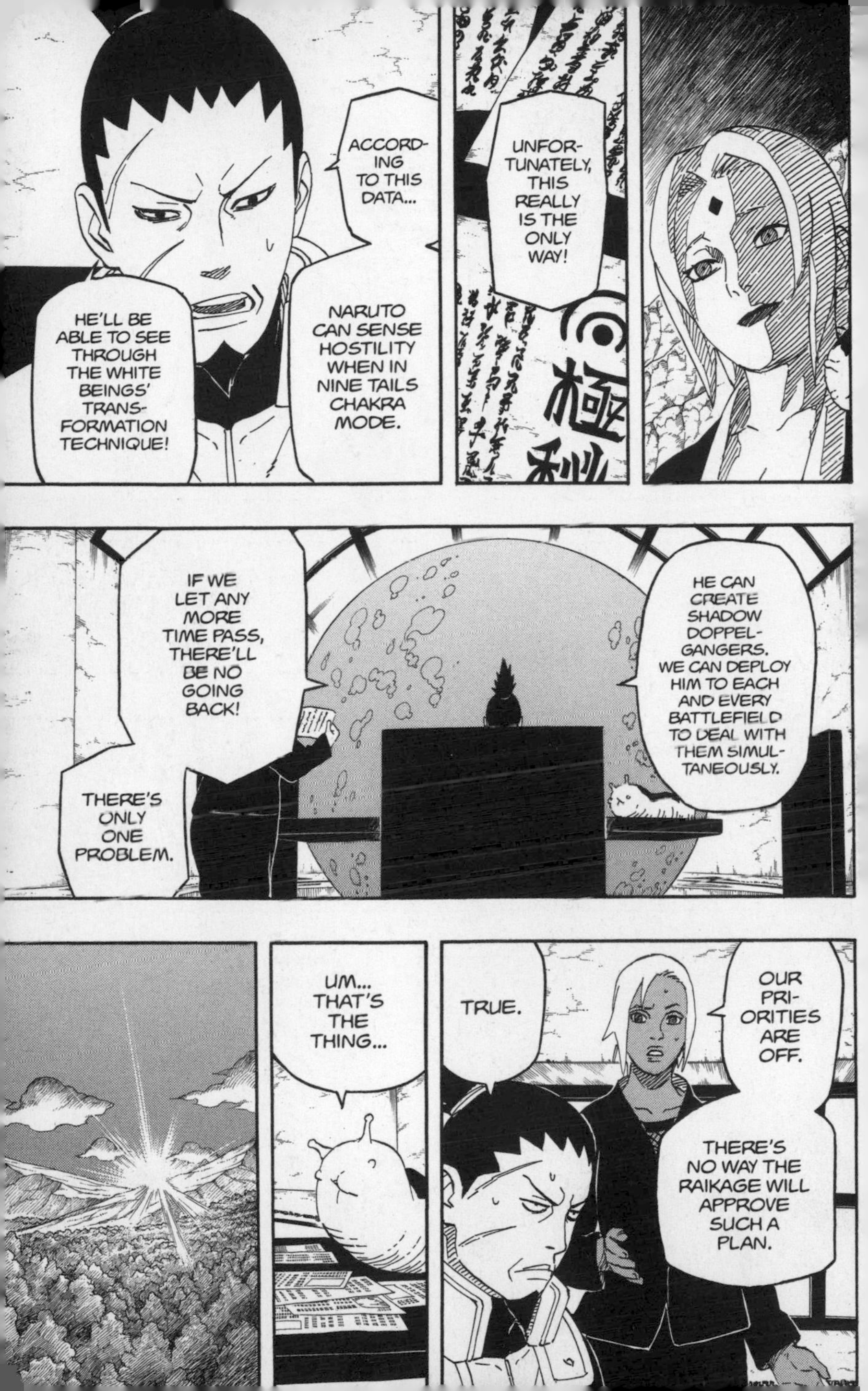

UNFORTUNATELY, THIS REALLY IS THE ONLY WAY!
ACCORDING TO THIS DATA...
NARUTO CAN SENSE HOSTILITY WHEN IN NINE TAILS CHAKRA MODE.
HE'LL BE ABLE TO SEE THROUGH THE WHITE BEINGS' TRANSFORMATION TECHNIQUE!
HE CAN CREATE SHADOW DOPPELGANGERS. WE CAN DEPLOY HIM TO EACH AND EVERY BATTLEFIELD TO DEAL WITH THEM SIMULTANEOUSLY.
IF WE LET ANY MORE TIME PASS, THERE'LL BE NO GOING BACK!
THERE'S ONLY ONE PROBLEM.
OUR PRIORITIES ARE OFF.
TRUE.
THERE'S NO WAY THE RAIKAGE WILL APPROVE SUCH A PLAN.
UM... THAT'S THE THING...

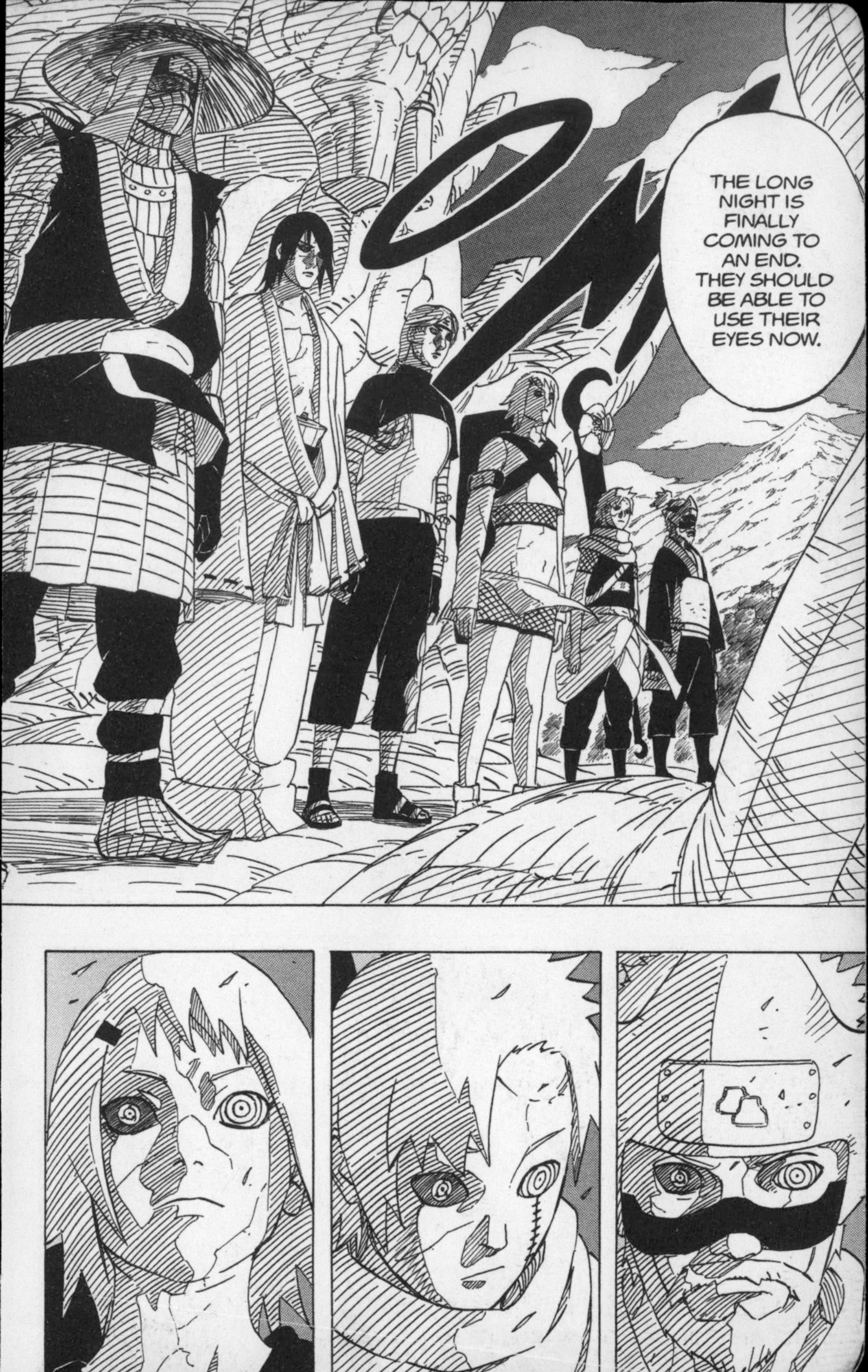
THE LONG NIGHT IS FINALLY COMING TO AN END. THEY SHOULD BE ABLE TO USE THEIR EYES NOW.

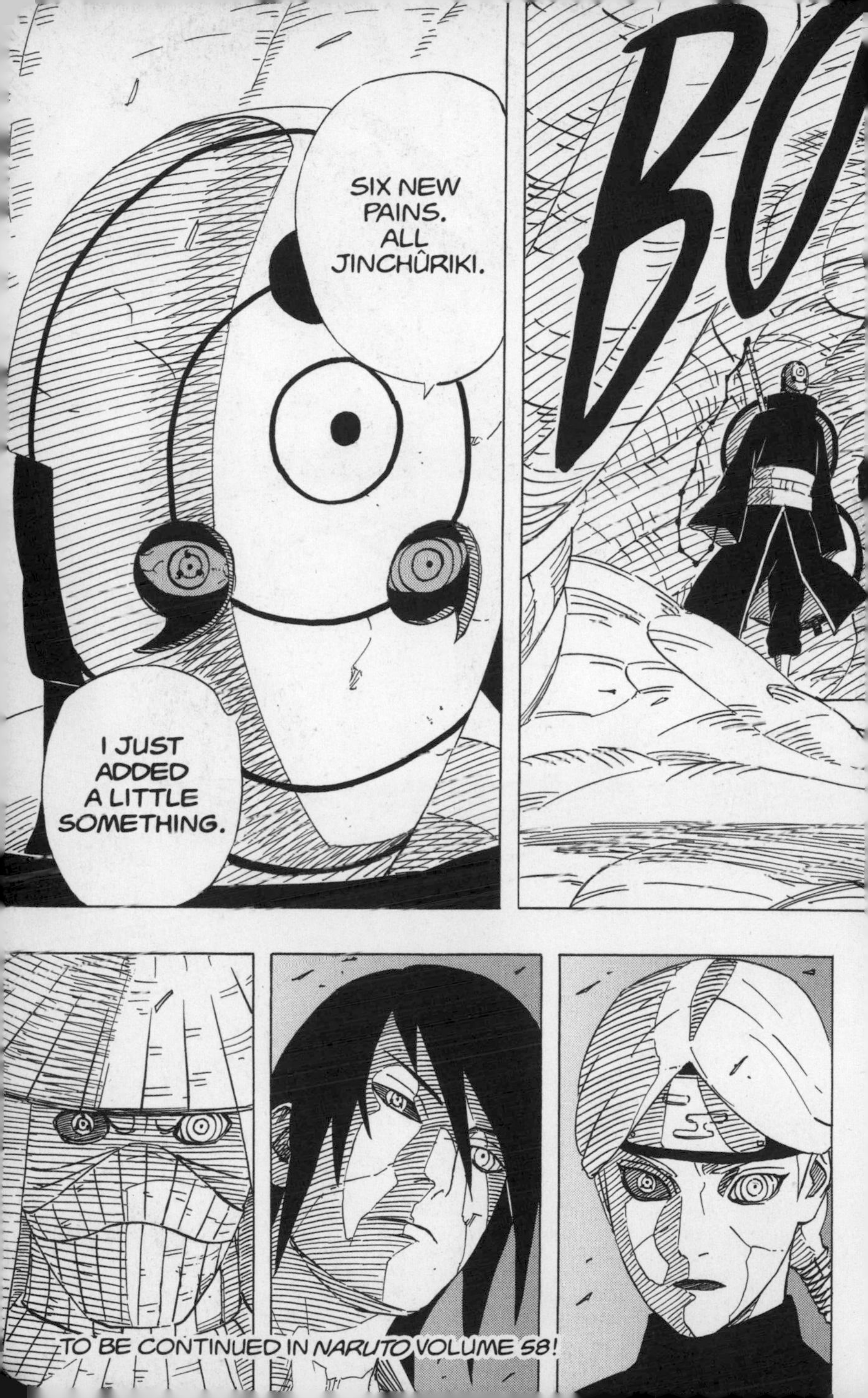
BO
SIX NEW PAINS. ALL JINCHÛRIKI.
I JUST ADDED A LITTLE SOMETHING.
TO BE CONTINUED IN *NARUTO* VOLUME 58!

IN THE NEXT VOLUME...

NARUTO VS. ITACHI

Kabuto's hold over his army of undead minions tightens as he senses that he's losing power over the stronger members of his Immortal Corps, including Nagato Pain. Sasuke's brother, Itachi, may have the best chance of breaking Kabuto's hold. But he's still not completely in control of his actions, which means Naruto may have to take him down once and for all.

AVAILABLE SEPTEMBER 2012!

© 2002 MASASHI KISHIMOTO /2007 SHIPPUDEN © NMP 2008

NOW AVAILABLE ON
DVD AND BLU-RAY

HEROES O.
ANIME

www.shonenjump.com

RATED
T
TEEN OLDER
TEEN
ratings.viz.com

25 / YEAR

For more Heroes of A
visit www.viz.com/25

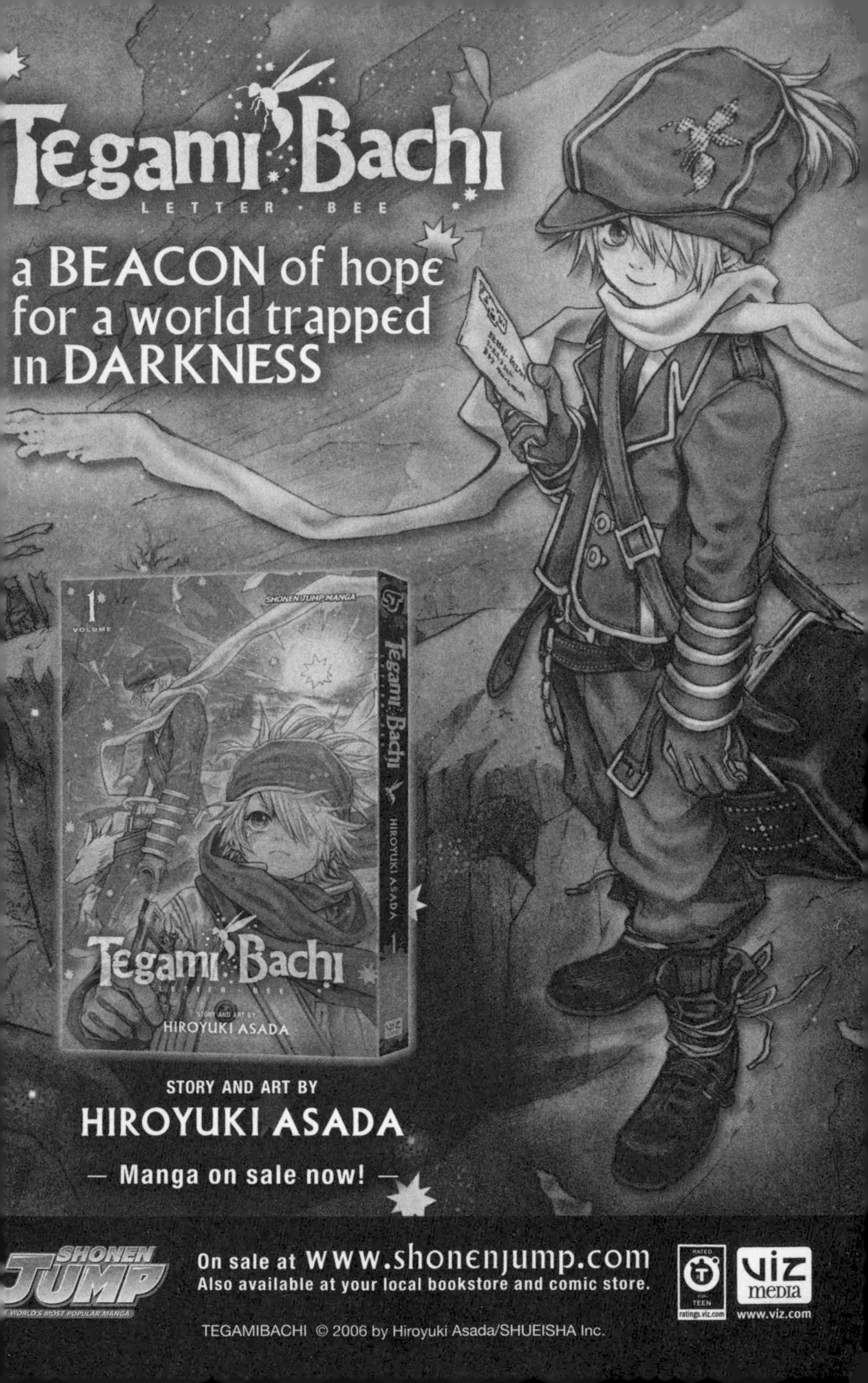

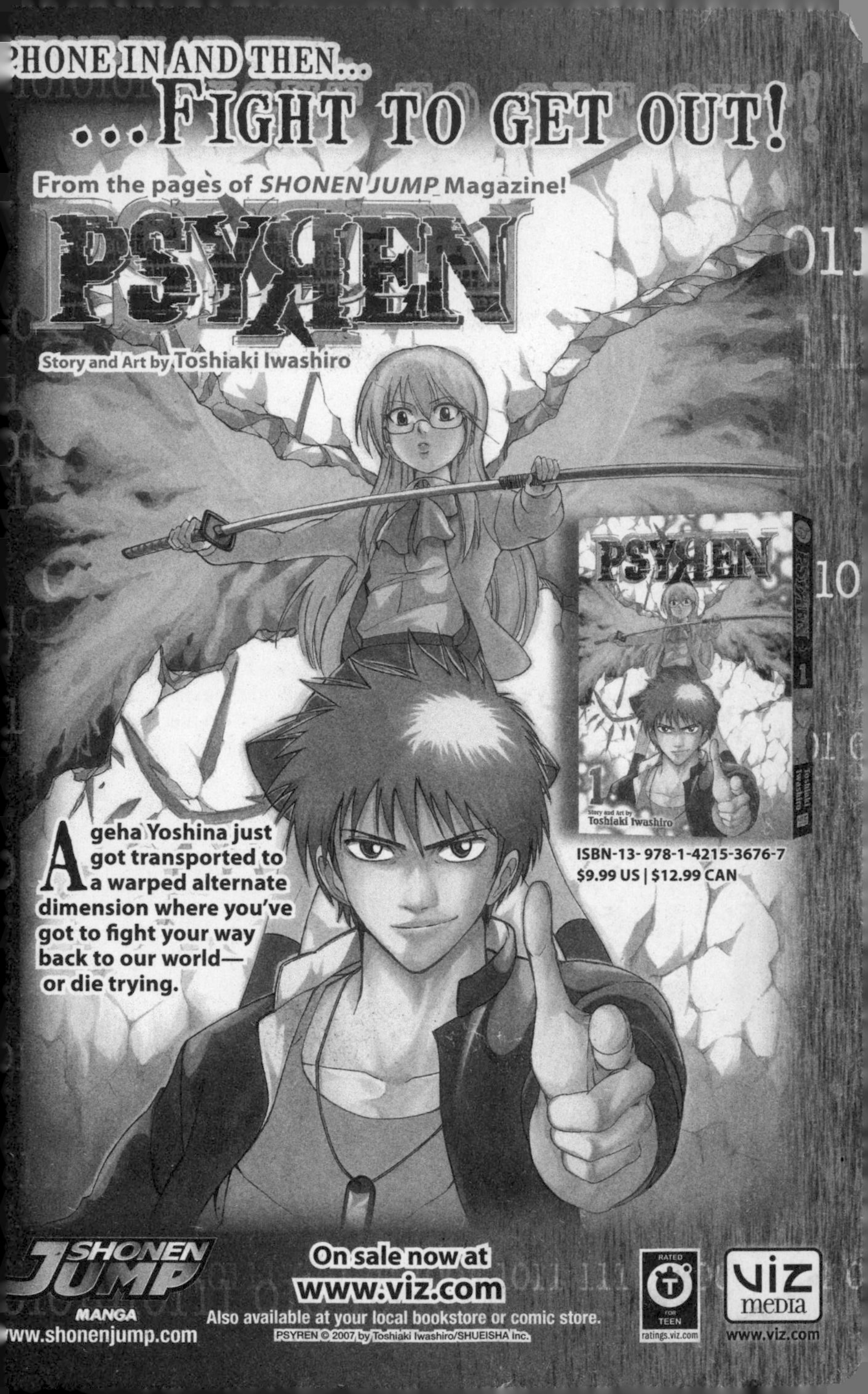

PHONE IN AND THEN...
...FIGHT TO GET OUT!
From the pages of SHONEN JUMP Magazine!
PSYREN
Story and Art by Toshiaki Iwashiro
Ageha Yoshina just got transported to a warped alternate dimension where you've got to fight your way back to our world—or die trying.
PSYREN
1
Story and Art by Toshiaki Iwashiro
ISBN-13- 978-1-4215-3676-7
$9.99 US | $12.99 CAN
SHONEN JUMP MANGA
www.shonenjump.com
On sale now at
www.viz.com
Also available at your local bookstore or comic store.
PSYREN © 2007 by Toshiaki Iwashiro/SHUEISHA Inc.
RATED T FOR TEEN
ratings.viz.com
VIZ media
www.viz.com